The Promise of THE SPIRIT

Charles G. Finney

Compiled & Edited by TIMOTHY L. SMITH

BETHANY HOUSE PUBLISHERS

MINNEAPOLIS, MINNESOTA 55438

A Division of Bethany Fellowship, Inc.

DR. TIMOTHY L. SMITH is professor of history and director of a doctoral program in American religious history at The Johns Hopkins University in Baltimore, Maryland.

Copyright © 1980
Timothy L. Smith
All rights reserved

Published by Bethany Fellowship, Inc.
6820 Auto Club Road, Minneapolis, Minnesota 55438

Printed in the United States of America

Library of Congress Cataloging in Publication Data

Finney, Charles Grandison, 1792-1875.
   The promise of the spirit.

   Bibliography: p.
   1. Theology—Addresses, essays, lectures.
I. Smith, Timothy Lawrence, 1924-
II. Title.
BR85.F426   1980   230   79-26286
ISBN 0-87123-207-3

PREFACE

The man chiefly responsible for the adoption among holiness people in America and England of the terms "filling" or "baptism of the Spirit" to describe the experience of entire sanctification was Charles G. Finney, New School Presbyterian evangelist and professor of theology after 1835 at abolitionist Oberlin College. Finney's breakthrough in biblical understanding and experience remained obscure to me until recently, despite the work which I and other scholars had done in clarifying his general alignment with the doctrine of Christian perfection. The reasons we scholars all missed the point are two: none of us realized how closely Finney's theological development, particularly his search for some means by which Christians would come up to the New Testament standard of holiness, paralleled developments in the so-called New England theology. For three decades before the Civil War that intensely ethical and tacitly Arminian theology dominated Congregationalist and New School Presbyterian preaching in both the Northeast and the Old Northwest. The second reason is more embarrassing: none of us seems to have read all the fine print.

Finney became interested in the subject of holiness when, after ten years of immensely successful evangelism, he accepted in 1833 a New York City pastorate, first at the Chatham Street Chapel and then at the Broadway Tabernacle. His *Lectures to Professing Christians* displayed that concern and his *Memoirs*, composed forty years later, recalled it. In the autobiography he says he examined the teachings of the Methodists on the subject during his years in the New York pastorate but laid them aside, thinking them to refer primarily to the emotions rather than to the will—a misimpression that probably flowed from John Wesley's use of the term "perfect love." For Finney, the will was absolutely central. "By the heart, I mean the will," he often said. He was sure, as were Nathaniel William Taylor and Lyman Beecher, who led the revolution in New England theology, that God had made men free and responsible. Moreover, grace reached men in the form of truth—truth so persuasive to their minds that in loving response to God's grace they could will to be all He would have them to be.

These doctrines of man's ability to exercise free will and of the moral nature of divine government flatly contradicted the notion of salvation by divine decree, or predestination, that during the preceding century had reigned triumphant in New England Calvinism. The new doctrines were so prominent in the preaching of Finney's generation of Congregationalist and New School Presbyterian leaders that Old School Calvinists accused them, with some degree of justice, of being Pelagians; that is, of teaching that salvation rested upon one's own determination and effort to be holy. But

Finney and Beecher and Albert Barnes were in fact affirming in a new way the primacy of grace. The truth of the gospel, they declared, is the "power of God for the salvation of everyone who believes." In that gospel the right-making power of God is revealed, bringing to those who will respond by committing themselves wholly to Him "a righteousness that is by faith from first to last." No such commitment was possible apart from the revelation of God in Jesus Christ—"full of grace and truth."

Finney, however, became concerned that the responses he saw even the most earnest Christians making, and the responses he saw in his own heart and life, had not yet brought them up to the biblical standard of righteousness. When, therefore, he began spending most of each year at Oberlin College, he was still in a quandary about how Christians could attain that standard. At Oberlin, of course, Finney became a close associate of Asa Mahan and the students who had rebelled from Lane Theological Seminary when the trustees attempted to curb their antislavery activities. The Oberlin College and community was from the day of its founding in 1835 the seedbed of American Christian radicalism, not only on the question of slavery but of racial brotherhood, women's rights, economic justice, peace, prohibition, and a whole range of concerns for the creation of a righteous social order, in the nation and in the world.

President Mahan, swept along by the intensity of the religious search characterizing the community, preceded Finney in the experience of what he called, uncompromisingly, "perfect sanctification." Finney did not profess a second work of grace at that point, however, though he played an important part in underlining, not only for Mahan but for the whole Oberlin community, the important distinction between *desire* and *will*. A man might wish to be holy until his dying day, Finney insisted, but until he willed to be so, as both the Old and New Covenants required, "with all his heart and mind and soul and strength," wishing made little difference. Here Finney exhibited what covenant theology had, since the Westminster Assembly of Divines, consistently affirmed: that God treated His children like persons, and expected them to respond fully to His grace and commit themselves heartily to Him. But the question for Finney, as always for the Methodists, was, by what means, by what experience, does God communicate His grace so perfectly as to enable us to will His will?

In the fall of 1838 Finney was restrained by ill health from making his usual evangelistic tour to the East, so set about delivering and publishing in the *Oberlin Evangelist* the series of lectures that comprise this book. He explained in an accompanying letter that he intended them to correct his long-standing neglect of the doctrine of sanctification. The lectures show us a splendid mind laying aside old views and adopting new ones, as the evangelist thought his way back through the Bible and revitalized the long-neglected promises of holiness that lay hidden in Puritan theology. He spoke of devotion to God, first; then of the law, which Christ had summed up in two "great commandments" to love God and our neighbors; and, finally, of the attainability in this life of an experience of Christian holiness such as God had commanded and His covenants had promised. The evangelist did not retreat from the New England theology's emphasis upon the ability of human beings, as distinct from their disposition, to choose God's will; but he restored to a crucial place in giving them that disposition the revelation of God's love, and their reception by faith of the sanctifying baptism of the Holy Spirit. He thus gave the idea of divine sovereignty a new and powerful meaning in Christian experience.

Moreover, in these lectures Finney worked his way through the whole of Old Testament theology, linking together Deuteronomy, the Psalms and the prophets, to demonstrate the overwhelming consistency and force of the biblical promises of the sanctifying Spirit. The renewal of those promises in the preaching of John the Baptist and in the assurances Jesus gave to the apostles on the eve of His crucifixion tied the Old and New Testaments together. The baptism of the Holy Spirit, poured out initially in a dispensational way at Pentecost upon the whole church, Finney declared, signalled the fulfillment of God's New Covenant, not simply with Israel but with all humankind.

The experience of the Spirit's fullness was, therefore, normative for all Christians; it was the source of the divine grace that sanctified their hearts and minds. Preachers must have it and they must lead their converts into it. By this means alone could such righteousness prevail in individual and social life, in church and nation, as the Lord had ordained for His people.*

I have provided a historical and theological introduction to the lectures that moves well beyond the general conclusions about the relationship between Oberlin and Methodist perfectionism to which I came in graduate school, while writing my book *Revivalism and Social Reform*.** It suggests also a firm link between the preaching of Finney and Mahan and the teachings about Christian holiness that were central to the Keswick movement in late-nineteenth-century England. Through the influence of Keswick, these teachings became briefly important also to Moody Bible Institute and other evangelistic centers that nurtured the evangelical and fundamentalist movements of the twentieth century. More generally, the introduction aims to set Finney's doctrine of the sanctifying Spirit in the broader context of the preoccupation of nineteenth-century Americans with biblical ideas of righteousness—a preoccupation that is the subject of my current research and, I hope soon, of a book.

In editing the lectures I have altered spelling, capitalization and punctuation to conform to modern practice, taking pains not to alter knowingly

---

*The foregoing paragraphs appeared originally in a commencement address at Western Evangelical Theological Seminary in June, 1877, and then in my article, "The Cross Demands, the Spirit Enables," *Christianity Today*, 33:10 (February 16, 1979), 22-26.

**Reading and placing in chronological order the sermons and doctrinal tracts of John Wesley and John Fletcher, and studying carefully their doctrine of the sanctifying Spirit, has sharply revised my understanding of Wesleyan teaching as well. The results will appear in the fall of 1980 at the Nazarene Publishing House in a volume of John Wesley's sermons on sanctification, entitled *Covenant, Cross and Comforter*.

by these changes the meanings of Finney's often very long sentences. I have corrected obvious typographical errors. And I have written out fully words for which standard abbreviations were used, except for "&c." and the names of books of the Bible, except when the latter appear with references to the chapter and verse or verses of a text quoted immediately afterward. Except for the two cases footnoted in Lecture 11, page 137, and 19, page 202, all the words in brackets in Finney's text are my additions, intended to clarify his meaning or correct his syntax. Most of the thirty-four cases of such additions consist of a single preposition and may in fact reflect a printer's omission. In only one case, footnoted in Lecture 4, page 68, have I left out a word of Finney's and substituted one of my own; and in one case, Lecture 9, I have supplied a title where none was printed.

I must acknowledge with thanks the support of my summer research in recent years provided by the Lilly Endowment and the National Endowment for the Humanities, for the cooperative study I and seven of my present and former student colleagues are preparing of "The Mosaic of Evangelical Protestantism in Modern America." The Lilly Endowment is also presently supporting my study of "The Bible in Nineteenth-Century America." The staff of the Congregational Library in Boston have been endlessly helpful in providing me photographic copies of Finney's lectures from their file of *The Oberlin Evangelist*. And Karen Rubinson, secretary to the Johns Hopkins Program in American Religious History, transcribed them with remarkable accuracy.

Timothy L. Smith
Boston, Ash Wednesday, 1979

TABLE OF CONTENTS

How Finney Helped Americans Discover the New Covenant:

    Righteousness Through Grace, by Timothy L. Smith 9

Professor Finney's letter of January 1, 1839 33

Lecture 1: Eternal Life, January 1, 1839 35

Lecture 2: Faith, January 16, 1839 40

Professor Finney's Letter of January 30, 1839 49

Lecture 3: Devotion, January 30, 1839 53

Professor Finney's Letter of February 13, 1839 58

Lecture 4: True and False Religion, February 13, 1839 61

Lecture 5: The Law of God, No. 1, February 27, 1839 68

Lecture 6: The Law of God, No. 2, March 13, 1839 82

Lecture 7: Glorifying God, March 27, 1839 94

Professor Finney's Letter of April 10, 1839 105

Lecture 8: True and False Peace, April 10, 1839 108

Lecture 9: Sanctification Under Grace, April 24, 1839 117

Lecture 10: Carefulness a Sin, May 8, 1839 125

Lecture 11: The Promises, No. 1, May 22, 1839 133

Lecture 12: The Promises, No. 2, June 5, 1839 142

Lecture 13: The Promises, No. 3, June 19, 1839 150

Lecture 14: The Promises, No. 4, July 3, 1839 156

Lecture 15: The Promises, No. 5, July 17, 1839 164

Lecture 16: Being in Debt, July 31, 1839 175

Lecture 17: The Holy Spirit of Promise, August 14, 1839 184

Lecture 18: The Covenants, August 28, 1839 191

Lecture 19: The Rest of Faith, No. 1, September 11, 1839 201

Lecture 20: The Rest of Faith, No. 2, September 25, 1839 210

Lecture 21: Affections and Emotions of God, October 9, 1839 216

Lecture 22: Legal and Gospel Experience, October 23, 1839 223

Lecture 23: How to Prevent Our Employments from Injuring

   Our Souls, November 6, 1839 231

Lecture 24: Grieving the Holy Spirit, No. 1, December 4, 1839 240

Lecture 25: Grieving the Holy Spirit, No. 2, December 18, 1839 249

Professor Finney's Letter of May 6, 1840 259

Professor Finney's Letter of June 3, 1840 263

INTRODUCTION

HOW FINNEY HELPED AMERICANS DISCOVER
THE NEW COVENANT:
RIGHTEOUSNESS THROUGH GRACE*

by Timothy L. Smith

A grand view of both the national and the Christian future began pervading popular culture in America from the moment the War for Independence ended in the generous peace terms England granted in 1783. Hopes for an early inauguration of Christ's rule on earth and a thousand years of peace took hold in every section of the country, despite the political conflicts surrounding the forming of the new nation. Millennial expectation was more religious than political in character, I believe, and preoccupied as much with the future of all mankind as with the special role of the United States in securing it.[1] The spread of religious awakenings after 1800 convinced clergymen in all parts of the country that the Spirit of the Lord was mightily at work, ushering in the millennium through the hallowing of America. This conviction sparked the movements for both foreign and home missions and sustained all sorts of moral crusades: peace, temperance, Sunday schools, public education, antislavery, women's rights and concern for the urban poor.[2]

The decade of the 1830's witnessed the flowering of this millennial vision among the leaders of every denomination. Although the vision reinforced the doctrine of America's mission, its perspective was international. Millennialists thought the foreign missionary movement an enterprise in which European and American Protestants were cooperating to bring all mankind under the judgment and into the kingdom of Christ.[3] Garth Rosell has recently demonstrated that Charles G. Finney's passion for social reform caught fire during his revival of 1828 in Rochester, and stemmed from his heady anticipation that Christ's kingdom was dawning.[4] In this belief, the young evangelist was not far ahead of the two most prominent Connec-

---

*Much of the content of this introduction has appeared in varying forms in my articles, "Charles G. Finney's Synthesis of Wesleyan and Covenant Theology," *The Wesleyan Theological Journal*, Volume 13 (Spring, 1978), 92-113; "Righteousness and Hope: Christian Holiness and the Millennial Vision in America, 1800-1900," *The American Quarterly*, Volume 31 (Spring, 1979), 21-45; and in the volume of the essays presented at the Oxford Institute of Methodist Theology, Lincoln College, Oxford University, in July, 1977, forthcoming from The Abingdon Press under the title *Sanctification and Liberation*.

ticut clergymen, Lyman Beecher and Nathaniel W. Taylor. These and many other New Englanders drew, as Finney did, upon the combination of millennial expectation and radical moralism which Samuel Hopkins, Congregationalist pastor at Newport, Rhode Island, had made central to his revision of Jonathan Edwards' Calvinism.[5] In the Ohio Valley, likewise, not only the Yankee home missionaries but influential Methodist, Baptist, and Presbyterian clergymen born and raised west of the Allegheny mountains were equally committed to the dream of a Christian society—one in which evangelism, education, social reform, economic progress and advancing democracy were all heralds of the approaching rule of Christ on earth.[6]

In this atmosphere of soaring hopes, there emerged out of the heart of Connecticut Calvinism a multi-faceted perfectionism which differed only in minor details from that long espoused by the Arminian Methodists, whose invasion of New England the Congregationalist establishment scorned but could not halt. This Yankee combined perfectionism with millennialism to make social radicals out of Christians reared in a section that had bitterly opposed Jeffersonian republicanism. The triumph of God's justice, peace and love in society, all sides came to agree, required the sanctification of individuals. Preachers, editors, and professors of moral philosophy drew hope for that triumph from the biblical promise that in the last days God would pour out His spirit on the faithful, writing His law on their hearts, and bringing them power to escape personal sin and conquer social evil. Finney's account of his initial grappling with the doctrine of sanctification after he moved to New York City in 1833 is well known, of course. This broader religious context makes understandable the biblical and perfectionist thought of William Lloyd Garrison and the evangelicals associated with him in the early years of the abolitionist crusade.[7] I was recently surprised to learn that the debate over holiness was also the context in which William Ellery Channing, gentle and beloved spokesman for Boston's Unitarian elite, preached during the early 1830's a series of twelve sermons later published under the title *The Perfect Life*. In them, Channing declared that the central principle of the Christian religion was God's purpose "TO PERFECT THE HUMAN SOUL; to purify it from all sin; to create it after His own image; and to fill it with His own spirit. . . . "[8] All these preachers, and a thousand others scattered from Maine to the Mississippi River, affirmed that the ethical renewal of persons was prerequisite to social righteousness. They disagreed only over whether and how much that renewal depended on human choices to respond to biblical truth, rather than upon the power of the Holy Spirit.[9]

The year 1835 was the *annus mirabilis* of both Christian liberation theology and the doctrine of sanctification in the United States. Phoebe Palmer professed the experience of perfect love at a weekly ladies' prayer meeting held at her sister's home in New York City that year, and for the next four decades made the "New York Tuesday Meeting for the Promotion of Holiness" the center of Methodist perfectionism and spiritual feminism, and the source of much of its social concern.[10] That year, also, Orange

Scott, presiding elder in Springfield, Massachusetts, won over a majority of the New England Methodist ministers to abolitionism by sending each one a three-month subscription to William Lloyd Garrison's *The Liberator*. Scott's subsequent agitation of this issue, in defiance of the bishops, led eight years later to the secession of the Wesleyan Methodists in Western New York and, in a move to prevent New England from joining them, to the division of the Methodist church, north and south, at the General Conference of 1844.[11]

Methodists scarcely dominated the scene, however. Evangelicals of New England Congregationalist backgrounds, who when residing west of the Hudson River were required by the terms of the plan of union of 1801 to become Presbyterians, moved in parallel directions in the year 1835. In January, John J. Shipherd and Asa Mahan came to New York City to persuade Arthur Tappan to locate at Oberlin, Ohio, the college he planned to support for the students who had withdrawn from Presbyterian Lane Theological Seminary, in Cincinnati, when the trustees forbade their antislavery activities the year before. Tappan, who had been a mainstay of Lane and who had supported the students during much of the year of feverish antislavery activity which followed their withdrawal, agreed to the plan and named Mahan, a Cincinnati Presbyterian pastor who had sustained the students against the trustees, to be president at Oberlin. Tappan's conditions were, however, that evangelist Charles G. Finney, recently pastor of the congregation of revivalists and reformers which he and his brother Lewis Tappan had helped organize in New York City, should spend half of each year in Oberlin as professor of theology; that the faculty, and not the trustees, should be in control of the college; and that it should be committed to "the broad ground of moral reform in all its departments."[12]

Oberlin became at once the vital center of Christian reflection and action aimed at the liberation of black people from slavery and racism; of women from the male oppression which excluded them from the higher professions, but exploited them in the oldest; of poor people from ignorance, alcohol, and the greed of merchants and land speculators; and of American society generally from all those forms of institutionalized evil which stood in the way of Christ's coming kingdom.[13] Theodore Dwight Weld, whose perfectionist view of Christian faith underlay his recent emergence as the most prominent evangelical abolitionist in the country, appeared at Oberlin in the fall of 1835, just as Finney completed his first half-year as professor there, to give a series of lectures on abolition and train students as antislavery agents.[14] Finney, whose New York congregation had meanwhile erected the Broadway Tabernacle for his church and revival center, began that fall the *Lectures to Professing Christians* that signalled his growing involvement with the doctrine of the sanctification of believers, which he thought crucial to further progress in Christendom's march toward the millennium.[15] The widespread merging of Christian perfection with moral reform, in a theology no longer Calvinist though professedly Puritan, was too much for the more conservative of the Scotch-Irish preachers in the Presbyterian church, U.S.A., and certainly too much for the Princeton Seminary faculty. Within two years, that denomination also divided, ostensibly over theological but in fact also over social issues.[16]

The broader significance of these events has been obscured by the tendency of historians, recently being reversed, to view perfectionists and abolitionists as an eccentric if not lunatic strain in American theology. Another series of events in the same year 1835 suggests, rather, that Christian radicalism was for the moment in the mainstream. Nathaniel W. Taylor, professor of theology at Yale and the chief architect with Lyman Beecher of the "New Divinity," or the "New England Theology," as it was called, published four essays in his journal, *The Christian Spectator*, that placed him firmly in the camp of those to whom sanctification had become the crucial issue. By grafting onto covenant theology the doctrine of the moral nature of divine government, which required the consent of the human will to all that God provided or demanded; by locating depravity not in our natures, as Jonathan Edwards had, but in our dispositions, our selfish wills; and by adopting Samuel Hopkins' idea that disinterested benevolence, or unselfish love toward God and man, was the sum of the Christian's duty, Taylor and Beecher transformed Calvinist dogma into a practical Arminianism, without having to jettison Calvinist verbiage.[17] Meanwhile, Lyman Beecher's son Edward, who joined the famous "Yale Band" to become the first president of Illinois College, spoke for many of the young New Englanders whom Yale and Andover seminaries sent out as missionaries to the Midwest in the 1830's.[18] He called in 1835 for "the immediate production of an elevated standard of personal holiness throughout the universal church—such a standard . . . as God requires, and the present exigencies of the world demand." With Finney, Edward Beecher believed that on its creation depended all hopes for the establishment of the kingdom of God on earth.[19]

The ethical seriousness of the New Divinity equalled that of the Methodists on one hand, or the Unitarians on the other. The title of the first of the four articles Taylor published indicated its content: "The Absolute Necessity of the Divine Influence for Holiness of Heart and Life." The second began with refreshing directness: "The promised agency of the Holy Spirit, for the conversion of sinners and the sanctification of saints, is the rock of safety to the church, and the hope to the world. All preaching and prayer which dispenses with the necessity of this divine influence . . . tends to drive revivals of religion, and religion itself, from the earth." This divine influence, however, the article went on to say, "never violates the great laws of moral action or contravenes the freedom of the subject." It does not leave man "the mere creature of passive impressions or a machine operated upon by compulsory force." [20]

The year 1835, finally, was crucial in the history of the movement to free the slaves. Lewis Tappan helped William Lloyd Garrison outmaneuver his brother Arthur and two other Tappan brothers, both of them Unitarians living in Boston, who wanted to moderate the abolitionist crusade for a moment in search of broader popular support. Arthur then joined Lewis in financing an immense expansion of abolitionist propaganda through four monthly journals, one appearing in each week of the month. They flooded the country in the twelve months after July, 1835, with a million pieces of abolitionist literature. The antislavery movement, having mounted this radical and "public" challenge to the South, could never again unite moderate Christians in a genteel moral consensus.[21]

That year also, Garrison embraced radically perfectionist piety as the only way to motivate the nation to free the slaves, liberate women, renounce warfare, and substitute love for force in the administration of justice. A company of able scholars have recently underlined the essentially evangelical commitments which governed the abolitionist crusade, not only in its earliest years, but during and after the year 1835, when Garrison began advocating a platform of "universal reform." He aimed to overthrow "the empire of sin" by an agitation whose only weapons were truth and love.[22] Aileen Kraditor has shown that biblical ideas of righteousness dominated his thought down until 1843, when he began to question the authority of the Scriptures, and 1845, when he discovered Thomas Paine. That before those dates Garrison's position paralleled that of Finney, Weld, and Orange Scott is evident from an editorial entitled "Perfection" which he published in *The Liberator* on October 15, 1841. "Whether this or that individual has attained to the state of 'sinless perfection' " is not the issue, the unsigned editorial began. What matters is "whether human beings, in this life, may and ought to serve God with all their mind and strength, and to love their neighbors as themselves!" Instead of assailing the doctrine "be ye perfect," Garrison continued, believers who were "not wholly clean, not yet entirely reconciled to God, not yet filled with perfect love," should acknowledge that "freedom from sin is a Christian's duty and privilege," and obey St. Paul's injunction to "put on the whole armor of God." [23]

Garrison's use of Wesleyan terms and concepts is a reminder that Methodist clergymen believed God had raised up their movement in order "to reform the nation, and spread scriptural holiness over the land." Since my days in graduate school, when I wrote *Revivalism and Social Reform*, evidence has multiplied that holiness preaching was from Francis Asbury's time onward an important catalyst to Methodist participation in American movements for social justice. Philip Bruce, a preacher stationed in Portsmouth, Virginia, wrote Bishop Thomas Coke on March 25, 1788, of immense revivals there among African slaves as well as free whites. "Here liberty prevails," he wrote. On one preacher's circuit in nearby Sussex and Brunswick Counties, between twelve and fifteen hundred whites besides a great number of blacks had been converted; and a friend had informed him that at the February court in Sussex, Methodists had filed deeds of manumission setting free over a hundred slaves.[24] In New England by the 1830's, Wesley's followers had established a reputation of commitment to the popular side in such political issues as universal white manhood suffrage, workingmen's rights, and a tax-supported system of free public schools. They generally endorsed the crusade for total abstinence earlier than others, in response not only to Wesley's influence but to the cry of their American Indian converts and of free blacks and workingclass whites in Northern cities, who insisted that liquor was for their peoples a tragic curse.[25] And at the end of the century, Norris Magnuson has shown, such Wesleyan organizations as the Salvation Army and the Door of Hope Mission learned from the poor people they served the necessity for a moral reconstitution of the social and legal structures which allowed the exploitation of the indigent. Evangelicals of many persuasions, including Methodist William Arthur, author of the famous holiness tract, *The Tongue of Fire*, had come by the same route to a similar conclusion during the 1850's.[26]

But on the American scene, at least, the denominational approach is myopic, as indeed I find it to some extent to be in Bernard Semmel's study of what he calls *The Methodist Revolution* in England. I have briefly examined the reports of Moravian missionaries in Antigua, in the years between 1800 and 1833, comparing them with those of the Methodists, who were equally effective on that island, and find little difference between the efforts of the two missions to liberate black people from the molds in which their African past and their American enslavement had imprisoned them. An immensely detailed plan of personal interviews and moral instruction for individual converts kept Moravian missionaries busy from dawn to dark of every day. True, they scorned preaching theology, being convinced that to tell the story of the cross of Jesus was the surest way to awaken the hearts and minds of the Africans. Once awakened, however, the converts found biblical teachings about purity, honesty, unselfishness, loyalty to marital bonds, and a forgiving spirit—in short, about the life of holiness—defined the character of a Moravian, despite what Methodists complained (and Semmel argues) was the antinomian character of their doctrine of justification.[27]

The same is true for the home missionary movement that swept American Congregationalism in the early decades of the nineteenth century. Whether at Yale College or along the advancing frontier of Yankee settlement in New York, Pennsylvania, and the upper Midwest, revivalists and home missionaries whose doctrines were still cast in Calvinist language displayed the same purpose as the Methodists: to produce, through a free response to the gracious truth of the gospel, the sanctification of disorganized and demoralized persons.[28] The rising expectations of the millennium which both home and overseas missions inspired did not glorify nationalism or westward expansion but demanded repentance. The millennial vision seems to have been at least as ecumenical as Wesley and Coke's view of the world parish. Those who shared it proclaimed the judgments of God upon all laws, governments, and social institutions, whether in the United States or elsewhere, that stood in the way of hope for a just and holy future for all humankind.[29]

Spokesmen for the New Divinity were never able to see, or at least to admit, what their critics readily perceived was their adoption of many Methodist doctrines.[30] In the same year 1835 when the columns of Nathaniel Taylor's *Christian Spectator* made the sanctifying work of the Holy Spirit the central issue in New England theology, he published an attack on Wesley's doctrine of the witness of the Spirit which misconstrued the founder of Methodism to teach that a subjective and personal revelation from God, rather than a transformed ethical life, attested one's conversion. Nathan Bangs remonstrated, but Taylor stuck to his charge. Methodists were only partially dismayed to hear themselves denounced by Congregationalism's greatest intellectual leader for not making personal holiness the only assurance of saving grace.[31]

For these reasons, then, the story of how Charles G. Finney forged in the crucible of Oberlin's social activism a Christian theology of liberation, in which the Arminianized Calvinism of the New Divinity was the chief element and the doctrine of what Finney called "perfect sanctification" through the baptism of the Holy Spirit was the catalyst, seems to me to illuminate best the history of radical religious thought in nineteenth-century America. Among New School Congregationalists and Presbyterians generally, the notion of Christian perfection was new and, therefore, almost impossible to associate with a traditional order. Methodists, however, tended to link that doctrine as much with loyalty to their Wesleyan past as with concern for a revolutionary future. A few of them preached and wrote about Christian holiness without any reference at all to the social crisis of the 1830's for which their message was newly relevant. Such antiquarian or individualistic perfectionism was not possible for preachers whose roots lay in New England Calvinism. At Oberlin especially, the interaction of theological reflection and spiritual experience with revolutionary ideology and political action was evident in all parties, and most especially in the evangelist whom Arthur Tappan made a professor of theology, Charles G. Finney.

Finney consented, after some initial reluctance, to accept the appointment at Oberlin because, during the previous two years, he had become convinced that the church could not save the nation unless its members found a way to translate the doctrine of sanctification into concrete experience. He had carried his evangelistic crusade from western New York to Philadelphia, New York, Providence and Boston, and then became pastor of Arthur Tappan's circle of revivalist and antislavery radicals in New York City. There, however, amidst the institutionalized evil evident in urban culture, the optimism with which he had in preceding years anticipated the early onset of the millennium was harder to sustain. Reform crusades—even one mounted to liberate "fallen women"—encountered withering opposition, some of it from less aggressive New School Calvinists. Finney saw in the invitation to Oberlin an opportunity to train a company of leaders who would make the idea of Christian holiness the center of a renewed campaign to place American society under the rule of Christ.[32] With the Tappans, Garrison, Beecher and Weld, he thought the times demanded a widespread raising of public consciousness that the old order was in crisis and that justice and love were destined to prevail in the new. Oberlin College could supply a trained corps of revivalists, ready to declare judgment upon all institutions which ran counter to the law of God and to affirm the dawn through His grace of a new day.[33]

Finney's role, as he conceived it, was not to agitate for particular reforms so much as to provide spiritual inspiration and a Christian ideology for them all. When Arthur Tappan guaranteed that the Oberlin faculty and students would be free of interference from trustees or other outsiders, and then guaranteed not only Finney's salary but whatever might become necessary to maintain the solvency of the school, the evangelist agreed to plant himself for half of each year at what he thought were the two arenas where America's moral destiny would be decided—New York City and the upper Midwest. The Oberlin venture did not in any sense, therefore, isolate him from the main currents of American social idealism. Rather, the college and community furnished him with a laboratory of both spirituality and radical social action, in which the idea of Christian perfection soon reigned supreme.[34]

Both Finney and Mahan left behind autobiographies, written in their old age, which recounted with some improvement from hindsight the events at Oberlin between 1835 and 1840. Far from fitting the image of a backwoods evangelist, Mahan was a moral philosopher of great sophistication. His textbook asserting an absolute standard of righteousness, and directly challenging the increasingly popular utilitarian views of Jeremy Bentham and John Stuart Mill, was the second most widely used in the standard course which college presidents taught for senior classes in nineteenth-century America. Both Mahan and Finney, moreover, were very close students of the English Bible; and their study aimed not only at understanding theology but at cultivating their own spiritual life. They freely acknowledged that during Oberlin's first five years a deep hunger for the highest personal achievements of piety and righteousness was their primary motivation. Mahan wrote that though he had been an effective evangelist and preached often at Methodist camp meetings, he found in St. Paul's writings evidence of a personal relationship with Christ that he did not know, and for which he continually prayed.[35] Never, since Luther and Wesley, had theology and experience been so closely intertwined.

In September, 1836, in the middle of the revival with which the college opened its second year, a student asked whether Christians had biblical grounds to anticipate a relationship with Christ which would enable them to live without committing such sins as produced guilt and condemnation—in short, to live a morally sanctified life. President Mahan answered, passionately, "yes," though acknowledging he had not yet attained such a relationship. During that evening and the following day, however, he broke through to what he saw was the way to experience Christian perfection: faith in Christ's atonement. "When I thought of my guilt, and the need of justification," he recalled, "I had looked at Christ exclusively, as I ought to have done; for sanctification, on the other hand, to overcome the world, the flesh and the devil, I had depended mainly on my own resolutions." [36] The next evening, he preached to the revival congregation on the text "the love of Christ constraineth us," declaring both from Scripture and his own experience "that we are to be sanctified by faith, just as we are justified by faith." Although he did not use in the sermon the phrase "baptism of the Holy Spirit," as he remembered having done when writing his autobiography over thirty years later, the version of the sermon which appeared in print in 1839 declared that "the appropriate office of the Holy Spirit" is to reveal the love of Christ so powerfully as to enable Christians fully to consecrate themselves to Him.[37] Later, in a thoughtful discourse entitled "The Divine Teacher," Mahan explained that the Holy Spirit "enlightens the intellect and carries on the work of sanctification in the heart," presenting Christ to our minds "in such a manner that we are transformed into His image" and freed from forlorn reliance upon "our own natural powers as moral agents." [38]

Finney was not present that second evening and probably did not yet approve Mahan's decisive turn toward the idea that a "second crisis" of Christian experience inaugurated the life of sanctity. But he began immediately what proved a three-year process of working his way through the teachings of the Bible concerning the covenant of holiness. As always, his head must go ahead of his heart. That fall and winter—which proved to be the last he spent in New York City—Finney included in the second series of his *Lectures to Professing Christians* one entitled "Sanctification by Faith," two on the subject of "Christian Perfection," another declaring "Love Is the Whole of Religion" and a final one entitled "Rest of the Saints." The last defined faith as "yielding up all our powers and interests to Christ, in confidence, to be led, and sanctified, and saved by Him." All of these lectures took as their starting point the general outlines of the New Divinity.[39]

In the fall of 1838, when ill health prevented his spending the winter traveling in evangelistic work, Finney undertook to deliver and publish in *The Oberlin Evangelist*, the faculty's new organ of religious and social reformation, the series of lectures on Christian perfection printed for the first time since then in this book. In a letter to readers, printed along with the third lecture, Finney explained that in the years before 1835 he had been wholly and, he believed in retrospect, wisely committed to revival preaching aimed at securing the conversion of sinners. During his years in New York City, however, he became "fully convinced that converts would die" and "that revivals would become more and more superficial and finally cease unless something effectual was done to elevate the standard of holiness in the church." He subsequently realized that he had known Christ "almost exclusively as an atoning and justifying Savior," but not as a sanctifying one. In the last two or three years, he continued, "I have felt as strongly and unequivocally pressed by the Spirit of God to labor for the sanctification of the Church, as I once did for the conversion of sinners. . . . God has been continually dealing with me in mercy. . . . How often I have longed to unburden myself, and pour out my whole heart to the dear souls, that were converted in those powerful revivals." Through the lectures, then, he hoped to correct the deficiencies of his earlier ministry.[40]

The suggestion some scholars have made, following William McLoughlin, that such high-blown spirituality indicated a turning away from the movement to reform society will not fit the facts. 1839 and 1840 were vintage years for Christian evolutionary ideology at Oberlin. Finney's

Skeletons of a Course of Theological Lectures published in the latter year included several on human government, in which he declared that "when one form of government fails to meet any longer the necessities of the people, it is the duty of the people to revolutionize. . . . In such cases it is vain to oppose revolution; for in some way the benevolence of God will bring it about. . . . God always allows His children as much liberty as they are prepared to enjoy." [41] Finney claimed, in a passage cut from his *Memoirs* before their publication in 1876, that he led the faculty in resistance to racism. When students from the South questioned the propriety of black students eating with them at the same tables, he wrote, the faculty adopted his proposal to set up separate tables where any who did not wish to eat with the blacks might take their meals; the historic arrangements thus being reversed, the separate tables remained empty.[42] Moreover, the lectures on sanctification themselves contained a radical attack on prevailing legal standards of business ethics that left little room for the profit motive.[43]

When in 1839 the Ohio legislature, as Donald Dayton has recently pointed out, adopted a statute which seemed to extend to all of Ohio the jurisdiction of Kentucky law over fugitive slaves, Finney introduced a resolution at the next meeting of the Ohio Anti-slavery Society declaring the statute "a palpable violation of the Constitution of this state and of the United States, of the common law and of the law of God," and announced it "as a well-settled principle of both common and constitutional law, that no human legislation can annul or set aside the law or authority of God." [44] At the commencement exercises in September, 1839, Jonathan Blanchard presented his famous address, "A Perfect State of Society," to the Oberlin Society of Inquiry. Over a thousand persons attended a meeting of the Lorain County Anti-slavery Society on commencement evening, denounced "the disgraceful 'Black laws' of Ohio," and resolved that the membership would "not support any man for the legislature" who did not favor the repeal of all Ohio laws "founded on a distinction of color." [45] The announcement of these events in the *Evangelist* accompanied a stirring account of schools for the children of fugitive slaves that Oberlin graduates were maintaining in Canada and a denunciation of the "blood-thirsty and land-coveting whites" of Florida who had waged a three years' war against the Seminole Indians and now were resisting their permanent settlement in the southern part of that state lest runaway slaves should find protection among them.[46]

The development of Finney's doctrine of Christian perfection reflected and reinforced his revolutionary concern, and that of the Oberlin community generally, to reform society. The lectures of 1838 and 1839, which we shall examine in a moment, demonstrate the essentially religious basis of this concern and thus explain why Oberlin's political radicalism won such widespread attention: it was rooted in the central theme of the Old and New Testament Scriptures. The God of eternity had bound himself in covenant with those who would be His people, making them morally responsible to Him and to one another to help His kingdom come, as Jesus put it, and His will to be done, on earth as it was in heaven. Like John Wesley,

Finney drew deeply upon Moses and the prophets, but reenforced that source by appeal to the long tradition of Puritan or covenant theology. Moreover, his starting point in New Testament studies was not Moravian pietism, but Samuel Hopkins' distillation of the ethical teachings of Jesus and Paul into the law of disinterested benevolence—what Wesley called perfect love.

When Finney discovered, apparently out of his own study of the English Bible, the logical and historical links between covenant and promise in the Old Testament, and Jesus' covenant promise in the New of His continuing presence through the sanctifying comforter, the Holy Spirit, the circle was complete. He then proclaimed, as Wesley himself had only rarely declared, that the entire sanctification of the believer's moral will was achieved through the baptism of the Holy Spirit. That proclamation did not reduce but in fact radicalized Christian concerns for social justice. For it offered to Calvinist, Pietist, and Arminian alike a way of repossessing the doctrine of the sovereignty of God over individuals as well as over the structures of society.

The result, Finney recognized, was a radical reshaping of what the next year he called the "science of theology." Like other branches of knowledge, he declared, theology must be open to "new truth" and ministers of the Gospel should cast aside the fear of changing their opinions about what the Scriptures teach. "I was to a wonderful extent blind to my profound ignorance of the Word of God, till about three years past," he wrote. "Since that time I have been able to read it with a degree of astonishment in respect to my former ignorance which I cannot express." And he added, "I pray the Lord to deliver me, and to deliver the ministry, from the absurd prejudice that chains them and the church to a set of stereotyped opinions on all religious subjects." [47]

Finney began the lectures, then, with one on "eternal life" which, based on a text from the fifth chapter of 1 John, equated it with the present experience of sanctity rather than a future experience of blessedness. True faith, he said, is "receiving Christ as indwelling Savior," who becomes *the eternal life of the soul*. God's presence does not alter human nature but enables the Christian to begin a life of complete obedience.[48] The second lecture, on faith, based on Jesus' response to those who asked Him "what shall we do," insisted that Calvinists and Arminians alike were trying to produce faith by obedience, despite God's directive that holiness flows from "faith which works by love." Finney declared that in his earlier *Lectures on Revivals* he had erred in not showing "that the exercise of faith is the first thing to be done." The key element in that faith, he wrote, was "the consent of the heart or will" to the truth of God's faithful love, as it is "perceived by the intellect." Trust stemmed from "confidence in the character of God." [49] The third in this trilogy on hope, faith, and love was entitled "Devotion." This Finney defined, with characteristic concreteness, as "that state of the will in which the mind is swallowed up in God, as the object of supreme affection." In such a life of devotedness, "we not only live and move *in* God, but *for* God." He renounced the tendency to separate devotion from duty, including faithfulness to the ordinary duties of business life. And he rebuked those who forget that "devotion belongs to the will," not to the "ever-varying states of emotion," which some "are prone to call religion." [50]

For lecture four, Finney revised one of his earlier *Lectures to Professing Christians* entitled "True and False Religion," from Galatians 5:1. The true, he said, is the opposite of slavery: genuine liberty to act out of love. "The true Christian never yields to the will of God by constraint" but is drawn and persuaded, engaged and committed, by joyous awareness that "infinite wisdom and love" makes Christ the soul's "supreme, eternal choice." Slavery consisted in being obliged to choose between two evils. The slaves in the American South were not strictly speaking in a state of involuntary servitude, he said, for they "prefer being as they are, to being in a worse condition—to being imprisoned or whipped for attempting to escape." Though the religion of many persons is analagous to such slavery, he said, true faith brings genuine liberty. [51]

Finney then turned to two lectures on "the law of God." Its demands were wholly fulfilled, he said, following both Moses and Jesus, in the commandment to love God with all your heart, soul and mind, and to love your neighbor as yourself. Drawing upon but expanding Samuel Hopkins' idea of disinterested benevolence, he made a crucial distinction between loving one's self as an act of benevolence, and mere self-indulgence. Even more important, however, was Finney's explanation that by "love of the heart" he did not mean simply an emotional attachment. "By the heart I mean the will," he wrote; "emotions, or what are generally termed feelings, are often involuntary states of mind . . . and of course do not govern the conduct. Love, in the form of an emotion, may exist in opposition to the will. . . . " Since "the will controls the conduct," he continued, "it is, therefore, of course, the love of the heart or will, that God requires." [52]

The second talk on divine law set forth the doctrine that behind the American constitution stood a higher law, defined by what Hopkins had declared was the nature of God and the sum of man's duty: disinterested benevolence, or pure love. "In the light of this law," Finney wrote, "how perfectly obvious is it, that slavery is from hell. Is it possible that we are to be told that slavery is a divine institution? What! Such a barefaced, shameless, and palpable violation of the law of God authorized by God himself? And even religious teachers, gravely contending that *the Bible sanctions this hell-begotten system*? 'Oh shame where is thy blush?' What! Make a man a slave—set aside his moral agency—treat him as a mere piece of property . . . and then contend that this is in keeping with the law of God . . . ?" [53]

The two lectures came to a climax, characteristically, in a concrete application of the law of radical love to the ethics of conducting business. Every violation of the rule of disinterested benevolence, or perfect love, "is fraud and injustice," Finney said, not only toward God but "toward every individual in the universe." To transact business merely upon the "principles of commercial justice" upheld by courts of law is "rebellion against

God"; in a Christian, such behavior is "real apostasy," for which restitution must be made in all cases possible "or there is no forgiveness." Fiercely denouncing on this ground not only slaveholders and merchants who priced goods beyond their real value but speculators in Western lands, Finney declared such offenders must "give back their ill-gotten gains" or suffer damnation. He then outlined the proper Christian attitude toward wealth in terms that differed from John Wesley's. "The law of love," he said, "requires that we should afford everything as cheap as we can, instead of getting as much as we can. The requirement is that we do all the good we can to others, and not that we get all we can ourselves. The law of God is, sell as cheap as you can— the business maxim, as dear as you can." [54] Not content to leave the matter there, Finney added a third lecture entitled "Glorifying God" that defined holiness as faith in practice. In it he decried the love of money and praised simplicity of life, particularly in clothing and food, then came back, grandly, to link the idea of holiness to the first question of the Westminster catechism.[55]

The eighth lecture, on "True and False Peace," followed a letter to readers of the *Evangelist* which revealed Finney's doctrine of "sin in believers" to be very close to Wesley's, as was his appeal to converts to have faith in Christ, the sanctifying Savior.[56] The lecture itself dealt with the psychic dimension of choice. When conscience and will unite in holy commitment to God, peace is complete. But to yield one's will to conscience or persuasion without a deep conviction that God is trustworthy—that is, without a motive rooted in the assurance of His love—is to paper over cracks in the wall.[57]

By late April both the lectures and Finney's accompanying letters revealed the results of his deepening personal quest for biblical understanding. The scriptural promise of a renewed covenant of grace, taken from the prophecy of Jeremiah as well as the epistle to the Hebrews, laid a basis in logic for the emphasis upon the work of the Holy Spirit that preoccupied him in the succeeding months. And his dawning awareness that the Christian needs divine help beyond that of merely the illumination of the intellect was evident in his thoroughly Wesleyan exposition of chapters seven and eight of the epistle to the Romans. Rejecting the traditional view that the bondage to sinning Paul described in the seventh chapter depicted his life as a converted Christian, Finney declared that those truly born of the Spirit experienced the victory described in chapter eight. The power of the spirit of life in Christ made them free from the principle of sin and death and, therefore, "more than conquerors" in every struggle with temptation.[58]

Five lectures on "The Promises," printed from May to July, bore the fruits of his study of the distinction between the Old and the New Covenants. The text for all five was St. Peter's word in his second epistle: "Whereby are given unto us exceeding great and precious promises, that by these ye might be partakers of the divine nature." The argument of each lecture, however, ranged across the entire spectrum of biblical promises of righteousness that were fulfilled in Pentecostal experience. "We never keep the commandments, only as we take hold of the promises," Finney began; "by this I mean that grace alone enables us, from the heart, to obey the commandments of God." In a vastly complex recitation of the Old Testament promises which, he said, "belong emphatically to the Christian church," and especially of God's pledge recorded in Jeremiah 31 and Ezekiel 36 to put a "new heart" within His people—passages that he quoted at length three or four times in the first lecture—Finney burst through to an assertion that "the Old Covenant left men to the exercise of their own strength" in responding to God's commands, whereas "the New is the effectual sanctification by the Holy Spirit." [59] Partaking of the divine moral nature did not mean, however, that God had promised "to change our constitution—to destroy our personal identity—and make our spiritual existence identical" with His. Rather, Christians were invited to become "partakers of the moral nature, or attributes or perfections of God" which are "by the Spirit, through the promises, begotten in our minds." This assertion, though couched in the language of God's moral government, was staggering to anyone not teethed on St. Paul. It clearly made the work of the Holy Spirit central to the New Covenant. And that covenant, Finney now saw, was not the promise itself, nor an "outward precept," nor "any outward thing whatever, but an inward holiness brought about by the Spirit of God—the very substance and spirit of the law written in the heart by the Holy Ghost." [60]

This study of the promises inspired Finney's decisive turn to the language of Pentecost to expound the covenant of grace. On further examination of the Scriptures, he concluded that "the blessing of Abraham" that Paul wrote had "come on the Gentiles through Jesus Christ" was not simply Christ himself but, rather, the Holy Spirit. The promises of His coming formed "one unbroken chain from Abraham to Christ," completed when the risen Lord pledged to His disciples that they should be baptized with the Spirit. This "blessing of Abraham," Finney declared, Christians must receive by faith. Though faith began in "perception of the truth," it was complete only when they yielded their wills to "the guidance, instruction, influences, and government of the Holy Spirit." [61] He now saw clearly, he said, that Christ and the apostles regarded the day of Pentecost "as the commencement of a new dispensation," in which the Old Covenant was set aside only in the sense that it was fulfilled in the New.[62]

In this rich context of scriptural and covenant theology, Finney placed before his readers the doctrine of sanctification through the baptism of the Holy Spirit. "Every individual Christian may receive and is bound to receive this gift of the Holy Ghost at the present moment," he proclaimed. Christians who have been born again do not have that gift "in such a sense as it is promised in these passages of the Holy Scripture, or in a higher sense than he was received by the Old Testament saints . . . , of whom it was said that 'they all died in the faith, not having received the promise.'" [63]

The next year, Finney's "Letters to Ministers of the Gospel" urged them to preach earnestly the doctrine he had so recently come to understand himself. They should spare no pains to help new converts realize their need of the experience of entire sanctification. He acknowledged again that his instruction to converts had in former times "been very defective," for he had not clearly seen "that the baptism of the Holy Ghost is a thing universally promised . . . to Christians under this dispensation, and that this blessing is to be sought and received after conversion." That baptism "is the secret of the stability of Christian character," he declared; new converts need "to be baptized into the very death of Christ, and by this baptism to be slain, and buried, and planted, and crucified, and raised to a life of holiness in Christ." [64]

Throughout all of their lectures and letters of these years, Finney and Mahan consistently declared that the only assurance that God was accomplishing His purpose in human lives was ethical: the righteousness which showed itself in radical rejection of all sin, whether stemming from individual choice or corrupt social institutions, through faith in Jesus Christ. Again and again, they and other members of the Oberlin faculty rang the changes on this theme, renouncing what they alleged was the antinomianism of the Oneida "perfectionists" on one hand and, on the other, the unwillingness of conservative Calvinists to trust the promises of God.[65]

Here was a theology cradled in experience and nurtured in Scripture, just as Wesley's had been. And the experience was of persons ready to organize their lives around the pursuit of a right relationship with God, that they believed would be attested by just and loving relationships with their fellow human beings and a holy war on the corrupted structures of society. The immediate background, however, was the revitalized Calvinist ethics of Samuel Hopkins, rather than the Anglican moralism that launched Wesley on his quest, or the pietism that helped him at a crucial juncture to see he could realize it through trust in Christ. The social context, moreover, was the optimism of a new nation, where hopes were blossoming of a social order hallowed by divine grace and hence characterized by justice and love.

Finney's earlier preaching had stressed so much the freedom and responsibility of human beings to repent and make a new life as to allow the charge that he ignored the role of God's grace in sanctification. Now, however, he was affirming that divine grace, poured out in the baptism of the Holy Spirit, was indispensable to the sanctification of both persons and the structures of society. Individual Christians must receive that divine gift by a faith so reasonable and a consecration so deliberate as to leave fully intact their moral responsibility to help build a righteous society and a holy character. Never a Pelagian, I think, Finney had found a way to reclaim the doctrine of God's sovereignty without becoming a Calvinist, either. He had discovered, he believed in Scripture, a Pentecostal version of covenant theology that opened the way to the evangelical unity that Wesley and Whitefield sought but were never able to establish. Rooting the experience of the baptism of the Spirit in the Old Testament covenant of holiness also insulated it against the anti-intellectual and mystical corruptions of it that Wesley feared and that, alas, forgetting Finney, twentieth-century Pentecostals seem often to have embraced.

Interestingly enough, Finney did not profess to have attained this experience himself until three years after these lectures were completed. They provide the context necessary to understand the little-noticed passage of his autobiography, describing his supply pastorate during the winter of 1843-1844 at Marlborough Chapel, in Boston. This was a newly organized Congregationalist group that he remembered as "composed greatly of radicals," most of them holding "extreme views" on such subjects as nonviolence, women's rights or antislavery. During this winter, he recalled, "my mind was exceedingly exercised on the question of personal holiness." After many weeks of Bible reading and prayer during which he avoided visiting with individuals, Finney found himself, as he remembered it, in "a great struggle to consecrate myself to God, in a higher sense than I had ever before seen to be my duty, or conceived as possible." In particular, he felt unable to give his ailing wife up without reservation to the will of God. "What if, after all this divine teaching, my will is not carried," he asked himself, "and this teaching takes effect only in my sensibility? May it not be that my sensibility is affected by these revelations from reading the Bible and that my heart is not really subdued by them?" The issue was the same one he had raised at the revival in Oberlin in 1836: desire versus will, sentiment versus choice.[66]

One memorable day, however, the evangelist was able, as he put it, "to fall back, in a deeper sense than I had ever before done, upon the infinitely blessed and perfect will of God." Then, in an act of consecration that fit precisely Samuel Hopkins' description of the Christian's duty but that Wesleyans thought outrageous, Finney recalled, "I went so far as to say to the Lord, with all my heart, that He might do anything with me or mine to which His blessed will could consent; that I had such perfect confidence in His goodness and love as to believe that He could consent to do nothing to which I could object," including "the salvation or damnation of my own soul, as the will of God might decide." In this moment he said he also gave up his former assurance of salvation and took it for granted from that day forward that he would be saved, as he put it, "if I found that . . . [God] kept me, and worked in me by His Spirit, and was preparing me for heaven, working holiness and eternal life in my soul."[67]

Looking back at this experience when writing his *Memoirs* thirty-two years later, Finney declared:

As the great excitement of that season subsided and my mind became very calm, I saw more clearly the different steps of my Christian experience, and came to recognize the connection of all things, as all wrought by God from beginning to end. But since then I have never had those great struggles and long protracted seasons of agonizing prayer that I had often experienced. It is quite another thing to prevail with God, in my own experience, from what it was before. . . . I have felt since then a religious freedom, a religious buoyancy and delight in God and in His word, a steadiness of faith, a Christian liberty and overflowing love that I had only experienced, I may say, occasionally before. . . . Since then I have had the freedom of a child with a loving parent.

This testimony to the fruits of a second work of grace would have suited any Methodist. Certainly the evangelist did not describe it in the terms of man's natural ability to obey God's absolute moral law which had pervaded his earlier preaching. The full cooperation of God with man, an immersion in the divine presence which both made possible and hallowed the free act of full consecration, had become for him, as for John Wesley's Methodists, the way to spiritual peace and moral triumph.[68]

The transfer of Finney's Pentecostal language into American Methodism was direct and immediate. George O. Peck, editor of the influential Methodist weekly, the *New York Christian Advocate*, paid close attention to Finney's lectures as they appeared in *The Oberlin Evangelist* in 1839 and 1840. In the fall of the latter year, he became the first Methodist I know since John Fletcher to have equated the experience of entire sanctification with the baptism of the Holy Spirit.[69] Others followed at once, and by 1855 reports of Methodist campmeetings and revivals in a variety of periodicals frequently referred to persons being "baptized" or "filled with the Spirit," and used the terms interchangeably with "heart purity," "perfect love," or "entire sanctification." [70] Phoebe Palmer, leader of the holiness awakening among Methodists, was so deeply involved in the elaboration of John Wesley's language of Calvary that she was one of the last to adopt the new terminology; but she did adopt it, in the fall of 1856, after a summer of immense spiritual refreshing in campmeetings in Western New York.[71] Her next major book, *Promise of the Father for the Last Days*, made Peter's text at Pentecost the basis of faith for the "second blessing" and the foundation as well of a biblical argument in favor of women's right to preach the gospel—a right that she had exercised, but refused to claim, for the previous twenty years.[72]

Ever since, Wesleyans, Presbyterians, Congregationalists and Friends devoted to the proclamation of Christian holiness in America have intermingled, in preaching and in witness, the language of Pentecost and the language of Calvary.[73] The imagery of the Spirit did not displace that of the cross, certainly. Holiness campmeetings, especially Methodist ones held along the eastern seaboard, closed with long Sunday night communion services, at the end of which Christians who had prayed throughout the week for the baptism of the Holy Spirit were urged to open their hearts and sing "The cleansing stream I see, I see. I plunge, and oh, it cleanseth me." [74]

Finney's new teachings, and Asa Mahan's elaboration of them, were also crucial in the early years of the "higher life" movement among English evangelicals and of the Keswick conferences that sustained it. William E. Boardman, a Presbyterian home missions leader in America and author of the immensely popular volume *The Higher Christian Life*, and R. Pearsall Smith and his wife, Hannah Whitall Smith, initiated the Oxford and Brighton "union meetings for the promotion of holiness" on the heels of Dwight L. Moody's first great crusades in England. Finney's evangelistic tours of Britain in 1849 and from 1858 to 1861 and the publication of his writings there had laid the foundation for the acceptance of the doctrine of holiness among Baptist, Presbyterian and Anglican clergymen searching for a gospel with redeeming power over both individual and social evil. Mahan moved to England permanently in the 1870's, published his autobiography and a book entitled *Baptism of the Holy Ghost* there and was a key participant in the union meetings at Oxford in 1873.

The influence of Finney and Mahan remained strong as the Keswick movement expanded from a single summer conference in the Lake Country to numerous affiliated conferences and year-round weekly meetings in many English cities. The reason for their influence was that they were not Methodists and did not subscribe to the Wesleyan doctrine that the experience of entire sanctification involved the destruction or cleansing away of the Christian's inward bent to sinning, the "carnal mind." No matter that Finney did not in fact affirm the existence of such a fallen nature and argued that humankind was fallen in its dispositions, not in its nature; he declared that the baptism of the Holy Spirit, the perfection of love, actually cancelled out selfishness and all the sinfulness associated with it. The English evangelicals of Calvinist background wanted both to escape association with what had become there the scandal of Methodism, its doctrine of complete deliverance from what Wesley called the "inbred enemy," and to preach entire deliverance from acts of sin. As contrasted with Finney, they affirmed in orthodox fashion the existence of the old nature or principle of "sin in believers," but declared that in the second experience of grace the Holy Spirit brought total triumph over its operation, so bound up "the man of sin" within that the believer who thereafter walked in the light would have no consciousness of His existence. To all other aspects of the doctrine of salvation upon which Oberlin and Methodist teachings were agreed—the promise of a life of perfect love and, hence, of full freedom from acts of selfishness; the deep grounding of this promise on the grace of God that flows from the atonement of Christ; and trust in the Holy Spirit rather than in any human effort to bring victory over all sin—the Keswick leaders down at least until the turn of the century were unanimously committed.

Thus did Charles G. Finney help spread through England and America a theology of salvation that brought the whole of the Old and New Covenants to bear upon God's promise to renew His children in righteousness and love. His deep consciousness of sin— especially his awareness of its stubborn social character—and his fierce loyalty to the law offered an alternative to the sentimentalizing of New Testament doctrine that lay immediately in the future. By the end of the century evangelicals of many backgrounds had romanticized the doctrine of the atonement, separating their understanding of God's love from His judgments that are "true and righteous altogether." The liberal heirs of the New England theology had meanwhile pulled loose the idea of the Incarnation from its rooting in God's covenant of grace. Moreover, the social gospel, which began in the sturdy biblical theology of Oberlin and Wesleyan preaching before the Civil War, was shorn of its strength when nothing but a humanized conception of the love of Jesus was its motive power. Charles M. Sheldon's question, "What would Jesus do?" is always a crucial one; but what God's law and our faithfulness to Him require needs always to be the context in which Christians ask the question. That context is precisely what the biblical idea of a covenant of righteousness offered to those who were awakened to the promise of a sanctifying Spirit.

In retrospect, this story of the maturing of Charles G. Finney's theology, and of its rooting in the clash of events and ideas in which the biblical notion of righteousness was central, bears in important ways on issues of great importance today. The central one, of course, is the ethical problem raised by the more ecstatic, subjective, and individualistic character of contemporary witnesses to the experience of the baptism of the Holy Spirit, both in and outside Wesleyan circles. These have allowed if not encouraged an unbiblical divorce of personal from corporate or social ethics, of individual from what Wesley called "social holiness."

Finney's systematic interpretation of biblical teachings also suggests a scriptural authentication for a set of beliefs about the baptism of the Holy Spirit that some have suspected were an imposition of folk theology upon Wesleyan doctrine. Dealing with that issue in biblical terms will, I think, shed important new light on the nature of the link (or, as I would incline to put it, the gap) between nineteenth-century Wesleyan and twentieth-century Pentecostal and charismatic perceptions of Christian experience.

The story also returns us to the problem of evangelical ecumenicity. Christ calls to unity in doctrine and practice those who believe the Bible to be a sufficient rule of both. Finney's labored effort to put together Wesleyan and covenant theology reminds us that since the days when Wesley and Whitefield found themselves pulled apart, their followers have never been able to pull themselves together. And the problem is larger than, merely, the dialogue between neo-Arminian and neo-Calvinist positions. For the worldwide mosaic of Bible-believing Christians today includes also the evangelicals in the Mennonite, Brethren and Quaker traditions; the Pentecostals and their new-found allies in the broader charismatic movement; the modern heirs of continental Pietism, whether in Lutheran, Reformed, or Moravian communities; the Southern Baptists and their extended family of spiritual kinfolk in the South, which in some ways includes and in other ways does not include the many millions who follow in Alexander Campbell's train and call themselves churches or Disciples of Christ; the Adventists, most of them now, perhaps, in the Seventh-Day Adventist Church; those properly called fundamentalists, who look back to the biblicist, millenarian and Christological doctrines forged into an antimodernist credo during the controversies of the first three decades of this century; and what I have called elsewhere the post-fundamentalist evangelicals of the center, mostly of Presbyterian, Baptist and Congregationalist backgrounds, who dominate the headlines of church life in the great cities of the nation, maintain theological seminaries such as Fuller, Gordon-Conwell, Westminster, Trinity and Bethel, and share in a network of evangelistic enterprises for which *Christianity Today* is the voice and Billy Graham the symbol. Finney's pilgrimage through New England theology to the doctrine of a baptism of the Holy Spirit, which he believed would both inwardly sanctify and consecrate to radical ethical ideals the

28

whole of the covenanted community of Bible-believing Christians, reminds us that Jesus concluded His last-supper homily on the coming of an illuminating and sanctifying spirit. He prayed there that His followers should be one, "as thou, Father, art in me, and I in thee."

Finally, Finney's intellectual pilgrimage through the Scriptures—passing from the nature of the original covenants of holiness made between God and His people, represented by Abraham, Moses and David; through the prophetic translation of the ideas of both blessing and covenant into the promise of the Holy Spirit's coming; and thence through the preaching of John the Baptist and the teaching of Jesus to the fulfillment of all these promises in the experience of Pentecost—challenges as a fundamental distortion of Christian theology the recent discussion of whether Christology or pneumatology are the vital center of Christian faith. What Finney proposed in the lectures I have summarized and what, in my judgment, the Old and New Testament Scriptures repeatedly affirm is that the three persons of the Trinity are united in all the mighty acts of redemption by which God renews and sanctifies His people. To extend the distorting dialectic between Christ-centered and Spirit-illuminated religion to a historical contrast of nineteenth- and twentieth-century faith compounds this bad theology with poor history; for from the 1830's forward, evangelical believers in America moved steadily toward the conviction that the God who came near in covenant with Israel and in redemption through the life and death and life again of His Son remains savingly near in all ages through the sanctifying presence of the Holy Spirit.

NOTES

1. Cf. Nathan O Hatch, *The Sacred Cause of Liberty; Republican Thought and the Millennium in Revolutionary New England* (New Haven: Yale, 1977), 139-175, with James West Davidson, *The Logic of Millennial Thought: Eighteenth-Century New England* (New Haven: Yale, 1977), 122-178, 255-297. Most influential of many contemporary essays on the subject was Samuel Hopkins, *A Treatise on the Millennium* . . . (Boston, 1793), which reveals not a trace of American nationalist ideology; see esp. pp. 34, 54.

2. Ernest Lee Tuveson, *Redeemer Nation: The Idea of America's Millennial Role* (Chicago: University of Chicago, 1968), 53-82, 101-126; Robert T. Handy, *A Christian America: Protestant Hopes and Historical Realities* (London: Oxford, 1971), 27-64, *passim*; Timothy L. Smith, *Revivalism and Social Reform in Mid-Nineteenth-Century America* (Nashville, Tenn.: Abingdon, 1957), chapters 5, 10, 14.

3. John Mott Smith, "The Kingdom," *The Methodist Preacher: or Monthly Sermons from Living Ministers*, III (1832), 250-256; review of Thomas H. Skinner, *Thoughts on Evangelizing the World* (New York, 1836) in *Quarterly Christian Spectator*, IX (June, 1837), 291, 295; and *The Oberlin Evangelist*, I, no. 1 (December 20, 1838), p. 3, and the masthead in succeeding issues, declaring the millennium to be a state of general holiness in the church.

4. Garth M. Rosell, "The Millennial Roots of Early Nineteenth-Century Reform: An Examination of Charles G. Finney's Theology of Social Action," presented to the Hopkins-Harwichport Seminar in American Religious History, 1975. For an impor-

tant source of this kind of thinking, see Missionary Society of Connecticut, *The Constitution . . . ; With an Address from the Board of Trustees . . .* (Hartford: The Society, 1800), 14.

5. Taylor's views appear in numerous articles for the 1830's in his journal, *The Quarterly Christian Spectator*, notably in "On the Study of Prophecy," IX (June, 1837), 320-324, and, in the same volume, 376-377. See, again, Hopkins, *Treatise on the Millennium*, 44, 48-49, 56-57; and the same author's, *An Inquiry Into the Nature of True Holiness* (Newport, 1773), 1-9.

6. I cite extensive evidence on this point in my essay, "Uncommon Schools: Christian Colleges and Social Idealism in Midwestern America, 1820-1950," Indiana State Historical Society, *Lectures, 1977-1977* (Indianapolis, Indiana: The Society, 1978).

7. Aileen S. Kraditor, *Means and Ends in American Abolitionism: Garrison and His Critics in Strategy and Tactics, 1834-1850* (New York: Pantheon Books, 1967), 59, 79-82, 90-91.

8. William Ellery Channing, "The Essence of the Christian Religion," from *The Perfect Life, in Twelve Discourses* (Boston: Roberts Brothers, 1873), quoted here pp. 244-245, was recently reprinted in Sydney E. Ahlstrom, *Theology in America: The Major Protestant Voices, from Puritanism to Neo-Orthodoxy* (Indianapolis; Bobbs-Merrill, 1967); but see also, in Channing, *Perfect Life*, 52-54, 74-75, 113-114, 117-119, and the closing passage of the sermon on "The Universal Father," proclaiming the coming of "a Better Day," pp. 78-79.

I have recently learned that the "Dr. C." to whom Charles G. Finney, *Memoirs* (New York, 1876), 356-357, refers is identified in the Ms. version at the Oberlin College Archives as William Ellery Channing.

9. See, generally, Daniel W. Howe, *The Unitarian Conscience: The Harvard Moral Philosophers, 1805-1861* (Cambridge: Harvard, 1970), 131-148; William R. Hutchison, *The Transcendentalist Ministers* (New Haven: Yale, 1959), 1-21; and the discussion of "Moral Society," in D. H. Meyer, *The Instructed Conscience: The Shaping of the American National Ethic* (Philadelphia: University of Pennsylvania Press, 1972), 109-120, esp. the concluding pages.

10. Documentation for this [as for other points in this essay where the work is cited] appears in my *Revivalism*, 105, 116-117.

11. *Ibid.*, 181, 184-185. Cf. Donald Dayton, *Discovering an Evangelical Heritage* (New York, 1976), 73-85; Donald G. Mathews, "Orange Scott: The Methodist Evangelist as Revolutionary," in Martin Duberman, ed., *The Antislavery Vanguard: New Essays on the Abolitionists* (Princeton, New Jersey, 1965), 71-101; and Smith, *Revivalism*, 181, 184-185.

12. Bertram Wyatt-Brown, *Lewis Tappan and the Evangelical War Against Slavery* (New York, 1971), 129-130.

13. Smith, *Revivalism*, 104-105, 108-113; Dayton, *Evangelical Heritage*, 15-24, 35-43.

14. Wyatt-Brown, *Tappan*, 131.

15. Charles G. Finney, *Lectures to Professing Christians* (New York, 1837), lectures no. 17, 19, 20. This work has appeared in many subsequent editions.

16. George M. Marsden, *The Evangelical Mind and the New School Presbyterian Experience: A Case Study of Thought and Theology in Nineteenth-Century America* (New Haven, Connecticut), 59-87; Nathaniel W. Taylor, "The Revolution in the Presbyterian Church," *The Quarterly Christian Spectator*, IX (December, 1837), 597-646, a little-noticed article in which Taylor equated New School Doctrine with the New England Theology and raised the slavery issue, 629; Smith, *Revivalism*, 26-27, 185-187.

17. Taylor, "Revolution in the Presbyterian Church," *loc. cit.*, 599, 604-617. Sidney E. Mead, *Nathaniel William Taylor, 1786-1858: A Connecticut Liberal* (Chicago, 1942), underplays the perfectionist ethics in Taylor's theology.

18. Robert Merideth, *The Politics of the Universe: Edward Beecher, Abolition, and Orthodoxy* (Nashville, Tennessee, 1968), 73-84.

19. Edward Beecher, "The Nature, Importance, and Means of Eminent Holiness Throughout the Church," *The American National Preacher: Or Original Sermons— Monthly*, X (June and July, 1835), 193-194, 197, 203. Merideth, *Politics of the Universe*, 91-101, shows the relationship of these sermons to Beecher's friendship and alliance with abolitionist Elijah P. Lovejoy from 1834 to the latter's death at the hands of a mob in October, 1837.

20. The articles, which appeared unsigned, as did all the others of which I presume Taylor to be the author, are: "Man's Dependence on the Grace of God, for Holiness of Heart and Life," *The Christian Spectator*, VII (March, 1835), 76-89; "The Nature and Application of Divine Influence in the Salvation of Man," the same (June, 1835), 301-321; "An Inquiry into the True Way of Preaching on Ability," the same, 223-257; and "The Scriptural View of Divine Influence," the same (December, 1835), 591-597, in which the discussion of the work of the Holy Spirit, 595-597, seems to me to lay down the basis in logic for Charles G. Finney's later use of the expression "baptism of the Holy Ghost."

21. Wyatt-Brown, *Tappan*, 131.

22. Kraditor, *Means and Ends*, 59, 79-82.

23. *Ibid.*, 90-91; cf. pp. 24-25, showing Garrison's agreement with the New Divinity and, hence, with Finney and Mahan, on the nature of depravity and of free will, a context for Garrison's thought of which Professor Kraditor is largely unaware.

24. Philip Bruce, "An Extract of a Letter . . . to Bishop Coke, dated Portsmouth, Virginia, March 25, 1788," *The Arminian Magazine* [American], II (November, 1790), 563-564, came to my attention through my student, Thomas C. Johnsen. Cf. the idea of sanctification as liberation from sin through love, "the inward law of the gospel, *the law of the Spirit of life*," in a sermon by "Dr. Cutworth," the same, I (September, 1789), 444-445.

25. George Claude Baker, *An Introduction to the History of Early New England Methodism, 1789-1839* (Durham, North Carolina, 1941), 37-38, 45-82; Smith, *Revivalism*, 154-159, 169-172, 184-185; James B. Finley, Dayton, Ohio, December 3, 1819, to the editor, *The Methodist Magazine*, III (January, 1820), 34-40, quoting statements by Indian chiefs praising the liberating power of the "good Spirit" from addiction to whisky; "State Legislation on The Temperance Question," *The A.M.E. Christian Recorder*, no. 18 (August 17, 1854), 70.

26. Norris Magnuson, *Salvation in the Slums: Evangelical Social Work, 1865-1920* (Metuchen, New Jersey, 1977), 165-178 and, generally, 101-102, 117, 124-126, 140-142; Smith, *Revivalism and Social Reform*, 148-177; William Arthur, *The Tongue of Fire; or, The True Power of Christianity* (New York, 1880), 52-57, 110-132, 145-146.

27. Accounts of British Methodist overseas missions in *The* [American] *Methodist Magazine*, I (1819), 30-36, 193-200, 313-319, and *passim* do not refer at all to the doctrine of sanctification, though the journal shows Methodists in the United States continuously interested in the subject. For the Moravians, see their American journal, *The United Brethren Missionary Intelligencer and Religious Miscellany . . .* , II (First Quarter, 1825), 9-10; and cf. *Periodical Accounts Relating to the Missions of the Church of the United Brethren*, I (1790), 7-15.

28. Handy, *Christian America*, 27-35; review of Thomas H. Skinner, *Thoughts on Evangelizing the World* (New York, 1836), in *The Christian Spectator*, IX (June, 1837), 291-295; and "Encouragement to Effort, for the Speedy Conversion of the

World," the same, VII (March, 1835), 1-8.

29. Rosell, "Millennial Roots," *loc. cit.*

30. Asa Rand's description of Lyman Beecher's New Divinity as resembling "in its prominent features and bearing *Wesleyanism*," a "strange mingling of evangelical doctrine with Arminian speculation, . . . tending to produce spurious conversions," quoted in *The Baptist Weekly Journal of the Mississippi Valley* (August 9, 1833), is typical of scores I have seen.

31. "Wesleyan Methodism on the 'Witness of the Spirit,' " *The Christian Spectator*, IX (June, 1837), 176-182 and *passim*, and W. M. B., "Letter to the Christian Spectator on the Witness of the Spirit," *Methodist Magazine and Quarterly Review*, n.s. VIII (October, 1837), 457-476, review the controversy.

32. Wyatt-Brown, *Tappan*, 65-70, 129-131, 138-141.

33. *Ibid.*, 109-114, 121-128; Kraditor, *Means and Ends*, 22-25, 78-81; Finney, *Memoirs*, 333-343.

34. William G. McLoughlin, *Modern Revivalism: Charles Grandison Finney to Billy Graham* (New York, 1959), 108-113, misunderstands Finney's choice of role to have been a pietistic withdrawal from social action, an interpretation which the events at Oberlin, described below, do not sustain. Cf. Dayton, *Evangelical Heritage*, 15-24.

35. Edward H. Madden, *Civil Disobedience and Moral Law in Nineteenth-Century American Philosophy* (Seattle, Washington, 1968), 44-45, and *passim*. Cf. Meyer, *The Instructed Conscience*, 89-97, on Mahan as moral philosopher; Finney, *Memoirs*, 340-351; and Asa Mahan, *Out of Darkness into Light . . .* (Boston, 1876), 125-131, 133-136.

36. Finney, *Memoirs*, 350-351, and Mahan, *Out of Darkness*, 133-136, 140, 146, are closely parallel accounts, though both were written nearly forty years later. I believe Mahan's personal testimony in his *Scripture Doctrine of Christian Perfection . . .* , (4th ed., Boston, 1840), 185-187, tells substantially the same story, and that his account of a question from "a brother in the ministry" which provoked a winter's study by him and Finney, the same, 188-189, refers to a different though related issue. Cf. Mahan, *Doctrine of the Will* (Oberlin, Ohio: Oberlin College, 3rd ed., 1847), 228, quoted in Madden, *Civil Disodedience*, 45, for contemporary evidence of the crucial nature of the distinction between will and sensibility in the form of Mahan's attack upon Jonathan Edwards.

37. Mahan, *Scripture Doctrine*, 186-187; cf. Mahan, *Out of Darkness*, 139-147.

38. Mahan, *Scripture Doctrine*, 163-193, prints this lecture, which includes his personal testimony cited above; the quotation is from p. 172. This volume, printed on a Methodist press in Boston, uses Wesleyan terms such as "perfect love" and "entire sanctification" freely.

39. Finney, *Memoirs*, 340; Finney, *Lectures to Professing Christians*, 213, and *passim*.

40. Charles G. Finney, "Letter to Readers," *The Oberlin Evangelist* [cited hereinafter as *OE*], January 30, 1839, and below, pp. 50-52.

41. Charles G. Finney, *Skeletons of a Course of Theological Lectures* (Volume I, Oberlin, 1840), 24.

42. Finney, Ms. for *Memoirs*, 1875, Oberlin College Archives, chapter 25, pp. 1-2. Garth Rosell called my attention to this passage in the manuscript.

43. *OE*, I (March 13, 1839), 51, and (March 27, 1839), 57, also below, pp. 86-91, 96, 106.

44. Dayton, *Evangelical Heritage*, 47.

45. *OE*, I (September 11, 1839), 157.

46. *Ibid.*

47. *OE*, II (March 27, 1839), 59-60, (April 22, 1840), 67-68.

48. *OE*, I (January 1, 1839), 9-10, and below, pp. 36, 38.

49. *OE*, I (January 16, 1839), 18-19, and below, pp. 41, 44-45.

50. *OE*, I (January 30, 1839), 26-27, and below, pp. 55-57.

51. *OE*, I (February 13, 1839), 34, below, pp. 55-57.

52. *OE*, I (February 27, 1839), 41. Cf. also I (April 10, 1839), 66, below, pp. 69, 71, 109.

53. *OE*, I (March 13, 1839), 50, and below, pp. 83, 85, 89.

54. *Ibid.*, 50-51, and below, pp. 86-93.

55. *OE*, I (March 27, 1839), 57-60, and below, pp. 95-97, 104-105.

56. *OE*, I (April 10, 1839), 65, and below, p. 106.

57. *Ibid.*, 66-68, and below, pp. 109, 112-114.

58. *OE*, I (April 24, 1839), 74-75, and below, pp. 118-121, 123. Compare Mahan, *Scripture Doctrine*, 52-58, 101-103, on Romans 7 and 8: John Wesley, "The Spirit of Bondage and Adoption," in *Works* (12 vols.; New York, 1826), V, 84-89; and Cutworth's sermon, *The* [American] *Arminian Magazine*, I (September, 1789), 429, 444, 446, on the "law of the Spirit of Life," in Romans 8.

59. *OE*, I (May 22, 1839), 89 (June 19, 1839), 105, and below, pp. 132, 135, 150.

60. *OE*, I (June 5, 1839), 96, (June 19, 1839), 105-106, and below, pp. 142, 154.

61. *OE*, I (August 14, 1839), 137-138, and below, pp. 186-188.

62. *OE*, I (August 28, 1839), 147, and below, p. 196.

63. *OE*, I (August 14, 1839), 138, and below, p. 190.

64. *OE*, II (May 6, 1840), 76, and below, pp. 259-263. Cf. the letters in the same series in the two succeeding issues: (May 20, 1840), 84, and (June 3, 1840), 92, and below, pp. 263-265. Finney composed these letters shortly after completing the last seven lectures in the series on Christian Perfection, printed in *OE* from January through mid-April, 1840, and published at Oberlin in July of the same year, in his volume titled *Views of Sanctification*. These concluding lectures recapitulated the logic of the earliest ones in the series and did not employ the terminology of Pentecost, prompting scholars (including myself), who previously relied chiefly on that volume and neglected to read the *Evangelist* carefully, to suppose Finney did not at this stage teach that entire sanctification was accomplished by the baptism of the Holy Spirit.

65. *OE*, I (August 14, 1839), 140 is one example of scores that year.

66. Finney, *Memoirs*, 350-351, 373-375.

67. *Ibid.*, 375-376.

68. *Ibid.*, 381, and, for testimony that his subsequent preaching promoted such a "second experience" of sanctification through the baptism or filling with the Spirit, 422-425. Charles G. Finney, *Sermons on Gospel Themes* (transcribed by B. J. Goodrich; Oberlin, 1876), of which I have seen an undated New York edition, contains, pages 406-410, a passage that replicates all the teachings of Phoebe Palmer on the experience of sanctification.

69. [George O. Peck], "Christian Perfection," *The Methodist Quarterly Review*, XXIII (January, 1841), 128-132, 151-152. The same author's *The Scripture Doctrine of Christian Perfection Stated and Defended* ... (New York, 1841), 224-244, set forth a detailed summary of literature pertaining to the Oberlin perfectionists that shows his close reading of *The Evangelist*; the volume consists of his lectures delivered in New York City in response to developments at Oberlin.

70. See "Faith an Element of Power," *Zion's Herald*, XXV (September 8, 1852) 2; "How Souls are Purified," the same (August 25, 1852), 4; Peck, *Scripture Doctrine*, 416; John H. Wallace, *Entire Holiness* (Auburn, New York, 1853), a Methodist tract, 91-95; and editor Fletcher Harper's use of the terms as synonyms in *Harper's Monthly*, XVIII, number 109 (June, 1859), 841.

71. Richard Wheatley, *The Life and Letters of Mrs. Phoebe Palmer* (New York,

1876), 312-317, 326-327, and, for an important quotation of an undated article of hers in *The Guide to Holiness*, 544-545.

72. Phoebe Palmer, *Promise of the Father, or a Neglected Specialty of the Last Days* . . . (Boston, 1859).

73. Mahan, *Out of Darkness*, 156, 169-170, 172-173.

74. Henry B. Ridgaway, *The Life of the Rev. Alfred Cookman* . . . (New York, 1874), 115, 193-198, 229, 235-236, 239, 258, 281, 292-293, 311, 345, 402-405. Cf. my *Revivalism and Social Reform*, 135-141, for numerous references, and, for surprisingly thoughtful discussions combining Wesleyan and Oberlin concepts in the seedbed of what became Midwestern holiness radicalism, *Proceedings of the Western Union Holiness Convention, held at Jacksonville, Ill., Dec. 15th-19th, 1880* (Bloomington, Ill., 1881), 28, 38, 41, 47-48, and 63-69.

Professor Finney's Letter of January 1, 1839*

TO THE YOUNG CHRISTIANS WHO HAVE BEEN CONVERTED IN THE GREAT REVIVALS OF THE FEW PAST YEARS, SCATTERED UP AND DOWN IN THE LAND, WHEREVER THE PROVIDENCE OF GOD MAY HAVE CAST YOUR LOT:

Beloved in the Lord: My body is so far worn and especially my organs of speech so far exhausted that I cannot visit and preach to you orally the word of life. I therefore address you through the press, as the most direct and effectual medium through which I can communicate my thoughts.

I propose, the Lord willing, to address to you through the columns of the *Oberlin Evangelist* from time to time a series of short sermons.

I. *On those practical subjects that I deem most important to you and to the kingdom of our Lord Jesus Christ.* When I shall have said what I desire on those more immediately and highly practical topics, if the Lord permit, I design

II. *To give you a series of sermons on some doctrinal topics, especially the moral government of God, including the atonement and the influences of the Holy Ghost in the administration of that government.*

A great many of you I know personally, and many more of you know me with whom I have not the honor of a personal acquaintance. You do me the honor to call me your spiritual father, and I have the unspeakable happiness of believing that God has made me instrumental in doing you good. Such of you as know me personally *know* that it is my manner to deal with great plainness of speech and directness of address to the souls and consciences of men. You remember that this was my manner when I was with you. That this is still the only way to do you good I have the greatest confidence.

---

*From *The Oberlin Evangelist*.

Now the thing that I desire to do is, so far as in me lies, to lay open before you the very secrets of your hearts, and also to lead you to an entire renunciation of everything that grieves the Spirit of God, to a relinquishment of selfishness, under every form and in every degree, and to hold out before you those "exceeding great and precious promises" whereby you may be made "partakers of the divine nature." The conductors of this paper are willing that I should make it the medium of spreading before you my thoughts, as the providence and Spirit of God shall enable me. I shall give you a sermon as often as my health and other duties will permit; and whenever you receive this paper containing one of my lectures, I wish you to consider yourself as personally addressed by me. I wish you to read for *yourself* and feel that I mean *you*, as much as though it were a private communication made to you from my own pen, or as if I had a personal interview and addressed you "face to face." If I probe you to the quick, I beg of you not to be offended and throw the paper aside and refuse to hear me. "I beseech you by the mercies of God," nay, I conjure you by our Lord Jesus Christ to hear me patiently and with candor. Nay, beloved, I expect candor from *you*; and many of you, I doubt not, will not only hear me with *candor* but with *joy*. I will try to write as if I had you all before me in one great congregation, as if I beheld your countenances and were addressing you "face to face." Nay, I will consider you, and I desire you to consider yourselves, as in such a sense members of my congregation as to attend statedly on my preaching. I shall take it for granted that you read every lecture, and of course address you from time to time as if you had candidly read and attentively considered what I had already said.

Unless I can engage you to grant me one request, I have little hope of doing you good. And that is, as soon as you receive this communication you will make me, yourselves and the subject of the proposed lectures subjects of earnest and constant prayer; and that whenever you receive a paper containing one of the proposed lectures, you go upon your knees before you read it and lay open your heart in solemn prayer before God and to the influence of truth, and implore the aid of the Holy Spirit to make the word to you quick and powerful. We shall all soon meet at the bar of God. I earnestly desire to do you all the good I can while I am in the flesh; and as I do not intend to write for your amusement but solely for your spiritual edification, will you pledge yourselves on your knees before God to examine the truth candidly—make a personal, faithful and full application of it to your own hearts and lives—and to improve it as you will answer to God in the solemn judgment? If these are your resolutions and purposes, I am confident the Lord will bless you. I shall not cease to pray for you and intend to make such of you as I can remember special and particular subjects of prayer; and I entreat you to do the same by me.

C. G. FINNEY,
A Servant of the Lord Jesus Christ

LECTURE 1

Eternal Life

1 John 5:10-11: "He that believeth on the Son of God hath the witness in himself: he that believeth not God hath made him a liar; because he believeth not the record that God gave of his Son. And this is the record, that God hath given to us eternal life, and this life is in his Son."

In discoursing upon this subject, the following is the order in which I intend to direct your thoughts:

I. Show what we are to understand by eternal life.
II. That Jesus Christ is the eternal life of the soul.
III. That God has given eternal life to all mankind, entirely irrespective of their knowledge or consent.
IV. That this gift may be rejected by unbelief or received by faith.
V. Whosoever believes on the Son of God, or receives this gift, has the witness in himself, or knows that he has eternal life by his own consciousness.

I. *I am to show what we are to understand by eternal life.*

1. Not merely eternal existence. This is implied in eternal life but does not constitute it. Death, as used in the Scriptures or in common language, does not mean annihilation. Nor does life mean mere existence.

2. Not merely exemption from eternal death or punishment. This, also, is implied in but does not constitute eternal life.

3. Not merely eternal happiness. All these are implied and included in eternal life but are not the principal thing intended by it.

4. But this life is the contrast or opposite of that death in "trespasses and sins" in which mankind are said to be by nature. Life is the opposite of death. If we can, therefore, understand what the Scriptures mean by death, as applied to the mind, we can ascertain what that life is which is brought to light in the gospel. Death as applied to the mind in the Scriptures is a state of entire sinfulness, of total depravity and alienation from God. Eph. 2:1, the Apostle, addressing those who had been converted, says, "And you *hath he quickened*, who were dead in trespasses and sins." And in the fifth verse again he says, "Even when we were dead in sins, hath quickened us together with Christ, (by grace ye are saved)." In Col. 2:13 he says, "And you, being dead in your sins and the uncircumcision of your flesh, hath he quickened together with him, having forgiven you all trespasses." And in Eph. 5:14 he says, "Wherefore he saith, Awake thou that sleepest, and rise from the dead, and Christ shall give thee light." These and other similar passages show what is meant by the death which is the contrast of that life which, in the text, is said to be given in Christ. This life includes exemption from eternal punishment together with eternal happiness. But the great

and leading thing implied is salvation from sin, or perfect and eternal holiness. Hence it is said in the very beginning of the gospel, Matt. 1:21, "Thou shalt call his name JESUS, for he shall save his people from their sins." And He is everywhere in the gospel represented as a Savior from sin.

II. *I am to show that Jesus Christ is the eternal life of the soul.*

This is shown by the text, and by John 11:25, "Jesus said unto her, I am the resurrection, and the LIFE: he that believeth in me, though he were dead, yet shall he LIVE." This text establishes the same point. In Col. 3:4 it is directly asserted, "When Christ, who is our LIFE, shall appear, then shall ye also appear with him in glory." In 1 John 1:1 he is called the "Word of LIFE." And in 1 John 5:12 it is said, "He that hath the Son hath LIFE, and he that hath not the Son of God hath not LIFE." That He is the eternal life of the soul is evident from John 5:40, "And ye will not come to me, that ye might have LIFE." And also from John 6:33 and onward, "For the bread of God is he which cometh down from heaven, and giveth LIFE unto the world. Then said they unto him, Lord, evermore give us this bread. And Jesus said unto them, *I* am the bread of LIFE: he that cometh to me shall never hunger; and he that believeth on me shall never thirst." Again, in the 48th verse and onward, He says,

> *I* am that bread of LIFE. Your fathers did eat manna in the wilderness, and are dead. This is the bread which cometh down from heaven, that a man may eat thereof, and not die. I am the LIVING bread which came down from heaven: if any man eat of this bread he shall LIVE for ever: and the bread that I will give is my flesh, which I will give for the LIFE of the world.
>
> The Jews therefore strove among themselves, saying, How can this man give us his flesh to eat? Then Jesus said unto them, Verily, verily, I say unto you, Except ye eat the flesh of the Son of man, and drink his blood, ye have no LIFE in you. Whoso eateth my flesh, and drinketh my blood, HATH ETERNAL LIFE; and I will raise him up at the last day. For my flesh is meat indeed, and my blood is drink indeed. He that eateth my flesh, and drinketh my blood, dwelleth in me, and I in him.
>
> As the living Father hath sent me, and I live by the Father; so he that eateth me, even he shall LIVE by me. This is that bread which came down from heaven: not as your fathers did eat manna, and are dead: he that eateth of this bread shall LIVE for ever.

At these words His disciples murmured, saying, verse 60 and onward, "This is an hard saying; who can hear it? When Jesus knew in himself that his disciples murmured at it, he said unto them, Doth this offend you? What and if ye shall see the Son of man ascend up where he was before? It is the Spirit that QUICKENETH; the flesh profiteth nothing: the words that I speak unto you, they are spirit, and they are LIFE." His disciples supposed Him to speak of His material body and blood. But in these verses He informs them that it was His *divine* nature which came down from heaven, and that constituted the bread and blood of which He spake—of

which, if they ate and drank, they should have eternal life. I need not multiply passages of scripture. You who read your Bibles know that Christ is
everywhere represented as "the resurrection and the LIFE," as "the way,
the truth and the LIFE," as "the bread and water of eternal LIFE," as the
"fountain of LIVING waters"; and in a vast variety of ways this truth is
taught throughout the Scripture.

III. *I am to show that God has given eternal life to all mankind, entirely
irrespective of their knowledge or consent.*

By this, I do not mean that they have received or are actually put in possession of eternal life, or if they remain in unbelief that they ever will be put
in possession of it, but that an act is passed conferring on them pardon and
eternal life. In proof that this gift must be irrespective of our believing it, I
remark that whatever is to be believed must be true, independent of our belief. If the truth of a proposition depended upon our believing it, then we
should be under the necessity of believing it before it was true, which would
be an absurdity. Every truth of the gospel which is an object of faith is true,
whether we believe it or not. Were it not so, we could not be required to believe it. It must, therefore, be true that God has given eternal life to all who
are under any obligation to believe the gospel.

The text represents the unbeliever as making God a liar "because he believeth not the record that God gave of his Son. And this is the record, that
God hath given to us eternal LIFE, and this life is in his Son." Now is the
unbeliever to believe that God has given to others eternal life and excluded
himself, or is he to believe *himself* to be included in the gift of eternal life?
If by *"us,"* he is to include himself with the rest of mankind, then it must
be true that eternal life was given him before he believed or received it. Did
the gift belong only to those that believe, and that too after they believe?
How then should our unbelief make God a liar?

This gift must extend to all for whom Christ died. In John 1:29 He is
called the "Lamb of God that taketh away the sin of the world." In John
3:16-17 it is said, "For God so loved the world, that he gave his only begotten Son, that whosoever believeth in him should not perish, but have everlasting life. For God sent not his Son into the world to condemn the world;
but that the world through him might be saved." In John 4:42 He is again
called the "Saviour of the world." In John 6:33 He is represented as "giving
life to the world"; and in the 51st verse the same fact is declared: "And the
bread that I will give is my flesh, which I will give for the life of the world."
In Heb. 2:9 it is said, "We see Jesus, who was made a little lower than the
angels for the suffering of death, crowned with glory and honour; that he by
the grace of God should taste death for EVERY man." These and many
other passages that might be quoted show that this gift respects all mankind.

IV. *I am to show that this gift may be rejected by unbelief or received by
faith.*

The gift is absolute, without any other conditions than those necessarily implied in the bequest. If I give a man anything, the condition is always implied that he receive it. The gift on my part may be absolute, but the condition, if not expressed, is always implied in the very nature of the case. A father may make a will and bequeath his estate to an heir; but in this bequest this condition is implied, that he receive it. The gift is an absolute gift, which may be received or rejected at the pleasure of the heir. Now faith is a *necessary* condition of the gospel. It is naturally impossible that an unbelieving mind should accept or receive the gift of eternal life. The gift is holiness. Holiness is love and active obedience. Unbelief is distrust. Now, it is impossible that there should be love and the obedience of the heart where there is distrust. Faith is trust, or confidence—that confidence of the heart that works by love. Faith is the yielding up the soul to the influence and truth of Christ.

And thus Christ is represented as being our sanctification. Not our sanctifier, as if He made us holy in ourselves, and left us to obey in the exercise of our own uninfluenced and unaided powers. When He is said to be our life, "our sanctification," and "bread of life," the "vine of which we are branches," I suppose these and such like expressions all mean the same thing; namely, that Christ is the perpetual author of all our holy feelings and actions. Faith is that act of the mind that submits to the control of Christ and of the truth. It is the receiving of Christ as an indwelling Savior; it is that opening of the door of the heart, spoken of in the Scripture, and receiving Christ as an indwelling and reigning king. Thus in Eph. 3:17, Christ is represented as "dwelling in the heart by faith"; and in many other passages He is represented as dwelling in the heart, and faith is represented as the door by which He enters. It is, as I have already said, the voluntary receiving of the divine influence of Christ and of His truth into the mind. It is the yielding of our voluntary powers to His divine control.

Hence He is represented as dwelling in us, which I suppose to be really and literally true, that by His Spirit He is personally present with the mind, and by His truth and persuasive influences controlling, guiding and directing it. Now distrust, or unbelief, rejects His teachings—refuses to receive and be guided and molded by truth; while faith, receiving the divine communication, surrenders the will and all the powers to His entire control. So that He is our sanctification, that is, He does not change our nature so that we become good in ourselves so that we have life in ourselves apart from Him. But as it is said in Col. 3:3-4, "Our life is hid with Christ in God," and "when Christ, who is our life, shall appear, then shall [we] also appear with him in glory." He is the life or the holiness of the soul; it is His presence and agency that produces holiness in us; and this holiness continues no longer and extends no farther than the divine agency that produces it.

By this, I do not mean that we are passive in holiness, or that we receive His holiness or righteousness by imputation, but that we actually become partakers of His holiness and of His life by the voluntary surrender of our powers to His control. Nor by controlling our powers do I mean that our own agency is, in any sense, suspended. Our own agency is never more freely and fully exercised than when under the divine influence of Christ. His influences are moral, that is, persuasive *only*, else they could not be received by faith. It were absurd to speak of receiving a physical or compulsory influence by faith. Nor in the nature of the case can eternal life, although absolutely given and left at the option of every man, be received in any other way than by simple faith. This gift is entirely irrespective of works of any kind on our own part. Nor do works of law or any other kind of works bring us any nearer the reception of it. Faith alone receives it. Unbelief alone rejects it.

V. *I am to show that whosoever believes on the Son of God, or receives this gift, has the witness within HIMSELF, or knows that he has eternal life by his own consciousness.*

This is expressly affirmed in the text. And I might quote various other passages to the same effect, but would observe that as eternal life consists in holiness, it must be a subject of consciousness. Holiness is supreme love. Now of what can we be conscious if not of the *supreme* affection of the mind? Is it possible that any of you should love God *supremely* and not be *conscious* of it? Many persons hope that they love God and hope that they have eternal life. But if they would consider that eternal life is holiness and that nothing short of *supreme love* is holiness, they would know at once that if any man believes he has the witness in *himself*—the testimony of his own consciousness, which is the highest and best possible evidence. Now if any of you have not this evidence, this witness of your own consciousness, I beg of you to put away your hope and your talk about eternal life. For what is a life worth which is not a matter of consciousness?

REMARKS

1. From what has been said, every one of you must know whether you have eternal life. Can you say with Paul "I am crucified with Christ: nevertheless I live; yet not I, but Christ liveth in me"? And "the life which I now live, . . . I live by the faith" in "the Son of God"? Do you know that you live in love and walk in love?

2. You who do not believe and thus receive eternal life are making God a liar. How horrible it would sound were the language of your unbelief put into words!

3. You see from this subject the great mistake of those who suppose that if persons were wholly sanctified, they would have no further need of Christ. You who think thus overlook the fact that Christ is the *eternal life* of the soul. The difference between those who are wholly and those who are partially sanctified is that the former are made to feel continually their entire dependence upon God—that "in him they live, and move, and have their being," that without Him, they are absolutely dead in "trespasses and sins," that every spiritual breath they breathe and pulse they tell is from

His influence. They know they have not and never expect to have any life but in Him, any more than the vine has life when severed from the branch. Constant faith receives the tide of eternal life as it flows continually from Christ. In other words, it receives a continual influence and the constant leadings and guidings of the spirit of Christ, whereas they that are but partially sanctified have so illy learned their dependence, as sometimes to look to Christ and at other times to turn away and depend upon the exercise of their own unaided powers.

4. If God has given to us eternal life, why should we not enter into and take possession of it? The gift is absolute; our elder brother, the Lord Jesus Christ, has it in possession and holds it as a trustee, or surety or guardian, and invites and continually urges us to accept it. And why, with such an inheritance as this, should we go about like swine and wallow in the filth of sin, instead of at once entering upon our inheritance and taking hold of the fullness of gospel salvation? Take hold at once; Christ your elder brother has in possession this eternal life. Believe in Him—believe now, at once, without any preparatory process whatever. Believe the record that God hath given to us "eternal life, and this life is in his Son," and you shall now enter into the rest of faith.

5. From this subject you see also the infinite guilt of those who reject the gospel. The gift is absolute; it is tendered to their acceptance, with all the sincerity of God; it was purchased by the blood and treasured up in the life of Christ. There is an infinite excellence and power and glory in it. And if "he that despised Moses' law died without mercy, under two or three witnesses, of how much sorer punishment, suppose ye, shall he be thought worthy, who hath trodden under foot the Son of God and hath counted the blood of the covenant, wherewith he was sanctified, an unholy thing?"

6. Lastly, let it be remembered, understood, realized and felt by every one of you that this bequest is made. The testator has died and sealed it with His blood. The infinite treasure, the pearl of great price, lies before you, waiting for your acceptance. Take it. Receive it. Hold fast to it by faith.

LECTURE 2

Faith

John 6:28-29: "Then said they unto him, What shall we do, that we might work the works of God? Jesus answered and said unto them, This is the work of God, that ye believe on him whom he hath sent."

The following is the train of thought I shall pursue:

I. Notice several erroneous answers commonly given to the question proposed in the text, namely, what shall we do that we may work the works of God?

II. Show that Christ gave the only proper answer, under the circumstances in which the question was asked.

III. Show that under other circumstances another answer might with propriety be given.

I. *I am to notice several erroneous answers commonly given to the question proposed in the text.*

1. Should the question be proposed to a Jew, "What shall I do that I may work the works of God," he would answer, keep the law, both moral and ceremonial, that is, keep the commandments.

2. To the same inquiry an Arminian* would answer, improve common grace and you will obtain converting grace, that is, use the means of grace according to the best light you have, and you will obtain the grace of salvation. In this answer, it is not supposed that the inquirer already has faith and is using the means of grace in faith, but that he is in a state of impenitency and is inquiring after converting grace. The answer, therefore, amounts to this: you must get converting grace by your *impenitent* works; you must become holy by your hypocrisy; you must work out sanctification by sin.

3. To this question most professed Calvinists would make, in substance, the same reply. They would reject the language while they retained the idea. Their direction would imply either that the inquirer already has faith or that he must perform works to obtain it, that is, to obtain grace by works.

Neither an Arminian nor a Calvinist would *formally* direct the inquirer to the *law* as the ground of justification. But nearly the whole church would give directions that would amount to the same thing. Their answer would be a legal and not a gospel answer. For whatever answer is given to this question that does not distinctly recognize *faith* as the foundation of all virtue in sinners is legal. Unless the inquirer is made to understand that this is the first grand fundamental duty, without the performance of which all virtue, all giving up of sin, all acceptable obedience is impossible, he is misdirected. He is led to believe that it is possible to please God without faith and to obtain grace by works of law. There are but two kinds of works, works of law and works of faith. Now if the inquirer has not the "faith that works by love," to set him upon any course of works to get it is certainly to direct him to get faith by works of law. Whatever is said to him that does

---

*Finney here uses the word "Arminian" in the sense usual among nineteenth-century Christians of Calvinist background, as a synonym for "Pelagian," that is, one who affirms salvation by good works. Methodists, understandably, deplored this usage.

not clearly convey the truth that both justification and sanctification are by faith, without works of law, is law and not gospel. Nothing before or without faith can possibly be done by the unbeliever but works of law. His first duty, therefore, is faith; and every attempt to obtain faith by unbelieving works is to lay works at the foundation and make grace a result. It is the direct opposite of gospel truth.

Take facts as they arise in every day's history to show that what I have stated is the experience of almost all, professors and nonprofessors. Whenever a sinner begins in good earnest to agitate the question, "what shall I do to be saved," he resolves as a first duty to break off from his sins, that is, in unbelief. Of course his reformation is only outward; he determines to do better, to reform in this, that and the other thing, and thus prepare himself to be converted. He does not expect to be saved without grace and faith but he attempts to get grace by works of law.

The same is true of multitudes of anxious Christians who are inquiring what they shall do to overcome the world, the flesh and the devil. They overlook the fact that "this is the victory that overcometh the world, even your faith," that it is with "the shield of faith" that they are "to quench all the fiery darts of the wicked." They ask, why am I overcome by sin? Why can I not get above its power? Why am I thus the slave of my appetites and passions and the sport of the devil? They cast about for the cause of all this spiritual wretchedness and death. At one time they think they have discovered it in the neglect of one duty, and at another time in the neglect of another. Sometimes they imagine they have found the cause to lie in yielding to one sin and sometimes in yielding to another. They put forth efforts in this direction and in that direction and patch up their righteousness on one side while they make a rent in the other. Thus they spend years in running around in a circle and making dams of sand across the current of their own corruptions. Instead of at once *purifying their hearts by faith*, they are engaged in trying to arrest the overflowing of its bitter waters. *Why* do I sin, they inquire; and casting about for the cause they come to the sage conclusion, it is because I neglect such a duty, that is, because I do sin. But how shall I get rid of sin? Answer: by doing my duty, that is, by ceasing from sin. Now the real inquiry is, *why* do they neglect their duty? Why do they commit sin at all? Where is the foundation of all this mischief? Will it be replied, the foundation of all this wickedness is in the corruption of our nature, in the wickedness of the heart, in the strength of our evil propensities and habits? But all this only brings us back to the real inquiry again: how are this corrupt nature, this wicked[ness] and these sinful habits to be overcome? I answer, by faith alone. No works of law have the least tendency to overcome our sins but rather confirm the soul in self-righteousness and unbelief.

The great and fundamental sin which is at the foundation of all other sin is unbelief. The first thing is to give up that—to believe the Word of God. There is no breaking off from one sin without this. "Whatever is not of faith is sin." "Without faith it is impossible to please God." Thus we see that the backslider and convicted Christian, when agonizing to overcome sin, will almost always betake themselves to works of law to obtain faith. They will fast and pray and read and struggle and outwardly reform, and thus endeavor to obtain grace. Now all this is in vain and wrong. Do you ask, shall we not fast and pray and read and struggle? Shall we do nothing but sit down in Antinomian security and inaction? I answer, you must do all that God commands you to do; but begin where He tells you to begin and do it in the manner in which He commands you to do it, that is, in the exercise of that faith that works by love. Purify your hearts by faith. Believe in the Son of God. And say not in your heart, "Who shall ascend into heaven?" (that is, to bring Christ down from above); or "Who shall descend into the deep?" (that is, to bring up Christ again from the dead), "But what saith it? The word is nigh thee, even in thy mouth, and in thy heart: that is, the word of faith, which we preach."

Now these facts show that even under the gospel almost all professors of religion, while they reject the Jewish notion of justification by works of the law, have after all adopted a ruinous substitute for it and suppose that in some way they are to obtain grace by their works.

II. *I am to show that Christ gave the only proper answer, under the circumstances in which the question was asked.*

In order to understand the propriety of the answer, we must understand the meaning of the question. The context shows that the question was asked by certain unbelieving Jews, who inquired what they could do to work the works of God—in other words, to obtain the favor of God. Christ understood them as inquiring what works would be acceptable without faith. He therefore answers, "This is the work of God, that ye believe on him whom he hath sent." As if He had said, nothing is a work of God which you would recognize as such. Faith is the first great work of God, without which it is impossible to please Him. To a Jew, this answer would imply that he believed Him to be the Messiah foretold in the Scriptures. And to all persons the answer implies not only a general confidence in the character of God but a trust in His atonement and saving grace in opposition to all works of law, for justification.

To show that this is the only proper answer to be given to a person in a state of unbelief, I will state

1. *What I DO NOT mean by the proposition;* and
2. *What I DO mean by it.*

1. I do not mean that it is the only proper answer because there is no good and acceptable work but faith.

2. Nor do I mean that faith without works is acceptable to God.

3. Nor do I mean that faith makes void the law and sets aside the obligation and necessity of good works. The Apostle, in James 2:17-26, sets the necessity of works, as the result of faith, in a strong light:

> Even so faith, if it hath not works, is dead, being alone. Yea, a man may say, Thou hast faith, and I have works: shew me thy faith without thy works, and I will shew you my faith by my works. Thou believest that there

is one God; thou doest well: the devils also believe, and tremble. But wilt thou know, O vain man, that faith without works is dead? Was not Abraham our father justified by works, when he had offered Isaac his son upon the altar? Seest thou how faith wrought with his works, and by works was made perfect? And the scripture was fulfilled which saith, Abraham believed God, and it was imputed unto him for righteousness; and he was called the Friend of God. Ye see then how that by works a man is justified, and not by faith only. Likewise also was not Rahab the harlot justified by works, when she had received the messengers and had sent them out another way? For as the body without the spirit is dead, so faith without works is dead also.

4. Nor do I mean that there are no other directions that may be given to an inquiring sinner or Christian that, if followed, would not in the end amount to the same thing as the direction in the text. In number eighteen of my "Revival Lectures" I said, "You may give the sinner any direction or tell him to do anything that includes a right heart." To repent, to submit, to give the heart to God and all the directions there specified *imply* faith. Were I to preach that sermon again, I should give a greater prominence to faith and show that the exercise of faith is the first thing to be done, and that upon the exercise of this, repentance, submission, love and every other grace depend.

5. But by the above proposition I do mean that no works are good works or are in any sense acceptable to God, only as they proceed from faith. Let it be forever remembered that "without faith it is impossible to please God," and "whatsoever is not of faith is sin."

6. It is the proper answer because both justification and sanctification are by faith alone. Rom. 3:30: "Seeing it is one God, which shall justify the circumcision by faith, and the uncircumcision through faith"; and 5:1: "Therefore being justified by faith, we have peace with God through our Lord Jesus Christ." Also, 9:30, 31: "What shall we say then? That the Gentiles, which followed not after righteousness, have attained to righteousness, even the righteousness which is of faith. But Israel, which followed after the law of righteousness, hath *not* attained to the law of righteousness. Wherefore? Because they sought it not by faith, but as it were by the works of the law."

But perhaps you will not clearly see the truth of this unless I make a remark or two upon the nature of faith.

The first element of saving faith is a realizing sense of the truth of the Bible. But this is not alone saving faith, for Satan has this realizing sense of truth which makes him tremble.

But a second element in saving faith is the consent of the heart or will to the truth perceived by the intellect. It is a cordial trust or resting of the mind in those truths and a yielding up of the whole being to their influence. Now it is easy to see that without the consent of the will, there can be nothing but an outward obedience to God. A wife without confidence in her husband can do nothing more than perform outwardly her duty to him. It is a contradiction to say that without confidence, she can perform her duty from the heart. The same is true of parental and all other governments. Works of law may be performed without faith; that is, we may serve from fear or hope or some selfish consideration, but without the confidence that works by love, obedience from the heart is naturally impossible. Nay, the very terms, obedience from the heart without love, are a contradiction.

7. By the above I mean that to seek the grace of faith by works of law is an utter abomination. It is as abominable as to attempt to purchase the Holy Ghost with money. It is to set aside the testimony of God with respect to our utter depravity and attempt to palm off our unbelieving, heartless works upon an infinitely holy God. It is an attempt to purchase His favor, instead of accepting grace as a sovereign gift.

8. It is as preposterous as it is wicked. It is seeking to please God by our sins—to purchase the grace of faith by making God a liar.

9. To give any other answer to one in unbelief, and to set him to perform any work with the expectation that by it he shall obtain faith, is to confirm him in self-righteousness, to prolong his rebellion, to lead him either to settle down in a self-righteous hope or to produce, in the end, discouragement and blasphemy.

10. Because that *repentance, faith, love and every other holy exercise* both imply and proceed from faith. Without confidence in the character and requirements of God it is impossible to repent. For what is repentance but heartily to justify God and condemn ourselves. So it is equally impossible to exercise a complacent love to God without faith. Submission to God also implies and presupposes the exercise of confidence in God and in His requirements.

11. This is a proper answer, because all right affection and all good works will necessarily proceed from faith. Christ was not afraid of begetting an Antinomian spirit by laying so much stress upon faith. He knew full well that true faith as naturally and necessarily begets every other inward grace and all outward good works as a cause produces its effects.

12. It is the only proper answer because faith is the only exercise that receives Christ with all His powerfully sanctifying influences into the heart. The Bible everywhere represents the sanctified soul as being under the influence of an indwelling Christ. Now the exercise of faith is that opening of the door by which Christ is received to reign in the heart. Who will pretend that any works are properly good or that any true faith exists in the mind except as the result of the operation or influence of Christ in the mind. Now if this is so, the proper direction plainly is to do that which receives Christ. If this is done, all else will be done. If this is neglected, all else will be neglected, of course.

III. *I am to show that under other circumstances another answer might with propriety have been given.*

1. The careless, unawakened sinner who knows nothing of his depravity or helplessness, it might be important and proper to direct to the law of God as the rule of his duty—not with the expectation of directly promoting

holiness thereby but of convicting him of sin. Thus we find Christ requiring the young man who was wrapped up in self-righteousness "to keep the commandments," and taking such a course as to bring out before his mind his supreme love of the world. This produced regret and discouragement in him; and when required to "part with all that he had" and follow Christ, he "went away sorrowful."

2. To the anxious sinner who makes this inquiry, Christ, as I have shown, gave the only appropriate answer. Also to the Christian, inquiring after sanctification, this is the only appropriate answer. In short, to anyone who is convinced of his real character this is the proper, and the only proper, answer.

3. But to one already full of faith and love and of the Holy Spirit, another answer may be given, simply because by the inquiry he means a different thing. When he asks, "What shall I do to work the works of God," his heart breaks forth with the inquiry, "what shall I do to honor and glorify God," not "what shall I do to be saved." Let such an one be directed to the whole preceptive part of the Bible. Do this and avoid that is just the instruction which he needs and upon which he will eagerly seize, to glorify God with all his heart. Such a mind needs instruction, not command and threatening. To him the preceptive part of the Bible is just what his circumstances and state of feeling demand. The commands of the Bible will not beget in him a legal spirit, and thus prove a stumbling block to his soul. He will not set himself self-righteously to perform the duties enjoined; but his *heart* goes forth to meet his responsibilities and perform the requirements of God.

REMARKS

1. You see from this subject how to understand Rom. 9:20-32, which I have before quoted, "What shall we say, then," &c. The Jews sought by their own doings to please God without faith; but all their righteousness was as filthy rags. While the Gentiles, who had lived in open rebellion, when they heard the gospel believed it at once, instead of betaking themselves to works of law; and thus exercising faith that works by love, they attained to the righteousness which is of God, by faith.

2. You see why the church is not sanctified. They overlook the office and necessity of faith as that which alone can produce acceptable obedience to God. They are engaged in efforts to obtain faith by works, instead of first exercising that faith which will beget within them a clean heart. In this way they seek in vain for sanctification. How common is it to see persons full of bustle and outward efforts and works—fasting and praying, giving and doing and struggling; and after all, they have not the fruits of the Spirit: love, joy, peace, longsuffering, gentleness, goodness, faith, meekness, temperance, against which there is no law. They have not, after all, crucified the flesh with its affections and lusts. They do not live in the Spirit and walk in the Spirit. They do not, in their own experience, realize the truth of that saying, "Thou wilt keep him in perfect peace, whose mind is stayed on

thee: because he trusteth in thee." Without that trust they cannot have peace, cannot be sanctified.

Others endeavor to force themselves to exercise the various Christian graces of love, submission, &c., without faith, overlooking the fact that it is faith that works by love, and that repentance and submission imply faith and are the results of faith. They are the surrendering of our wills to the will of God. But this certainly cannot be, without confidence in the character of God. In short, every Christian grace implies the exercise of faith as its foundation.

3. You see why the Bible lays so much stress upon faith.

4. You see what is the difficulty with those who are constantly in a complaining state on the subject of religion. They seem to know they are wrong, but do not understand wherein the foundation of their wrong consists. They sometimes think that a neglect of this duty is the grand difficulty, and sometimes something else is that upon which their minds fasten as the prime difficulty in the case. They set themselves to break off from one sin and another, and practice this self-denial and that duty, and all without that faith that fills the heart with love. Thus they go round and round in a circle and do not see that unbelief is their great, their damning sin, without the removal of which no other sin can be repented of or forgiven. All their efforts are entirely legal, hypocritical and vain till they exercise faith.

5. You see the mistake of Antinomian perfectionists in setting aside all preceptive religion and understanding obedience to the commands of God as legality. They do not make the discrimination here made. If persons without faith, in an unsanctified state, set themselves to obey the commandments of God, their efforts must necessarily be legal, self-righteous and ruinous. To them the precepts of the gospel, as well as the commandments of the law, are a horrible pit of miry clay. You cast a man into a horrible pit of miry clay, and the more he struggles the deeper he sinks. Now to a man without faith, the precepts of the law and gospel are fitly compared to miry clay. Every effort at obedience without faith is sin and, as it confirms self-righteousness, is sinking him farther and farther from God and rational hope. And the more vehemently he struggles, the more desperate and alarming his case becomes. The clay surrounds him and cleaves to him, suffocates and kills him. Just so the commands of God to an *unbelieving* heart are a snare and a pit. They are miry and suffocating clay. Without faith there is *ruin* and *damnation* in them.

6. You see how to the Jews and to all unbelievers, the commandments of God are a stumbling block. All outward conformity to them is useless, yea, ruinous. Love without faith is impossible. And consequently the merciful direction and instructions contained in the preceptive parts of the gospel are made the food of self-righteousness and the snare of death. But to those whose souls are full of faith and love, the commandments of God are just the instruction which they need when, in their ignorance, they earnestly inquire what they shall do to glorify God. Do this and avoid that, and the like, are just the things upon which hearts of love will seize, as the needed directions of their heavenly Father.

7. But someone may inquire, do not men learn to exercise faith by what you call legal efforts and in obedience to legal directions? No. They only learn by experience that all such directions are vain and that they are totally depraved and dependent, which they *ought* to have *believed* before. They set themselves to pray and read and struggle, expecting at every meeting they attend, every prayer they make, to obtain grace and faith. But they never do until they are completely discouraged and despair of obtaining help in this way. And the history of every self-righteous sinner's conversion and every anxious Christian's sanctification would develop this truth: that deliverance cometh not until their self-righteous efforts were proved by their own experience to be utterly vain, and abandoned as useless, and the whole subject thrown upon the sovereign mercy of God. This submitting a subject to the sovereign mercy of God is that very act of faith which they should have put forth long before, but which they would not exercise until every other means had been tried in vain.

8. But perhaps you will say, if by this self-righteous struggle they learn their depravity and dependence and in this manner come to prove by their own experience the truth of God, why not encourage them to make these efforts as, at least, an indirect way of obtaining faith? Answer: blasphemy and drunkenness and any of the most shocking sins may be and often have been the means of working conviction which has resulted in conversion. Why not encourage these things, as such is sometimes their indirect effect? The truth is, when a sinner's attention is awakened and he is convicted and puts forth the inquiry "what shall I do"; and when a Christian, struggling with his remaining corruption, puts forth the same inquiry, why should they be thrown into the horrible pit of which I have spoken? Why not tell them at once, in the language of the text, "This is the work of God, that ye believe on him whom he hath sent"?

9. Let me say to you who would make the inquiry in the text, don't wait to fast, read, pray or anything else; don't expect to break off from *any sin* in your unbelief. You may break off from the outward commission—you may substitute praying for swearing, reading your Bible for reading novels, outward industry and honesty for theft and idleness, sobriety for drunkenness, and anything you please—and it is, after all, only exchanging one form of sin for another. It is only varying the *mode* of your warfare. But remember that in unbelief whatever your conduct is, you are in highhanded rebellion against God. Faith would instantly sanctify your heart, sanctify all your doings, and render them, in Christ Jesus, acceptable to God. Unbelief is your great, your crying, your damning sin, against which the heaviest thunderbolts of Jehovah are hurled.

10. Don't wait for any particular view of Christ before you believe. When persons in the state of mind of which I have been speaking hear those who live in faith describe their views of Christ, they say, "Oh, if I had such views I could believe; I must have these before I can believe." Now you should understand that these views are the result and effect of faith. These views of which you speak are that which faith discovers in those passages of scripture which describe Christ. Faith apprehends the meaning of those

passages and sees in them these very things which you expect to see before you exercise faith, and which you imagine would produce it. Take hold, then, on the simple promise of God. Take God at His word. Believe that He means just what He says. And this will at once bring you into the state of mind after which you inquire.

11. Let what has been said be an answer to that sister in New York who inquired, by letter, what she should do to obtain the blessing of sanctification. My dear child, you inquire whether you shall obtain by reading the Bible, or by prayer, fasting or by all these together. Now let this sermon answer you and *know* that by *neither* nor by *all* these, in the absence of faith, are you to grow any better or find any relief. You speak of being in darkness and of being discouraged. No wonder you are so, since you have plainly been seeking sanctification by works of law. You have "stumbled at this stumbling stone." You are in the horrible pit and miry clay of which I have just spoken. Immediately exercise faith upon the Son of God. It is the first, the only thing you can do to rest your feet upon the rock; and it will immediately put a new song into your mouth.

Professor Finney's Letter of January 30, 1839*

TO THE CHRISTIAN READERS OF
THE OBERLIN EVANGELIST

Beloved: You perceive that I have already commenced one of the promised courses of lectures. Before I proceed any farther, permit me to bring distinctly before your minds the main object I have in view and the reasons for the course I intend to pursue.

My object is the sanctification of "your whole spirit and soul and body."

My reasons are the following:

When I was first converted and entered the ministry, my mind was powerfully drawn, as I then thought and now think, to labor for the conversion of sinners. Upon that one grand object my heart was set, and to the accomplishment of it many of you can bear witness that all my powers were devoted. My study, preaching, prayers, visiting and conversation were devoted to that end. My mind was, of course, occupied almost exclusively with that class of truths that were calculated to work the conviction and conversion of the impenitent.

I generally spent but a few months in a place, and during that time my preaching and influence were directed, as I have said, almost exclusively to

---

*From *The Oberlin Evangelist*.

the conversion of the ungodly. I only spent so much time in preaching to the church as was indispensable to arouse them and get them out of the way of sinners.

About the same time, and subsequently to my laboring as an evangelist, a number of other evangelists were and have been called forward by the Spirit of God, who have labored mainly for the same object. The attention and labor of pastors have also been directed mainly to the same end during the extensive revivals of the few past years.

To my own mind it appears that this unity of design and effort were, to say the least, to a great extent indispensable to the accomplishment of the great work that has been undeniably achieved. That hundreds of thousands of sinners have been converted to God by these instrumentalities I have no doubt. And I think I can see very clearly the wisdom of God in calling up the attention of so many evangelists, pastors and churches to the immediate conversion of the ungodly.

It has been represented, as perhaps some of you know, that I wholly disapprove of my own course as an evangelist and that I wholly disapprove of the course of other evangelists and pastors in this great work. Now this is by no means true. I do not by any means pretend to justify all that I have done, nor suppose that my course was faultless. Nor do I pretend to justify all that other evangelists and pastors have done to promote this work. Nor do I pretend that in everything our views of what was best to be done have been exactly alike. But with respect to myself, I feel bound to say that the more I have looked over the course in which I was led, the class of truths I preached, and the means that I adopted, the more deeply have I been impressed with the conviction that, considering the object I had in view, namely, the conversion of sinners, the course in which God led me was upon the whole wise, and such an one in almost all respects as I should pursue again, with my present experience, had I the same object in view.

I am also convinced that God has been wise in leading other evangelists and pastors in their preaching and measures. And although much of human infirmity may have and doubtless has appeared in what we have done, yet upon the whole I do not see what better could have been expected or done, under the circumstances of the case, for the accomplishment of so great and good a work.

In the midst of my efforts, however, for the conversion of sinners (and as far as my knowledge extends, it has been so with other evangelists and pastors) we have overlooked in a great measure the fact that converts would not make one step of progress only as they were constantly plied with means as well adapted to their sanctification and growth in grace, as were the means for their conversion. Believing and feeling as I did then and do now that if persons were once converted God in faithfulness would save them, I overlooked the necessity of the constant and vigorous and pointed use of means to effect this end. By this I do not mean that I did not at all feel this necessity. But it was not so fully before my mind as the necessity of the use of vigorous means for the conversion of the ungodly.

It is true that had I been impressed with this necessity, my stay in every place was too short to accomplish much in the work of leading converts to manhood in religion. The same has been true of my brethren who have been and are evangelists. And I have reason to believe that the great desire of pastors for the conversion of sinners in those congregations where revivals have prevailed, and the great success that under God has attended the use of means for their conversion, has led them in a great measure to neglect the church—to leave out of view the more spiritual truths of the gospel that constitute the food of Christians and are essential to their sanctification.

In revisiting some of the churches in which I had formerly labored, my mind was some years since from time to time deeply impressed with the necessity of doing something for the sanctification of Christians. And after I had been settled two or three years in the city of New York and had labored almost exclusively for the conversion of sinners, I was fully convinced that converts would die, that the standard of piety would never be elevated, that revivals would become more and more superficial and finally cease, unless something effectual was done to elevate the standard of holiness in the church. And in attempting to present to the church the high and pure doctrines of grace and all that class of truths which are the food and life of the Christian soul, I found to my sorrow that I had been so long in pursuit of sinners with the law, to convict them, and only enough of the gospel just to convert them, that my mind had, as it were, run down. And those high and spiritual truths had not that place in my own heart which is indispensable to the effectual exhibition of them to others. I found that I knew comparatively little about Christ, and that a multitude of things were said about Him in the gospel of which I had no spiritual view and of which I knew little or nothing.

What I did know of Christ was almost exclusively as an atoning and justifying Savior. But as a JESUS to save men from sin, or as a sanctifying Savior, I knew very little about Him. This was made by the Spirit of God very clear to my mind. And it deeply convinced me that I must know more of the gospel in my own experience and have more of Christ in my own heart, or I could never expect to benefit the church. In that state of mind, I used often to tell the Lord Jesus Christ that I was sensible that I knew very little about Him; and I besought Him to reveal himself to me that I might be instrumental in revealing Him to others. I used especially to pray over particular passages and classes of passages in the gospel that speak of Christ, that I might apprehend their *meaning* and feel their *power* in my own heart. And I was often strongly convinced that I desired this for the great purpose of making Christ known to others.

I will not enter into detail with regard to the way in which Christ led me. Suffice it to say, and alone to the honor of His grace do I say it, that He has taught me some things that I asked Him to show me. Since my own mind became impressed in the manner in which I have spoken, I have felt as strongly and unequivocally pressed by the Spirit of God to labor for the sanctification of the church as I once did for the conversion of sinners. By multitudes of letters and from various other sources of information I have learned, to my great joy, that God has been and is awakening a spirit of inquiry on the subject of holiness throughout the church, both in this country and in Europe.

You who read my lectures in the *N.Y. Evangelist* while I was in the city of New York may remember the manner in which God was leading my own mind—through what a process of conviction and to what results He brought me previously to my leaving there. Since then God has been continually dealing with me in mercy. And oh how often I have longed to unburden myself and pour out my whole heart to the dear souls that were converted in those powerful revivals.

And now, dearly beloved, I have commenced this course of lectures in the hope that, should God spare my life, He will make them the instrument of doing you good. You need searching and trying and purifying and comforting. You need to be humbled, edified, sanctified. I think I know, very nearly, where great multitudes of you are in religion and will endeavor, God helping me from time to time, to adapt truth to what I suppose to be your circumstances and state of mind. As I said in my former letter, I cannot visit you and preach to you orally, on account of the state of my health. And besides, I think the Spirit of God calls me for the present to remain here. But through the press, I can hold communion with you and preach to you the gospel of Christ.

In addition to the sermons which I design to preach to you, I shall probably from time to time address letters to you, when I have anything particular to say that cannot well be said in a sermon. If any spiritual advice is asked by letter, as is often the case, upon any subject that can be answered in a sermon, you may generally expect to find my answer in some of my lectures—concealing, of course, the fact that I have a particular case under my eye. If, in any case, the answer cannot well be given in a sermon, should providence permit you may expect an answer, either privately to the individual who makes the request or in a letter in the *Evangelist*, which may not only assist the inquirer but that class of persons who are in a similar state of mind. In this case also, of course, I shall not disclose the names of the particular inquirers.

And now, dearly beloved, do not suppose that I do this because I suppose that I am the only man who can give you spiritual advice, but because I am willing to do what I can. And as I have freely received, I wish freely to impart whatever of the gospel the blessed God has taught me.

One word more. I have noticed in several papers a garbled extract from a remark that I made in one of my lectures published in the *N. Y. Evangelist*, which I here mention simply because it is dishonorable to God and injurious to you. In that lecture I said "that those converted in the great revivals in the land, although real Christians, as I believed, and the best Christians in the church at the present day, were nevertheless a disgrace to religion on account of the low standard of their piety; and if I had health again to be an evangelist, I would labor for a revival in the churches and for the elevation of the standard of piety among Christians."

Now you perceive that I have here asserted my full conviction that those revivals were genuine works of God, "that the converts were real Christians," that "they are the best Christians in the church," and yet that on many accounts they are a disgrace to religion. Now this I fully believe and reassert. And it is to win you away, if possible, from the last remains of sin that I have undertaken this work. The papers to which I allude have injuriously represented me as admitting that those revivals were spurious and the converts not Christians. I do not complain of this on my own account nor speak of it, if I know my own heart, because I have any regard to its bearing upon myself, but because it is a slander upon those precious revivals, and injurious to you, as in substance denying that the grace of God ever converted you.

And now, dearly beloved, I must close this letter, beseeching you to make me a subject of earnest prayer that God will enlighten and sanctify me, fill me with the spirit of the gospel of His Son, and help me to impart to you the true bread and water of life, rightly dividing truth and giving to everyone a portion in due season.

May the grace of our Lord Jesus Christ be with you forever.

C. G. FINNEY,
A Servant of the Lord Jesus Christ

LECTURE 3

Devotion

1 Cor. 10:31: "Whether therefore ye eat, or drink, or whatsoever ye do, do all to the glory of God." Col. 3:17, 23: "And whatsoever ye do in word or deed, do all in the name of the Lord Jesus, giving thanks to God and the Father by him; and whatsoever ye do, do it heartily, as to the Lord, and not unto men." Rom. 6:13: "Neither yield ye your members as instruments of unrighteousness unto sin: but yield yourselves unto God, as those that are alive from the dead, and your members as instruments of righteousness unto God." Rom. 14:7, 8: "For none of us liveth to himself, and no man dieth to himself. For whether we live, we live unto the Lord; and whether we die, we die unto the Lord: whether we live therefore, or die, we are the Lord's."

These texts teach the nature and duty of devotion to God. In discussing this subject, I design to show:

  I. What is not true devotion to God.
  II. What is true devotion.
  III. That devotion and nothing short of devotion is true religion.

IV. Notice several mistakes commonly made upon this subject.

I. *I am to show what is not true devotion.*

1. Devotion does not consist in reading the Bible nor in praying nor in attending meetings. These may be or may not be instances of particular acts of devotion but are not to be regarded as devotion itself.

2. Devotion does not consist in closet, public or social consecration of ourselves to God. These are to be regarded as special acts of devotion and pledges or promises on our part of devotion, rather than as constituting devotion.

3. Devotion does not consist in individual acts or exercises of any kind. Acts or exercises may be devotional acts, that is acts of devotion; but let it be remembered that no acts or exercises constitute devotion.

II. *I am to show what is true devotion.*

It is a state of the mind or of the heart. It is that state of the will in which everything—our whole life and being and possessions—are a continual offering to God, that is, are continually devoted to God. True devotion, so far from consisting in any individual act or feelings, must of necessity be the supreme devotion of the will, extending to all we have and are—to all times, places, employments, thoughts and feelings.

Let your own ideas of what a minister ought to be illustrate my meaning. You feel that a minister, in preaching the gospel, should have but one design, and that should be to glorify God in the sanctification and salvation of sinners. You know that he is professedly a servant of God. You feel that he ought to study and preach and perform all his ministerial duties not for himself, not for his salary, not to increase his popularity, but to glorify God. Now you can easily see if a minister has not this singleness of eye, his service cannot be acceptable to God. It is not an offering to God; it is not a devotion to God, but a devotion to himself.

Devotion, then, in a minister, is that state of mind in which all his ministerial duties are performed with a single eye to the glory of God and where his whole life is a continual offering to God.

Again, you feel that a minister ought to be as devoted in everything else as he is in praying and preaching; and in this you are right, for he not only ought to be but really is as devoted out of the pulpit as he is in the pulpit. If he is influenced by selfish and worldly motives during the week, he is influenced by the same motives on the Sabbath. If during the week he is studying his own interests and endeavoring to promote his own ends, it must be that he is so on the Sabbath.

You feel also that if a minister is not truly devoted, he will go to hell. Should you know that a minister preached, prayed, visited and performed his ministerial duties mainly for the purpose of supporting his family or in any way honoring or benefiting himself—whatever zeal he might manifest—you would say he was a wicked man, and unless he is converted he must inevitably lose his soul. If these are your views on the subject, they are undoubtedly correct. Here, where you have no personal interest, you form a right judgment and decide correctly concerning the character and destiny of such a man.

Now remember that nothing short of this is devotion in you. Bear it in mind that no particular acts or fervor or gushings of emotion, or resolutions or purposes of amendment or of future obedience are devotion.

But devotion is that state of the will in which the mind is swallowed up in God as the object of supreme affection, in which we not only live and move *in* God, but *for* God. In other words, devotion is that state of mind in which the attention is diverted from self and self-seeking and is directed to God—the thoughts and purposes and desires and affections and emotions all hanging upon and devoted to Him.

III. *I am to show that devotion, and nothing short of devotion, is true religion.*

Devotion and true religion are identical.

1. Because devotion implies and includes supreme love to God. It is impossible that we should be devoted to an object unless it be the object of our supreme affection.

2. It is impossible that we should not be devoted to an object of supreme affection. If we love God supremely, He will be the end for which we live; for that which we love supremely is always necessarily the end and object for which we live. If an individual loves God supremely, he will be as conscious that he lives for God as that he lives at all.

3. Nothing short of this state of mind which I have described is consistent with true religion. Supreme love to an object is a state, and not a mere act of the mind. By state, I mean a *voluntary* state of mind. Where, therefore, there is a supreme love, devotion or consecration to God, [it] must be a state, a voluntary state of mind, in opposition to individual acts of mind.

4. Nothing short of this can be acceptable to God. Unless devotion be a habit or state of mind, unless the whole being be an offering to God, He must have a rival in our hearts. This He will not endure. And to attempt to please Him by isolated acts of devotion, when it is not the habit and state of our minds, is infinitely more abominable than for a wife to attempt to please her husband with an occasional smile, when she lives only to please and gain the affections of another man.

5. Nothing short of this can be the result of evangelical faith. Evangelical faith is that state of mind in which eternal things are apprehended as realities. The things of time and of eternity—God's interests and our own interests, His character and claims and loving kindness—are apprehended by the mind as facts, and as they are.

Now a mind in the exercise of this faith will as naturally live for eternity and not for time, for God and not for self, as an unbeliever who apprehends none of these things as they are would live for time and self, and not for God.

6. A departure from this state is *heart* apostasy. Whatever a man's outward deportment may be, the moment he turns aside from sincere devotion to God, from a supreme consecration of his whole being to the service of God, he has in heart apostatized from true religion. He is no longer in the service of God but is serving the object upon which his heart is set; and that is the object of his devotion, that is, it is his God.

IV. *I am to notice several mistakes commonly made upon this subject.*

1. Many imagine that there is a real distinction between devotion and other duties, as if a man could be doing his duty in that which is not devotion to God. The duties of devotion are generally supposed to be closet and family prayer, reading the Scriptures, together with singing and praying in the public exercises of God's house. These are called the devotional parts of worship, while the preaching and hearing are called less devotional. On the Sabbath men imagine themselves to be devotional, while on the weekdays, excepting in those few acts which they call religious duties, they are serving themselves and are supremely devoted to their own interests. Now all such ideas as these arise out of the total absence of true devotion; and individuals who entertain such views have not yet understood what true religion is. Nothing is duty that is not performed for God. A man that is truly religious is as truly devotional in his daily business as on the Sabbath. The business of the world is performed by him in the same spirit and with the same design as he prays and reads his Bible and attends the worship of God on the Sabbath. If this is not the case, he has no true religion.

2. Some who seem to do all for God and are manifestly in a devotional state of mind do not, after all, seem to realize that every act devoted to God is as acceptable as prayer or praise. If by necessary duties they are kept from spending much time in their closets and going a great deal to meetings, Satan takes advantage of their ignorance and brings them into bondage. He endeavors to persuade them that they are neglecting their duties to God and attending to other things. Now you who are devoted to God should understand that if the providence of God confine you at home to nurse the sick or prevent you from observing those hours of secret prayer which you are wont to observe, you are not to be brought into bondage on this account, if you are conscious that these other duties are performed for God.

3. Others think that devotion may be sincere and yet extend only to certain duties, that is, that a man may pray sincerely and from right motives and yet be worldly in the transaction of business. Now a little reflection will convince any honest mind that it is naturally impossible. Devotion to God cannot be sincere any further than it annihilates selfishness. Devotion and selfishness are eternal opposites.

4. It is a very common idea that we are to be more devotional, that is, more religious on the Sabbath and in secret and social prayer than at other times and in other things. But the text shows that whatever we do, whether we eat or drink, at all times, in all places and in all things we are to do all for the glory of God.

5. Many mistake the religion of emotion for that of the will or heart. This is manifest from their lives. You will often witness the gushings forth of their emotions. They weep and appear to melt and break down. They promise reformation and entire consecration to God. But attempt to trade with them the very next day and you will find them supremely selfish—that they are not devoted to God but to their own interest, and are ready to take any advantage, even of their brethren, to benefit themselves. Now in this case it is manifest that their melting and breaking down was merely a gushing of the emotions and not a will subdued and devoted to God. Devotion belongs to the will; and there may be many paroxisms of emotion where the consecration of the will to self remains supreme.

6. Many mistake the consecration and devotion of the imagination for that of the heart. They can write poems or sermons or religious articles for the paper; they can talk and pray and preach and exercise any degree of zeal in the cause of religion; and yet meet them on any ground where the deep foundations of their hearts are developed and you find they will be supremely selfish.

7. Many expect devotion without faith. This is naturally impossible. The mind cannot be devoted to God without confiding in Him.

8. This shows that they confound faith with hope, or the expectation of salvation. A man may be devoted without a hope, and may consecrate his whole being to God while he thinks nothing of his own salvation.

9. Many do not distinguish between that naked faith in the simple truth, which invariably begets devotion, and their ever-varying states of emotion, which they are prone to call religion. Simple faith in the character of God, as revealed in the Bible, naturally and necessarily begets a spirit of consecration to God. But there may be any amount of emotion without any true devotion.

REMARKS

1. A spirit of devotion will make the most constant cares and the most pressing labors the means of the deepest and most constant communion with God. The more constant and pressing our duties are, if they are performed for God, the deeper and more incessant is our communion with Him; for whatever is done in a spirit of devotion is communion with God.

2. They are not Christians who do not hold communion with God in their ordinary employments. If you do not hold conscious communion with God in your ordinary business, it is because it is not performed with a spirit of devotion. If not performed in a spirit of devotion, it is sin. But if your ordinary employments are sin, then certainly you have no religion, unless a man can be truly religious and yet ordinarily a servant of the devil.

3. They are certainly not in a sanctified state who cannot attend to the ordinary and lawful business of life without being drawn away from God.

4. That is unlawful which cannot be done in a spirit of devotion. If you feel the incongruity of performing it as an act of devotion to God, it is unlawful, yourself being judge.

5. That is unlawful which *is not* so done; that is, whatever the act may

be in itself, if it is not actually performed as an act of devotion to God, it is sin. Hence "the plowing of the wicked is sin." Eating and drinking and the most common acts of life, if not done in a spirit of devotion, are sin.

6. Anything not right or wrong in itself may be either right or wrong as it is or is not done in a spirit of devotion. Hence:

7. A selfish mind may condemn a sanctified mind for what is no sin in that particular individual; for the selfish man might naturally enough suppose the other to be actuated by the same motives by which he knows himself to be actuated.

So, again, a sanctified mind might give credit to a selfish mind where it is not due, taking it for granted that when the act is right the motive is right. So the sinner may sin in copying the example of a Christian—I mean the example of the Christian when he does not sin. Christian example may influence him to go to meetings but still, if his motives are not right, it is sin.

8. Sinners may and often do give themselves credit for outwardly imitating the example of Christians when, in reality, the very thing for which they give themselves credit is among their greatest sins.

9. There is no peace of mind but in a state of devotion. No other state of mind is reasonable. In no other state will the powers of the mind harmonize. In any other state than that of devotion to God there is an inward struggle, and mutiny and strife in the mind itself. The conscience upbraids the heart for selfishness. Hence "there is no peace, saith my God, to the wicked."

10. They have "perfect peace whose minds are thus stayed upon God" in an attitude of constant devotion. It is impossible that they should not have peace, for devotion implies and includes peace.

And now, beloved, have you the spirit of true devotion? Do not reply, I hope so; for nothing but consciousness should satisfy you for a moment. If you are devoted to God, you are conscious of it; and if you are not conscious of being devoted to God, it is because you are not so devoted. "Be not deceived, God is not mocked, for whatsoever a man soweth, that shall he also reap; for he that soweth to the flesh shall of the flesh reap corruption, and he that soweth to the Spirit, shall of the Spirit reap life everlasting."

Professor Finney's Letter of February 13, 1839*

TO THE CONVERTS OF THE GREAT REVIVALS THAT
HAVE PREVAILED IN THE UNITED STATES WITHIN THE FEW
LAST YEARS.

Beloved: I closed my last letter by adverting to the fact that several pro-

---

*From *The Oberlin Evangelist*.

fessedly religious periodicals have so referred to what I had said in regard to your being "a disgrace to religion" as virtually to represent me as denying the reality, genuineness and power of those glorious revivals in which you were converted. I denied having said anything in that connection to that effect. But I did assert in my lecture and reassert in my last letter that I believed many of you were by your lives a disgrace to the religion of Christ. Now, beloved, I said not this nor do I now say it to bring a railing accusation against you, but for the purpose of preparing the way to put some questions to your conscience, with the design to turn your eyes fully upon your own life and spirit as exhibited before the world.

And here let me say that when you receive this number I desire each of you to consider this letter as directed to you individually, as *a private letter to you*, although communicated through this public channel.

I will write upon my knees, and I beg you to read it upon your knees. And when you have read it as written to *yourself* and received it, as I conjure you to do, as a private communication to *you from me*, in the name of the Lord Jesus Christ, I entreat you to hand it to all your Christian friends in your neighborhood and within your reach, beseeching them to receive it and consider it as a private letter to *them*, in the name of the Lord Jesus Christ.

Hereafter, should the providence of God permit, I may more particularly address different classes of individuals than I can in this letter. I intend to address fathers, mothers, husbands, wives, children, ministers, church officers, editors of religious papers, young men and young women, as so many distinct classes of individuals to whom particular truths may be applicable. In this, I address you without reference to your age or sex or station or calling, simply as a professor of the religion of Jesus Christ.

I have said that I fear and believe that many of you, at least, are a disgrace to the religion you profess. By this I mean that instead of fairly and truly representing the religion of Christ in your life and spirit, you in many respects grossly misrepresent it. Do not here suffer your temper to rise and turn upon me and say, "Physician, heal thyself." I might, to be sure, confess my own sins; but my business now as "an ambassador of Jesus Christ" is with your own conscience.

And now, dearly beloved, bear with me while I put the questions home to you, as by name.

Are not your life and spirit and habits a miserable *misrepresentation* of the religion you profess?

You are a professor of the religion of Jesus Christ. Your profession of religion has placed you on high, as "a city that cannot be hid." You are not hid. The eyes of God, of Christians, of the world, of hell are upon you.

And now, precious soul, do you sincerely believe that you *feel* and *act* and *live* and *do* as the Lord Jesus Christ would under similar circumstances?

Are those around you forced by your *life* and *spirit* to recognize the lineaments divine of the character of Christ in you?

Would those that know nothing of Christ be able to catch and *understand* the true *spirit* and *meaning* of the religion of Jesus by an acquaintance with you?

Would they obtain from your *life* and *example* such an idea of the *nature, design* and *tendency* of the gospel as would lead them to value it, to understand its necessity and importance?

Are your spirit and temper and conversation so *unearthly*, so *heavenly*, so *divine*, so much like *Christ*, as fairly to represent Him? Or do you misrepresent Him?

Is not the *temper* that you manifest, the *life* that you lead, your *conversation*, your *pursuits*—are not all these in many respects the very opposite and contrast of the spirit of the religion of Christ?

My beloved brother, sister, father, mother, whoever you are, *remember* that while you read these questions God's eye is pouring its *searching blaze* into your *inmost soul*.

What is your temper in your *family*, among your *friends*, in your *private* life, in your *domestic* relations and in your *public* walks?

Is your conversation in heaven or is it "earthly, sensual, devilish"?

What is the testimony of your *closet*? Can it bear witness to your sighs and groans and tears over the wickedness and desolations of the world?

Are men by beholding your good works constrained to "glorify your Father who is in heaven"? Or is the name of God blasphemed on account of your earthly and unchristian life and spirit?

Can those that remain unconverted in the place where you live bear witness that a great and divine change was wrought in you by the Spirit of God?

I beseech you in the name of Christ to inquire, are your impenitent acquaintances *constrained* to confess that that *must* have been a work of God that could have wrought so great a change in you, as they daily witness?

Do you think that the interests of religion are *really advanced* by your life and that you are continually making an impression in favor of holiness on those around you?

Do they witness in you the "*peace* of God that passeth understanding"?

Do they behold in you that *sweet* and *divine complacency* in the will and ways of God that spreads a heavenly *serenity* and *calm* and *sweetness* over your mind, in the midst of the *trials* and *vicissitudes* to which you are subjected?

Or do they behold you vexed, anxious, careful, easily disturbed and exhibiting the spirit of the world? My dear soul, if this is so you are a horrible disgrace to religion; you are unlike Jesus. Was this the spirit that Jesus manifested?

Let me inquire again: what are you *doing* for the *conversion of sinners* around you, and what for the conversion of the world?

Would one hundred million such Christians as you are, and living just as you live, be instrumental in converting the world?

Suppose there are a thousand million of men upon the earth and suppose that one hundred million of these were just such Christians as you are, in your present state and at your present rate of usefulness; when would the world be converted?

Is the church and the world *better* and *holier* on account of your profession? And are they really *benefited* by your life?

If not, your profession is a libel upon the Christian religion. You are, like Peter, *denying* your Savior; and like Judas, you have kissed but to *betray* Him.

Now, beloved, I will not take it upon me to decide these questions that I have put to you on my knees and in the spirit of love. Will you be honest and, on your knees, spread out this letter to God your Maker and Christ your Savior? Will you not upon your knees read over these questions, one by one, and ask God to show you the real state of your life as it relates to each of them?

And here, beloved, I leave you for the present; and may the Savior aid you and make you honest in meeting cordially and answering honestly these questions. You must be searched and humbled and broken down in heart before you can be built up and made strong in Christ.

Do be *honest* and in *haste*, and address yourself to the work of self-examination without delay. I beg of you to prepare yourself to receive the consolations of the gospel of Christ, for my soul is panting to spread them out before you.

Providence permitting, you may expect to hear from me again soon.

C. G. FINNEY,
A Servant of the Lord Jesus Christ

LECTURE 4

True and False Religion

Gal. 5:1: "Stand fast therefore in the liberty wherewith Christ hath made us free, and be not entangled again with the yoke of bondage."

The observances of the ceremonial law were designedly a typical representation of the gospel. The Jews had misunderstood them, and supposed that their observance was the ground of justification and acceptance with God. After the introduction of Christianity, many of the Christian Jews were exceedingly zealous for their observance, and for uniting the ceremonial dispensation with Christianity. On the contrary Paul, the great "Apostle of the Gentiles," insisted upon justification by faith alone, entirely irrespective of any legal observances and conditions whatever. There were a set of teachers in the early days of Christianity who were called Judaizers, from the fact that they insisted upon uniting legal observances with Christianity as a ground of justification. Soon after the establishment of the Galatian churches by St. Paul, these Judaizers succeeded in introducing this corruption into the Christian churches. To rebuke this error and overthrow it was the design of this epistle. The yoke and bondage spoken of in the text was the yoke of legal observances. The liberty here mentioned is the liberty of love—of justification and of sanctification, by faith alone.

In discussing this subject I design to show:

    I. What it is to make a man a slave.
    II. What it is to be a slave.
    III. What true liberty is.
    IV. That the religion of many persons is mere slavery.
    V. That true religion is genuine liberty.

I. *I am to show what it is to make a man a SLAVE.*

To enslave a man is to treat a person as a thing—to set aside moral agency and to treat a moral agent as a mere piece of property.

II. *I am to show what it is to be a SLAVE.*

It is not to be in a state of involuntary servitude for, strictly speaking, such a state is impossible. The slaves in the Southern States are not, strictly speaking, in a state of involuntary servitude. Upon the whole, they choose to serve their masters rather than do worse. A man cannot act against his will, but his will may be influenced by considerations that set aside his liberty. To be a slave is to be under the necessity of choosing between two evils. Thus the slaves in the Southern States prefer being as they are to being in a worse condition: to being imprisoned or whipped for attempting to escape. But plainly this is a choice between two evils, neither of which, if left to themselves, would they choose. So a wicked man may choose to obey human laws rather than suffer the consequences of disobedience; still he may *abhor the laws* and *feel* himself shut up to the necessity of choosing between two evils. So a wife who does not love her husband may choose, upon the whole, to live with him rather than break up her family, lose her character and subject herself to poverty and reproach. And yet if she does not love her husband, she will consider living with him merely as the least of two calamities. She feels shut up to the necessity of choosing between two courses, neither of which is agreeable to her. All that can be said is that she chooses that course which, upon the whole, is the least *disagreeable.*

To be obliged to choose against our feelings and inclinations—to be shut up to the necessity of pursuing a course of life not chosen for its own sake, but as the last of two evils—is the very essence of slavery.

III. *I am to show what true liberty is.*

1. True liberty does not consist in the unrestrained indulgence of lust and selfishness.

2. Nor in freedom from all law, or rule of action.

3. But true liberty consists in the privilege of choosing and pursuing that course which is preferred for its own sake—that course of life in which our whole moral being will harmonize, where violence is done to no law of the mind.

4. In other words, and more particularly, it consists in pursuing that course of life which is not chosen as the least of two evils, but of all possible courses is that which the mind prefers. For example, a wife who loves her husband and prefers his society to that of any other man is free, in the proper sense of the term, in living with him, whereas if she preferred another man to him, and lived with her own husband from other considerations than love, she would be a slave and not free.

A man who obeys wholesome laws from love to virtue and good order is free in the highest sense; but when he obeys law from restraint, not because he loves virtue but from fear of punishment, he is a slave. Here it is plain that his choice of obedience is, by him, considered as a choice of two evils and not that course of conduct which he prefers for its own sake.

IV. *The religion of many persons is mere slavery.*

1. Their religion is not that in which they are *most deeply interested.* Their conduct shows that many other things interest them more deeply than the subject of religion—upon which they are more excited and engaged. Their religion seems to be like the labor of children. Children choose to *play* for its own sake; in that they are deeply interested. Therein you see their engagedness and zeal. But when put at work it is manifest that this is submitted to as the least of two evils. They don't love work for its own sake but prefer it to punishment. Just so it seems to be with the religion of many professors. Religion is not that to which they naturally turn as the great central object of their affections, and to which they return with the force of gravity as soon as the pressure of any object that has diverted their attention for a time is removed. On the contrary, their *attention* is somewhere else, even while they are outwardly and languidly attending to what they call religion.

2. Their religion is altogether a *secondary business.* It is not the great, absorbing, commanding, prominent object of their lives but is so far huddled into a corner that everyone may see that religion is not their *main business,* that they have some other *business,* and that religion is a matter by the bye. Thus what they call their religious duties—their prayers, reading the Scriptures, &c.—are hurried over or for slight causes wholly omitted, while that which constitutes their *main business* commands their time

and thoughts and hearts.

3. Religion, with them, is a matter rather of *conscience* than of the *heart*. They feel themselves driven by the remonstrances of conscience to the performance of their religious duties, rather than drawn by the deep love of religion itself.

4. That their religion is slavery is evident from the fact that it does not constitute their *happiness*. This demonstrates that it is not a thing chosen for its own sake. True, they cannot be happy without it; nor can they be happy with it. Conscience will not suffer them to rest without something they can call religion. And yet they do not choose it for its own sake. The mind is not satisfied with it nor is it made happy by it.

5. They are religious upon the same principle that men take medicine in time of sickness. It is *submitted* to for the benefits of it. The medicine may be nauseous and offensive in itself but is *submitted* to as the least of two evils.

6. Just so religion is by many *submitted* to as something they *must* attend to—not that it is loved for its own sake, nor that the mind chooses it as that course which, on every account, is most desired and valued by the mind, but as something that it will not do to neglect.

7. Religion is regarded by this class of persons as the most *important* yet not the most *loved* employment. Their *reason* affirms that it is the one thing needful. But their *hearts* do not affirm that it is the one thing most loved and rejoiced in for its own sake.

8. The real state of mind in which this class of persons are may be learned from the fact that in exhorting others to attend to the subject of religion, they rather dwell on the danger of *neglect* than on the *blessedness* of the thing itself.

9. And that this does not arise merely out of the fact that they expect such considerations to be most influential with those to whom they speak, you will observe that in speaking about or considering their own case they are influenced mainly by the same reason they press upon others. Religion is, with them, something that it will not do to neglect. The hazard of neglect—the stings of conscience, and the misery that neglect brings with it—are the things which most influence them.

10. They are under circumstances of constraint. They *must* serve God; they *must* attend to their duty; they *must* prepare for death.

11. Their enjoyment consists mostly in their *hope* and not in the exercise of religion itself. Did they never expect to be more happy in their religion than they are now, they would be "of all men the most miserable." Hence they drag out their religion in obedience to the dictates of conscience, knowing that it does not constitute their happiness here; but somehow they hope it will be more agreeable to them in heaven.

12. Their religion acts by way of restraint and *constraint*. It serves as a bridle to rein in and restrain their rampant, sinful propensities on the one hand, and a whip to urge them forward in their religious duties on the other. It is not that course of life which of all possible or conceivable courses is the most agreeable to them for its own sake. But they have an existence

and there is no alternative. They *must* be religious, or they *must* be damned. They must continually be thrown upon the terrors of their conscience or drag on in duty, however much their heart may reluctate.

13. Consequently you hear them calculating about how much is their part, in any religious or benevolent enterprise; and they seem to be glad when they think they have done what they suppose falls to their share. Then they think they have done up their duty and may rest awhile, or attend to their own affairs. Hence,

14. The inquiry, how little can they get along with doing and giving and praying, and still maintain a hope? How little religion is compatible with going to heaven?

In short, it is plain that their religion, instead of being their happiness, as something chosen for its own sake and pursued on its *own account*, is their misery, as the least of two evils. Instead of making them *happy*, enough of it would be *hell*.

V. *I am to show that true religion is genuine liberty.*

1. Because it is that which is chosen for its *own sake*—that course which the mind prefers to all other conceivable courses of life.

2. It is the *highest good*, in the estimation of the mind that possesses it.

3. If left entirely unbiased by every other consideration, and having all other possible and conceivable courses of life and conduct spread out before it, the religion of Christ would be its *supreme, eternal choice*.

4. It is that in which the whole being, in all its powers, unites and harmonizes. The reason, the conscience, the understanding, all the affections and emotions—in short, the volitions and all that makes up the moral being—unite and sweetly harmonize in the exercise of this divine religion.

5. Consequently it constitutes real, permanent happiness.

6. It casts out *fear*—fear of hell, fear of disgrace, fear of man; and all fear that hath torment is annihilated, and the mind sweetly bathes itself in an ocean of love and peace.

7. The soul yields obedience to all the requirements of God *joyfully*. For the will of God marks out to it the very course, of all others, which it *delights* to pursue. The affectionate wife obeys her husband, and his wish is her law, not of constraint but willingly, because her happiness is wrapped up in doing his will. She loves him, and to please him is her element and her life. Just so it is with the true Christian. To please God is his supreme joy.

8. The true Christian never yields to the will of God by constraint but always prefers the will of God, whenever that will is known. In other words he really wills what God wills, as soon and as far as he knows what that is. He may have desires for this and the other object and may express those desires to God in prayer. He may think this or that course would be most for the glory of God. But true religion always prefers that God's will should be done. His will is controlled by infinite wisdom and love. It is impossible, therefore, that true religion should ever be made miserable by being obliged or constrained to submit to the will of God.

9. True religion is not submitted to, by him that possesses it, as *medicine*, but is like *food* that we eat for its own sake. We love our food and should eat it for the pleasure of eating, whether we expect to be benefited by it or not. Just so in religion: the mind is not mainly influenced by the benefit to be received, but it is the *food of the mind*, the *natural aliment* on which it lives.

10. The truly religious man does not inquire how little religion he can get along with, but how much he may possess.

11. Not how much sin may be indulged in, and yet he get to heaven, but how he can be rid of all sin, whether he goes to heaven or not. Not how sinful he may be and still be a child of God, but how holy he *may* and *can* be.

12. His religion makes up his happiness. It is the continual exercise of it that mainly makes him blest; and enough of the same kind would make heaven.

REMARKS

1. From what has been said, it is manifest that many professors of religion in reality regard God as a great slaveholder. I do not mean that they would say this in words, nor that they understand that they do regard him in this light. The reason is that they do not *understand* themselves to be *slaves*. If they realized what slavery is, and that they themselves have the spirit of slaves and are, in their religion, all that is meant by being slaves, they would then be shocked with the irresistible inference that they do regard God as a *Slaveholder*.

2. What an abomination such a religion must be in the sight of God. Instead of seeing His professed children engaged, heart and soul, in His service—finding it the essence of true liberty, and their supreme joy—He beholds them groaning under it as a severe burden, submitted to only to escape His frown.

3. You see, in this discourse, the true distinction between the religion of *law* and that of the *gospel*. The religion of many professors seems to set as painfully on them as a straitjacket. It is evidently not their natural element. It is the bondage of law and not the religion of peace.

4. Many express indignation against Southern slavery, as they may well do, but who are slaves themselves. They know full well that if they would be honest with themselves, their religion is to them a yoke of bondage. They are *afraid* of death, *afraid* of the judgment, *afraid* of God.

They submit to religion as the only method of escaping "the wrath to come." But yet let it be known to them that there is no hell, no solemn judgment, that men will universally be saved, do what they will, and they will feel relieved of a weighty burden. They will feel rid of the responsibilities of moral agents and cast off their religion as of no consequence.

5. This slavery is utterly inexcusable and consists in the perverse state of the heart.

6. Such religion is worse than no religion.

(1) It is not any more safe than no religion.

(2) It is more hypocritical than none.

(3) It confirms self-righteousness.

(4) It begets and perpetuates a delusion in the mind.

(5) It ruins the soul of the professor and is a stumbling block to others. What is a greater stumbling block, for example, than for an impenitent husband to see his wife possessing this painful, legal religion? Instead of observing her happy, humble, sweet, heavenly-minded and peaceful, like an angel, he perceives that her religion makes her complaining, uneasy and irritable—in short, that it is the lashings of conscience by which she is actuated, and not the constant flow of the deep feelings of her heart.

(6) This kind of religion is more dishonorable to God than none. It is really the contrast of true religion. "The fruit of the Spirit is love, joy, peace, long-suffering, gentleness, goodness, faith, meekness, temperance, against which there is no law." Now the religion of which I have been speaking is the very opposite of all this. To be sure, a man who is openly irreligious, dishonors God. But [for] a man . . . [to profess]* to be God's representative, to exhibit God's spirit and to be the reflection of His image, and then go about the duties of religion as a task to be submitted to instead of pouring out the overflowings of His benevolence—to unclench His hard hand at the stern biddings of conscience—is to publish as gross a libel upon the character of God and the religion of the gospel as is possible.

(7) It is worse than none, inasmuch as it prevents conviction and true conversion. Persons in this state suppose themselves to be truly religious and seem not to dream that this is the very opposite of true religion. Now, while under this delusion, it is vain to expect their eyes to be opened and to anticipate a real and thorough conversion to God.

7. All who have left their first love are again entangled in the yoke of bondage. If any of you have known what it was to love God with all your heart, you have known what it was to be free. You know by your own consciousness that your religion was then the essence of true liberty. But if you have laid aside your love, no matter by what other principles you are actuated, you are "entangled again in the yoke of bondage." Your religion has ceased to be liberty and you have become a slave. Now I ask you, "Where is the blessedness" you once spoke of? Have you that great peace that they possess who love the law of God? Does the peace of God rule in your hearts? Is Christ's joy fulfilled in you? Or are you lashed along by your conscience, actuated by hope and fear and any and every other principle than love?

And now, beloved, I ask you in the name of the Lord Jesus Christ whether you have the religion of the gospel. I have in this discourse endeavored to set before you in as simple a form as is possible the grand distinction between true saints and hypocrites. To which of these classes do you belong? Remember the eye of God is upon you. "Be ye not deceived, for God is not mocked." "If the Son hath made you free, then are ye free indeed." And I exhort you in the words of the text, "Stand fast therefore in the liberty wherewith Christ hath made you free, and be not entangled again with the

*Finney's words were "But a man who professes to be. . . ."

yoke of bondage." But on the other hand, if the Holy Ghost sees you with the chains of slavery upon your soul, driven on by conscience as by a slave-holder, working out your painful religion lest you should lose your soul, I beseech you in the name of Christ, get up out of this bondage, lay aside these chains. "Loose thyself from the bands of thy neck, O captive daughter of Zion," lay aside this legal yoke and come forth from slavery and death, that Christ may give you liberty and life.

LECTURE 5

The Law of God, No. 1

Matt. 22:36-40: "Master, which is the great commandment in the law? Jesus said unto him, Thou shalt love the Lord thy God with all thy heart, and with all thy soul, and with all thy mind. This is the first and great commandment. And the second is like unto it, Thou shalt love thy neighbour as thyself. On these two commandments hang all the law and the prophets."

In discussing this subject, I shall show:

I. That obedience to these two commandments comprises the whole of true religion.
II. What constitutes true obedience.
III. Notice several mistakes into which men have fallen on this subject.

I. *I am to show that obedience to these commandments comprises the whole of true religion.*

1. This is evident from the text itself. Upon these two precepts, said the Savior, "hang all the law and the prophets," that is, the whole of what is required in the law and the prophets is here epitomized.

2. In Rom. 13:8-10, it is said, "Owe no man any thing, but to love one another: for he that loveth another hath fulfilled the law. For this, Thou shalt not commit adultery, Thou shalt not kill, Thou shalt not steal, Thou shalt not bear false witness, Thou shalt not covet; and if there be any other commandment, it is briefly comprehended in this saying, namely, Thou shalt love thy neighbour as thyself. Love worketh no ill to his neighbour, therefore love is the fulfilling of the law." Here it is declared that *love*, with corresponding action of course, comprises our whole duty to our fellowmen.

Reason affirms that there is no virtue without love and that perfect love to God and man, with its natural fruits, is the consummation and the whole of virtue. This is also agreeable to the dictates of conscience and common sense.

3. The law of God is the standard of right and wrong. The whole law of God is summed up in these two precepts. Consequently, obedience to these is the whole of virtue or true religion. In other words, it is the whole of what God requires of man. But I need not insist at large upon this, as it will not probably be denied or doubted.

II. *I am to show what constitutes true obedience.*

Love is the sum of the requirement. But I may and should be asked what is the kind of love required by these commands? I shall consider:

1. *The kind of love to be exercised towards God.*

(1) It is to be love of the *heart*, and not a mere emotion. By the heart I mean the will. Emotions, or what are generally termed feelings, are often involuntary states of mind; that is, they are not choices or volitions and of course do not govern the conduct. Love, in the form of an emotion, may exist in opposition to the will; for example, we may exercise emotions of love contrary to our conscience and judgment, and in opposition to our will. Thus the sexes often exercise emotions of love towards those to whom all the voluntary powers of their mind feel opposed and with whom they will not associate. It is true that in most cases the emotions are with the will. But they are sometimes, nay often, opposed to it.

Now it is a voluntary state of mind that the law of God requires, that is, it lays its claims upon the will. The will controls the conduct. And it is therefore, of course, the love of the heart or will that God requires.

(2) *Benevolence* is one of the modifications of love which we are to exercise towards God. Benevolence is good will. And certainly we are bound to exercise this kind of love to God. It is a dictate of reason, of conscience, of common sense and of immutable justice that we should exercise good and not ill will to God. It matters not whether He needs our good will or whether our good or ill will can, in any way, affect Him. The question does not respect the *necessities* but *deserts*.

God's well-being is certainly an infinite good in itself, and consequently we are bound to desire it, to will it, to rejoice in it—and to will it and rejoice in it in proportion to its *intrinsic* importance. And as His well-being is certainly a matter of *infinite* importance, we are under infinite obligation to will it with all our hearts.

(3) Another modification of this love is that of *complacency* or *esteem*. God's character is infinitely good. We are therefore bound not merely to love Him with the love of benevolence, but to exercise the highest degree of complacency in His character. To say that God is good and lovely is merely to say that He deserves to be loved. If He deserves to be loved on account of His goodness and love, then He deserves to be loved in proportion to His goodness and loveliness. Our obligation, therefore, is infinitely great to exercise towards Him the highest degree of the love of complacency of which we are capable. These remarks are confirmed by the Bible, by rea-

son, by conscience, and by common sense.

(4) Another peculiarity of this love which must by no means be overlooked is that it must be *disinterested*, that is, that we should not love Him for selfish reasons, but that we should love Him for what He is: with benevolence, because His well-being is an infinite good; with complacency, because His character is infinitely excellent; with the heart, because all virtue belongs to the heart. It is plain that nothing short of disinterested love is virtue. The Savior recognizes and settles this truth in Luke 6:32-34: "For if ye love them which love you, what thank have ye? for sinners also love those that love them. And if ye do good to them which do good to you, what thank have ye? for sinners also do even the same. And if ye lend to them of whom ye hope to receive, what thank have ye? for sinners also lend to sinners, to receive as much again." These words epitomize the whole doctrine of the Bible on this subject, and lay down the broad principle that to love God or anyone else for selfish reasons is not virtue.

(5) Another peculiarity of this love is that it must be in every instance *supreme*. The text plainly requires this. Besides, anything less than *supreme* love to God must be idolatry. If anything else is loved more, *that* is our God.

Observe that God lays great stress upon the degree of love, so that the *degree* is essential to the *kind* of love. If it be not *supreme* in *degree*, it is wholly defective and in no sense acceptable to God.

2. I will consider *the kind of love to be exercised towards our fellowmen.*

(1) It must be the love of the *heart* and not mere desire or emotion. It is very natural to desire the good of others—to pity the distressed and to feel strong emotions of compassion towards those who are afflicted. But these emotions are not virtue. Unless we *will* their good as well as *desire* it, it is of no avail. James 2:15, 16: "If a brother or sister be naked, and destitute of daily food, and one of you say unto them, Depart in peace, be you warmed and filled; notwithstanding ye give them not those things which are needful to the body, what doth it profit?" Now here the Apostle fully recognizes the principle that mere desire for the good of others, which of course will satisfy itself with good words instead of good deeds, is not virtue. If it were good *willing* instead of good *desiring*, it would produce corresponding action; and unless it is good willing there is no holiness in it.

(2) *Benevolence* to men is a prime modification of holy love. This is included in what I have said above, but needs to be expressly stated and explained. It is a plain dictate of reason, of conscience, of common sense and immutable justice that we should exercise good will towards our fellowmen; that we should will their good, in proportion to its importance; that we should rejoice in their happiness and endeavor to promote it, according to its real value in the scale of being.

(3) *Complacency* towards those that are virtuous is another modification of holy love. I say towards those that are virtuous because while we exercise benevolence towards all, irrespective of their character, we have a right to exercise *complacency* towards those only who are holy. To exercise

complacency towards the wicked is to be as wicked as they are. But to exercise entire complacency to those that are holy is to be ourselves holy.

(4) This love is to be in every instance equal. By equal I do not mean that degree of love which selfish beings have for themselves, for this is supreme. There is a grand distinction between self-love and selfishness. Self-love is that benevolence to self or regard for our own interest which its intrinsic importance demands. Selfishness is the excess of self-love, that is, it is supreme self-love. It is making our own happiness the supreme object of pursuit because it is our *own*, and not attaching that importance to others' interests and the happiness of other beings which their importance demands. A selfish mind is therefore in the exercise of the supreme love of self.

Now the law of God does not require or permit us to love our neighbor with this degree of love, for that would be idolatry. But the command "to love our neighbour as ourselves" implies:

(a) That we should love ourselves less than supremely and attach no more importance to our own interests and happiness than they demand. So that the first thing implied in this command is that we love *ourselves less* than supremely, and that we love our neighbor with the same degree of love which it is *lawful* for us to exercise towards ourselves.

(b) *Equal* love does not imply that we should neglect our own *appropriate* concerns and attend to the affairs of others. God has appointed to every man a particular sphere in which to act and particular affairs to which he must attend. And this business, whatever it is, must be transacted for God and not for ourselves. For a man, therefore, to neglect his particular calling under the pretense of attending to the business of others is neither required nor permitted by this law.

Nor are we to neglect our own families and the nurture and education of our children and attend to that of others. "But if any provide not for his own, especially for those of his own house, he hath denied the faith, and is worse than an infidel." To these duties we are to attend for God. And no man or woman is required or permitted to neglect the children God has given them, under the pretense of attending to the families of others.

Nor does this law require or permit us to squander our possessions upon the intemperate and dissolute and improvident. Not that the absolute necessities of such persons are in no case to be relieved by us, but it is always to be done in such a manner as not to encourage but to rebuke their evil courses.

Nor does this law require or permit us to suffer others to live by sponging out our possessions, while they themselves are not engaged in promoting the good of men.

Nor does it require or permit us to lend money to speculators or for speculating purposes, or in any way to encourage selfishness.

(c) But by *equal* love is meant, I have said, the same love in *kind* and *degree* which it is lawful for us to exercise towards ourselves. It is lawful, nay, it is our duty to exercise a suitable regard to our own happiness. This is benevolence to self, or what is commonly called self-love. The same, both in kind and degree, we are required to exercise to all our fellowmen.

(5) Another feature of holy love is that it must be *impartial*, that is, it must extend to *enemies* as well as *friends*, else it is selfish love and comes under the reprobation of the Savior in the passage before quoted, Luke 6:32, 34, "For if ye love them who love you, what thank have ye? for sinners also do even the same."

Now observe that this test must always be applied to the kind of love we exercise to our fellowmen in order to understand its *genuineness*. God's love is love to enemies. It was for His enemies that He gave His Son. Our love must be the same in kind; it must extend to enemies as well as friends. And if it does not, it is partial and selfish.

III. *I am to notice several mistakes into which men have fallen on this subject.*

1. It seems to be a very general opinion among men that love to God and men may be genuine in *kind* but deficient in *degree*, that is, that we may have some true love to God that is not supreme love.

Now this cannot be true. For God lays great stress in His law upon the degree of love. Besides it is perfectly plain if it be not supreme in degree that the mind loves something else more and is consequently in a state of idolatry, instead of having any degree of holy love.

2. It seems to be a very general opinion that there is such a thing as imperfect obedience to God, that is, as it respects one and the same act.

Obedience may be imperfect in respect to its constancy; an individual may obey at one time and disobey at another. But I cannot see how an imperfect obedience, relating to one and the same act, can be possible. *Imperfect* OBEDIENCE! What can be meant by this but *disobedient* OBEDIENCE! a *sinful* HOLINESS!

Now to decide the character of any act we are to bring it into the light of the law of God. If agreeable to this law, it is obedience—it is right, *wholly right*. If it is in *any respect* different from what the law of God requires, it is disobedience—it is wrong, *wholly wrong*. Consequently,

3. It is supposed that a person may be partly *holy* and partly *sinful* in the same act and exercise.

I was formerly of this opinion myself; and I believe in some one of my reported lectures it is expressed. I formerly reasoned in this way: that an exercise might be put forth in view of several motives, some of which were right and some wrong, and that the exercise, therefore, had the complex character of the motives that produced it. But I am now persuaded that this philosophy is false. Whatever may have preceded a given exercise that may have led the way to its being put forth is not the question, nor does it alter the character of that exercise. For whenever the exercise is put forth, it must be in view of some *one* consideration which the mind contemplates at the instant. If the reason which the mind has for the exercise be disinterested, the action is holy. If otherwise, it is sinful. By disinterested I do not mean that the mind must necessarily feel that it has no personal interest in the thing, but that the degree of self-interest that is felt should not be disproportioned to the interest which the mind takes in the matter on account of its own intrinsic importance. In other words, if the mind's interest in it is selfish the action or exercise, whatever it may be, is sinful. If it be not selfish, it is holy, although there may be a suitable regard to our own interest at the moment of decision.

But that the action or affection must be either right or wrong—that when the test of God's law is applied it must be pronounced an act of obedience or disobedience—seems to me to be very plain. That it should be of such a mixed character as both to be obedience and disobedience, if the nature of God's law be considered, appears to me to be impossible. It should be understood that holiness and sin belong to the will or choice of the mind. Where the mind is under the influence of an existing sinful choice, it should be understood that this choice is sinful because it is selfish. Now a multitude of considerations may from time to time present themselves to the mind that may diminish the power of a wrong or sinful preference or choice. But however much the power of a selfish choice may be weakened, yet there is no virtue till the mind comes to exercise an opposite or disinterestedly benevolent choice. Now whenever the mind puts forth a holy choice, it is absurd and contradictory to say that any degree of selfishness is exercised by the mind in putting forth that choice. For selfishness is supreme love [for self]. Therefore, it is naturally impossible that selfishness should mingle with holiness. It is the same contradiction as to say that supreme self-love co-exists with supreme disinterested love. Therefore the volition cannot possibly have a mixed character, that is, it cannot be partly selfish and partly holy. If any degree of sin can be affirmed of it, if in any way it is defective, it must be on account of the degree of its strength and not on account of its co-existence with some degree of selfishness.

But here let it be understood that it cannot be defective in degree and yet be holy, unless it can be holy without being agreeable to the law of God. It must be supreme in degree to have the character of holiness at all. It must be disinterested in opposition to selfish[ness] or it is wholly sinful. If, therefore, it is disinterested in kind and supreme in degree, it is wholly a right affection. Otherwise, it is wholly wrong.

4. Another mistake is that holiness may be deficient in *degree* as well as in *permanency*. This is only another form of expressing nearly the same idea. But I aim at perspicuity, and I choose to reassert the mistake in this form, namely, that holiness may be *real* while deficient in *degree* as well as in permanency.

Now, holiness is love. To say, therefore, that holiness may be deficient in *degree* is the same as to say that love may be true, acceptable love to God while it is less than supreme in degree—which is plainly contrary to both the letter and spirit of the law of God—or, in other words, it may be acceptable to God while we love something else more and are in fact idolaters.

5. That we may be conscious of loving God *less* than something else and yet have some *genuine love* and some true religion.

Now love, to be genuine, must possess all the attributes which the law of God requires. And as God lays great stress upon its being supreme, if we are conscious that we love other things more than God, it is impossible that we should be in the exercise of any true religion.

6. That *emotions* of love, while the heart or will is selfish, is true religion.

Now that there may be emotions and strong emotions of love to a being or thing to which our will is opposed is the experience of every day. And I see not why emotions of *love* to God as well as emotions of *gratitude* to God may not exist while the will is selfish, and therefore the heart entirely depraved. I know from my own experience that such emotions can exist in an unconverted mind; and it appears to me that herein consists the grand delusion of vast multitudes of professors of religion, as well as of those who are professedly impenitent. When some flashes of light in regard to some of the attributes of God are witnessed—when he is exhibited in certain relations and his feelings of compassion are thrown out before the mind, as exhibited in the death of Christ—I think I know by experience, and I see not why it is not in accordance with true philosophy, that there should be a gush of emotion which may be and often is taken for true religion, while the heart or will is entirely selfish. This is illustrated in the character of those who, in revivals and seasons of religious excitement, will manifest a high degree of religious emotion, while in their business operations they prove to be completely selfish.

7. That some degree of *selfishness* may co-exist with some degree of *holiness.*

I say *co-exist.* I do not mean to deny that a mind may be selfish at one time and benevolent at another. But I do deny that a mind can be selfish and benevolent at one and the same time, or that any degree of holiness can exist in the mind in the exercise of selfishness. Selfishness, as we have already seen, is the supreme love of self. It is always the supreme affection of the mind and cannot be exercised in any one instance in any other form than that of supreme regard to self. It is what God expressly forbids. Every exercise of it, therefore, not only implies that we love ourselves more than we love our neighbor but, as it is a violation of the law of God, it is loving ourselves more than we respect the authority of God.

To say, therefore, that some degree of selfishness may co-exist with some degree of holiness is the same absurdity as to say that we can love ourselves supremely and God supremely at one and the same time.

8. That we may be conscious of loving our neighbor *less* than ourselves and still love our neighbor with some degree of *acceptable* or *holy* love.

Now this is a radical and ruinous mistake. That we should feel compassion or pity for a person in distress is natural, whatever be the state of our will. But if our love only amount to desire, if it is not good willing as well as good desiring, there is not a particle of anything good in it. It must be love of the heart or will—that which will control the conduct. Again I repeat James 2:15, 16: "If a brother or sister be naked, and destitute of daily food, and one of you say unto them, Depart in peace, be you warmed and filled;

notwithstanding ye give them not those things which are needful for the body; what doth it profit?"

Now there can be no doubt that multitudes are radically deceived upon this point. They mistake their kind feelings, which are merely constitutional, for that love which the law of God requires them to exercise. Hence they will be very pitiful and benevolent in word but not in deed.

9. That a man can be selfish in his business, both in its design and in the manner of performing it, and yet be truly though defectively religious; that in establishing himself in business he may have a supreme regard to his own interest—that it is neither love to God nor man that mainly actuates him in the establishment of his business, but that his great object may be to make property for himself and family—and yet be truly religious; that the transaction of his business may be on the same principle upon which it was established; that in his dealings with men he may aim mainly at promoting his own interest, and may consult his own side of the bargain with very little reference to the individual with whom he is trading or the community in which he lives.

I believe this to be a sad and ruinous mistake. A man's business is that in which he is engaged, or at least is supposed to be engaged, six days in seven of his whole life. It is that which mainly occupies his time and thoughts and energies. Now if in this he is selfish, either in his object or manner of performing it, it is as impossible that he should have any degree of true religion as that he should be supremely selfish and religious at the same time.

It is supposed by many that selfish love to God is true religion. In my lecture to Christians, published in the last volume of my sermons, is a whole discourse devoted expressly to the discussion of this question. As you can consult that, I will not dwell upon it here.

10. That *selfish* or *partial* love to man is true religion.

There are many who cannot speak peaceably of an enemy who are nevertheless very affectionate to their friends—who seem to have adopted the corrupt maxim of the Jews, "Thou shalt love thy neighbour and hate thine enemy," which Jesus Christ so severely reprobates. Christ insists that to be like God we must "love our enemies," "do good to them that hate us" and "pray for those that despitefully use us." Here also, doubtless, many make a ruinous mistake. They have a great affection to individuals who are friendly to them—of their own sect, or party, or way of thinking—while they exhibit and manifest anything but love towards those that differ from them.

11. That entire holiness implies a high and constant and, of course, insupportable degree of *excited emotion.*

Whatever may be true of the mind when separated from the body, it is certain while it acts through a material organ that a constant state of excitement is impossible. When the mind is strongly excited, there is of necessity a great determination of blood to the brain. A high degree of excitement cannot long continue, certainly, without producing inflammation of the brain and consequent insanity. And the law of God does not require any degree of emotion or mental excitement that is inconsistent with life and health.

Our Lord Jesus Christ does not appear to have been in a state of continual excitement. When He and His disciples had been in a great excitement for a time, they would turn aside "and rest awhile."

Who that has ever philosophized on this subject does not know that the high degree of excitement which is sometimes witnessed in revivals of religion must necessarily be short, or that the people must become deranged? It seems sometimes to be indispensable that a high degree of excitement should prevail for a time, to arrest public and individual attention and to draw people off from other pursuits to attend to the concerns of their souls. But if any suppose that this high degree of excitement is either necessary or desirable or possible to be long continued, they have not well considered the matter.

And here is one grand mistake of the church. They have supposed that the revival consists mostly in this state of excited emotion rather than in conformity of the human will to the will of God. Hence when the reasons for much excitement have ceased and the public mind begins to grow more calm, they begin immediately to say that the revival is on the decline, when in fact with much less excited emotion there may be vastly more real religion in the community.

Excitement is often important and indispensable. But the vigorous actings of the will are infinitely more important. And this state of mind may exist in the absence of highly excited emotions.

12. That entire conformity to the law of God implies that the attention of the mind is *continually* and *exclusively* directed to God, so that God is the direct object of thought, volition, and feeling.

Now holiness implies no such thing. The law of God requires supreme love of the heart. By this is meant that the mind's supreme preference should be of God, that God should be the great object of its supreme love and delight. But this state of mind is perfectly consistent with our engaging in any of the necessary business of life— giving to that business that attention and exercising about it all those affections and emotions which its nature and importance demand.

If a man love God supremely and engage in any business for the promotion of His glory, if his eye be single, his affections and conduct are entirely holy, when necessarily engaged in the right *transaction* of his business, although for the time being neither his thoughts or affections are upon God.

Just so a man who is supremely devoted to his family may be acting consistently with his supreme affection and rendering them the most important and perfect service while he does not think of them at all. As I have endeavored to show in my lecture on the text "make to yourselves a new heart, and a new spirit," I consider the moral heart to be the mind's supreme preference. As I there stated, the natural, or fleshly heart, is the seat of animal life and propels the blood through all the physical system. Now there is a striking analogy between this and the moral heart. And the analogy consists in this, that as the natural heart by its pulsations diffuses life through the physical system, so the moral heart, or the supreme governing preference of the mind, is that which gives life and character to man's moral actions.

For example, suppose that I am engaged in teaching Mathematics. In this, the supreme desire of my mind is to glorify God in this particular calling. Now in demonstrating some of its intricate propositions I am obliged, for hours together, to give the entire attention of my mind to that object. Now, while my mind is thus intensely employed in this particular business, it is impossible that I should have any thoughts directly about God or should exercise any direct affections or emotions or volitions towards Him. Yet if in this particular calling all selfishness is excluded and my supreme design is to glorify God, my mind is in a sanctified state even though, for the time being, I do not think of God.

It should be understood that while the supreme preference of the mind has such efficiency as to exclude all selfishness and to call forth just that strength of volition, thought, affection and emotion that is requisite to the right discharge of any duty to which the mind may be called, the heart is in a sanctified state. By a suitable degree of thought and feeling to the right discharge of duty, I mean just that intensity of thought and energy of action that the nature and importance of the particular duty to which for the time being I am called, demand.

In this statement, I take it for granted that the brain together with all the circumstances of the constitution are such that the requisite amount of thought, feeling, &c., are possible. If the constitution, physical or mental, be in such a state of exhaustion as to be unable to put forth that amount of exertion which the nature of the subject might otherwise demand, even in this case the languid efforts, though far below the importance of the subject, would be all that the law of God requires. Whoever, therefore, supposes that a state of entire sanctification implies a state of entire abstraction of mind from everything but God labors under a grievous mistake. Such a state of mind is as inconsistent with duty as it is impossible while we are in the flesh.

13. That entire holiness implies an equal degree of strength in the affections of the mind at all times.

Now this is neither consistent with duty nor possible. Every particular duty to which we are called does not demand the same degree of mental action. Nor, as I have already said, is the brain, the physical organ through which the mind acts, capable of sustaining the same degree of mental affections. If in performing any work for God the affections be as high as the nature of the particular subject requires in order to its right performance; and in every case where the action of the mind is equal in strength to the present capacity of the brain, or physical organ through which the mind acts; it is all that the law of God requires. Here it should be distinctly remembered that the holiness of the mind, when some kind of business or labor for God is the object of the mind's attention, does not consist so much in the strength of those particular affections, which may be more or less energetic as the state of the brain may admit or the nature of the subject may require; but it does consist in the supreme preference of the mind—in that state of supreme devotedness to God that has called the mind to the performance of this particular work and for this particular reason, that is, for the glory of God.

14. That a state of entire holiness implies *equal* strength in all the volitions of the mind.

But this is absurd. It is neither requisite nor possible. All volitions do not need the same strength. They cannot have equal strength because they are not produced by equally powerful reasons.

Should a man put forth as strong a volition to pick up an apple as to extinguish the flames of a burning house? Should a mother, watching over her sleeping nurseling when all is quiet and secure, put forth as powerful volitions as might be requisite to snatch it from the devouring flames? Now suppose that she was equally devoted to God in watching her sleeping babe and in rescuing it from the jaws of death. Her holiness would not consist in the fact that she exercised equally strong volitions, in both cases, but that in both cases the volition was equal to the accomplishment of the thing required to be done. So that persons may be entirely holy and yet continually varying in the strength of their affections, according to their circumstances, the state of their physical system, and the business in which they are engaged.

15. That no degree of mental *languor* or *rest* is consistent with a state of entire holiness.

This is so far from true that every degree of rest and languor which the nature of man requires is consistent with a state of *entire* sanctification.

16. Another mistake respects what constitutes *partial*, and what *entire* sanctification.

As I have already said, some seem to suppose that partial sanctification relates as well to the *degree* of holy affection as to its *constancy*. I trust I have already said enough to show that partial sanctification cannot relate to the degree of holy love, but that love must be supreme in degree to be holiness at all. And here let me remind you again that all holy affections, thoughts and volitions have not necessarily God for their direct objects, but may be employed about other things and are entirely holy when the design of the mind, in engaging in these callings and pursuits, is supremely to glorify God. You will here understand also that by the constancy of holy affections is not meant, as I have just said, that they should have God for their immediate object, or that it is an interruption of obedience for the mind to think and act and feel upon any subject to which duty calls it.

By partial sanctification, I mean that state of mind in which it sometimes acts selfishly and at other times benevolently.

17. That entire holiness in man implies the same degree of holiness that is in God.

No such thing is implied, for God's holiness is infinite. For us to be holy as God, is not to be as holy as He is in degree but to have as single an eye as He has.

Nor does entire sanctification imply the same strength of holy affections that Adam may have had before the fall, before his powers were debilitated by sin.

Nor does it imply that we exercise the same strength or consistency of holy affection that we might have done had we never sinned. If we love Him with what strength we have, be it more or less, however debilitated our powers may be, it is all that the law of God requires.

Nor does it imply that we love Him as much as we should were we not so ignorant, or had we as much knowledge of Him as we might have had, had we improved our time and opportunities of gaining information. The law of God requires nothing more than the right use of our powers as they are, without respect to whatever might and would have been had we never sinned.

18. That a state of entire holiness is inconsistent with the existence and exercise of our constitutional susceptibilities.

A great portion of the temptations to which the mind is subject consists in the excited state of the susceptibilities of the body and mind that are purely constitutional. All the susceptibilities of our nature Christ must have had, or He could not have been "tempted in all points like as we are." It was the excitement of Adam's constitutional appetites and susceptibilities that led him to sin. But his sin consisted not either in the existence of these susceptibilities and appetites or in their being excited, but in consenting to gratify them in a prohibited manner. If our constitutional susceptibilities were annihilated, our activity would cease. So that if anyone supposes that to be sanctified "wholly, body, soul and spirit," implies the extinction of any appetite or susceptibility that is purely constitutional, he is deceived. A state of sanctification consists in subordinating all these to the will of God and not in their annihilation.

19. That it implies a cessation of spiritual warfare.

If by this they mean a war with our selfishness, they are right. But if they mean that our war with the world, the flesh and the devil will ever cease in this life, they are mistaken.

20. That it is inconsistent with growth in grace.

I suppose that saints will continue to grow in grace to all eternity, and in the knowledge of God. But this does not imply that they are not entirely holy, when they enter heaven or before.

21. That it is entirely inconsistent with any sorrow, or mental suffering.

It was not so with Christ. Nor is it inconsistent with our sorrowing for our own past sins, and sorrowing that we have not now the health and vigor and knowledge and love that we might have had, if we had sinned less; or sorrow for those around us, sorrow in view of human sinfulness or suffering. These are all consistent with a state of entire sanctification and indeed are the natural results of it.

22. That it is inconsistent with our living in human society, with mingling in the scenes and engaging in the affairs of this world. Hence the absurd and ridiculous notions of papists in retiring to monasteries and convents, in taking the veil and, as they say, retiring to a life of devotion.

Now I suppose this state of voluntary exclusion from human society to be utterly inconsistent with any degree of holiness and a manifest violation of the law of love to our neighbor.

23. That a state of entire holiness would be recognized as such by all men.

Now this is as far as possible from being true. It was insisted and positively believed by the Jews that Jesus Christ was possessed of a wicked, instead of a holy, spirit. Such were their notions of holiness that they no doubt supposed Him to be actuated by any other than the Spirit of God. They especially supposed so on account of His opposition to the current orthodoxy and the ungodliness of the religious teachers of the day. Now, who does not see that when the church is in a great measure conformed to the world, that a spirit of holiness in any man would certainly lead him to aim the sharpest rebukes at the spirit and life of those in this state, whether in high or low places? And who does not see that this would naturally result in his being accused of possessing a wicked spirit?

24. That a state of entire holiness implies a state of entire moroseness of temper and manners.

Nothing is farther from the truth than this. It is said of Xavier, whom perhaps few holier men have ever lived, that "he was so cheerful as often to be accused of being gay." Cheerfulness is certainly the result of holy affections. And sanctification no more implies moroseness in this world than it does in heaven.

25. That entire holiness is inconsistent with any further dependence on Christ and the Holy Spirit.

Now this idea arises out of the very obscure notions that people have with regard to what constitutes entire sanctification. They seem to suppose that in sanctification the Holy Spirit changes the *nature*, so that men remain holy without any further influence from the Spirit of Christ, whereas a state of entire and permanent sanctification is nothing else than a state of entire and perpetual dependence on Christ and on the Holy Spirit. It is the state in which the mind throws itself entirely upon the supporting grace of Christ.

REMARKS

1. From what has been said, you can see the error of those who suppose we are incompetent witnesses of our own sanctification.

It is true that our testimony may not be satisfactory to others. But still it *is* true that so far as we are regarded as honest men, our testimony should be as satisfactory upon this as upon any other subject. It is a point upon which we have the testimony of our own consciousness, which is the highest kind of evidence. And we are just as competent witnesses to testify to our entire sanctification as that we have any religion at all.

But it is objected that we may be deceived. True; but is this any good reason why a man should not be a competent witness to that of which he has the testimony of his own consciousness?

But it is said that many profess sanctification who are manifestly deceived; therefore it is a suspicious circumstance, not to say ridiculous, for a person to profess sanctification. Now this is the very reason urged by Unitarians against all spiritual religion. They say that men may be and many manifestly are deceived, and therefore it is ridiculous for men to profess spiritual regeneration.

Again, it is objected that it is dangerous to preach the doctrine of holiness because it may lead to deception—that many may and will think themselves sanctified when they are not, and will consequently be puffed up with pride and fall into the condemnation of the devil. Now who does not know that this is the very objection to insisting upon spiritual religion at all? And the argument is just as forcible against our having any knowledge of our being regenerated as against our knowing that we are entirely sanctified.

2. I said that religion is always a matter of co sciousness. This must be true if religion consists in supreme love to G͡. If we are not conscious of the supreme affection of the mind, of what are we conscious? And here let me guard you against a mistake. Do not suppose that I mean by this that every thought, volition and feeling has God for its direct object and is an act of supreme conscious love to God. A man may be engaged in transacting some business for God that may require, for the time being, his whole attention. In this state of mind he cannot be conscious all the while that God is the direct object of thought and affection, for this is not the fact. But he may, all the while, be conscious that he is doing this for God, and that it is the supreme preference of his mind for God that has engaged him in his present business.

3. True religion does not abrogate the law of God but fulfills it.

Hence Paul declares, Rom. 8:4, "that the righteousness of the law might be fulfilled in us, who walk not after the flesh but after the Spirit."

Here let me remark that it is a strange infatuated dream that persons in a sanctified state are under no obligation to obey the moral law. If they are under no such obligation, then obedience is not virtue. And it is the aggregate of all that is absurd and contradictory to say that a man is entirely holy, and yet under no obligation to obey law. What is law but a rule of action, and what is holiness but conformity to this rule, and what is sin but a violation of it? Now if the rule is abrogated, then there is neither holiness nor sin in men, any more than there is in brutes.

It is true that a person in a sanctified state does not obey the law through fear of the penalty. Nor does he love God simply because God commands it. But grace gives him such an acquaintance with God, and Christ, as to produce the very spirit of the law, that is, perfect conformity of heart to the law. The very love which the law requires is thus begotten in the mind. Hence the Apostle says, "Do we make void the law through faith? God forbid; yea, we establish the law."

I design to continue this subject in my next lecture, and shall then show more particularly that the law of God can never be repealed or altered.

LECTURE 6

The Law of God, No. 2

Matt. 22:39: "And the second [commandment] is like unto it, Thou shalt love thy neighbour as thyself."

In continuing the discussion of this subject, I design to show:

    I. The real spirit and meaning of this commandment.
    II. Its tendency, and the natural results of perfect and universal obedience.
    III. The tendency and natural results of universal disobedience.
    IV. That it is the universal and unalterable rule of right.
    V. Wherein it differs from human laws.
    VI. That every violation of this rule is fraud and injustice.
    VII. That the public and, to a great extent, the private conscience is formed on the principles of commercial justice.
    VIII. That the transaction of business upon principles of commercial justice merely is a violation of the law, rebellion against God, and in a professor of religion is real apostasy.
    IX. That restitution must be made, whenever restitution is practicable, in all cases where this law is violated or there is no forgiveness.

I. *I am to show the real spirit and meaning of this commandment.*

1. It prohibits supreme *self-love*, or selfishness. In my last lecture I attempted to show that the command "love thy neighbour as thyself" implied not that we should love our neighbor supremely, as selfish men love themselves, but that we should love ourselves, in the first place, and pursue our happiness only according to its real value in the scale of being. But I need not dwell upon this, as it will not probably be doubted that this precept prohibits *supreme* self-love.

2. It prohibits all *excessive* self-love, that is, every degree of love that is disproportioned to the relative value of our own happiness.

3. It prohibits the laying of any practical stress upon any interest because it is our *own*.

4. It prohibits, of course, every degree of *ill will*, and all those feelings that are necessarily connected with selfishness.

5. It prohibits *apathy and indifference* with regard to the well-being of our fellowmen.

I will show what the law *requires*.

1. It requires the practical recognition of the fact that all men are

brethren; that God is the great Parent, the great Father of the universe; that all moral agents everywhere are His children; and that He is interested in the happiness of every individual, according to its relative importance. He is no respecter of persons. But so far as the love of benevolence is concerned, He loves all moral beings in proportion to their capacity of receiving and doing good.

Now the law of God evidently takes all this for granted, and that "God hath made of one blood all nations of men, to dwell on all the face of the earth."

2. It requires that every being and interest should be regarded and treated by us according to its *relative value*, that is, that we should recognize God's relation to the universe and our relation to each other and treat all men as our brethren—as having an inalienable title to our good will and kind office, as citizens of the same government and members of the great family of God.

3. It requires us to exercise as tender a regard to our neighbor's *reputation, interest* and *well-being*, in all respects, as to our own, to be as unwilling to mention his faults as to have our own mentioned, to hear him slandered as to be slandered ourselves. In short, he is to be esteemed by us as our brother.

4. It justly reprobates any violation of the great principle of equal love as *rebellion* against the whole universe. It is rebellion against God because it is a rejection of His authority; and selfishness, under any form, is a setting up of our own interests in opposition to the interests of the universe of God.

II. *I am to show the tendency and natural effect of universal obedience to this law.*

1. The tendency and effect of obedience is to make the obedient individual *happy*. The state of mind required by the law is itself happiness. And if there were but one individual who was obedient, he would be happy for that reason.

2. But were obedience universal, the tendency and effect would be the greatest sum of *public* happiness. Public happiness is made up of the happiness of individuals. Now as I have said, the universal exercise of the spirit of this law would make any individual who exercised it happy. Furthermore, *universal* obedience implies that everyone is engaged in making others happy; so that the aggregate amount of happiness would be made up not only by the happiness which each one would experience by conformity to the law, but to this must be added the vast amount of good from each one endeavoring to make all around him happy.

3. It would destroy all *selfish* competition among men and, consequently, all that brood of infernal passions and all the great and crying evils that are the legitimate offspring of selfish competition.

4. It would promote a *benevolent* competition that would greatly increase public and individual happiness. Take an illustration. Suppose two

book-sellers to be actuated by principles of pure benevolence, and one of them should print an edition of the Bible with a design of furnishing the book to every person at as cheap a rate as possible, from motives of pure benevolence. Now suppose the other could print a cheaper edition, equally valuable, and could thus supply the poor with the bread of life at a still cheaper rate. Now, would not the first of these rejoice in the fact that the Bibles were afforded at this low rate, even if he should never sell his own? The great object that he had in view, to supply the poor with Bibles, is accomplished, and in a better manner than he could do it himself. And it is easy to see that in this he would heartily rejoice.

So with the American, and British and Foreign Bible Societies. Suppose them to vie with each other in furnishing the world with Bibles at the lowest possible rate. Now their object being the same, each would rejoice to be outdone by the other. Thus the competition would be holy and not selfish. And instead of engendering every infernal passion, it would increase "that love which is the bond of perfectness."

It is easy to see that perfect obedience to this law would create a perfect state of society; and for any community to live together in conformity to this principle would be heaven itself.

III. *I am to show the tendency and natural results of disobedience.*

1. It would cause *individual* misery, because selfishness is misery. And to say nothing of the internal war and mutiny that selfishness creates in the mind, it is misery because it can never be gratified. From the very nature of the case there could be but one selfish being in the universe gratified. Nor even one; for did he possess all actual and existing good—did he possess all that is to be possessed and govern all that are to be governed—instead of satisfying him it would only "enlarge his desires as hell."

2. It would produce the greatest sum of *public* misery. Public misery is made up of the misery of the individuals who compose the public. Now each of these is miserable in the exercise of his own selfishness. And where selfishness is universal and unrestrained, each one is engaged in making all around him miserable. In this state of things, every evil passion would be generated, perpetuated, increased and perfected. And universal grasping after each other's possessions would produce universal war. Indeed, it would result in universal hell.

IV. *I am to show that . . . [this law] is the universal and unalterable rule of right.*

Because it is founded in the *nature* and *relations* of moral beings. It is *universal* because it is entirely suited to the nature of moral beings, in whatever world they may exist. It is *unalterable* because the nature of moral beings is unalterable. And as their nature is unalterable so are their relations, of course. While these natures and relations exist even God himself has no right to abrogate this law. He has created these natures and established these relations, and while they exist this law must exist, of course.

And here let me say that any system of religion, any pretended revelation, any scheme of doctrine that sets aside, repeals or alters this law is certainly from hell. *No proof* can sustain the claims of such a book or scheme of doctrine to be a revelation from God.

V. *I am to show wherein . . . [this law] differs from human laws.*

And let me begin by saying that it is one of the first principles of common law that whatever is contrary to the law of God is not law, that is, is not obligatory upon men. So that the difference between human laws and the law of God is not that they are contrary, the one to the other; for properly speaking, any human enactment that is contrary to the law of God is, after all, not law. The difference lies in the fact that human laws do not require enough. Their requirements are good so far as they go, and should be strictly obeyed. But as they fall short of the requirements of God's law, they may be strictly obeyed without one particle of virtue or holiness. But to be more particular, I remark,

1. That human laws are of a negative character. They are designed to prohibit outbreaking selfishness. And although they are said by legal writers to command what is right and prohibit what is wrong, yet it will be seen on close examination that they are far from prohibiting all that is wrong, and that in no case do they require what God's law esteems to be really right. In their prohibitions, they necessarily stop short at the outward act, without pretending to judge or restrain the thoughts and affections of the mind any further than as they are developed in the outward actions. So that in every case, all that constitutes the real moral character of the crime may exist in any mind without being recognized as a crime by any human law. The moral character lies in the *disposition* of the mind. But if this disposition be not acted out, human laws take no cognizance of it.

2. They only prohibit *outward* acts of selfishness or the open violation of other men's rights and do not require even *outward* benevolence. They leave every man to be as selfish as he will, provided he restrains his selfish conduct within certain limits. Now it is easy to see that all this falls entirely short of the spirit and letter of the law of God.

3. The law of God is *positive.* It not only restrains outward but all *inward* selfishness. It not only prohibits outward selfish acts but the inward selfish thoughts and feelings. It regards the outward act as crime, and deserving of punishment, only because it is the result of the inward feelings and affections of the mind. Hence it aims its prohibitions at the heart and spreads out its claims over all the movements of the mind.

4. It commands perfect *inward* and *outward* benevolence, that is, not only that men should not hate each other but should love each other as they do themselves; that they should not only abstain from injuring one another but should positively engage in promoting each other's happiness, to the extent of their ability.

5. Another difference is that perfect obedience to human laws would not necessarily secure one particle of happiness. It would only lessen the amount of misery. As we have just seen, there might be perfect obedience to human laws and yet supreme selfishness exist in every mind. So that perfect obedience to the wisest and best of human enactments may consist with a vast amount of individual and public misery. But on the other hand, perfect and universal obedience to the law of God, as we have seen, would secure the greatest amount of individual and public happiness.

VI. *I am to show that every violation of this rule is fraud and injustice.*

1. Because this is the *only rule of right.* Remember that it is not by human law but by His own law that God will judge the world. The question is not, what is fraud and dishonesty in the light of human laws, but what is *real* fraud, what is *real* injustice? This can only be known by a reference to the law of God. And every violation of this rule wears upon its front the seal of God's eternal reprobation. It is not enough, in the light of the law of God, that you abstain from trespassing upon your neighbor's possessions. If you do not actually love him, and love him as you do yourself, you as actually invade his rights and deny him that which is his due as if you should steal his property. He has as absolute a right to your equal love as he has to any article of property which he may have in possession. And you have no more right to withhold the one than to take the other. You are as much bound to consult his interest in your dealings with him as your own; and he has as actual a right to expect you to consult his interests as well as to consult your own, as he has to expect that you will not steal his money. And to omit the former is as absolute fraud and injustice as to do the latter.

Every violation of this law is injustice, fraud and dishonesty towards God and towards every individual in the universe. It is setting aside the rights and authority of God and trampling upon the rights of our neighbor. And as all mankind are one family and have one common interest, to defraud *one* is to injure the *whole.*

VII. *I am to show that the public and private conscience is formed on the principles of commercial justice.*

By the principles of commercial justice, I mean mere human laws in relation to human dealings.

In proof of this position, I observe that men generally satisfy themselves with acting legally and, at most, equitably. But the courts, both of law and equity, lay down rules for the government of human conduct, as we have seen, that fall entirely short of the law of God.

By the public and individual conscience being formed on the principles of commerical justice, I do not mean that men are always satisfied with mere obedience to human laws, for this is far from being true; and many a man feels in his conscience what an elder in a Presbyterian church once said to me, "that he was avoiding the payment of his debts, by the public sale of his property, through the *finesse* of the law."

The truth is that men often feel as if they were guilty in the sight of God when they have acted in strict conformity with human laws. Nevertheless, it is true to an astonishing and alarming extent that men generally, and even professors of religion, content themselves with transacting business in conformity with the principles of human laws.

VIII. *I am to show that the transaction of business upon principles of commercial justice merely is a violation of this law, rebellion against God, and in a professor of religion is real apostasy.*

1. Because it is setting aside the law of God and establishing another rule of action.

2. It is a total rejection of the divine authority.

3. This self-constituted rule, with which we blind our mind and stifle our conscience, only restrains selfishness within certain limits, while it is consistent with the deepest selfishness of heart. Who does not know that the principles of commercial justice are established to regulate the selfish transaction of business? They are instituted by selfish men for selfish purposes; that is, they are so framed as to aid every man in securing all his selfish ends, so far as is consistent with a certain degree of respect for the selfish pursuits of others.

Now if casting off God's authority be rebellion in any individual, as it really is, in a professor of religion it must be outrageous apostasy. Obedience to God's law is the rejection of all selfishness and the practical adoption of the principle of universal benevolence. For any individual, therefore, to engage in selfish business is a total departure from God. And it includes in it all that really constitutes apostasy.

And what is still worse, it adds shameless *hypocrisy* to apostasy; for while men really apostatize in heart, instead of openly avowing, as in all honesty they ought to do, their rejection of the law of God, they remain in the church and keep up a hypocritical show of obedience.

IX. *I am to show that restitution must be made in all practicable cases where this law has been violated, or there is no forgiveness.*

This is evident from the fact that without restitution there can be no repentance. Certainly in no proper sense can a man be said to repent who has defrauded his neighbor and refuses to make him the satisfaction that is in his power. But without repentance God has no right to forgive. What would you say if the governor should forgive a man who had stolen your money, while he refused to restore it? He has no right to do this; nor has God any right to forgive fraud and injustice without repentance and restitution. It would, therefore, dishonor God and ruin the universe should He connive at your sins and not hold you bound to restore your ill-gotten gains.

Now I beseech you to remember that the restitution demanded of you is not merely where you have defrauded men at common law, but in every case so far as you can remember where you have not acted agreeably to the law of God. Wherever you have not consulted your neighbor's interest equally with your own in your business transactions, you have been guilty of fraud. God's law has pronounced that transaction dishonest and unjust, and has aimed its eternal thunders at your head.

REMARKS

1. The church can compel the world to transact business upon the principles of the law of God. The church members often excuse themselves in the transaction of their worldly business, by saying that they cannot compete with worldly men without dealing upon the same principles with them. To this I answer,

(1) That if this were true, then worldly business cannot be engaged in by men without absolute ruin to their souls.

(2) But this is not true. It is as far from the truth as possible. Now suppose that professors of religion were universally to transact their business upon the principles of the law of God—consulting, in every instance, the real good of those with whom they deal as much as they do their own. This would immediately result in their doing the entire business of the world, or in compelling worldly men to follow their example; for who would trade with a selfish man, who would consult only his own interest, while those were at hand with whom he might trade with the assurance that he should not be over-reached but that the business would be transacted upon principles of entire benevolence?

2. Almost any individual of any calling may compel those in the same business to conduct their affairs upon the principles of God's law. Let him but adopt this principle in his own dealings, and he would soon force others to come to the same standard, or drive them to bankruptcy through loss of business.

3. You can see the desert of every act of selfishness—that it includes in it the entire rejection of the authority of God and a trampling upon the rights of the universe. In this there is certainly infinite guilt and the desert of eternal punishment.

4. You see what is the duty of God in relation to selfishness, that as the Father and Supreme Executive Magistrate of the Universe He is bound to punish it in every case, with unsparing severity, where there is not repentance.

5. That the government of God is very little understood in this world; and human law, instead of the law of God, has come to be very generally regarded as the rule of right. This has blinded the world and the church in regard to what real religion is. So that much passes current among men for true religion that is, after all, an entire violation of the law of God. Multitudes in the Christian church are regarded as pious men who are daily transacting business upon principles of entire selfishness.

6. Infidels are always fighting a shadow and making war not upon Christianity itself but on something else falsely called by this name. Where can

an infidel be found who will have the hardihood to object to these two great principles of the government of God? But these constitute the whole of the Christian religion. It is then some corrupt dogma of the church, the lives of hypocrites, and a spurious representation of the Christian religion against which they array themselves. But let them march up and object anything, if they can, to the Christian religion as it is taught in the Bible, and to the government of God as it is embodied in these two precepts.

7. You see why there is so little conviction among men, both in and out of the church. It is because they judge themselves by a false standard. If they live in conformity with human laws and keep up the morality of public sentiment, they feel in a great measure secure. But be assured that God will judge you by another standard.

8. In the light of this law, how perfectly obvious is it that slavery is from hell. Is it possible that we are to be told that slavery is a divine institution? What! Such a barefaced, shameless, and palpable violation of the law of God authorized by God himself? And even religious teachers, gravely contending that *the Bible sanctions this hell-begotten system?*

"O shame, where is thy blush?" What! Make a man a slave, set aside his moral agency, treat him as a mere piece of property,

> "Chain him—and task him,
> And exact his sweat, with stripes
> That Mercy, with a bleeding heart, weeps
> When she sees inflicted on a beast"

and then contend that this is in keeping with the law of God which, on pain of death, requires that every man should love his neighbor as himself! This is certainly, to my mind, one of the most monstrous and ridiculous assertions ever made. It is no wonder that slaveholders are opposed to the discussion of this subject. It cannot bear the light; it retires from the gaze and inspection and reprobation of the law of God, as darkness retires before the light.

9. We see the true character of those speculations in provisions and in the necessaries of life with which the land is becoming filled. The custom of buying up the necessaries of life so as to control the market and raise the price of provisions, while there is an abundance of them in the country, is a plain and manifest violation of the law of God.

Suppose there were a famine in this land, and a multitude of vessels should be freighted with flour and sail from Europe to supply the starving population. Suppose the owners to instruct their captains to sell it for five dollars per barrel. And now, suppose certain speculators in New York should receive advices of the arrival of the fleet upon our coast; they charter a boat and go out and purchase all the flour. And when the fleet comes in sight, the docks and every passage in the city is thronged with starving people, with their bags and whatever money they can command to supply their starving families. But on the fleet's coming to anchor, they are informed that the speculator demands seventy-five dollars per barrel for the flour. In this case, no doubt, the public would set the seal of reprobation on such an outrage. But how does this differ in *principle* from that which is becoming so common, even among professed Christians: to secure as far as possible, and so as by all means to control the market, the bread stuffs and to a great extent the other provisions throughout the length and breadth of the land, and then enrich themselves by selling them at their own prices? Is this loving their neighbor, or is it supreme and horrible selfishness?

In speaking of this speculation in provisions, I have taken it for granted that they were not in reality scarce, but merely rendered so by speculators controlling the market. But suppose they were really scarce; suppose that a great drought, such as we have had the past summer, should extend throughout the whole land and produce a universal scarcity of provisions. In this case, it is contrary to the law of God for those who have them to spare to increase their price simply because they are scarce. I say *simply* because they are scarce, for cases may occur in which the raising of them may have cost more than in ordinary seasons. I have for many years known one man, of whom it is said that he has practically recognized the principle of the government of God in his transactions upon this point. When there has been a scarcity of provisions, and of course the prices were greatly increased, he would receive no more than the common prices of articles when there was no scarcity. If questioned in regard to the reasons of his conduct, he would simply answer that they cost him no more than formerly, and what his family did not want the consumers might have at former prices.

Now the corrupt maxim of businessmen is this, that an article is worth all that it will bring in market; and they will cause it to bring in market just what the necessities of people may compel them to give. So that if the scarcity of an article will permit, they make no conscience of demanding any price for it. Now the real question should not be what, under the circumstances, may you compel a man to give, but what did it cost and how cheap can you afford it to him without injuring yourself more than you will benefit him? For it should be borne in mind that the law of love requires that we should afford everything as cheap as we can instead of getting as much as we can. The requirement is that we do all the good we can to others, and not that we get all we can ourselves. The law of God is, sell as cheap as you can—the business maxim, [sell] as dear as you can.

But suppose it should be asked, by what rule am I to be governed in the sale of an article when, in the purchase of it, I gave more than it has since proved to be worth? I answer, the loss is yours. You have no right to sell it or to expect to sell it for more than its real value, whatever price you may have paid for it.

But here another question may arise. What is the duty of the individual who sold me the property for so much more than it afterwards proved to be worth? I answer that he is bound to act upon the law of love. And if at the time of the purchase you and he were both deceived with regard to the real value, he has a right to receive of you no more than the real *ascertained* value. But if he will insist upon the wrong and compel you to pay what you agreed to pay, or not refund what you have already paid, you are nevertheless bound to be governed by the law of love in the sale, and not to ask or receive more than its real value.

To illustrate this, suppose that you had purchased a piece of land under the impression that it contained a mine of gold, that it was sold to you in good faith, both you and the seller supposing that this was the matter of fact. If afterwards it should prove that you were deceived, that no such mine existed and that, therefore, the land is of no more value than any other land, it were contrary to the law of God for him to insist upon the fulfillment of this bargain and that you should pay what, under the circumstances, you had agreed to pay.

10. You see the character of those speculations in government lands that have become so common. The government proposes to sell their lands to those who will improve them for one dollar and twenty-five cents per acre, designing thereby to encourage the settlement of the country. But speculators rush forth and purchase all the most eligible locations and raise the price, and thus retard the settlement of the country. When the laborer who would cultivate the land with a small amount of means comes, he finds that instead of being able to purchase at the government prices he must pay ten, twenty, thirty or even one hundred dollars per acre—and that, too, when no improvement has been made by the speculator.

Now it is in vain to attempt to justify this, as some have done, by saying that those lands are really worth what the speculator demands for them. Suppose they are; what right has he to demand that price? He did not design to cultivate the land; and but for him the laborer might have had it at the government price. Now the violation of the principles of God's law in this case is just as manifest as it would be if my family were starving for a barrel of flour and I was on the point of purchasing it for five dollars, all the money I had; and a speculator, knowing my circumstances, should forestall me and buy the barrel and then demand seventy-five dollars for it, and should say to me, "O sir, it is worth that to you." True, it may be worth that rather than that my family should starve. But I ask, what right had he to purchase it and then make this demand?

But for all this there are many hypocritical excuses urged. Many pretend to be making money for God. This is truly a strange manner of serving God, to rob His children to give to Him—to violate the law of God, to set aside God's authority for the sake of making money for Him! But as a general thing this is a mere pretense; for it is seen to be true that in proportion as the speculators grow rich they increase their expenditures, until men of the greatest wealth are among the first to complain of poverty when called upon to give. Now they can never convince mankind that they are honest in pretending to be driving their speculations for God, until it is seen as a matter of *fact* that they do not increase their expenditures with the growth of their property and lay out this money upon their lusts, but that they really appropriate it to benevolent purposes.

But if it were true, as it sometimes may be, that they really intend to appropriate money obtained in this way to build up the kingdom of God, still the manner of getting it can never be justified by the law of God and can never be acceptable in His sight. Will the end sanctify the means?

11. Much restitution is to be made by speculators or they must go to hell. Those that have enriched themselves by speculations that involved a violation of the law of love must give back all their ill-gotten gains—must renounce their wealth and render obedience to the government of God—or they must be damned.

12. It is very obvious that many persons have involved themselves in a snare from which probably they never will escape. They plunged into a series of speculations and at the time, no doubt, were so blinded by public sentiment that its utter inconsistency with the law of God was not seen; and now, when the test is applied and the law comes to pour its light upon them, they will either hide away in darkness and strive to conceal the true character of their conduct even from their own eyes or, seeing it, they will "go away sorrowful, because they have great possessions," and will not make the restitution that the law of God demands.

13. In the light of this subject you can easily judge what kinds of business are lawful, and that for any person to engage in selling articles that are injurious is rebellion against God and a trampling upon the rights of the universe. Such is the sale of alcohol, tobacco and narcotics of every kind that are used as articles of luxury or diet. Their sale for these purposes is utterly unlawful. It is no excuse to say that people will have them and that you may as well sell them as anybody else. I beseech you to remember the words of the Savior: "It is impossible but that offences should come, but *woe* unto HIM through whom they come."

14. It is objected that the adoption of this principle in the present state of human society is impossible. To this I reply,

(1) That it is the law of God and must be adopted and practiced by you, or you must be damned.

(2) It is the simplest and most practicable rule of conduct conceivable. To a selfish mind, I grant, it may be a stumbling block; but to a truly benevolent mind it is, in almost all cases, as plain as sunlight. In those cases where individuals do really love each other as they love themselves— as husbands and wives, parents and children—do they find any difficulty in the application of this rule? No. And should they extend their benevolent regards to all mankind, and did all mankind recognize their relations to each other and regard themselves as one family, this rule would be found to be of the easiest application.

15. It is objected that its application would overturn nearly all the business transactions of the world. It would certainly revolutionize nearly all the business of the world and produce changes in the state of society that to most people are wholly inconceivable. As business is now transacted, the more business, the more jealousy, envy and strife. But were all men really benevolent, they would universally vie with each other in seeing who could accomplish the greatest good and produce the greatest amount of human happiness.

16. I said that the government of God was very little understood in this world. Now it is plain that a leading object of Jesus Christ was to put the world in possession of the true spirit and meaning of the law of God. It is

astonishing to see how slow of heart a selfish mind is, to understand the law of God and the nature of true religion. For a mind whose whole object is to get and appropriate to itself all it can, it is difficult to conceive of the nature of that religion which finds its happiness in giving, instead of getting.

The preaching of Christ, but more especially His example, put His followers in possession of the idea "that it is more blessed to give than to receive." The life of Christ was designed as an illustration of this cardinal principle, that the proper happiness of a moral agent lies in doing good, in denying self for the benefit of others. In diffusing happiness, it finds its own happiness.

Now the apostles and early Christians caught this same idea, preached it, carried it out in living illustration before the world; and it was soon said of them that they had "turned the world upside down."

If I mistake not, an infidel writer has somewhere attempted to account for the rapid spread of Christianity in the apostles' days by saying that "it was the natural result of the spirit and conduct of the primitive Christians. They gave themselves up to acts of benevolence and in laboring for the good of others." Now this is true, and it is also true that the natural result of this would be powerfully to influence mankind in favor of Christianity. But how could he overlook the fact that such a spirit and temper must be *divine*?

It is true, as a modern writer has said, that "the Church now is the exact contrast of the primitive Church." Primitive Christians rushed forth, at the hazard of their lives, and millions of them sacrificed their lives without hesitation for the salvation of the world. They were seen denying themselves and offering themselves upon the altar of benevolence for the salvation of those who were perishing in sin.

But for centuries, selfishness has been the most prominent feature of the church. And instead of sacrificing herself for the salvation of men, she is sacrificing the world, to gratify her own lusts.

17. It is naturally impossible that a selfish church should ever succeed in converting the world. They cannot possibly make the world understand the gospel. The light which they hold up is darkness. Their "salt has lost its savor," their benevolence is selfishness, their religion is rebellion against God. Suppose Jesus Christ had come, as the Jews expected, as a great temporal prince—living and reigning in mighty earthly splendor, overawing and subduing the nations and exterminating His enemies by the sword. Could He, by any *precepts* whatever, have put the world in possession of the true spirit of religion? Could they have possibly received from Him the idea of what constitutes obedience to the law of God? Certainly not. Nor could the apostles and primitive Christians have possibly possessed the world with the right idea of religion in any other manner than by offering themselves up a living sacrifice for their salvation. And never can the world be converted, never can missionary enterprises succeed, until true religion is taught in the lives of its professors—until benevolence, and not selfishness, is exhibited by the church.

18. I beg of you to remember that this law is to be the rule of judgment, by which all the secrets of your heart and soul and life shall be judged. Do

therefore, I beseech you, bring yourselves to the true test, examine your-selves by this rule, decide your former life and your present character by in-specting it in the light of this law. You have never embraced the gospel any further than you are under the practical influence of the law of God. The gospel was designed to annihilate selfishness, to produce true obedience. If it does not produce this result in you, you are lost forever.

Now will you go down on your knees, will you open your heart before God, will you spread this discourse before Him, will you be honest in decid-ing upon the real character of your business transactions—of your daily life and walk and spirit?

Now I urge this upon you at the conclusion of every lecture; for these truths must be to you "a savor of life unto life, or of death unto death." I be-seech you, do not cover up your sins nor try to avoid the light. It will do you no good to cavil. Truth is truth, whether you receive it or not. And I pray God that you may receive it, so that your whole body, soul and spirit may be sanctified through the truth and preserved blameless unto the coming of our Lord Jesus Christ.

LECTURE 7

Glorifying God

1 Cor. 10:31: "Whether therefore ye eat, or drink, or whatsoever ye do, do all to the glory of God."

In this discussion, I design to show:

I. What is to be understood by the glory of God.
II. How we may glorify Him.
III. To what extent we are to apply this rule in practice.
IV. The importance of glorifying God.
V. Whatever is short of this is enmity against God.

I. *I am to show what is to be understood by the glory of God.*

Theologians speak of the *essential* and *declarative* glory of God. His essential glory is the intrinsic excellence of His general and moral attri-butes. His declarative glory is His renown or reputation, or the estimation in which He is held by moral beings.

It is in the latter sense that the term is manifestly used in the text. In the former sense, our conduct has nothing to do with the glory of God. But in the latter sense, as we shall see, it has everything to do with it.

II. *I am to show how we may glorify God.*

1. By exhibiting His spirit and temper and character, as Christ did. The *man* Christ Jesus was a living illustration of the spirit and temper and character of the invisible God. As a *man* He was constantly engaged in glorifying God. And it is easy to see that by thus representing God He highly honored His heavenly Father and gave the world occasion to admire and love and obey Him.

2. We are to illustrate by *precept* and *example* the excellence of His law and the glorious tendency of His government. We are to embody in our lives the very heart and meaning of the law, and thus possess the world of the idea that God is love. It is easy to see to what an extent this would constrain the world to acknowledge the glorious excellency of His "glorious majesty."

3. We are to glorify Him by holding forth, both in *precept* and *example*, the true light and doctrines of the gospel. The *gospel* can never be understood by precept without a corresponding example. By precept we are to lay down the principle of the law, and our lives are to be a living illustration of it. The truths of the gospel are in themselves exceedingly simple. They are, however, at so great a remove from the common prejudices of men that no truths in the world need so much to be illustrated in order to be understood; and no illustration can be effectual but the deeds and spirit of Christians. And herein is the great source of the ignorance of impenitent men on the subject of religion. Many of them attend the preaching of the Word; but to them it is a mere abstraction, a dead letter, for want of living illustration among professors of religion around them. It is impossible that the gospel should take effect without being understood; and it is impossible that it should be understood by selfish minds without illustration; and it is impossible that it should be illustrated but by the lives of Christians. Hence Christ's life first illustrated it to the apostles, [and] the lives of the apostles and primitive Christians to the impenitent of their day; and precisely as living illustrations are found, the gospel is seen to be the "power of God unto salvation."

4. By acting the part of *faithful witnesses* for God. "Ye are my witnesses, saith the Lord." Now the appropriate business of Christians is to bear testimony continually for God; and the success of His cause on earth depends upon the fullness and faithfulness of their testimony. If His witnesses contradict by their practice what they inculcate in precept, their testimony is destroyed. If at one time, during a revival of religion, they live and talk and act so as practically to represent God, yet if they suffer a reaction to come over them, they then contradict their former testimony. And like a witness who contradicts himself on a cross-examination, their testimony goes for nothing.

III. *I am to show to what extent we are to apply this rule in practice.*

1. In the *arrangement* of our business. We are bound to make it manifest to all around us that our business is calculated and designed to promote the happiness of our fellowmen. If this does not appear, we do not represent God but misrepresent Him. It is manifest that all the works of God are designed to promote happiness; and if in our works the same design is not manifest, we are not glorifying but dishonoring God. If, therefore, our business be of such a nature as to show that it is a selfish employment, and especially if the business is in itself injurious to the interests of society, scarcely a greater abomination than this in a professing Christian can be named. Is this like God? No; it is like the devil. It is representing hell and not heaven.

But if the business be in its *nature* lawful, yet if it be transacted in a selfish manner—if it be manifest to those with whom you deal that your main object is to get and not to communicate good, to accumulate property and not to diffuse happiness abroad—this is exactly the reverse of glorifying God. It is a misrepesentation of His character and religion; and there are no more effectual agents of the devil than those professors of religion who are selfish in the transaction of their business. God's temper and spirit is to give, *give*, GIVE; their spirit and temper is to get, *get*, GET. This is the exact contrast of true religion.

2. In our *houses*, *equipage* and *furniture* we are to glorify God. We are to so arrange our houses, equipage and furniture as to show that our hearts are not set upon these things, and especially to demonstrate that it is utility and not ornament at which we aim.

By this I do not mean that we are not to regard a correct taste in these things. God has everywhere in His works displayed a most exquisite and infinitely refined taste; and to pay no regard to this is to violate a fundamental law of our nature and to misrepresent God.

But in our houses and equipage and furniture we are to see to it that we do not appear to have our hearts upon such things and as if we sought our happiness in them, but on the contrary should show to the world that we seek those things only that are convenient, and have no fellowship with display and useless and worldly ornament.

There are two extremes upon this subject, both of which are as ridiculous as they are wicked. One is to launch forth into all manner of extravagance; and the other is to discard all taste, decency and utility and rush back to barbarism. Now both these extremes are to be avoided by Christians. While they do not neglect the decencies and conveniences of life, they are to avoid useless display and ornament.

3. In the furnishing of our *tables* we are to glorify God. In this we are continually to demonstrate that we are not creatures of appetite, that our belly is not our God, and that we do not live, like swine, merely to eat and drink. Scarcely anything is more injurious to the cause of Christ than for Christians to show that they are fond of high living. This disposition in some of the primitive professors of religion greatly distressed the Apostle and caused him to say, whose "god is their belly, whose glory is in their shame, whose end is destruction." The text expressly enjoins upon us to

glorify God in eating and drinking. This must respect,

(1) The *quality* of our food. This should be such, and only such, as is healthful, nutritious and calculated in the highest degree to promote the activity of our bodies and the clearness and energy of our minds. It is sin in us to eat and drink those things which we know to be injurious to our health, and the eating and drinking of which violates the laws of life.

(2) In respect to the *quantity*. We are to eat no *more* and no *less* than our health requires. It is astonishing to see to what an extent mankind are under the government of their appetites and how much time and thought and labor are expended in procuring something that will gratify their taste, regardless of health and duty to God or man. And so much are even some professors of religion under the influence of a depraved and artificial appetite that you can hardly produce a greater excitement on any subject than will be created by calling in question their manner of living in regard to "meat and drink." You touch their tea and coffee—those fashionable narcotics—and you touch the apple of their eye. They are ready to cry out, "The kingdom of God consists not in meat and drink, but in righteousness, and peace, and joy in the Holy Ghost." Now the quotation of this passage comes with a very ill grace from this class of persons. For their practice would indicate that *their* living did consist in meat and drink, and their fierce contentions in support of the gratification of their tastes would seem to demonstrate that "meat and drink" is, to them, of much more importance than "righteousness, and peace, and joy in the Holy Ghost."

Now it is manifest that for Christians to show that they are creatures of appetite is exceedingly to misrepresent and dishonor God. And we are bound, as we value the honor or regard the authority of God, so to eat and drink as to show that we have a higher source of enjoyment than the pleasure of eating and drinking, and to illustrate the truth of that saying, "Man shall not live by bread alone, but by every word that proceedeth out of the mouth of God." In short, it should be manifest that we eat and drink not to gratify our palates but that we may be able in the best manner to do the work of God.

4. In the choice of our *books* we are to glorify God. Our books are our companions—their authors, the spirits with whom we hold communion; and if a "man may be known by the company he keeps," surely a man's favorite books will tell the story of what is in his heart. Our books, therefore, are always to be chosen with reference to the glory of God, to prepare our minds in the best manner to serve Him. They are to be so chosen as to manifest that we regard the knowledge of God as infinitely more important than any other knowledge.

Few things are more dishonorable to God than for a Christian to load down his table or pollute his closet with plays and novels, with Shakespeare, Byron and Walter Scott. Are these the spirits with whom Christians are to commune? Do these promote the knowledge of God? Can a Christian make these his favorite companions and yet make the world believe that he considers the knowledge of God as of the greatest importance? The Bible represents the knowledge of God as the sum of all that is desirable in knowledge and declares that to "know God is life eternal."

Take the following Bible declarations of the importance of true wisdom, that is, of a knowledge of God, Job 28:12-28:

> But where shall wisdom be found? and where is the place of understanding? Man knoweth not the price thereof; neither is it found in the land of the living. The depth saith, It is not in me; and the sea saith, It is not with me. It cannot be gotten for gold, neither shall silver be weighed for the price thereof. It cannot be valued with the gold of Ophir, with the precious oynx, or the sapphire. The gold and the crystal cannot equal it: and the exchange of it shall not be for jewels of fine gold. No mention shall be made of coral, or of pearls: for the price of wisdom is above rubies. The topaz of Ethiopia shall not equal it, neither shall it be valued with pure gold. Whence then cometh wisdom? and where is the place of understanding? Seeing it is hid from the eyes of all living and kept close from the fowls of the air. Destruction and death say, We have heard the fame thereof with our ears. God understandeth the way thereof, and he knoweth the place thereof. For he looketh to the ends of the earth, and seeth under the whole heaven; to make the weight for the winds; and he weigheth the waters by measure. When he made a decree for the rain, and a way for the lightning of the thunder: then did he see it, and declare it; he prepared it, yea, and searched it out. And unto him he said, Behold, the fear of the Lord, that is wisdom; and to depart from evil is understanding.

Now can a Christian believe this and spend his time with novels? He can scarcely give a higher demonstration that he neither believes nor loves the Bible than in choosing such companions for his closet. Certainly it is not paying God a very high compliment—nor attaching much value to a knowledge of Him nor making the impression upon mankind that divine knowledge is infinitely more important than any other—for Christians to spend their time in the light and miscellaneous reading of the day.

5. In all our *employments* and *spirit* and *temper* and *conversation*, in *everything* we are to glorify God by exhibiting that which is the very reverse of the spirit and temper of the world—in other words, in *everything* as fully as possible to represent God, that is, to glorify Him.

IV. *I am to show the importance of glorifying God.* I remark,

1. That God's government is moral, that is, a government of moral suasion and not of force. Consequently the stability and strength of this government depend upon His reputation, or the estimation in which His subjects hold Him. The devil ruined the world by shaking the confidence of our first parents in God. While their confidence continued their obedience was perfect; and thus it always is. Perfect confidence naturally secures perfect obedience in the subjects of any government, while distrust, or unbelief, certainly and necessarily results in disobedience.

2. That unconverted men and women form their opinions of religion by the lives and temper of professing Christians. Now it is as important that your lives and temper should be just what they ought to be as that their opinions of God should be just what they ought to be. Their hearts cannot

be right unless their opinions are right; and as *their* opinions depend upon *your* lives, if you sin and exhibit a wrong spirit you are not only chargeable with all the sin which you thus cause, but their blood will be required at your hands.

3. The efficacy of Christ's death depends on your living in such a manner as to illustrate its design. Unless your life is full of love—unless you breathe the spirit and exhibit the temper that led Christ to die for sinners—you misrepresent Him, contradict the gospel, and throw a cloud of impenetrable darkness around the cross of Christ. If on the contrary you exhibit disinterested love in all your life, you will be a living illustration of the spirit of the glorious gospel and will thus glorify God.

4. That Christians under God will save or ruin the world; and that in proportion as they live for the glory of God or not, Christ represents them as "the light of the world," as "the salt of the earth"—thus plainly teaching that if their "light be darkness" and their "salt have lost its savor," the world must sink down to hell in darkness.

V. *I am to show that whatever is short of this is enmity against God.*

1. Because it is slandering God. For a professor of religion to misrepresent God is to do his utmost to dethrone Him. It is the highest influence that can be brought against any government, to misrepresent and slander it. It is by slander and falsehood that Satan has always maintained his influence in this world. Whoever then misrepresents and slanders God is in league with the devil against God.

But none are so efficient agents of the devil as inconsistent professors of religion. They are enemies in the camp. They are God's professed children, and it is taken for granted that they know God and that their testimony may be relied on; and as they are God's own witnesses, if they testify against and misrepresent Him His cause must fail. It is more injurious than the slander of a legion of devils. It is by no means true, as some have supposed, that Satan wishes to have everybody openly wicked. The testimony of one worldly professor is more influential in favor of Satan than that of a host of infidels. He would doubtless be glad to have all men professors of religion if they would be inconsistent enough to misrepresent and thus betray God.

Now there is no neutral ground upon this subject. Christ has said, "He that is not with me is against me, and he that gathereth not with me scattereth abroad." It is impossible that you should not in all your life and walk and spirit either honor or dishonor God. Your whole spirit and temper and deportment are watched and scrutinized by those around you; and inferences are continually drawn either in favor of or against the God you profess to worship.

2. He who does not live to the glory of God is the common enemy of the universe, just as he is the common enemy of any government who sets himself to slander, betray and ruin that government.

REMARKS

1. You see why God is represented in the Bible as seeking His own glory, as a thing of the highest importance to the universe. Infidelity has objected to the idea of God's seeking His glory, as if in this He was proud and jealous and ambitious of being esteemed. But when it is understood that by His glory is meant His reputation, it is easy to see that in a moral government of such an extent and duration as His, the estimation in which the great head of the government is held by the subjects is of infinite importance. And should He not pursue His glory as of the greatest good, He would not estimate things according to their real value.

This text lays down an easy rule by which to judge of the lawfulness of any employment in which we propose to engage. If it is *business* the question is, is it such an employment as Christ would engage in under the circumstances? Is it that kind of business in which you can reasonably expect to represent and honor God? If any *amusement* invites us, the question is easily settled. Should anyone see me engaged in it, would it be honorable to God and fairly represent the spirit of His religion?

2. We are not only bound to live to the glory of God but to choose those *employments*, and pursue them in that *manner*, which will best glorify God. We are to enquire for what employment we are best suited—in what way we can not only do good but do the most good. And when we have understood ourselves—our adaptedness and calling to any employment—we are cheerfully and with all our hearts to engage in it for the glory of God.

3. Herein may be seen the true point of distinction between real saints and hypocrites. The true Christian loves God supremely; God's honor and glory are, of course, dearer to him than anything and everything else. He just as naturally devotes himself to the glory of God and lives only for that end, as a man naturally pursues that in which he has supreme delight. If a man is not conscious that this is the end for which he lives, that the glory of God is dearer to him than all things else, he certainly has not the Spirit of God and it is preposterous to call himself a Christian.

Now right over against this is the hypocrite. He *professes* to live for the glory of God; but yet he certainly knows or ought to know by his own consciousness that if he seeks God's glory at all, it is with him a subordinate and not a chief end. He knows full well, if he will be honest with himself, that selfishness lurks in all the religion he has. Instead of having a strong and permanent consciousness that he is living for God, the most that he can say is, he hopes he is thus covering up his hypocrisy.

4. From this subject, it is easy to see how shocking and abominable are the *pretensions* of many professing Christians. How many of them are engaged in employments in which they cannot hope to glorify God and can make no such pretension without rendering themselves ridiculous.

5. Public sentiment seems to have restricted the obligation of this rule to ministers. They are expected to live for the glory of God. Everybody feels that a minister, in his particular employment, should aim at the glory of God. And should a minister engage in many branches of business in which

laymen think it lawful for themselves to engage, it would shock common sense.

It is wonderful to see, . . . where selfishness does not blind them, how ready men are to form right opinions. Previously to the commencement of the Temperance Reformation, I recollect of having heard of a minister who, by ill health or for some other cause, was prevented from preaching; and for the maintenance of his family he established a grocery in which he sold alcohol. This was, even then, universally reprobated. It seemed to shock the common sense of the whole community. And yet multitudes of laymen, and even Christian laymen, were engaged in the same employment without supposing themselves to be doing anything wrong.

Now why should the operation of this rule be thus by public sentiment restricted to ministers? It certainly cannot be, unless salvation is also restricted to them. Every man is as much bound to observe this rule as a minister; and the same reasons that make it obligatory upon a minister make it obligatory on every man. Now you would say, and say truly, that a minister was no Christian, that he could not be saved, if in his employment he did not aim at the glory of God. If his *main* object was to support his family, under the pretense of complying with the command to provide for his own household, you would say that he could not be saved. Now a minister may have and is bound to have just as much respect to the maintenance of his family as any other man may *lawfully* have to the maintenance of his. But neither has any right to pursue any worldly object, or any heavenly objects whatever, as an end other than the glory of God. Every man who has a family is bound to make the maintenance of his family one of the ways and one of the means of glorifying God. But to pursue this as an end is ruin and death.

6. Every man is bound to pursue that employment to which he is called of God, as much as a minister is. He is bound to be as careful and diligent in ascertaining his duty, and mark the leadings and providences of God in relation to his employment for life, as a minister is. And he has no right to pursue any business to which he is not called by the providence and Spirit of God, any more than a minister has to preach without such a call.

7. It seems sometimes as if nearly all the laymen in the church must go to hell. You find them driving in different directions and pursuing almost every kind of business and, in great multitudes of instances, without the least pretense that they were ever called to that particular employment by the Spirit or providence of God.

I some time since asked a lawyer if he supposed God called him to that particular employment, and if he engaged in it from such motives as he supposed a minister ought to engage in the work of the ministry. He frankly said, No. How then, I inquired, can you be saved? Are you not bound to live for the glory of God as much as any minister? Are you not living in the habitual neglect of known duty? Is not the whole tenor of your life selfishness and a palpable violation of the commandment of God? In the light of this text, he could not deny that it was so. Now there are hundreds and thousands of such laymen in the church. They know themselves to be pursuing courses of life from such motives as they would utterly condemn in a minister. And they would judge, and rightly judge, that he had no religion at all. Know then assuredly that in your employment, whatever it is, unless you have such an eye to the glory of God as you know a minister ought to have in his employment, you cannot be saved.

8. From this subject you can see the great wickedness of dishonoring God in our *methods* of obtaining property under the pretense that we shall devote it to benevolent purposes. Unless we get money in a manner which is honorable to God, it is in vain to pretend to make any amends for the manner of getting it by the use we make of it.

9. You see how absurd and wicked it is to engage in any business that is dishonorable to God for the purpose of paying debts. Because it is dishonorable to God to be in debt, some persons will engage in employments that violate the law of love and trample on God's commandments for the sake of getting money to pay their debts. Now why not as well steal to pay your debts, or engage in highway robbery or piracy? It is as absolute a violation of the law of God to obtain property by any selfish means as to steal or engage in piracy.

10. Every pretended conversion that does not result in shaping the man's business and life and spirit in conformity with this precept is a spurious conversion. Have you seen a man engaged in the selfish transaction of any business and professing conversion? Now mark me, if one of the first-fruits be not the reformation of his business, that man is deceived. If his business was unlawful in *kind*, he will renounce it altogether. If the fault was in the manner of *transacting* a business lawful in its kind, he will instantly reform the manner. And it is an outrage to common sense to call that man a Christian, the secret of whose life and thoughts and especially whose business transactions are not turned manifestly into the channel of glorifying God.

11. The same is true of those seasons of religious awakening in which great multitudes profess conversion to God. If the fruits of these excitements fall short of the principle laid down in this text— if it does not break up and reform the business transactions of selfish men, no matter how great their excitement of mind may have been—they have, after all, fallen short of true conversion; they have not yet taken the first step in religion and do not yet understand in what it consists.

12. Since my last lecture was written, a question has been proposed to me by a brother, an answer to which may well be given here. It is, does the law of love, when applied to business transactions, require that a man should merely support his family by his business, and have nothing more, or less, reserved to himself? I answer,

(1) That the support of a man's family is not to be the end at which he aims; but as I have already said, the support of ourselves or families is to be regarded by us as one of the *means* of glorifying God.

(2) That the support of one's self or family is by no means to be the criterion by which we are to be governed in the transaction of business; that is, whatever it may cost to support ourselves or families is not to regulate the

prices at which we are to buy or sell. If a man should keep one cow and, under the pretense of her being the support of his family, should attempt to sell milk at two shillings per quart, this certainly would not be lawful, any more than keeping one hen and attempting, under the pretense of supporting his family, to sell eggs for one dollar each would be lawful. The truth is that no man has a right to attempt to support himself or family in such a way as this.

So, on the other hand, if a man be engaged in an extensive business, the amount of his necessary expenditures in the maintenance of his family is not to be the criterion by which he is to be governed in his established prices. But in buying and selling he is to have the same regard to the interest of every individual with whom he trades as to his own. He is to sell as low as he can, without injuring himself more than he benefits others. And the amount of what he makes must depend upon the amount and nature of his business.

Suppose a wholesale merchant to employ an immense capital and perform a vast amount of business, and suppose him to supply one hundred country merchants with goods; and in this suppose him to consult the good of each, equally with his own. In this case the aggregate of his income would be equal to the aggregate of all their incomes together, so that in fact he might become very rich and have it in his power to exercise great hospitality and greatly promote benevolent objects, and still consult every man's interest, with whom he trades, equally with his own.

13. Here another question may be and has been recently asked. It is said, if every man is bound to sell so low as to consult every customer's interest equally with his own, then those who have a small capital cannot live by their business. To this I answer that no man has a right to live by [a] business by which he cannot support himself and transact it upon the principle of the law of God.

I was asked the other day this question: Suppose a certain man, in the employment of an immense capital, should conduct his business upon the principle of the law of God and, in consulting his customers' interests as much as his own, should undersell those of smaller capital, or sell at prices so low that they would become bankrupt in attempting to support their families at these prices? Now in this case, it is said the man of great capital would ruin the business of all the rest.

To this I reply, it is every man's duty to benefit the public as much as possible. And if one man can supply the market at a lower rate than others, he ought to supply it, and no others have a right to complain. Individuals and their families are not to be supported at the expense of public and higher interests. If other individuals cannot afford to act upon the law of love, their business ought to cease. And they are bound to engage in some employment in which they can conform themselves to the law of God. The very question I have been answering is founded upon the supposition that every man has a right to engage in any particular calling and support his family by it, whether consistent or inconsistent with the public good. But this is the direct reverse of the truth.

If one man, therefore, is so circumstanced that he can supply the whole demand in any market more advantageously to the public than another, he not only has a right but is bound to do so and the other is under obligation to retire.

Another question has been proposed, namely, if persons are to sell as cheap as they can, without injuring themselves more than they benefit those with whom they deal, would not their profits be so small as to prevent their accumulating property with which to do good? Now this is indeed a strange question. If a man is living and conducting business upon the principles of the law of God, or of love, he is all the time doing good upon the largest scale possible. And can it be imagined that he would really do more good by over-reaching his customers for the sake of giving his property to others? Shall a man do injustice to one man, and violate the law of God, for the sake of giving to another man? As well might a man steal to give to the poor or support the gospel, under the pretense of doing good, as in any other respect to violate the law of love for the sake of acquiring property to do good with. It should be understood that the man who lives and feels and acts and transacts business upon the principles of the law of God is *continually* doing all the good in his power. He is diffusing more happiness, by far, than if he were grinding the faces of his customers one day, to give to some benevolent object the next.

It is as *ridiculous* as it is *wicked* for a man to violate the law of benevolence under the pretense of having something to give away. Suppose that every man were conformed to the law of love; then every man would be continually doing all that he possibly could do for benevolent objects. And in such a case, where would be the necessity of one man *laying up* money to give to these objects? He is giving *as fast as he receives* to benevolent objects. The fact is that in such a case the coffers of all benevolent institutions would immediately overflow. The ice that has so long locked up the channels of love would be universally dissolved, and the streams of light and life and love would flow on, until what are now commonly called objects of charity and benevolence could not be found.

14. I have often been led to inquire, in what do Christians of the present day suppose religion to consist? It seems as though they thought it consisted in praying in their closets, reading their Bibles, attending church on the Sabbath and occasionally giving something for the support of the institutions of religion. Now religion consists in no one nor in all these things together. And millions of such things would not make a particle of true religion. Religion consists in the true benevolence of the heart—not a mere *desire* to do good but a *willing* good, a benevolence that controls the conduct, that is active, blessed, godlike.

15. To glorify God is the only object for which you have any right to live for one hour. And you can live for no other purpose with the least reasonable hope of being saved. If this be not the end and object of your life, I forewarn you that your hope will perish "in the giving up of the ghost."

16. And now, beloved, let me ask you, have you ever laid your all upon the altar and rendered yourselves a living sacrifice, holy and acceptable to God?

Is it your daily prayer and constant endeavor to be used all up with the most divine economy for God?

Do you husband your time, your strength, your all, in such a way as to make the most of your influence for the promotion of the glory of God?

Is it really in your heart to live and die for Him?

Are you willing—nay, are you supremely desirous and are you conscious of this desire—to live or die, to be sick or well, rich or poor, or in any other circumstances that will make the most of you and use you up with the greatest economy for God?

Do those with whom you sit at table see that you eat and drink for the glory of God, that you have made yourself acquainted with dietetics so far, at least, as to exclude whatever is injurious?

Do you prove to them by the quantity and quality of your food that you are not a creature of appetite—that you live not to eat but eat to live, and live to glorify God? "Whether therefore ye eat, or drink, or whatsoever ye do, do all to the glory of God."

Professor Finney's Letter of April 10, 1839*

TO THE CHRISTIAN READERS OF
THE OBERLIN EVANGELIST

Beloved: The object of this letter is to state a little more definitely than I have hitherto done some of the reasons why young converts have not grown in grace more, and why I have feared, as I said in a former letter, that revivals would become more and more superficial till they would finally cease.

I have from my earliest conversion been led to notice more and more particularly the fact that there are four classes of professors in the church.

The first class seems to have had very little conviction of sin, and consequently there is not light enough in their experience; that is, they have not experience enough so to understand the Bible as to be able, under God, to convict others of sin. They pass along, and nearly their whole lives seem to be worse than useless so far as the interests of religion are concerned.

A second class seems to have had frequent and deep conviction of sin but appear never to have been truly regenerated. They understand the Bible measurably on the subject of depravity, so as to be able under God to bring others under conviction and distress of mind; and here they stop. They rarely if ever are instrumental in the regeneration of a sinner. Having no experience on the subject of conversion themselves, they are all in the dark. And when the inquiry is made by an anxious sinner, "What shall I do

---

to be saved?"—although they may give him directions in the language of Scripture, yet as a matter of fact they cannot so answer his inquiries and shape their directions and remove his difficulties as to bring him into the kingdom of God. This class is very numerous. And I have been astonished to find how seldom it is that professors of religion know what to say to anxious sinners. From long and close observation, I am led to believe that the difficulty lies in their total want of *experience* on the subject of regeneration.

The third class have been really converted and understand the way through the gate of regeneration well enough to direct others. Knowing themselves what it is to be converted, thus far they can go with sinners. They know measurably how to use the law to produce conviction, and enough of the atonement and of Christ as a justifying Savior instrumentally to bring sinners fairly into the kingdom; for in this they have personal experience.

But they have gone no further than this. Their time and thoughts and lives have been employed with these two classes of truths—the law, and so much of the gospel as to produce conversion. They have, though, advanced no further than "the first principles of the oracles of God." They continue to lay again and again "the foundation of repentance from dead works and of faith toward God, of the doctrine of baptism and the laying on of hands, the resurrection of the dead and eternal judgment." They go round and round in the circle of these first principles of the doctrine of Christ and never "go on to perfection," either in doctrine or in practice.

Hence, having never given their attention to those higher and more spiritual truths of the gospel which are the more appropriate food of the Christian soul and indispensable to his growth in grace, they make little or no progress in holiness and often in a few years become mechanical in their efforts to convert sinners. Their spirit, not being sweetened by deep and constant and increasing intercourse with Christ, becomes bitter and censorious. They know very little what to say to an anxious Christian struggling against remaining sin. Let them be consulted by a Christian who has made any considerable attainments in piety and who understands measurably the plague of his own heart and is panting after the utter annihilation of sin in all its forms and to be raised up "to the measure of the stature of the fulness of Christ," and they are in the dark. They will generally insist upon such persons going to work for the conversion of sinners, [and] reproach them with not being at work for God and for thinking so much about themselves and their own sins. The fact is, they are in the dark in regard to the real state and necessities of such persons. This state of mind is entirely beyond their experience. They seem to be totally destitute of that to which Paul refers in 2 Cor. 1:3-6: "Blessed be God, even the Father of our Lord Jesus Christ, the Father of mercies, and the God of all comfort; who comforteth us in all our tribulation, that we may be able to comfort them which are in trouble, by the comfort wherewith we ourselves are comforted of God. For as the sufferings of Christ abound in us, so our consolation also aboundeth by Christ. And whether we be afflicted, it is for your consolation and salvation, which is effectual in the enduring of the same sufferings which we also suffer: or whether we be comforted, it is for your consolation and salvation."

Here the Apostle found that God gave him deep Christian experience and comfort that he might be able to understand the distresses and administer comfort to those in like circumstances.

Now as a general thing I do not believe it is possible for a Christian to go much beyond his own experience in administering the consolations of the gospel or in removing the difficulties that obstruct the paths of others. Even Christ himself was, in this respect, made perfect through sufferings; "for in that he hath suffered, being tempted, he is able to succor those that are tempted." The New Testament, and especially the Epistle to the Hebrews, seems plainly to recognize this truth that Christ having been in the flesh "and tempted in all points like as we are" is thereby qualified to sympathize with us, because he "can be touched with the feelings of our infirmities." It seems plain from the very nature of mind that in order to lead others, we ourselves must be acquainted with the way; and it is alarming and affecting to see how few Christians there are in the church who have experience enough to direct those who are struggling after high attainments in piety. Whenever a teacher attempts to go beyond his own experience, he becomes a blind leader of the blind.

This class of converted Christians who are able, at least for a time, to labor successfully for the conversion of others, without ever having grown much in grace themselves and in the knowledge of our Lord Jesus Christ, has been much increased during the great revivals.

The fourth class, and I am constrained to say that they are comparatively few, have learned so much of Christ as a *sanctifying* as well as a *justifying* Savior, have drunk so deeply at the fountain-head of love and of the waters of the sanctuary, as to be able not merely to direct an inquiring *sinner* but an anxious *Christian*. I have always observed that this class of Christians feel peculiarly solicitous for the weak lambs of the church. The weak and stumbling and God-dishonoring state of the church is what most peculiarly afflicts them. Their compassions are greatly moved when they behold the haltings, complainings, anxieties and follies of the church.

Now it seems to me that there is something in the history of Paul that ought to be instructive to the church on this subject. He seems to have spent a number of years almost exclusively in the conversion of sinners and in the establishment of churches. But during his confinement at Rome and in the latter part of his ministry, he appears to have had his attention turned particularly to the subject of strengthening the church. And it is very edifying to see in all his epistles this prominent feature of his character: a great solicitude to promote growth in grace among Christians. It is not to be supposed that he omitted to labor for the conversion of sinners. But it is, I think, manifest beyond all dispute that his mind was mainly engrossed with the sanctification of the church. And it is evident from his epistles that he did not believe that the church would ever be sanctified merely by pressing them to labor exclusively for the conversion of sinners or by dwelling upon that particular class of subjects that were denominated by him "the beginning of the doctrine of Christ." His letters were, I think, undeniably designed to lead Christians into a fuller knowledge of Christ, in all his relations—to the necessity, means and practicability of entire sanctification. The same seems to have been true of all the apostles whose epistles have come down to us.

But I have made so many preliminary remarks that I must omit my main design, that is to notice some of the reasons why converts have not grown more in grace, till my next.

C. G. FINNEY,
A Servant of the Lord Jesus Christ

LECTURE 8

True and False Peace

Ps. 119: 165: "Great peace have they who love thy law, and nothing shall offend them."

In this lecture I design to show:

I. What we are to understand by law in this passage.
II. What it is to love the law of God.
III. That the natural result of this love is great and constant peace of mind.
IV. That nothing shall offend them that love the law of God.
V. Notice a delusion upon this subject that is very common among professed Christians.

I. *I am to show what we are to understand by law in this passage.*

Law is the revealed will of the law-giver. The whole revealed will of God is to be understood as His law, however that revelation is made—whether in the Bible, in the providence, or by the Spirit of God. The term law, as used in this Psalm and very often in the Bible, is doubtless to be understood in this extended and indeed its most proper sense.

In a more restricted sense, all the commandments of God are to be considered as His law. And in a sense still more limited, the Ten Commandments are His law. And these, again, are condensed into the two precepts, "Thou shalt love the Lord thy God with all thy heart, and thy neighbour as thyself."

But God's will—His *whole will*—is His law. And whenever this will is revealed in any way whatever, it becomes binding on us. So that when we are informed by His Word or providence that anything is agreeable to the divine will, that is to settle the question with us, and we are sweetly to acquiesce in it.

II. *I am to show what it is to love the law of God.*

It is a *disinterested preference of the will of God*—a preferring with all our heart that the will of God, whatever it is, should be done because it is holy, wise and good. It is not the making a *virtue* of *necessity,* and yielding by constraint because resistance will do no good, but it is the mind's supreme choice that God's will shall be done, on earth as in heaven. It is a sweet and entire complacency in the will of God, however that will may be revealed. It is that state in which the mind continually cries, and echoes and re-echoes, "Thy will be done on earth as it is done in heaven." It is a supreme and sweet delight in whatever is the will of God, because it is His will. It is not that forced submission of the mind when it is prostrated and the will broken down by absolute agony. But it is a sweet and heavenly rest in the will of God—a spontaneous gushing forth of the heart that meets, and responds Amen, to all the will of the blessed God.

III. *I am to show that the natural result of this love is great and constant peace of mind.*

By peace I do not mean *indifference,* or that quiet of the mind that results from diverting the attention from that which had before agonized it.

Peace is opposed to war. A war of mind is a state of mutiny, where the heart and conscience and perhaps other powers of the mind are in conflict with each other. The heart chooses what the conscience condemns, and the conscience demands what the heart refuses. And the emotions, in such cases, may be thrown into a state of great excitement and agitation, filling the mind with agony and every hateful passion.

Now peace is the opposite of this state of mind, not the mere absence of it—not the mere absence of agony and inward mutiny, but a delightful and sweet harmony in the exercise of all the powers of the mind. The will and the conscience are at one, the heart sweetly choosing and delightfully reposing in that which is agreeable to the decisions of the conscience, and the conscience, as it were, sweetly smiling approbation upon the decisions of the will, and the emotions flowing like a gentle streamlet in delightful accordance with both the conscience and the heart.

This is far from being a mere negative or quiescent state of mind, which is often mistaken for peace. It is a positive, active and heavenly state of mind. It is a wakeful and deep composure of the soul, like the deep, pure, calm ocean—clear, composed and heavenly. It is a state of mind far better understood by experience than described in words. It is "the peace of God, that passeth understanding." This peace have they that love the law of God.

To show this, let me observe that in this state of mind they certainly can know no resistance to whatever they discover to be the will of God. And whatever desires they may have or prayers they may make in relation to any particular event, when by any means they are led to understand the will of God respecting that event, they joyfully acquiesce. We have an illustration of this in the case of David, who mourned sorely when his child was sick. He "besought God for the child and fasted and went in and lay all night upon the earth"; for he said, "Who can tell whether God will be gracious to me that the child may live?" But as soon as the child was dead, and he was thereby informed what the will of God was, "he arose from the earth, and washed, and changed his apparel, and came into the house of the Lord and worshipped, and said, I shall go to him but he shall not return to me."

This peace will be a *great* peace; that is, it will extend to every providence and to all the will of God. How can it be otherwise, if the heart is in such a state as to have a supreme preference for His will? What can occur, in such a state of mind, that shall break or disturb its deep repose in God?

IV. *I am to show that nothing shall offend or stumble those that love the law of God.*

You will observe that in the margin it is written, they shall have no stumbling block—that is, that they shall so acquiesce in all the will of God as not to stumble and fall into rebellion on account of anything revealed in the Bible, or on account of any providence of God.

By this is not meant that persons in this state of mind can know no such thing as sorrow or distress. Various things may occur to disturb the emotions of the mind while the heart or will is as undisturbed as the great deep of the ocean. We have an illustration of this in the great agony of Christ in the garden. His conflict was so severe and the excitement of His emotions so great that "he sweat great drops of blood." And yet it was manifest that His heart, or will, was firmly settled to do the will of God, as unmoved as the everlasting mountains. His will was not disturbed or shaken. And in this respect His peace was undisturbed; and while He cried out in the anguish almost of death, "If it be possible, let this cup pass from me," the deep stedfastness of His heart in the will of God concluded every time, "Not as I will, but as thou wilt." Here was an instance of great desire existing for a certain blessing, and yet the will most stedfastly clinging to the will of God.

Now when I said above that the peace spoken of in this text includes the harmonious action of all the powers of the mind, I did not mean, certainly, that the *emotions,* which are involuntary states of mind, are always at rest or composed. They generally accord with the state of the will. But sometimes circumstances occur, as in this case of Christ, when the emotions or desires are greatly excited, while the will remains unshaken. Nor is this to be considered as really disturbing the peace of mind. These are accidental or, perhaps more properly, providential fluctuations of the involuntary powers of the mind. And the emotions may be exceedingly joyous without any true peace, as they often are in fits of laughter and merriment.

So they may on the other hand be painful and agonizing without breaking up or affecting the deep repose of the will, as was manifestly the case with Christ. When the will is at rest in the will of God the emotions will sweetly acquiesce, unless it be in cases of strong temptation and trial, as in the case of Christ and David, just mentioned. But in such cases, a Christian's sorrows may be stirred and yet their peace, properly speaking, remain unbroken. So a Christian who loves the law of God may be exercised with great compassion for sinners, with deep travail of soul for Zion, with distress and indignation at sin; and in many ways the surface of the mind, as it were, may be ruffled while, like the ocean, its deep fountains are unmoved.

The text says, "They have great peace who love thy law, and nothing shall offend [or stumble] them." Nothing can occur that can throw them into a state of discontent or repining at God. They shall not be disappointed in anything. Dr. Payson could say, "He had not known what disappointment was, since he had given up his own will."

To love the law or will of God is to have our will submerged in His will—to have no will of our own separate from His, but to will with all our heart that His will should be done. Now this state of mind absolutely precludes a state of discontent, resistance, repining or disappointment at the revealed will of God.

Nothing certainly can occur which is not, upon the whole, according to the will of God; that is, He has either actively brought it about by His own agency or seen it wise, upon the whole, not to prevent its being accomplished by the agency of others. So that whatever is, is upon the whole "according to the counsel of his own will"; that is, He upon the whole prefers its being just as it is to such an alteration of His providential and moral government as to have brought about a different result. The enlightened Christian that knows this—and every Christian who can be truly said to love the law of God is enlightened enough to know this—will find as a matter of fact that nothing shall offend or stumble him.

V. *I am to notice a delusion upon this subject that is very common among professing Christians.*

The delusion consists in their obtaining a *false peace* from time to time, by a natural process of mind which they do not seem to understand. In an impenitent state the heart is selfish, and the conscience and heart are opposed to each other. Instead of their being at one, and thus creating a great calm and peace in the mind, there is often a great conflict, the conscience sternly demanding and insisting upon sacrifices which the heart is unwilling to make. It is often the case that the conscience continues to distress the mind and press the will with its claims, until from some consideration purely selfish the heart will yield one point after another, and thus afford the mind a temporary relief.

Suppose, for example, the conscience to upbraid the mind with the indulgence of any particular form of sin. This throws the mind into distress, and in its agony it casts about for relief. Suppose the sin to be intemperance. It is easy to see that the mind, in contemplating the subject, may see a great many reasons for yielding the point and giving up intemperance; and it may be yielded, and intemperance really abandoned, from any other and every other consideration than love to the will of God and hatred of sin, as such. Now if the point is yielded, from whatever motive, although true peace does not follow, yet a natural reaction takes place in the mind which is often mistaken for peace. Thus when anything is proposed and pressed upon the heart which it resolutely resists, the tendency is to throw the mind into an agony. But if the point is yielded, there is naturally induced a quiescent state of mind and sometimes a verging to the opposite extreme of joyousness which, though a common fact, does not seem to be generally understood.

Perhaps some of you have witnessed a case of this kind, where a proposal of marriage has been made to a lady, on many accounts highly honorable and advantageous, but to which her heart is strongly opposed, either from a want of interest in the person or on account of a pre-existing attachment. Now if the proposal be pressed by the person himself and by her friends, urging considerations upon her as inducements to consent, she becomes agonized, can neither eat nor sleep, and in her distraction casts about for relief until, overcome by argument and persuasion and flattery and appeals to her ambition, she consents. Now the will is carried, but not from proper motives. The conflict ceases and a natural reaction of the mind takes place. A calm ensues that verges towards sweetness and affection for her admirer and complacency in the proposal. But still he is not the object of her choice. It is not love to him but other considerations that have influenced the will. Now as soon as they are united and his will comes to be the rule of her action, she will discover her mistake and find that it was a forced submission. And not loving her husband, it is impossible for her to be at peace. At every turn she will find her will opposing his will. And conscience, a regard for reputation or some other like inducement must force submission from time to time, after a protracted and agonizing struggle.

Now this is exactly the conduct and character of many a convicted sinner who obtains a false hope, and many a deceived professor of religion. Enlightened by the Spirit, conscience gives them no rest. Their distress increases till a forced submission is produced. The fear of punishment, the hope of pardon, a desire for peace and the consolations of the gospel, and many other selfish inducements may come in to influence the will till there is a forced submission of some point upon which the mind is particularly pressed. Perhaps it is the duty of family prayer, which the mind is resisting; perhaps it is the confession of some sin, the making restitution, the taking an anxious seat, attending a meeting of inquiry, the opening the mind to a minister, or something of this kind. Now when inducements are held out to yield this *point,* instead of the character of God being so presented as to make the mind fall in love with Him, it is plain that multitudes of selfish considerations may cause the mind to yield when, after all, it has no knowledge of God and no love to Him—when the mind is as far as possible from true repentance or faith or love to God or man. Conscience has forced the will upon such a dilemma that it has yielded the point, yet from selfish considerations. It has not at all changed its attitude toward God. It has only substituted one form of selfishness for another. When driven to desperation and looking all around for peace, it has taken sanctuary in yielding the point from some selfish motive.

Now it often occurs that when a sinner sits upon his seat and a call is made for the inquirers to come forward, as soon as he makes up his mind to go, from whatever motive, his distress leaves him. He felt a desperate struggle till the question was decided. But as soon as the decision was made to go, although it was the anxious seat and not God or Christ that was in all his thoughts, perhaps he became calm; he felt as if a mountain weight had rolled off from his soul. Now how natural for him to mistake the calm, which is the legitimate effect of a reaction in his mind, for the peace of God. He has yielded the point that occasioned so great struggle. Others have gone to the anxious seat and obtained hopes. He knew he was kept back by pride. His conscience and reason and a thousand inducements clustered around him and bade him go, if peradventure he might be blessed.

Now while the pride of his heart resisted there would of course be a tremendous struggle; and whatever inducements caused him to yield would produce calm and that calm might, and doubtless often is, fatally mistaken for true peace. For it should be understood that this natural reaction may be sudden and great, in proportion to the greatness of the distress that had preceded it. The reaction may go much further than a calm and the absence of distress. A joyousness may and naturally will succeed which, being mistaken for true religion, will encourage hope; and hope encouraged in the mind will increase joy, and joy increased will strengthen hope. This strengthened will, in its turn, strengthens joy, until the deluded soul persuades himself that he is filled with the love of God.

Now the true distinction between this state of mind and that peace which they have who love the law of God is this: instead of enforcing submission to the performance of some particular duty, the mind apprehends and loves the character of God. The will yields not to the biddings of conscience or force of circumstances or selfish considerations; but the mind, being diverted from all selfishness, looks away to God and Christ and sweetly yields *to,* and acquiesces *in,* His will.

Now the difference in these two states of mind will be apparent in this: the deluded sinner, not having his will merged in the will of God, will soon find that what he calls his peace is continually broken. Instead of finding that he is not stumbled or offended with the providences and will of God, he will find that he is almost continually stumbled. He is thrown into an excitement of mind at every providence and every commandment of God that crosses his path. The *will* of God is not the *law* of his being. So far from it, he often finds himself in such a state of mind that conscience must enforce its claims upon the heart, and sometimes a severe conflict compels him to yield one form of sin after another. Thus he submits and yields one point today from some selfish consideration, and tomorrow there is some new call to duty—some demand of self-denial, or something else—which brings him up to a stand of strong resistance and throws him into great confusion. This, perhaps after a severe struggle, the mind will yield, and retreat to some refuge, prepared to resist the next demand upon its selfishness.

Now right over against this is that state of mind that constitutes true peace. True peace is the result of the heart's having yielded to God, that is, in its loving God and preferring the will of God to all other things. Instead of being fretted and stumbled and thrown into agony and disappointment and discontent by every call to self-sacrifice and duty, all these calls are so many joyful occasions on which to gratify its love and in which it feels the sweetest and most profound complacency. As it turns over the leaves of the Bible, as it listens to sermons, as the unfoldings of providence point out new paths of duty and call afresh for self-denial, instead of being thrown in an agony at these demands it is delighted with these opportunities of manifesting its love; and it finds that its repose is deepened and its joy heightened and rendered more exquisite by how much the more frequently these demands are made.

Now perhaps I am relating the very experience of some of you. How is it, when duty is pointed out? Do you find that the pressure of obligation disturbs your peace? Does conscience, the law and the Spirit of God point out your duty, and does your heart hold back? It is then to you a stumbling block and a rock of offense. And if you find it impossible to divert your mind, you may take shelter in the outward performance of duty and so far yield the point as to perform the duty without any love to God. A calm succeeds which you mistake for true peace. You rest in your delusion for a day, to be called, perhaps tomorrow, to a new conflict with your conscience and the will of God.

Now rest assured, if this is your character and this your experience, "you are in the gall of bitterness, and in the bonds of iniquity." How many such persons have I seen who would appear to be very happy in religion while no sacrifice was called for and no demand made upon their selfishness. But attack their lusts, call on them for self-denial, ask their money for benevolent objects, point at some of their intemperate practices in eating and drinking, reprove some favorite indulgence, and instantly you have destroyed all their religion. Their peace is all gone. Conscience and the will are up in arms, and mutiny and war immediately ensue.

Now let me place beside this picture the experience of a Christian. In him, so far as he is a Christian, selfishness is subdued and his conscience and heart are at one. In such a case the office of conscience is not to force the heart, for the heart needs no force. Conscience is that power of the mind that points out the moral qualities of actions and enables the mind to distinguish between what is right and what is wrong. Now the Christian heart is in love with what is right, that is, with the will of God, whenever it discovers what it is. So that the dictates of conscience are readily, spontaneously and joyfully obeyed by the heart. In this case, the peace of mind is unbroken and there is a joyful acquiescence in all the will of God. Let there be new calls to duty, new occasions for self-denial, new demands upon life and health and strength for the promotion of God's glory; no mutiny results, but peace and a joyful yielding, a supreme and delightful preference of the will of God, reigns throughout the soul.

REMARKS

1. *Selfish* professors *cannot understand religion.* They continually make conscience and selfish resolutions supply the place of love. They do not distinguish between being influenced in their conduct by selfish resolutions and purposes and by the reproaches of conscience, and that love which begets a joyful acquiescence in all the will of God.

2. Many persons are spending their time in putting a *conscientious restraint* upon selfishness instead of *giving it up.* They are, like children, building dams of sand that by the slight risings of the water are instantly driven away. They see the risings of their pride, the rufflings of their temper, their worldly-mindedness and their sin, under many forms. These they are busied in putting down. They resolve, and re-resolve; they vow, and break their vows; they purpose, and fail to fulfill—and for the best of all reasons: their heart does not love God. And selfishness is too strong for their conscience; and sin will break over their dams of sand.

But here, it may be asked, are we to have no regard to conscience in our daily walk and conversation? I answer, yes. No man can walk with God unless he "keeps a conscience void of offence towards God and towards man." But observe, there is no virtue, no real holiness, except the heart loves what the conscience pronounces to be right. To comply with conscience from some other motive than love is not religion. Saul of Tarsus, it is said, "lived in all good conscience before God." But his conformity to the dictates of conscience was legal, that is, he was influenced by legal or self-righteous considerations and not by love.

3. In this discourse, you can see the *true distinction* between a professor *under the law* and a Christian who has entered into the *rest of the gospel.*

4. From what observation I have been able to make, I cannot but fear that only a comparatively *few* of the visible church *are converted to God.* It is a matter of fact that they have not the peace expressly promised in the text to those that love the law of God. Indeed, I should not say that this peace is *promised*—it is expressly declared to be the state in which they now *are* who love the law of God: "Great peace HAVE they, that love thy law."

Now have you this peace? Have the church this peace, as a matter of fact? As God is true, they only love the law of God who do, as a matter of fact, have this peace.

5. Much of the instruction given to anxious sinners and professors of religion *is only calculated to give and encourage a false peace.* When they are convicted and anxious, instead of spreading out before them the objects of faith and love to engage their attention and win their affections, they are

perhaps pointed to some form of sin and required to give that up and to resolve never to commit it again, and then to another and another, leading them, perhaps by various and selfish considerations, to yield some point or points upon which there is a conflict in the mind; and thus inducing, as I have already shown, a false peace, while there is not a particle of the right knowledge or of the love of God.

It appears to me to be impossible that true religion and true submission should be produced in the mind, without pressing upon the attention the character of God and of Christ as presented in the Bible. Those great and commanding objects of love and of faith must be presented and embraced: and there must be a yielding up of selfishness, through the power of truth and the Holy Ghost, or there is no true religion in the soul. But if selfishness is subdued, you will not witness these perpetual conflictings that are so common when professors of religion are pressed up to duty.

6. And now I must conclude by pressing home upon you the solemn inquiry, are you a Christian? Do you love the law of God? Is the will of God your rule of action? Or do you merely acknowledge that it *ought* to be while, as a matter of fact, you do not make it so?

Have you so renounced your own will as to find yourself undisturbed, peaceful and joyous when anything turns out, in the providence of God, different from what you had hoped and expected?

Whenever a sin is pointed out to you or any duty to perform, do you find that it distresses you to sacrifice that sin or to perform that duty? Do you yield by constraint, or willingly, joyfully?

Beloved souls, be ye not deceived. To love the law of God is to love the will of God—to prefer His will to your own will. Now do you, as a matter of fact, find your mind to be in this state? Or is it true of you that instead of yielding your own will to the will of God, without debate or distress, you only yield after a severe conflict, and are compelled by conscience rather than sweetly constrained by love?

Now just mark what this text says: not that they *may* have, *ought* to have, or *shall* have great peace that love the law of God; but that they actually DO HAVE great peace.

This is a matter of fact, and the natural result of yielding the will to the will of God. Indeed, I should rather say that this peace *consists* in your yielding to the will of God and preferring His will to your own.

Now your own consciousness must teach you, with absolute certainty, whether you are in this state of mind.

Will you be honest before God?

Will you decide this question, as before the solemn judgment?

I pray you to settle these solemn questions; and remember that your salvation or damnation is suspended upon their being decided according to truth.

LECTURE 9

Sanctification Under Grace*

Rom. 6:14: "For sin shall not have dominion over you; for ye are not under the law: but under grace."

I shall attempt to show:

I. What sin is.
II. When it may be said that sin has dominion in the soul.
III. What it is to be under the law.
IV. What it is to be under grace.
V. That under the law sin will have dominion over an unsanctified mind, of course.
VI. That sin cannot have dominion over those who are under grace.

I. *I am to show what sin is.*

Sin is a state of mind which is the opposite of the law of God. As I have shown in a former lecture, the whole of true religion consists in obedience to this law, which requires supreme, disinterested love to God and disinterested and equal love to our neighbor. This is the opposite of selfishness or a supreme regard to our own interest. Selfishness, therefore, under all its forms, is sin; and there is no form of sin that is not some modification of selfishness.

Sin then is not any part of our physical or mental constitution. It is no part or principle of nature itself but a voluntary state of mind, that is, an action or choice of the mind, a preferring our own interest, because it is our own, to other and higher interests. It does not consist in any defect of our nature, but in a perversion or prohibited use of our nature.

II. *I am to show when sin has dominion in the soul.*

It cannot be properly said that sin has *dominion* because the soul has fallen under the power of an occasional temptation. Some have supposed this passage to teach that a person under grace could not sin under any circumstances. They have maintained that to sin once is to be brought under the dominion of sin.

Now although I am for making the promises mean all they say, yet I do not believe that such language as this can be justly interpreted to mean all that such persons contend for. For example, if a man should be once intoxicated, under circumstances of peculiar temptation, it would be neither fair nor true, in speaking of his general character, to say that he was under the

---

*Untitled; this title supplied by the editor.

dominion of ardent spirits and a slave to his appetite.

As an illustration of my meaning take a parallel promise, John 4:14. Christ says, "But whosoever drinketh of the water that I shall give him shall never thirst; but the water that I shall give him shall be in him a well of water springing up into everlasting life." Now some have understood this promise to mean that if a person became a partaker of the Holy Ghost, he could never again know what it was to thirst for the divine influence in any sense—that he would have such a fullness of the Spirit of God as to have at no time any thirsting for more. But this is certainly a forced construction of this passage. It is not in accordance with what we should mean in the use of similar language. Should you promise your neighbor if he came and boarded with you he should never hunger nor thirst, would he understand you to mean that he should never have a good appetite for his food, or merely that he should not be hungry or thirsty without being supplied? He would doubtless understand you, and you would expect him to understand you, to promise that he should have enough to eat and to drink—that he should not suffer the gnawings of hunger or the pains of thirst without the supply that nature demands.

Just so I understand this promise of Christ: that if any man have partaken of these waters of life, he has the pledge of Christ that he shall have as great a measure of His Spirit as his necessities demand—that whenever his soul thirsts for more of the waters of life, he has a right to plead this promise with an assurance that Christ will satisfy his thirsty soul with living waters.

I suppose this text to have a similar meaning. It does not mean that no person, under temptation, can fall under the power of an occasional sin, but that no form of sin shall be habitual, that no form of selfishness or lust shall in any such case be habitual in the soul that is under grace; that no appetite or passion or temptation of any kind should in this sense be able to bring the soul into bondage to sin.

III. *I am to show what it is to be under the law.*

1. *To be under the law is to be subject to the law, as a covenant of works*—in other words, to be under the necessity of perfectly fulfilling the law in order to obtain salvation thereby.

2. To be under the law is to be influenced by *legal motives or considerations*—to be constrained by the fear of punishment, or influenced by the hope of reward.

3. To be under the law is to be *constrained* by *conscience* and a sense of duty, and *not by love*. Individuals seem to go painfully about their duty, under the biddings of conscience, and submit with about as much pain and reluctance as a slave to his master.

4. To be under the *condemning sentence of the law*, like a state criminal, and of course shut out from communion with God. A state criminal, under sentence, is of course shut out from all friendly intercourse with the government—is considered and treated as an outlaw. Just so with a sinner

under the sentence of God's law. While he remains in a state of spiritual death and alienation from God, the sentence of eternal death is out against him; he is shut out from communion with God, and consequently sin will have dominion over him.

IV. *I am to show what it is to be under grace.*

1. *To be under a covenant of grace* is in opposition to a *covenant of law*. By a covenant of grace, I mean the covenant which confers all the blessings of salvation as a mere gratuity, and more than a gratuity, as being the direct opposite of our deserts.

2. To be influenced by *love*, excited by *grace* and not by legal motives.

3. To be put in *possession of the blessings* of the new or gracious covenant.

Jer. 31:31-34: Behold, the days come, saith the Lord, that I will make a new covenant with the house of Israel, and with the house of Judah: not according to the covenant that I made with their fathers in the day that I took them by the hand to bring them out of the land of Egypt; which my covenant they brake, although I was an husband unto them, saith the Lord: but this shall be the covenant that I will make with the house of Israel: After those days, saith the Lord, I will put my law in their inward parts, and write it in their hearts, and will be their God, and they shall be my people. And they shall teach no more every man his neighbour, and every man his brother, saying, Know the Lord: for they shall all know me, from the least of them unto the greatest of them, saith the Lord: for I will forgive their iniquity, and I will remember their sin no more.

Heb. 8:8-13: Behold, the days come, saith the Lord, when I will make a new covenant with the house of Israel and with the house of Judah: not according to the covenant that I made with their fathers in the day when I took them by the hand to lead them out of the land of Egypt; because they continued not in my covenant, and I regarded them not, saith the Lord. For this is the covenant that I will make with the house of Israel after those days, saith the Lord; I will put my laws into their mind, and write them in their hearts: and I will be to them a God, and they shall be to me a people: and they shall not teach every man his neighbour, and every man his brother, saying, Know the Lord: for all shall know me, from the least to the greatest. For I will be merciful to their unrighteousness, and their sins and their iniquities will I remember no more.

4. To be under grace is to be so united to Christ, by faith, as to receive a continual life and influence from Him. He represents himself as a vine, and His children as the branches. And to be under grace is to be united to Him as a branch is united to the vine, so as to receive our continual support and strength and nourishment and life from Him.

To be under grace is to pass from death unto life, to be translated from the kingdom of darkness into the kingdom of God's dear Son, to pass from the state of a condemned criminal into a state of redemption, justification and adoption.

V. *I am to show that under the law sin will have dominion over an unsanc-*
tified mind.

1. Because this is the certain effect of law *upon a selfish mind*. A selfish
mind is seeking its own interests, of course. And if it attempts to obey the
law it will be through selfish considerations, either through hope or fear.
But in every such attempt the mind must fail, of course, for selfishness is
the very thing which the law prohibits. And every attempt to obey from
selfish motives is only a grievous breach of the law. Therefore, if all former
sins were cancelled and salvation depended upon future obedience to the
law, salvation would in this way be forever impossible. Hence, if the mind
attempted to obey for the sake of obtaining salvation, this would be selfishness and disobedience; and in every such attempt the mind must fail, of
course.

2. Sin must have dominion over a selfish mind that is under law, or it
would amount to this absurdity: that the disinterested love demanded by
the law would flow from selfish motives—a thing naturally impossible.

3. To produce disinterested love, salvation must be *gratuitous*, that is,
the soul must understand that obedience to law is not the condition to salvation. For if it understood legal obedience to be the condition of salvation,
it is impossible that this consideration should not influence a selfish mind
in its efforts to obey. So that this consideration would render all attempts
at obedience ineffectual, and sin would continue to have dominion.

4. Selfishness will of course seek *present* and *selfish* gratification until
compelled by deep conviction to desist, in which case the will certainly
takes refuge in a self-righteous attempt to obey the law, unless it understands that salvation is gratuitous, or a matter of grace. There seems to be,
as a matter of fact, no other way in which the power of selfishness can be
broken, except to annihilate the reasons for selfish efforts by bringing home
to the soul the truth that salvation is by grace, through faith.

The effect of law upon a selfish mind is beautifully illustrated by the
Apostle in the seventh chapter of Romans. The case here supposed is what
the Apostle, as is common with him, represents as if it were his own experience. It appears, from its connection, to illustrate the influence of law over
an unsanctified mind. It is plainly a case where sin was habitual, where it
had *dominion*, where the law of sin and death in the members so warred
against the law of the mind as to bring the soul into captivity. Now some
have contended and continue to contend that the Apostle in this chapter
describes the experience of a saint under grace. But this cannot be, because
in this case it would flatly contradict the text upon which I am preaching.
As I have said, the case described in the seventh of Romans is a case in
which sin undeniably has dominion—the very thing of which the Apostle
complains. But the text affirms that sin shall not have dominion over the
soul that is under grace. Besides, it is very plain that in the seventh of Romans it was the influence of *law*, and not of *grace*, which the Apostle was
discussing.

5. Another reason why sin will have dominion under the law is that
under law men are left to the unaided exercise of their own powers of moral

agency, without those gracious helps which alone can induce true holiness. The law throws out its claims upon them and requires the perfect use and entire consecration of all their powers to the service of God, and then leaves them to obey or disobey at their peril. It neither secures nor promises to them any aid, but requires them to go forth to the service of God—to love Him with all their heart and their neighbor as themselves—in pain of eternal death. Now in such circumstances, it is very plain that a mind already selfish will only be confirmed in selfishness under such a dispensation.

VI. *I am to show that sin cannot have dominion over those who are under grace.*

1. Because the law is *written in the heart*, that is, the spirit of the law has taken possession of the soul and made us forever "free from the law of sin and death" which was in our members.

2. Because the soul has become *acquainted with God and with Christ* and has fallen deeply in love with their character. It delights in God and exercises the very temper required by the law, uninfluenced by the hope of its rewards or by the fear of its penalty. It is overcome and swallowed up with that love that naturally results from a right acquaintance with God. Now in this state of mind, sin can no more have dominion over the soul; no form of selfishness can be habitual, any more than a wife who loves her husband supremely can become a habitual adulteress. A woman who loves her husband might, by force of circumstances and by some unexpected and powerful temptation, be led to sin against her husband; but for this to become *habitual* while the supreme love of her husband continues is a contradiction.

3. Sin cannot have dominion over the soul because *Christ has become its life*. He is represented not only as the life of the soul but as the head of the church, and Christians as members of His body and flesh and bones. Now as the vine supplies the branch and as the head controls the members, so Christ has become the mainspring, the well spring, of life in the soul; and sin cannot have dominion over such a soul unless it can have dominion over Christ. Christ may find it necessary to permit the soul to fall into an occasional sin, to teach it by experience what perhaps it will not learn in any other way. But that sin, under any form, should become habitual cannot be necessary to give the soul a sense of its dependence; and Christ, by express promise, has secured the soul against it.

4. Because the soul so *reposes in the blood of Christ* for justification and salvation as to have no motive to selfish efforts, being released from the responsibility of working out a legal righteousness. It is constrained by such a sense of abundant and overflowing grace that it loves and serves God, having no reason to serve itself.

5. Because it is so constrained by a sense of the *love of Christ* as to be as unable to indulge in sin, and vastly more so, than the most dutiful and affectionate child is to indulge in habitual and willful disobedience to its parents.

6. It is impossible for sin to have dominion over a Christian because it implies a *contradiction*. To be a Christian is habitually to love and serve and honor God. Obedience is the rule and sin is the exception. It is therefore impossible that sin should have dominion over a Christian, for this would be the same as to say that a person might be a Christian while sin was his rule and obedience the exception or, in other words, that sin is habitual and obedience only occasional. If this is the definition of a Christian, then I know not what a Christian is.

7. Sin cannot have dominion because the veracity of the God of truth is pledged that it shall not.

8. Because the very terms of the covenant of grace show that to be under grace is to have the law written in the heart—to be made or rendered obedient to God by the residence of the Spirit of Christ within us.

9. Because every form of sin is hateful to the soul, and can have no influence—[save] only during a moment of strong temptation, when the involuntary powers or emotions are so strongly excited by temptation as to gain a momentary ascendancy over the will, while the deep preference of the mind, although for the time being comparatively inefficient, yet remains unchanged.

10. Because the soul, under grace, is led by the Spirit to such an understanding and use of its powers as to make the soul a partaker of the divine nature. John says a man "born of God, doth not commit sin, for his seed remaineth in him," that is, the Spirit of Christ dwelling in him renders it unnatural for him to sin.

11. Because *old things are passed away and all things are become new*. The grand leading design of the mind has undergone a radical change. And as the leading design of the mind must of course control the habitual conduct of the soul, and as deviations from its influence will only be occasional and not habitual, so the soul under grace will not, cannot be under the dominion of sin.

REMARKS

1. There is no sound religion where there is not universal reformation. It should be constantly and strictly observed, in all cases of professed conversion, whether the reformation in habits and life is *universal*—whether it extends to selfishness and sinful lusts and habits of every kind and under every form. If any lust is spared, if selfishness under any form is indulged and habitual, if any sinful habit still remains unbroken and unsubdued, that is not a sound conversion. No form of sin will have dominion where conversion is real. Occasional sin may occur through the force of powerful temptation, but no form of sin will be indulged.

2. Want of attention to this truth has suffered a great many unconverted persons to enter the church. In some respects a reformation has been apparent. In such cases, without sufficient discrimination, hope has been indulged by the individual himself and encouraged by members of the church, and he has been admitted to the communion to the great disgrace

of religion. It does not appear to me to have been sufficiently understood that grace not only ought but actually does, in every case where piety is real, so overcome sin as to leave no form of it habitual. It has indeed been a common maxim that where sin is habitual there is no real religion. But this has manifestly not been adopted in practice: for great multitudes have been admitted and are still permitted to continue as members in good standing in Christian churches, who habitually indulge in many forms of sin. I think the gospel demands that no professed convert should be thus encouraged to hope or suffered to become a member of the church, whose reformation of life and habits is not *universal*.

3. You see that all those persons who have frequent convictions and conflicts with sin, and yet are habitually overcome by it, are still under the law and not under grace, that is, they are convicted but not converted. The difficulty is their hearts are not changed so as to hate sin under every form. Temptation is too strong, therefore, for their conscience and for all their resolutions. Their hearts pleading for indulgence will of course render them an easy prey to temptation. This seems to have been exactly the case described in the seventh chapter of Romans, to which I have referred. Where regeneration has taken place and the *heart* as well as the *conscience* has become opposed to sin—in every such case the power of temptation is, of course, so broken as that sin will at most be only occasional, and never habitual. In all cases, therefore, where individuals find themselves to be or are seen by others to be under the dominion of sin or lust of any kind, they should know or be told at once that they have not been regenerated, that they are under the law and not under grace.

4. What can those persons think of themselves, who know that they are under the dominion of selfishness in some of its forms? Do they believe this text to be a direct and palpable falsehood? If not, how can they indulge the hope that they are Christians? This text asserts, as plainly as it can, that they are under the law and not under grace.

5. You see the state of those who are encouraged by the seventh chapter of Romans, supposing that to be a Christian's experience. If they have gone no further than *that*, they are still under the law. I have been amazed to see how pertinaciously professors of religion will cling to a legal experience, and justify themselves in it by a reference to this chapter. I am fully convinced that the modern construction of the chapter from the 14th to the 24th verses, interpreting it as a Christian experience, has done incalculable evil and has led thousands of souls there to rest and go no further, imagining that they are already as deeply versed in Christian experience as Paul was when he wrote that epistle. And there they have stayed, and hugged their delusion till they have found themselves in the depths of hell.

6. There may be much legal reformation without any true religion.

7. A legal reformation, however, may generally 'e distinguished by some of the following marks:

(1) It may be only partial, that is, extend to certain forms of sin, while others are indulged.

(2) It may and almost certainly will be temporary.

(3) In a legal experience, it will also generally be manifest that some forms of sinful indulgence are practiced and defended as not being sin. And where there has not been a powerful conviction that has deterred the soul from indulgence, selfishness and lust are still tolerated.

A *gospel* or *gracious* experience will manifest itself in a *universal* hatred of sin and lust, *in every form*. And, as I have said, sin will have no place, except in cases of such powerful temptation as to carry the will for the time by the force of excited feelings, when a reaction will immediately take place and the soul be prostrate in the depths of repentance.

8. By reference to this test and the principles here inculcated, not only may the genuineness of each pretended conversion be decided, but also the genuineness or spuriousness of religious excitements. That is not a revival of true religion, but falls entirely short of it, that does not produce universal reformation of habits in the subjects of it. There is many a revival of conviction, and convictions are often deep and very general in a community where, for want of sufficient discriminating instruction, there are very few conversions.

9. You see the mistake of those sinners who fear to embrace religion lest they should disgrace it by living in sin, as they see many professing Christians now do.

Sinner, you need not stand back on this account. Only come out from under the law and be truly converted, submit yourself to the power and influence of sovereign grace, and no form of sin shall have dominion over you, as God is true.

10. This text is a great encouragement to real Christians. They often tremble when they have once fallen under the power of temptation. They greatly fear that sin will gain an entire ascendancy over them. Christian, lift up your head and proclaim yourself free. The God of truth has declared that you are not and shall not be a slave to sin.

11. This is a proper promise, and an important one, for Christians to plead in prayer. It is like a sheet anchor in a storm. If temptations beat like a tempest upon the soul, let the Christian hold onto this promise with all his heart. Let him cry out, O Lord, perform the good word of Thy grace unto Thy servant, wherein Thou hast caused me to hope that sin shall not have dominion over me, because I am not under law but under grace.

12. Let those who are under the law—over whom sin, in any form, has dominion—remember that under the law there is no salvation; that "whatever things the law saith, it saith to them that are under the law"; and that "cursed is every one that continueth not in all things written in the book of the law to do them."

LECTURE 10

Carefulness a Sin

Phil. 4:6: "Be careful for nothing."

In this discussion, I design to show:

I. What carefulness, as used in this text is.
II. That this state of mind is sin.
III. How to avoid it.

I. *I am to show the meaning of the word carefulness.*

The terms care and carefulness are used in two different senses in the Bible—one good, the other bad. The one kind of care is virtue, the other kind is vice. I will quote a few passages to illustrate both these senses. In some of the passages, the words care and carefulness are not used in the translation; but in every instance the same word is used in the original that in the text is translated careful. In 1 Cor. 12:25, the Apostle says "the members should have the same care one for another." In Phil. 2:20, ne also says, "For I have no man like minded, who will naturally care for your estate." In 1 Pet. 5:7, care is spoken of as being exercised by God.

It is manifest that the state of mind described in these passages is a virtuous state; it is that degree of wakeful desire and solicitude for our own or the happiness of others that begets due attention and produces that prompt and diligent use of means necessary to obtain a desirable end. This state of mind does not imply doubt, distress, corroding anxious suspense, and concern. This kind of care, however, may be very intense, and in its degree amount to real travail of soul and even to those "groanings which cannot be uttered," and yet be a virtuous and highly commendable state of mind. For this, instead of being the peevishness of unbelief and the corroding anxiety and carefulness which are the result of unbelief, is faith mightily wrestling with God for promised blessings.

But in the following passages we have the term used in a different sense: Matt. 6:25, "Therefore I say unto you, Take no thought for your life, what ye shall eat, or what ye shall drink; nor yet for your body, what ye shall put on." And in the 27th verse, "Which of you by taking thought can add one cubit unto his stature?" And verse 28, "Why take ye thought for raiment?" &c. And verse 31, "Therefore take no thought, saying, What shall we eat? or, What shall we drink? or, Wherewithal shall we be clothed?" Luke 10:41, Christ says, "Martha, Martha, thou art careful and troubled about many things." 1 Cor. 7:32-34, "But I would have you without carefulness. He that is unmarried careth for the things that belong to the Lord, how he may please the Lord; but he that is married careth for the things that are of the world, how he may please his wife. There is a difference also between a

126

wife and a virgin. The unmarried woman careth for the things of the Lord, that she may be holy both in body and in spirit; but she that is married careth for the things of the world, how she may please her husband." And in the text, the Apostle says, "Be careful for nothing."

Now it is manifest from these passages, in which the same original word is used as in the text, that the term is used in a bad sense. It implies doubtfulness, anxiety, absorbing and anxious concern, and unhappiness. This state of mind is but too common and needs very little description to be understood by almost everyone.

II. *I am to show that this kind of carefulness is sin.*

1. It is sin *because it is expressly forbidden by God himself.* Not only does the text forbid it, but it is expressly or impliedly forbidden in all the texts I have quoted, where it is used in a bad sense. It is, therefore, as much a violation of the law of God as profanity, drunkenness or any other abomination. It is as expressly forbidden and as diametrically opposed to the command of God as a lustful, covetous, thievish or licentious state of mind.

2. Because it is *distrust of the wisdom and benevolence of God.* Who that believes in a divine providence can suffer himself to be exercised with carefulness, without directly impeaching or denying the wisdom and benevolence of the blessed God. If God exercises a universal providence, then whatever comes to pass is in some way, directly or indirectly, brought about by the providence of God. To suffer ourselves then to be made unhappy—to be filled with anxiety, solicitude and suspense—is either to deny that God is wise and good in bringing about these events or is a virtual declaration on our part that, however wise and good He may have been in producing them, we are very far from being pleased with His providence. So that carefulness is either infidelity in regard to the providences of God or downright rebellion against Him.

3. Because it is *setting aside all the evidence which God has given that He cares for us.* He has given us the most ample assurances—by His providences, in His Word, and by giving His only begotten Son to die for us—that He cares for us and all our interests with all the tender solicitude of an infinitely benevolent Father; and yet we set aside all His declarations and all these evidences and refuse to cast our care upon Him. We suffer our minds to be corroded and borne down, and banished out of the presence of God, by carefulness.

4. Because *it can do no good.* It is a waste and worse than a waste of time and energy and life. Who among you ever found yourselves benefited in any respect by this kind of carefulness? Does your worldly business prosper any better for indulging this state of mind—do you pay your debts or manage any part of your business any better by suffering your mind to be borne down with care? Do you get along any better in religion? Are your prayers any more prevalent—do you use any better directed and successful means for your own or the spiritual improvement of others when oppressed with carefulness? And let me ask, can you in any instance recollect that

this kind of carefulness ever resulted in any good?

5. Because *it is highly injurious to yourself.* I beseech you to reflect upon your past history. Have you not found, in multitudes of instances, that this kind of carefulness was a real obstruction to your worldly business? And have you not found that the more you indulged this state of mind, the more embarrassed and perplexed your secular affairs became? And no wonder, for in this state you are in some sense a maniac and not qualified to manage business of any kind. How many persons there are who, instead of keeping calm and preserving a state of mind in which they can act with discretion and wisdom, will become so filled with carefulness as to incapacitate themselves for superintending their affairs with discretion; and they wonder that, after all their attention and carefulness and anxiety, they do not succeed any better. They seem to think that the providence of God is wholly adverse and is designed to perplex them, while in reality nothing uncommon has happened in the providence of God; and their foolish and wicked carefulness is that to which they may ascribe their failure.

It is just so in matters of religion. Multitudes suffer themselves in the peevishness of their unbelief to be so distracted and confounded with carefulness about their spiritual state or the spiritual state of those around them that they are forever whining, complaining, and murmuring—as if it were the most difficult matter in the world to persuade God to be good and kind and gracious. They seem to act as if it were as difficult a matter to get hold of the grace of God as to be saved by the law. And not withstanding all the declarations in regard to the freeness of gospel salvation, it would seem as if they supposed the wells of salvation were infinitely deep and their waters infinitely beyond their reach, and the promises of eternal life were infinitely high above their heads. Indeed, they are in that state of mind that from its own nature excludes the grace of the gospel and sets aside all the promises of God.

Now let me ask, did you ever find that this kind of carefulness has resulted in anything else than evil to your own souls? Why then indulge in it? Persons in this state are very apt to think their circumstances and condition deserve commiseration. They look around for sympathy and pity, and often secretly blame God for not pitying them when they have so carefully sought Him. Now this is a state of horrible rebellion against God. Here is an ocean of the waters of eternal life flowing at your feet; here is a table spread before you with infinite provisions for your souls and as free as the heart of God; and yet you stand and distress yourself and complain and are filled with vast cares and anxieties, lest you should lose your soul—starving, thirsting, dying with these provisions and waters of eternal life before you. Precious soul, lay aside your carefulness, I beseech you, and believe, or you must perish.

6. Because your carefulness *is a great stumbling block and injury to those around you.* Are they professors of religion—they are emboldened to exercise this same temper because they see it in you. Are they impenitent sinners—they wonder what religion is good for. They see you fretted with the same cares and anxieties that others are who have no hope in Christ.

What inference can they draw from witnessing your state, only that religion is a name that has no consolation or salvation in it.

7. Because *it grieves the Spirit of God*. What would a husband say should he observe that his wife had no confidence in his providence, and was perpetually exercised with great carefulness lest he should not fulfill to her the duties implied in his relation to her? And suppose that your children should groan about the house under the distressing apprehension that their wants would be overlooked. Would not husbands and parents feel themselves grieved and insulted by such a course? How, then, must this shameful carefulness appear to the Spirit of the blessed God? He is your comforter, but you refuse to be comforted; He cares for you, but you refuse to cast your care upon Him and insist upon bearing your own burdens. Do not, I beseech you, thus grieve the Holy Spirit of God, "whereby ye are sealed unto the day of redemption."

8. Because *it is as highly dishonorable to God as it is grievous to the Holy Ghost*. What can be more dishonorable to the father of a family than for its members to be filled with carefulness through distrust of His providence. And how does it gratify hell to see the children of God weighed down with carefulness, as if their heavenly Father were unable or unwilling to provide for them.

9. Because it is *selfishness*. Persons are never filled with carefulness unless they have some selfish interest in that which excites their care. You see the most diligent and efficient clerks and those employed in other people's business; and while they have a sufficient solicitude to be prompt and energetic in the business of their employers, yet they are not filled with care about it. When they have performed their duty they can eat and sleep calmly, and quiet themselves without corroding carefulness with regard to the results of their business.

Just so with the servants of God, if their hearts are right. They perform everything for Him and consider nothing as their own business, are prompt and energetic in the discharge of their duties, and calmly and quietly leave all the results to the disposal of His providence. It is just so with them on all religious subjects. They know that themselves and all they have are His, for time and eternity. And they can as cheerfully submit their spiritual as their temporal interests to His disposal without carefulness, "always rejoicing in the Lord."

III. *I am to show how to avoid carefulness.*

1. *Consider the reasons against it.* Many persons are so inconsiderate as never to avoid any sin of heart or life to which they are strongly tempted. But without consideration it is not to be expected that sin of any kind will be avoided. Consideration might and doubtless would have prevented the sin of our first parents. And it is not probable that any being does or would sin with all the considerations against sin fully before and subject to the attention of the mind. Let a mind fully consider the moral character of this state and all the reasons against it, even should it go no further than I have

described in this discourse—that it is forbidden of God, that it is infidelity, that it is rebellion, that it is setting aside all the evidences of God's love, that it can never benefit you nor anyone else, that it destroys your own happiness and the happiness of those with whom you are connected, that it is a stumbling block to the church and an occasion of blasphemy to the world, that it grieves and dishonors the blessed God and is one of the most loathsome and detestable forms of selfishness—let the mind, I say, consider these things and it would put away this sin from the heart.

2. *Consider the reasons for an opposite state of mind*—that you may and ought to be in a state of cheerful serenity and calmness and peace; that God's providences and promises and grace are such a sure foundation and afford such infinite reasons for repose in God that calmness, quietude, a deep unbroken repose in God, is the most reasonable state of mind that can be conceived. Consider that God requires you always to rejoice in Him and has made such infinite provisions for your help, consolation and eternal salvation and to meet the necessities of the church and the world, that there is no room left for carefulness, except it exists in the form of downright rebellion against God.

3. *Cultivate a considerate state of mind.* Let no temptation to carefulness prevail without taking time to consider the reasons against it and for an opposite state of mind.

4. *Put away selfishness.* If selfishness is suffered to reign, carefulness will be a thing of course. Examine yourself, therefore, attentively, and exclude selfishness under every form. You may find sometimes that to decide what is and what is not selfishness will require considerable thought and attention. Your neighbor may make a selfish demand of you or selfishly ask you for a favor that it may not be your duty to grant, and yet he may attribute your refusal to selfishness.

In all such cases you are to weigh the matter well, and decide in the presence of God whether the law of love requires you to act in one way or in the other. Persons are very apt in this matter to fall into a mistake and to suppose themselves to be doing as they would be done by, and to censure others for not doing as they desire, because they are unacquainted with the circumstances. For example, I ask a favor of a man which perhaps I have no right to ask. I think that in asking it I am doing what, under the circumstances, I should be willing to grant myself; and yet were I to know all the circumstances, I should perceive that I had no right to make the request and should heartily approve of his refusal to comply. In a world where there is so much selfishness, a truly benevolent mind needs to be wide awake to avoid, on the one hand, the appearance of selfishness (which will, after all, in some cases be impossible) and on the other hand, to avoid being devoured by the selfishness of others.

But whenever selfishness does exist, it must be sought out, it must be put away; and wherever this kind of carefulness exists there is selfishness. Of this you may be certain. Search, then, for this leaven of wickedness. Bring it forth to the light, and go and cast it into the valley of the son of Hinnom, among the abominations that defile that image of hell.

5. *Put away unbelief.* Unbelief is always the cause of all this kind of carefulness. This may easily be seen by a moment's reflection. Confidence in God would instantly banish all this distrustful carefulness from the mind.

6. *Dwell much upon grace received.* Cultivate a spirit of thankfulness. Instead of reflecting much upon what they have received of temporal and spiritual mercies, many persons reflect much upon the things which they yet need. Being taken up with their wants instead of their mercies, they naturally fall into a state of repining. Now it is of great importance that you should dwell much upon your temporal and spiritual good things, and spend much time in blessing and thanking God for existence, life, health, sickness, poverty, or wealth or whatever His providence has allotted you; that you were born in this age in this land under such circumstances. In short, you ought to realize that God is equally good in everything, and that all things are subjects of thankfulness and praise to God. Go over, then, and over again, often and often, your mercies; and cultivate such a spirit of gratitude and thankfulness as shall naturally beget a spirit of trust in God for future blessings.

7. *Reflect much upon the fact that God has always been better to you than your fears*—how your former anxieties and fears proved in the end to have been all uncalled for. In how many instances can you look back upon your former carefulness and say, "How have I been disquieted in vain?"

8. *Commit everything to God in prayer,* and know assuredly that the result will be just what you would wish it to be, when you know all the circumstances and reasons. The Apostle says in the verse of which the text is a part, "In every thing by prayer and supplication, with thanksgiving, let your requests be made known unto God." Now many persons, instead of carrying anything that lies upon their minds to God and committing it all to Him, undertake to bear their own burdens—to work it out by their own thoughts and exertions, without committing their way unto the Lord with the assurance that He will bring it to pass. Nothing should be undertaken without prayer; and anything and everything that cannot consistently be made a subject of prayer is to be avoided of course, as you would avoid the devil. Now observe what I say. I do not advise you *merely* to pray about everything, but to commit your way in all respects unto the Lord, so to give up your affairs to His guidance and control as to render all this carefulness impossible; so commit them to Him as to leave the event cheerfully with Him, and make up your mind to be satisfied with the result, be it what it may. Be solicitous to do your duty, leaving consequences most cheerfully and joyfully with Him who careth for you.

9. *Trust in Christ for grace in this thing.* Do not suppose that by any unaided efforts of your own you are to avoid carefulness. Selfishness is one of your most powerful enemies, and you may as well attempt to grapple with Satan in your own strength as to put down selfishness without the aid of Christ. Remember that He is your life, your strength, your righteousness, your salvation and redemption—not only from the curse of the law, but from every form of sin. Cleave to Him, and whenever you find yourself

tempted to carefulness, be sure to lay all your cares upon Him. He is able and desirous to bear all your burdens.

10. *Be sure to give up your own will.* While you have a will of your own, separate from that of God, you will of course be often filled with care, lest you should be disappointed. Lay aside your own will and make up your mind to be joyful always in the will of God.

11. *Cultivate a calm and quiet state of mind.* If temptation assail you to ruffle and disturb the deep repose of your soul in God, be quiet, keep calm, lift up your heart to God, keep still, and if possible suffer yourself not to speak until your mind becomes composed. Let it be the fixed purpose of your heart not to suffer yourself to be thrown into a state of carefulness and anxiety on any occasion whatever.

REMARKS

1. This requirement extends to everything, temporal and spiritual. Many persons think themselves to do well in being perpetually filled with great carefulness about their spiritual concerns. But this spirit is just as inadmissible and wicked in spiritual as in temporal things. It is God-provoking and dishonoring unbelief on whatever subject it is exercised.

2. How seldom is this state of mind looked upon as a sin, even by the Christian himself. Many persons claim and receive as much sympathy in this state as if it were a dire calamity instead of a sin. Nay, they make it a matter of self-righteousness, and pride themselves in their great anxiety and trouble about spiritual things. To "rejoice in the Lord" is wholly out of the question with them. They lament over themselves, and are mourned over by others, as if they deserved infinite pity rather than to be blamed for their unbelief.

Now, beloved, you ought to know that your carefulness is sin, and nothing but sin—that it no more calls for commiseration, sympathy or pity than the crime of adultery or drunkenness or any abomination whatever. It is unbelief. Away with it. It is the enemy of God.

3. This carefulness is as ridiculous as it is wicked. What would you say, should you see the children of a great and mighty prince filled with carefulness and anxiety about their daily food, when millions were at their disposal? You could account for it only upon the principle that they were monomaniacs. But what shall we say of the children of the King of kings and Lord of lords, whose Father is not a mere temporal prince but possesses all the attributes of God, everywhere present with them, ever wakeful to their interests; whose infinite resources, moral and physical, are at their disposal; and yet they are weighed down with care. What is the matter with you, my dear soul? Are you deranged? What do you mean? What ails you? Surely you dream and disquiet yourself in vain.

> Isa. 40:28-31: Hast thou not known? hast thou not heard, that the everlasting God, the Lord, the Creator of the ends of the earth, fainteth not, neither is weary? there is no searching of his understanding. He giveth power to the faint; and to them that have no might he increaseth strength. Even the

youths shall faint and be weary, and the young men shall utterly fall: but they that wait upon the Lord shall renew their strength; they shall mount up with wings as eagles; they shall run, and not be weary; and they shall walk, and not faint.

4. How destructive to your peace and growth in grace is the indulgence of this spirit.

5. What advantage it gives Satan. It is just cutting yourself loose from your moorings upon the promises of God and giving yourself up to the merciless buffetings of the prince of hell.

6. It is our duty freely and frequently to admonish one another upon this point. There is a great fault among Christians in this respect. Whenever care is depicted upon a brother's or sister's countenance, inquiry should instantly be made into the cause. They should be reproved for the sin, and admonished and entreated to desist from it immediately. They should be conjured by every consideration that is lovely and of good report to entertain no carefulness for a moment.

7. From this subject, it is easy to see how important it is for husbands and wives and those associated in the more intimate relations of life to bear each other's burdens, and as far as possible to diminish the amount of temptations to carefulness.

8. It is very important to resist the beginnings of this sin. Many Christians and, I have reason to believe, some ministers have fallen into great trouble by not resisting the beginnings of this "evil and bitter thing." They have begun perhaps by indulging carefulness about temporal things and, having by this grieved the Spirit, they are plunged into darkness in regard to their spiritual state. And as you pass by you may hear their groanings; but there is no relief, because they will not "encourage themselves in God."

9. This truth is very applicable and very important to indigent students, who are often so straitened in their temporal circumstances as to indulge a degree of carefulness that is very destructive, both to intellectual attainments and to growth in grace. Such persons should remember that their carefulness will in no instance help them. But if they indulge it, it will defeat the very ends of their education. Who can study? Who can pray? Who can walk with God in such a state of mind?

10. This requirement is applicable to all persons in all circumstances and at all times.

And now, beloved, will you put this sin away? Shall it be from this moment the fixed purpose of your hearts, in the strength of God to overcome it forever? Will you confess it and repent of it as a sin before God? Will you be as much ashamed of it as you would be of committing adultery, of being guilty of theft? Will you consider it as really disgraceful, in the sight of God, and as injurious to the interests of His kingdom as other sins and abominations are? Do, I beseech you, spread this whole subject, in tears of deep repentance, before the Lord. Put it away from you forever. Let the deep repose and patience and gratitude of your soul shed a balmy and a holy influence on all around you.

LECTURE 11

The Promises, No. 1

2 Pet. 1:4: "Whereby are given unto us exceeding great and precious promises, that by these ye might be partakers of the divine nature, having escaped the corruption that is in the world through lust."

I. I shall preface what I have to say upon this subject with several preliminary remarks with regard to the promises of the Scripture.

II. Show the design of the promises.

III. Show that they are adequate to that for which they are designed.

IV. Show why they are not fulfilled in us.

I. *I am to make several preliminary remarks upon the nature of the promises.*

1. The promises made to the church under the old dispensation belong emphatically to the Christian church. Thus the promise made to Abraham was designed more for his posterity and for the Christian church than for himself. That part of the promise which related to the temporal possession of Canaan never was fulfilled to him. He lived and died "a stranger and sojourner in the land of promise." In Heb. 11:13 we are expressly informed that Abraham did not receive the fulfillment of the promises but that they belonged especially to Christians under the New Testament dispensation. "These all died in faith not having received the promises but having seen them afar off, and were persuaded of them and embraced them, and confessed that they were strangers and pilgrims on the earth"; that is, Abraham and the patriarchs died without receiving the fulfillment of the promises. Again, verses 39-40, "And these all, having obtained a good report through faith, received not the promises, God having provided some better thing for us, that they without us should not be made perfect." So the New Covenant in Jer. 31:31-34:

> Behold, the days come, saith the Lord, that I will make a new covenant with the house of Israel, and with the house of Judah. Not according to the covenant that I made with their fathers in the day that I took them by the hand to bring them out of the land of Egypt; which my covenant they brake, although I was an husband unto them, saith the Lord; but this shall be the covenant that I will make with the house of Israel; After those days, saith the Lord, I will put my law in their inward parts, and write it in their hearts; and will be their God, and they shall be my people. And they shall

teach no more every man his neighbour, and every man his brother, saying, Know the Lord: for they shall all know me, from the least of them to the greatest of them, saith the Lord: for I will forgive their iniquity, and I will remember their sin no more.

Also Jer. 32:39-40: "And I will give them one heart, and one way, that they may fear me for ever, for the good of them, and of their children after them: and I will make an everlasting covenant with them, that I will not turn away from them, to do them good; but I will put my fear in their hearts, that they shall not depart from me." Also Ezek. 36:25-27: "Then will I sprinkle clean water upon you, and ye shall be clean: from all your filthiness, and from all your idols, will I cleanse you. A new heart also will I give you, and a new spirit will I put within you: and I will take away the stony heart out of your flesh, and I will give you an heart of flesh. And I will put my Spirit within you, and cause you to walk in my statutes, and ye shall keep my judgments, and do them."

And numerous other kindred promises made to the church under the Old Testament dispensation belong particularly to the church under the Christian dispensation. Consequently the Apostle in Heb. 8:8-12 maintains that the covenant in Jer. 31:31-32 respects particularly the gospel dispensation.

Behold, the days come, saith the Lord, when I will make a new covenant with the house of Israel and with the house of Judah: not according to the covenant that I made with their fathers in the day when I took them by the hand to lead them out of the land of Egypt; because they continued not in my covenant, and I regarded them not, saith the Lord. For this is the covenant that I will make with the house of Israel after those days, saith the Lord; I will put my laws into their mind, and write them in their hearts: and I will be to them a God, and they shall be to me a people: and they shall not teach every man his neighbour, and every man his brother, saying, Know the Lord; for all shall know me, from the least to the greatest. For I will be merciful to their unrighteousness, and their sins and their iniquities will I remember no more.

2. The promises made to the church as a *body* belong to *individuals* of the church. The church is composed of individuals, and the promises are of no avail any further than there is an individual application of them.

3. Promises made to the patriarchs and individuals, under the Old Testament dispensation as well as under the new, belong to all individuals in every age and land, under similar circumstances. Thus we find the inspired writers recognizing the principle, everywhere in their writings, in the use they make of the promises. As an illustration see Heb. 13:5, "I will never leave thee, nor forsake thee." If you turn to Gen. 28:15, you will see that the promise which the Apostle applies to all Christians was originally made to Jacob, on his way to Padan-aram. "And, behold, I am with thee, and will keep thee in all places whither thou goest, and I will bring thee again into this land; for I will not leave thee, until I have done that which I have spoken to thee of." So in Heb. 13:6 the Apostle continues, "The Lord is my helper, and I will not fear what man shall do unto me." This also is quoted from

Ps. 56:4, 11, "In God I have put my trust; I will not fear what man can do unto me."

Let these serve as specimens of the manner in which inspired writers make an application of the promises. In the experience of every Christian, it is manifest that the Spirit of God makes the same application of the promises to their minds. And thus the promises are a kind of common property to the saints. Who has not been edified and refreshed, in reading the biographies of highly spiritual men, by observing the copious use of the promises which the Spirit of God makes in refreshing the souls of the saints?

4. The promises made to Israel and Judah in the Old Testament are promises made to the whole Christian church, both Jews and Gentiles. Thus the church of Christ is called the "Israel of God." And the Apostle expressly affirms that "they are not all Israel which are of Israel." But this fact is abundantly confirmed, that the true Israel of the Scriptures is the true church of God in every age—to whom, collectively and individually, all the promises of the Bible belong.

5. The promises mean all they say; in other words, they are to be interpreted by the same rules by which we interpret the commandments. For example, the promise in Deut. 30:6, "And the Lord thy God will circumcise thine heart and the heart of thy seed, to love the Lord thy God with all thine heart and with all thy soul, that thou mayest live," is to be interpreted by the same rule by which we interpret the commandment, "Thou shalt love the Lord thy God with all thy heart and with all thy soul." So the promise in Ezek. 36:25-26 ("Then will I sprinkle clean water upon you, and ye shall be clean; from all your filthiness, and from all your idols, will I cleanse you. A new heart also will I give you, and a new spirit will I put within you: and I will take away the stony heart out of your flesh, and I will give you an heart of flesh") is to be understood as implying just as much as the commands in Ezek. 18:30-31, "Repent and turn yourselves from all your transgressions, so iniquity shall not be your ruin. Cast away from you all your transgressions, and make you a new heart and a new spirit." So also the promise, "I will put my Spirit within you and cause you to walk in my statutes, and ye shall keep my judgments and do them," is to be construed as meaning just as much as the commands "walk in my statutes" and "keep my commandments" mean.

6. We never keep the commandments, only as we take hold of the promises. By this I mean that grace alone enables us from the heart to obey the commandments of God. It is therefore only when we lay hold of the promise by faith and receive its fulfillment in ourselves that we really, in heart, obey the commandments of God. For example, we never love the Lord our God according to the first great commandment, only as we lay hold on and receive the fulfillment of some such promise as this: "I will circumcise thine heart and the heart of thy seed, to love the Lord thy God with all thy heart and with all thy soul, that thou mayest live."

7. The promises are held out to all who will believe them.

8. The promise of spiritual blessings cannot be fulfilled to us without

the exercise of faith on our part. This is naturally impossible.

9. The promises cannot be believed unless they are known to exist. This is self-evident.

10. They cannot be believed unless their application is understood.

11. Promises of particular blessings cannot be believed without a general confidence in the character and truth of God. Our confidence in any specific promise of any being must depend upon our confidence in His truth, willingness and ability. Thus if a man come to God to plead any promise, it is indispensable in the outset for him to believe that "God is and that he is a rewarder of those that diligently seek him."

12. There are promises in the Bible of all kinds of blessings, suited to all our wants and circumstances, temporal and spiritual.

13. There are promises suited to all classes and conditions of men.

14. There are promises suited to all possible states of mind.

Upon these last thoughts I shall have occasion to enlarge under another head.

15. Some of the promises are without any *condition,* expressed or implied. The fulfillment of these does not depend in any degree upon our own agency. The covenant made with Noah is an example of this kind. "While the earth remaineth, seed time and harvest, cold and heat, summer and winter, and day and night shall not cease."

16. There is, however, almost always some condition at least *implied* in every promise—a condition which, though not expressed, arises out of the nature of the case. For example, should I promise to pay a sum of money for value received, here, although no condition is expressed, yet it is plain that the individual must consent to receive it. So if a testator leave a legacy to an heir, the *terms* of the bequest may be absolute and without condition, yet it is always *implied* that the heir believe that a bequest was made and take the necessary steps to enter into the possession. So with the promises of God. Many of them appear to be absolute because there is no *expressed* condition. But a condition is *implied,* namely, that we believe the promise and are willing to receive the proffered blessing.

17. Multitudes of the promises of God are made upon *expressed* conditions. Thus the promises in Ezek. 36:25-27 ("Then will I sprinkle clean water upon you, and ye shall be clean; from all your filthiness, and from all your idols, will I cleanse you. A new heart also will I give you, and a new spirit will I put within you; and I will take away the stony heart out of your flesh, and I will give you an heart of flesh. And I will put my Spirit within you, and cause you to walk in my statutes, and ye shall keep my judgments, and do them") seem to be expressed in full, without any condition. Yet in the 37th verse this condition is expressed: "I will yet be inquired of by the house of Israel to do it for them, saith the Lord."

So in James 1:5 you find this promise, "If any of you lack wisdom, let him ask of God, that giveth to all men liberally, and upbraideth not; and it shall be given him." It seems to be expressed without condition; but in the sixth verse the condition is expressly annexed, "But let him ask in faith, nothing wavering"; and we are informed that without faith it shall not be fulfilled. In Matt. 7:7 you have another illustration of the same principle: "Ask and it shall be given you, seek and ye shall find, knock and it shall be opened unto you." Here asking (of course in faith) is made the condition of receiving.

18. I have already said that many of the promises are made to particular states of mind, and applicable only to persons in that state, for example:

(1) There are promises made to the impenitent sinner. Isa. 55:7: "Let the wicked forsake his way, and the unrighteous man his thoughts: and let him return unto the Lord, and he will have mercy upon him; and to our God, for he will abundantly pardon." Now the conditions of these promises are that the sinner "forsake his way" and "return unto the Lord." Without the fulfillment of this condition the sinner can never receive the benefit of the promise. In Isa. 1:19 there is a promise to the sinner: "Come now and let us reason together, saith the Lord. Though your sins be as scarlet, they shall be white as snow; though they be red like crimson, they shall be like wool." And in the nineteenth verse the condition is expressed, "if ye be willing and obedient."

(2) Again, there are promises to the backslider, as in Hosea 11:7-9: "And my people are bent to backsliding from me: though they [the prophets]* called them to the most High, none at all would exalt him. How shall I give thee up, Ephraim? How shall I deliver thee, Israel? how shall I make thee as Admah? how shall I set thee as Zeboim? Mine heart is turned within me, my repentings are kindled together. I will not execute the fierceness of mine anger, I will not return to destroy Ephraim; for I am God, and not man; the Holy One in the midst of thee: and I will not enter into the city." And in chapter 14:4-9:

> I will heal their backsliding, I will love them freely; for mine anger is turned away from him. I will be as the dew unto Israel: he shall grow as the lily, and cast forth his roots as Lebanon. His branches shall spread, and his beauty shall be as the olive tree, and his smell as Lebanon. They that dwell under his shadow shall return; they shall revive as the corn, and grow as the vine: the scent thereof shall be as the wine of Lebanon. Ephraim shall say, What have I to do any more with idols? I have heard him, and observed him: I am like a green fir tree. From me is thy fruit found. Who is wise, and he shall understand these things? prudent, and he shall know them? for the ways of the Lord are right, and the just shall walk in them.

Also in Jer. 3:12, 15, 22:

> Return, thou backsliding Israel, saith the Lord; and I will not cause mine anger to fall upon you: for I am merciful, saith the Lord; and I will not keep mine anger forever. Only acknowledge thine iniquity, that thou hast transgressed against the Lord thy God, and hast scattered thy ways to the strangers under every green tree, and ye have not obeyed my voice, saith the Lord. Turn, O backsliding children, saith the Lord; for I am married unto you: and I will take you one of a city, and two of a family, and I will bring you to Zion. And I will give you pastors according to mine heart, which shall

*The brackets and the words they enclose are Finney's.

feed you with knowledge and understanding. . . . Return, ye backsliding children, and I will heal your backslidings.

In both of these passages the conditions lie upon the face of the promises.

(3) Again there are promises especially to weak believers. Isa. 41:10-14:

Fear thou not; for I am with thee: be not dismayed; for I am thy God: I will strengthen thee; yea, I will help thee; yea, I will uphold thee with the right hand of my righteousness. Behold, all they that were incensed against thee shall be ashamed and confounded: they shall be as nothing; and they that strive with thee shall perish. Thou shalt seek them, and shalt not find them, even them that contended with thee: they that war against thee shall be as nothing, and as a thing of nought. For I the Lord thy God will hold thy right hand, saying unto thee, Fear not; I will help thee. Fear not, thou worm Jacob, and ye men of Israel; I will help thee, saith the Lord and thy Redeemer, the Holy One of Israel.

Also Isa. 35:3-10:

Strengthen ye the weak hands, and confirm the feeble knees. Say to them that are of a fearful heart, Be strong, fear not: behold, your God will come with vengeance, even God with a recompense; he will come and save you. Then the eyes of the blind shall be opened, and the ears of the deaf shall be unstopped. Then shall the lame man leap as an hart, and the tongue of the dumb sing: for in the wilderness shall waters break out, and streams in the desert. . . . And an highway shall be there, and a way, and it shall be called The way of holiness; the unclean shall not pass over it; but it shall be for those: the wayfaring men, though fools, shall not err therein. No lion shall be there, nor any ravenous beast shall go up thereon, it shall not be found there; but the redeemed shall walk there. And the ransomed of the Lord shall return and come to Zion with songs and everlasting joy upon their heads: they shall obtain joy and gladness and sorrow and sighing shall flee away.

Also Isa. 40:29-31: "He giveth power to the faint; and to them that have no might he increaseth strength. Even the youths shall faint and be weary, and the young men shall utterly fall: but they that wait upon the Lord shall renew their strength; they shall mount up with wings as eagles; they shall run, and not be weary; and they shall walk, and not faint."

(4) Again there are promises to those who are spiritually blind, and in darkness. Isa. 42:7: "To open the blind eyes, to bring out the prisoners from the prison, and them that sit in darkness out of the prison house." Also verse 16: "I will bring the blind by a way that they knew not; I will lead them in paths that they have not known: I will make darkness light before them, and crooked things straight. These things will I do unto them, and not forsake them."

(5) Again there are promises to those that are tempted. 1 Cor. 10:13: "God is faithful, who will not suffer you to be tempted above that ye are able; but will with the temptation also make a way to escape, that ye may be able to bear it." 2 Pet. 2:9: "The Lord knoweth how to deliver the godly out of temptation, and to reserve the unjust unto the day of judgment to be punished." Ps. 34:17-19: "The righteous cry, and the Lord heareth and

delivereth them out of all their troubles. The Lord is nigh unto them that are of a broken heart, and saveth such as be of a contrite spirit. Many are the afflictions of the righteous, but the Lord delivereth him out of them all."

(6) Again there are promises to those who are struggling to overcome sin and are weighed down with a sense of guilt. Matt. 11:28-29: "Come unto me, all ye that labour and are heavy laden, and I will give you rest. Take my yoke upon you, and learn of me; for I am meek and lowly in heart: and ye shall find rest unto your souls."

(7) There are promises to those who are seeking for sanctification. Matt. 5:6: "Blessed are they who do hunger and thirst after righteousness, for they shall be filled." Isa. 55:1-3:

> Ho, every one that thirsteth, come ye to the waters, and he that hath no money and without price. Wherefore do ye spend money for that which is not bread? and your labour for that which satisfieth not? hearken diligently unto me, and eat ye that which is good, and let your soul delight itself in fatness. Incline your ear, and come unto me: hear, and your soul shall live; and I will make an everlasting covenant with you, even the sure mercies of David.

1 Thess. 5:23-24: "And the very God of peace sanctify you wholly; and I pray God your whole spirit and soul and body be preserved blameless unto the coming of our Lord Jesus Christ. Faithful is he that calleth you, who also will do it." See also Jer. 31:31-34:

> Behold, the days come, saith the Lord, that I will make a new covenant with the house of Israel, and with the house of Judah: not according to the covenant that I made with their fathers in the day that I took them by the hand to bring them out of the land of Egypt; which my covenant they brake, although I was an husband unto them, saith the Lord; but this shall be the covenant that I will make with the house of Israel; After those days, saith the Lord, I will put my law in their inward parts, and write it in their hearts; and will be their God, and they shall be my people. And they shall teach no more every man his neighbour, and every man his brother, saying, Know the Lord: for they shall all know me, from the least of them unto the greatest of them, saith the Lord: for I will forgive their iniquity, and I will remember their sin no more.

Also Ezek. 36:25-27: "Then will I sprinkle clean water upon you, and ye shall be clean: from all your filthiness, and from all your idols, will I cleanse you. A new heart also will I give you, and a new spirit will I put within you: and I will take away the stony heart out of your flesh, and I will give you an heart of flesh. And I will put my Spirit within you, and cause you to walk in my statutes; and ye shall keep my judgments, and do them."

(8) There are also promises to those who fear future relapses into sin. Psalm 121 is a specimen of these:

> I will lift up mine eyes to the hills, from whence cometh my help. My help cometh from the Lord, which made heaven and earth. He will not suffer thy foot to be moved: he that keepeth thee will not slumber. Behold, he that

keepeth Israel shall neither slumber nor sleep. The Lord is thy keeper: the Lord is thy shade upon thy right hand. The sun shall not smite thee by day, nor the moon by night. The Lord shall preserve thee from all evil: he shall preserve thy soul. The Lord shall preserve thy going out and thy coming in from this time forth, and even forevermore.

Ps. 37:31: "The law of his God is in his heart; none of his steps shall slide."

(9) Again there are promises to those who are seeking divine influence. Luke 11:11-13: "If a son shall ask bread of any of you that is a father, will he give him a stone? or if he asks a fish, will he for a fish give him a serpent? or if he shall ask an egg, will he offer him a scorpion? If ye then, being evil, know how to give good gifts to your children, how much more shall your heavenly father give the Holy Spirit to them that ask him." Rev. 21:6: "I will give unto him that is athirst of the fountain of the water of life freely." And 22:17: "And the Spirit and the bride say, Come. And let him that heareth say, Come. And let him that is athirst, come. And whosoever will, let him take the water of life freely."

That the water here mentioned is the divine influence is evident from Isa. 12:3: "Therefore with joy shall ye draw water out of the wells of salvation." John 4:10, 14: "Jesus said unto her [the woman of Samaria], If thou knewest the gift of God, and who it is that saith to thee, Give me to drink; thou wouldest have asked of him, and he would have given thee living water. . . . Whosoever drinketh of the water that I shall give him shall never thirst, but the water that I shall give him shall be in him a well of water springing up into everlasting life." Also John 7:37-39: "Jesus stood and cried, saying, If any man thirst, let him come unto me, and drink. He that believeth on me, as the scripture hath said, out of his belly shall flow rivers of living water. (But this spake he of the Spirit, which they that believe on him should receive.)"

(10) There are promises to those who pray for their friends. Luke 11:5-9:

> Which of you shall have a friend, and shall go unto him at midnight, and say unto him, Friend, lend me three loaves; for a friend of mine in his journey is come to me, and I have nothing to set before him? And he from within shall answer and say, Trouble me not; the door is now shut, and my children are with me in bed; I cannot rise and give thee. I say unto you, though he will not rise and give him, because he is his friend, yet because of his importunity he will rise and give him as many as he needeth. And I say unto you, Ask, and it shall be given you; seek, and ye shall find; knock, and it shall be opened unto you.

One thing taught in this passage is that we may come and expect to receive blessings for our friends. So in Matt. 15:22-28:

> And, behold, a woman of Canaan . . . cried unto him saying, Have mercy on me, O Lord, thou Son of David; my daughter is grievously vexed with a devil. But he answered her not a word. And his disciples came and besought him, saying, Send her away; for she crieth after us. But he answered and said, I am not sent but unto the lost sheep of the house of Israel. Then came she and worshipped him, saying, Lord, help me. But he answered and said,

It is not meet to take the children's bread, and to cast it to dogs. And she said, Truth, Lord: yet the dogs eat of the crumbs that fall from their masters' table. Then Jesus answered and said unto her, O woman, great is thy faith: be it unto thee even as thou wilt. And her daughter was made whole from that very hour.

Although in this and the last quoted passage encouragement is held out to perseverance in prayer, yet it is especially taught that perseverance in prayer *for our friends* is indispensable to secure the blessing.

(11) There are promises to those who pray for the church. Every promise in the Bible that relates to its future prosperity is held out to all who will pray for the church.

(12) Again there are promises so general in their nature as to cover all our necessities, temporal and spiritual. Let Mark 11:24 stand as a specimen of this class of promises: "Therefore I say unto you, What things soever ye desire when ye pray, believe that ye receive them, and ye shall have them." Of this class of promises, that cover all our desires, I remark:

(a) That we must desire right things, that is, such things as will glorify God.

(b) It is implied that we desire them for right reasons, that is, that we have a benevolent and not a selfish design in wishing to obtain them.

(c) If these states of mind are implied, it is also of course implied that the suppliant should be under a divine influence in his request, and that his desire should be begotten by the Holy Spirit. None but the highly spiritual will ever rightly understand and apply this class of promises.

(13) There are promises to parents for their children. Isa. 44:3: "I will pour my Spirit upon thy seed, and my blessing upon thine offspring." Now this promise is as express to every Christian parent as it was to any parent that ever belonged to the church of God. The Apostle expressly informs us in Ephesians 2 that the Gentiles are made fellow heirs with the Jews and inheritors of the same promises. So that if this promise could ever have been claimed and appropriated by a Jew, it can be and ought to be so appropriated by every Gentile.

(14) Promises are made to persons under all kinds of trials and afflictions. These promises are so numerous that I need not quote any of them.

(15) Again there are promises to widows and to the fatherless. Ps. 68:5: "A father of the fatherless, and a judge of the widows, is God in his holy habitation." Jer. 49:11: "Leave thy fatherless children, I will preserve them alive; and let thy widows trust in me." Hosea 14:3: "In thee the fatherless shall find mercy." This class of promises is also numerous.

(16) Again there are promises to persons in all the stations and relations of life. Let these suffice as specimens of the vast multitudes of promises in their application to all classes of persons. You who read your Bibles know that I have quoted only a few under each head of the great multitude of promises that are made to each of these particular classes, and that I might easily continue to an indefinite extent the quotation of promises to all conditions of persons, in all the stations and relations of life.

I must defer the remaining heads of this discourse till my next lecture.

LECTURE 12

The Promises, No. 2

2 Pet. 1:4: "Whereby are given unto us exceeding great and precious prom- ises, that by these ye might be partakers of the divine nature, having escaped the corruption that is in the world through lust."

In continuing this subject I am to show:

II. *The design of the promises.*

The design of the promises, as stated in the text, is to make us partakers of the divine nature. I will state what I do not and what I do understand by being made partakers of the divine nature.

1. I do not understand that we are to be made partakers of the spiritual essence or natural attributes of God.

(1) For this would destroy our personal identity.

(2) It is naturally impossible, as it would be in effect making us divine beings.

(3) There is no such change promised in the Bible.

(4) Such a change would not be a moral but a physical change.

(5) The promises have no tendency to change our constitution—to de- stroy our personal identity and make our spiritual existence identical with that of God.

I do understand our being made partakers of the divine nature to mean,

1. That we are to be made partakers of the moral nature or attributes and perfections of God. By this I mean that the moral perfections of God cause the like moral perfections in us, so that the same exercises in kind that are in the divine mind are, by the Spirit, through the promises, begot- ten in our minds. In other words, that the exhibition of the moral character, nature and attributes of God, as exhibited by the Spirit, transforms us into the same image. Thus the Apostle expresses it in 2 Cor. 3:18: "We all, with open face beholding as in a glass the glory of the Lord, are changed into the same image from glory to glory, even as by the Spirit of the Lord." The Bible everywhere abounds with declarations and representations to this effect. It represents us as participating deeply, in His exercises, both of holiness and of happiness. I will quote a few of the many passages that might be given to sustain this position.

(1) We are called partakers of His *holiness*. Heb. 12:10: "For they verily for a few days chastened us after their own pleasure, but he for our profit,

that we might be partakers of his HOLINESS."

(2) We are made partakers of His *love*. Rom. 5:53: "And hope maketh not ashamed, because the LOVE of God is shed abroad in our hearts by the Holy Ghost which is given unto us."

(3) We are called partakers of His *fullness*. John 1:16: "And of his FULNESS have all we received, and grace for grace." By this I understand that the graces in Christians are answerable to the graces in Jesus Christ, that is, that the Christian graces are the same in kind that existed in the Son of God.

(4) We are partakers of His *joy*. Matt. 25:21: "Enter thou into the JOY of thy Lord." John 15:11: "These things have I spoken unto you, that my JOY might remain in you, and that your joy might be full." John 17:13: "And these things I speak in the world, that they might have my JOY fulfilled in themselves."

(5) We are made partakers of His *rest*. Ps. 95:11: "Unto whom I sware in my wrath, that they should not enter into my REST." Ps. 116:7: "Return unto thy REST, O my soul." Matt. 11:28-29: "Come unto me, all ye that labour and are heavy laden, and I will give you REST. Take my yoke upon you, and learn of me; for I am meek and lowly in heart: and ye shall find REST unto your soul." Heb. 3:11: "So I sware in my wrath, They shall not enter into my REST." Heb. 4:1, 3, 9, 11: "Let us therefore fear, lest, a promise being left us of entering into his REST, any of you should seem to come short of it. For we which have believed do enter into REST. There remaineth therefore a REST for the people of God. Let us labour therefore to enter into that REST."

(6) We are made partakers of His *peace*. John 14:27: "PEACE I leave with you, my PEACE I give unto you." John 14:33: "These things have I spoken unto you, that in me ye might have PEACE." Phil. 4:7: "And the PEACE of God, which passeth all understanding, shall keep your hearts and minds through Christ Jesus." Col. 3:15: "And let the PEACE OF GOD rule in your hearts, to the which also ye are called in one body."

(7) We are made partakers of His *happiness*. Ps. 36:7-8: "How excellent is thy loving-kindness, O God! therefore the children of men put their trust under the shadow of thy wings. They shall be abundantly satisfied with the fatness of thy house; and thou shalt make them drink of the river of thy PLEASURES." Ps. 16:11: "Thou wilt show me the path of life: in thy presence is fulness of joy: at thy right hand there are PLEASURES FOR EVERMORE."

Let these serve as specimens of the scripture representations on this subject. By a careful examination of the Bible, it will be found that every feature of the moral nature and character of God is begotten in the Christian, by the provisions of the gospel.

2. A state of entire sanctification is also included in the idea of being made partakers of the divine nature. The principal proof of this I shall examine when I come to show, under the next head, that the promises are adequate to that for which they are designed. But here I would suggest the following considerations in support of the position that entire sanctification

is included in being made partakers of the divine nature.

(1) If the saints are ever sanctified, it is plain that it must be done through the influence of the promises, including the whole revealed will of God. That the truth, and especially the truth contained in the promises, is the Spirit's grand and indispensable instrument for the saint's sanctification, no reader of the Bible can deny.

(2) If they are not sanctified in this life, there is no reason from the Bible to believe that they ever will be sanctified. The provisions made for the sanctification of the church, whether adequate or inadequate, are for this life; and I know of no reason to believe that these means will follow them into eternity, to change their characters there.

(3) In Eph. 4:11-13 we have the following declaration: "And he gave some, apostles; and some, prophets; and some, evangelists; and some, pastors and teachers, for the perfecting of the saints, for the work of the ministry, for the edifying of the body of Christ. Till we all come in the unity of the faith, and of the knowledge of the Son of God unto a perfect man, unto the measure of the stature of the fulness of Christ." Now here the perfecting of the saints is said to take place under this ministry; and these are the means by which this work is actually accomplished, until they come "unto a PERFECT man, unto the measure of the stature of the fulness of Christ." Where is this ministry to be exercised? This work is to be completed in the same world in which the ministry is exercised—the ministry of the apostles, prophets, evangelists, pastors and teachers.

(4) If the gospel has not provided for the entire and permanent sanctification of the saints, then no such provision is made anywhere that we know of.

(5) But if the gospel *has made* such provision, then sanctification must take place in this life; for it is in this life that the *gospel* must do its work.

(6) I recently saw a letter which had a remark to this effect, "that she [the writer] had seen so much of the depravity of her nature that she believed she could not be wholly sanctified, except by the sickle of death." Perhaps the form of expression here is somewhat singular, but the idea is a common one. Many believe that death is to complete the work of sanctification. It has been a common remark that one great reason why we should be willing to die is that by death we shall get rid of sin. Now I would ask, do any of the inspired writers ever urge this as a reason for being willing to die—that by death or at death we shall be rid of sin? "Blessed are the dead who die in the Lord," says John; "yea, saith the Spirit, for they shall rest from their labours, and their works do follow them." Now it is manifest that that from which they rest follows them. Does John here mean to say that men rest from their sins, and that their sins follow them?

I cannot but think that one reason and the prime reason for thinking that death only can terminate our sins is that the bodily appetites are supposed to be in themselves sinful, and that every excitement of men's constitutional propensities is in itself a sin. This opinion would naturally lead to the conclusion that the destruction of the body, and the annihilation of the bodily appetites alone, could free us from sin. I do not suppose that we have any promise in the gospel or any means that can make a physical or *constitutional* change in soul or body. And those who believe that the change required is a *constitutional* one would naturally conclude that death and not the promises is the means of our sanctification.

III. *I am to show that the promises are adequate to the effect ascribed to them.*

It appears to me that the reason why so much doubt is entertained upon the subject of the entire sanctification of the saints in this life is that the grand distinction insisted upon in the Bible between the Old and New Covenants is overlooked; that because saints under the Old Testament were not perfect, it is inferred that they will not be under the New; that inasmuch as the legal dispensation was not able entirely and permanently to sanctify saints, it is inferred that the Gospel dispensation cannot sanctify them, even when administered by the Holy Ghost. If I understand the Bible, the difference between the two dispensations and covenants is exceedingly great; that what was lacking under the Old Covenant is abundantly supplied by the New; that the New Covenant was designed to secure what the Old required, but failed to secure. Because the Old Covenant made nothing perfect, it was therefore set aside and the New introduced, founded upon better promises.

In order to show distinctly the difference between the two covenants, I will lay before you the scripture declarations of the peculiarities of each. By thus contrasting them step by step, you will be able to see whether the promises are adequate to the perfecting of the saints.

I am to show that the first or Old Covenant was the law written on the tables of stone. This was the substance of the covenant, to which was added the Ceremonial Law. Ex. 34:27, 28: "And the Lord said unto Moses, Write thou these words: for after the tenor of these words I have made a covenant with thee and with Israel. And he was there with the Lord forty days and forty nights; he did neither eat bread nor drink water. And he wrote upon the tables the words of the covenant, and the ten commandments." Deut. 9:9-15:

> When I was gone up into the mount to receive the tables of stone, even the tables of the covenant which the Lord made with you, then I abode in the mount forty days and forty nights, I neither did eat bread nor drink water: and the Lord delivered unto me two tables of stone written with the finger of God; and on them was written according to all the words, which the Lord spake with you in the mount out of the midst of the fire in the day of the assembly. And it came to pass at the end of forty days and forty nights, that the Lord gave me the two tables of stone, even the tables of the covenant. And the Lord said unto me, Arise, get thee down quickly from hence; for thy people which thou hast brought forth out of Egypt have corrupted themselves; they are quickly turned aside out of the way which I commanded them; they have made them a molten image. Furthermore the Lord spake unto me, saying, I have seen this people and, behold, it is a stiff-necked people: let me alone, that I may destroy them, and blot out their name from

under heaven: and I will make of thee a nation mightier and greater than they. So I turned and came down from the mount, and the mount burned with fire: and the two tables of the covenant were in my two hands.

Heb. 9:4: "Which had the golden censer, and the ark of the covenant overlaid round about with gold, wherein was the golden pot that had manna, and Aaron's rod that budded, and the tables of the covenant."

These, with many other passages that might be quoted, show what we are to understand by the first or Old Covenant. It should be known that the words covenant and testament mean the same thing, and are only different translations of the same original word.

I will now show what we are to understand by the New Covenant. Jer. 31:31-34:

Behold, the days come, saith the Lord, that I will make a new covenant with the house of Israel, and with the house of Judah: not according to the covenant that I made with their fathers in the day that I took them by the hand to bring them out of the land of Egypt; which my covenant they brake, although I was an husband unto them, saith the Lord: but this shall be the covenant that I will make with the house of Israel; After those days, saith the Lord, I will put my law in their inward parts, and write it in their hearts, and will be their God, and they shall be my people. And they shall teach no more every man his neighbour, and every man his brother, saying, Know the Lord: for they shall all know me, from the least of them unto the greatest of them, saith the Lord: for I will forgive their iniquity, and I will remember their sin no more.

Jer. 32:39-40: "And I will give them one heart, and one way, that they may fear me for ever, for the good of them, and of their children after them: and I will make an everlasting covenant with them, that I will not turn away from them to do them good; but I will put my fear in their hearts, that they shall not depart from me." Heb. 8:8-12:

Behold, the days come, saith the Lord, when I will make a new covenant with the house of Israel and with the house of Judah: not according to the covenant that I made with their fathers in the day when I took them by the hand to lead them out of the land of Egypt; because they continued not in my covenant, and I regarded them not, saith the Lord. For this is the covenant that I will make with the house of Israel after those days, saith the Lord; I will put my laws into their mind, and write them in their hearts, and I will be to them a God, and they shall be to me a people: and they shall not teach every man his neighbour, and every man his brother, saying, Know the Lord: for all shall know me, from the least to the greatest. For I will be merciful to their unrighteousness, and their sins and their iniquities will I remember no more.

Ezek. 36:25-27: "Then will I sprinkle clean water upon you, and ye shall be clean: from all your filthiness, and from all your idols, will I cleanse you. A new heart also will I give you, and a new spirit will I put within you; and I will take away the stony heart out of your flesh, and I will give you an heart of flesh. And I will put my Spirit within you, and cause you to walk in my statutes, and ye shall keep my judgments, and do them." Here, then, we have the two covenants distinctly spread before us.

I will now refer you to those passages which set them in contrast and point out, step by step, wherein they differ, as laid down in the Bible itself.

1. The Old Covenant was mere law, to which was added a typical representation of the gospel. Heb. 10:1: "For the law having a shadow of good things to come, and not the very image of the things, can never with those sacrifices which they offered year by year continually make the comers thereunto perfect."

The second or New Covenant is the writing of this law in the heart.

The first said "thou shalt love the Lord thy God with all thy heart, and with all thy soul, and with all thy mind and strength."

The New, as promised in Jer. 31:31-34, is the fulfillment of what the Old required. . . .*

Here, then, it is plain that the New is the fulfillment, in the heart, of what the Old *required*, and of *all* that the Old required.

2. The Old Covenant required perfect obedience on pain of death. Deut. 27:16: "Cursed be he that confirmeth not all the words of this law to do them. And all the people shall say, Amen." Deut. 28:15: "But it shall come to pass, if thou wilt not hearken unto the voice of the Lord thy God, to observe to do all his commandments and his statutes, which I command thee this day; that all these curses shall come upon thee, and overtake thee." Gal. 3:10: "For as many as are of the works of the law are under the curse; for it is written, Cursed is every one that continueth not in all things which are written in the book of the law to do them."

The New Covenant is the CAUSING God's people to render perfect obedience. Ezek. 36:25-27: "Then will I sprinkle clean water upon you, and ye shall be clean: from all your filthiness, and from all your idols, will I cleanse you. A new heart also will I give you, and a new spirit will I put within you: and I will take away the stony heart out of your flesh, and I will give you an heart of flesh. And I will put my Spirit within you, and cause you to walk in my statutes, and ye shall keep my judgments, and do them." Heb. 8:8-11. . . .**

Jer. 32:39-40: "And I will give them one heart, and one way, that they may fear me for ever for the good of them, and of their children after them: and I will make an everlasting covenant with them, that I will not turn away from them to do them good; but I will put my fear in their hearts, that they shall not depart from me."

Now it should be observed that the New Covenant is not a promise, but it is the thing promised; that is, the promise itself is not the New Covenant, but the state of mind produced by the Spirit of God writing the law in their hearts and CAUSING them "to walk in his statutes and keep his judgments and do them." The "new heart" and the "new spirit"—these are the New Covenant itself; and the promise of this New Covenant is quite another thing. The New Covenant and the promise differ as a promise and its ful-

---

*Finney here quotes again not only this passage, but Heb. 8:8-12.

**Finney repeats the long quotation of this passage.

fillment differ. The New Covenant is a fulfillment of this promise, Jer. 31:31: "Behold, the days come, saith the Lord, that I will make a new covenant with the house of Israel, and with the house of Judah." Here is the promise of a covenant to be made. Now what is the covenant to be made? This is it: "I will put my law in their inward parts, and write it in their hearts; and I will be their God and they shall be my people." It cannot be too distinctly understood that the New Covenant is neither law nor promise, but the very spirit required by the law produced in the heart by the Holy Ghost.

3. The Old Covenant *required* a holy heart. Ezek. 18:31: "Cast away from you all your transgressions, whereby ye have transgressed, and make you a new heart and a new spirit: for why will ye die, O house of Israel?"

The New is the giving of this holy heart. Ezek. 36:26: "A new heart also will I give you, and a new spirit will I put within you: and I will take away the stony heart out of your flesh, and I will give you an heart of flesh." Jer. 31:31-34. . . .*

4. Obedience was enforced under the Old Covenant by penal sanctions. "The soul that sinneth, it shall die." The New is the production of this obedience in the heart by the Spirit of God. Ezek. 36:27: "And I will put my Spirit within you, and cause you to walk in my statutes, and ye shall keep my judgments, and do them." Jer. 31:31-34. . . . and Heb. 8:8-11. . . .**

5. The Old Covenant promised *life* only upon the conditions of perfect and perpetual obedience. Lev. 18:5: "Ye shall therefore keep my statutes and my judgments, which if a man do, he shall even live in them: I am the Lord." Ezek. 20:11, 13, 21: "And I gave them my statutes, and shewed them my judgments, which if a man do, he shall even live in them." "But the house of Israel rebelled against me in the wilderness: they walked not in my statutes, and they despised my judgments, which if a man do, he shall even live in them; and my sabbaths they greatly polluted: then I said, I would pour out my fury upon them in the wilderness, to consume them." "Notwithstanding the children rebelled against me: they walked not in my statutes, neither kept my judgments to do them, which if a man do, he shall even live in them; they polluted my sabbaths: then I said, I would pour out my fury upon them, to accomplish mine anger against them in the wilderness." Luke 10:28: "And he said unto him, Thou hast answered right: this do, and thou shalt live." Rom. 10:5: "For Moses describeth the righteousness which is of the law, that the man which doeth those things shall live by them." Gal. 3:12: "And the law is not of faith: but, the man that doeth them shall live in them."

The New is the producing of this perfect and perpetual obedience. That it is *perfect* see Deut. 30:6: "And the Lord thy God will circumcise thine heart, and the heart of thy seed, to love the Lord thy God with all thine heart, and with all thy soul, that thou mayest live." Ezek. 36:25: "Then will I sprinkle clean water upon you, and ye shall be clean: from all your

---

*Finney again quotes this entire passage.

**He quotes these two long passages again here.

filthiness, and from all your idols, will I cleanse you." Jer. 50:20: "In those days, and in that time, saith the Lord, the iniquity of Israel shall be sought for, and there shall be none: and the sins of Judah, and they shall not be found: for I will pardon them whom I reserve." 1 Thess. 5:23-24: "And the very God of peace sanctify you wholly; and I pray God your whole spirit and soul and body be preserved blameless unto the coming of our Lord Jesus Christ. Faithful is he that calleth you, who also will do it." Jer. 24:7: "And I will give them a heart to know me, that I am the Lord; and they shall be my people, and I will be their God: for they shall return unto me with their whole heart." Jer. 33:8: "And I will cleanse them from all their iniquity, whereby they have sinned against me; and I will pardon all their iniquities, whereby they have sinned, and whereby they have transgressed against me." That it is *perpetual*, see Ezek. 36:27: "And I will put my Spirit within you, and cause you to walk in my statutes, and ye shall keep my judgments, and do them." Jer. 32:39-40: "And I will give them one heart, and one way, that they may fear me for ever, for the good of them, and of their children after them: and I will make an everlasting covenant with them, that I will not turn away from them, to do them good; but I will put my fear in their hearts, that they shall not depart from me." 1 Thess. 5:23, 24: "And the very God of peace sanctify you wholly; and I pray God your whole spirit and soul and body be preserved blameless unto the coming of our Lord Jesus Christ. Faithful is he that calleth you, who also will do it." It has been objected that this last is a mere prayer, and may not be answered; but the 24th verse promises "will do it."

Now if this covenant is to be everlasting, so that "they shall fear him for ever," that "they shall not depart from him"; if [it is] to cleanse the church from "all her idols," "from ALL iniquities, and ALL sins," so that when her "iniquities are sought for, NONE shall be found"; if [it is] to "give her a new heart and a new spirit," and "*cause* her to walk in his statutes"; if [it is] "to sanctify her wholly, body, soul, and spirit, and *preserve* her *blameless* unto the coming of our Lord Jesus"—if these are not perfect and perpetual obedience, I know not in what terms such obedience could be expressed.

It has been objected by some that the promises in the Old Testament were made to Jews and applied only to the Jews. I answer, it is plain that these promises respected the whole church under the New Covenant dispensation, and that the New Covenant included the Gentile nations. The Christian church is the Israel of God, as I have shown in a former lecture.

LECTURE 13

The Promises, No. 3

2 Pet. 1:4: "Whereby are given unto us exceeding great and precious promises, that by these ye might be partakers of the divine nature, having escaped the corruption that is in the world through lust."

In continuing the contrast between the Old and New Covenants, I remark:

6. The Old Covenant left men to the exercise of their own strength. The New is the effectual sanctification by the Holy Spirit. Ezek. 36:25-27: "Then will I sprinkle clean water upon you, and ye shall be clean; from all your filthiness and from all your idols, will I cleanse you. A new heart also will I give you, and a new spirit will I put within you: and I will take away the stony heart out of your flesh, and I will give you an heart of flesh. And I will PUT MY SPIRIT WITHIN YOU, and cause you to walk in my statutes, and ye shall keep my judgments, and do them." Gal. 3:14: "That the blessing of Abraham might come on the Gentiles through Jesus Christ; that we might receive the PROMISE OF THE SPIRIT through faith." I r.eed not quote the numerous promises which sustain this point. But here let me say that this is one of the grand distinctions between the Old and New Covenants, that the *New Covenant is the effectual indwelling of the Holy Spirit, producing the very temper required by the law, or Old Covenant.* There is a grand and mighty difference between the Old and New Covenants in this respect; and let it be forever understood that the difference does not lie merely or mainly in the fact that the New Covenant is a fuller revelation than the Old. Which brings me to say,

7. The Old was a mere outward covenant, written upon tables of stone—the mere "letter that killeth." The New is an inward covenant. It is the indwelling of the Spirit of God, writing the law in the heart, begetting and maintaining the *very obedience required* by the Old Covenant. If this be overlooked, the New Covenant is thrown away. And herein is the great error of the church, that they make the Old and New Covenants substantially the same thing while, in fact, the Old Covenant was the mere requirement of that of which the New Covenant is the *fulfillment,* by the indwelling and effectual influences of the Spirit of God.

8. The Old Covenant had properly two parties. We find both the parties recognized in Ex. 19:8—"And all the people answered together and said, All that the Lord hath spoken we will do. And Moses returned the words of the people unto the Lord"—and [in Ex.] 24:3-8:

> And Moses came and told the people all the words of the Lord, and all the judgments; and all the people answered with one voice, and said, All the words which the Lord hath said will we do. And Moses wrote all the words of the Lord, and rose up early in the morning, and builded an altar under the hill, and twelve pillars, according to the twelve tribes of Israel. And he

sent young men of the children of Israel, which offered burnt offerings of oxen unto the Lord. And Moses took half of the blood and put it in basins; and half of the blood he sprinkled on the altar. And he took the book of the covenant, and read in the audience of the people: and they said, All that the Lord hath said will we do, and be obedient. And Moses took the blood, and sprinkled it on the people, and said, Behold the blood of the covenant, which the Lord hath made with you concerning all these words.

This covenant had no surety. But the New Covenant unites the parties in a mediator, who is also the surety of the New Covenant. Heb. 7:22: "By so much was Jesus made a surety of a better testament." Now observe the Old has no surety pledged for its fulfillment, while the New has the most ample surety pledged for the fulfillment of every jot and tittle of it.

9. The Old Covenant, I have said, was broken. Jer. 31:32: "Which my covenant they brake, although I was an husband unto them, saith the Lord." Now this was the grand reason why this covenant was set aside. Heb. 8:7: "For if that first covenant had been faultless, then should no place have been sought for the second." Heb. 7:11, 18-19: "If therefore perfection were by the Levitical priesthood (for under it the people received the law), what further need was there that another priest should rise after the order of Melchisedec, and not be called after the order of Aaron?" "For there is verily a disannulling of the commandment going before for the weakness and unprofitableness thereof. For the law made nothing perfect, but the bringing in of a better hope did; by the which we draw nigh unto God." But the New Covenant shall not be broken by those who receive it. The great difficulty with the Old Covenant was that it had not sufficient efficiency to secure holiness. And if the New Covenant is not holiness, wherein is it better than the Old? In Heb. 8:6 it is said, "But now hath he [Christ] obtained a more excellent ministry, by how much also he is the mediator of a better covenant, which was established upon better promises."

But see the tenor of the covenant itself. The reason why it was not faultless was because it did not secure obedience. This was the very reason why God found fault with it and introduced a new one which *consisted in obedience.* See again Heb. 8:7-11:

For if that first covenant had been faultless, then should no place have been sought for the second. For finding fault with them, he saith, Behold, the days come, saith the Lord, when I will make a new covenant with the house of Israel and with the house of Judah: not according to the covenant that I made with their fathers in the day when I took them by the hand to lead them out of the land of Egypt; because they continued not in my covenant, and I regarded them not, saith the Lord. For this is the covenant that I will make with the house of Israel after those days, saith the Lord; I will put my laws into their mind, and write them in their hearts: and I will be to them a God, and they shall be to me a people: and they shall not teach every man his neighbour, and every man his brother, saying, Know the Lord; for all shall know me, from the least to the greatest."

Jer. 31:31-34:

> Behold, the days come, saith the Lord, that I will make a new covenant with the house of Israel, and with the house of Judah: not according to the covenant that I made with their fathers in the day that I took them by the hand to bring them out of the land of Egypt; which my covenant they brake, although I was an husband unto them, saith the Lord: but this shall be the covenant that I will make with the house of Israel; After those days, saith the Lord, I will put my law in their inward parts, and write it in their hearts, and will be their God, and they shall be my people. And they shall teach no more every man his neighbour, and every man his brother, saying, Know the Lord: for they shall all know me, from the least of them unto the greatest of them, saith the Lord: for I will forgive their iniquity, and I will remember their sin no more.

Jer. 32:39, 40: "And I will give them one heart, and one way, that they may fear me for ever, for the good of them, and of their children after them: and I will make an everlasting covenant with them, that I will not turn away from them, to do them good, but I will put my fear in their hearts, THAT THEY SHALL NOT DEPART FROM ME." Ezek. 36:26: "A new heart also will I give you, and a new spirit will I put within you: and I will take away the stony heart out of your flesh, and I will give you an heart of flesh." Ezek. 11:19-20: "And I will give them one heart, and I will put a new spirit within you; and I will take the stony heart out of their flesh, and will give them a heart of flesh: that they may walk in my statutes, and keep mine ordinances, and do them: and they shall be my people, and I will be their God." Jer. 24:7: "And I will give them an heart to know me, that I am the Lord: and they shall be my people, and I will be their God: for they shall return unto me with their whole heart." To these I might add many other passages to the same effect.

10. The Old Covenant was designed to develop sin. Rom. 5:20: "Moreover, the law entered, that the offence might abound. But where sin abounded, grace did much more abound." Rom. 7:8-13:

> But sin, taking occasion by the commandment, WROUGHT IN ME ALL MANNER OF CONCUPISCENSE. For without the law sin was dead. For I was alive without the law once: but when the commandment came, SIN REVIVED, and I died. And the commandment, which was ordained to life, I found to be unto death. For sin, TAKING OCCASION BY THE COMMANDMENT, deceived me, and by it slew me. Wherefore the law is holy, and the commandment holy, and just, and good. Was then that which is good made death unto me? God forbid. But sin, that it might appear sin, WORKING DEATH in me by that which is good; that sin by the commandment might become exceeding sinful.

Now the design of the Old Covenant, as declared in these texts, was not to make men holy but to develop their real character—to bring out their depravity to their own observation and thus convict and condemn them, rather than make them holy and justify them.

Read the New Covenant again, Jer. 31:31-34. . . ,* and also Jer.

---

*The whole passage he quotes again here.

32:39-40: "And I will give them one heart, and one way, that they may fear me for ever, for the good of them, and of their children after them. And I will make an everlasting covenant with them, that I will not turn away from them to do them good; but I will put my fear in their hearts that they shall not depart from me." Jer. 50:20: "In those days, and in that time, saith the Lord, the iniquity of Israel shall be sought for, and there shall be none; and the sins of Judah, and they shall not be found: for I will pardon them whom I reserve." Ezek. 36:25-27: "Then will I sprinkle clean water upon you, and ye shall be clean; from all your filthiness, and from all your idols, will I cleanse you. A new heart also will I give you, and a new spirit will I put within you: and I will take away the stony heart out of your flesh, and I will give you an heart of flesh. And I will put my Spirit within you, and cause you to walk in my statutes, and ye shall keep my judgments, and do them."

Rom. 6:1-14:

What shall we say, then? Shall we continue in sin, that grace may abound? God forbid. How shall we, that are dead to sin, live any longer therein? Know ye not, that so many of us as were baptized into Jesus Christ were baptized into his death? Therefore we are buried with him by baptism into death: that like as Christ was raised up from the dead by the glory of the Father, even so we also should walk in newness of life. For if we have been planted together in the likeness of his death, we shall be also in the likeness of his resurrection: knowing this, that our old man is crucified with him, that the body of sin might be destroyed, that henceforth we should not serve sin. For he that is dead is freed from sin. Now if we be dead with Christ, we believe that we shall also live with him: knowing that Christ being raised from the dead dieth no more; death hath no more dominion over him. For in that he died, he died unto sin once: but in that he liveth, he liveth unto God. Likewise reckon ye also yourselves to be dead indeed unto sin, but alive unto God through Jesus Christ our Lord. Let not sin therefore reign in your mortal body, that ye should obey it in the lusts thereof. Neither yield ye your members as instruments of righteousness unto sin: but yield yourselves unto God, as those that are alive from the dead, and your members as instruments of righteousness unto God. For sin shall not have dominion over you: for ye are not under the law, but under grace.

Rom. 7:4-6:

Wherefore, my brethren, ye also are become dead to the law by the body of Christ, that ye should be married to another, even to him who is raised from the dead, that we should bring forth fruit unto God. For when we were in the flesh, the motions of sins, which were by the law, did work in our members to bring forth fruit unto death. But now we are delivered from the law, that being dead wherein we were held; that we should serve in newness of spirit, and not in the oldness of the letter.

Rom. 8:2: "For the law of the Spirit of life in Christ Jesus hath made me free from the law of sin and death." Gal. 5:16-18: "This I say, then, Walk in the Spirit, and ye shall not fulfil the lust of the flesh. For the flesh lusteth against the Spirit, and the Spirit against the flesh: and these are contrary the one to the other: so that ye cannot do the things that ye would. But if ye be led of the Spirit, ye are not under the law."

I continue to quote these texts, and to write them out, that you may read them attentively in the different connections in which they occur in this discourse. I wish you by all means to consider them attentively in all the different connections in which I quote them, and see if they prove the points for which they are quoted.

Now I ask you, beloved, if these texts do not prove that the New Covenant is *the death of sin,* in opposition to the Old which is the "STRENGTH OF SIN"? 1 Cor. 15:56: "The STRENGTH of sin is the law."

Now observe again that the New Covenant is not an outward precept nor an outward promise nor any outward thing whatever, but an inward holiness wrought by the Spirit of God—the very substance and spirit of the law written in the heart by the Holy Ghost. Hence in Rom. 6:1-14, persons that are baptized by the Holy Ghost are said to be *"dead," "crucified," "buried,"* &c. I have just quoted it, but consult it again. . . . [and] Rom. 7:4-6 . . . .*

Rom. 8:2: "For the law of the Spirit of life in Christ Jesus hath made me free from the law of sin and death." Gal. 5:16-18: "This I say, then, Walk in the Spirit, and ye shall not fulfil the lust of the flesh. For the flesh lusteth against the Spirit, and the Spirit against the flesh: and these are contrary the one to the other: so that ye cannot do the things that ye would. But if ye be led of the Spirit, ye are not under the law."

Now what do these passages mean, if they do not teach *a death to sin?* And this certainly is not spoken of a future state of existence but is affirmed of saints in this world. If these passages do not contain an account of a state of entire sanctification, I believe there are none in the Bible that contain such an account, either in reference to this world or heaven itself.

Again, if these passages do not speak of a state of entire sanctification, then there are none that speak of a state of entire depravity. If to be "dead *in* trespasses and sins" is not a state of total depravity, then I do not know that the doctrine of total depravity is taught in the Bible. But if to be dead *in sin* is total depravity, then to be dead *to sin* must be total or entire holiness.

Now by what rule of biblical interpretation can this conclusion be denied or evaded?

11. The Old Covenant was the ministration of *death,* but the New of *righteousness* and *life.* 2 Cor. 3:6-16:

Who also hath made us able ministers of the new testament; not of the letter, but of the Spirit: for the letter *killeth,* but the Spirit giveth *life.* But if the ministration of death, written and engraven in stones, was glorious, so that the children of Israel could not stedfastly behold the face of Moses for the glory of his countenance; which glory was to be done away: how shall not the ministration of the Spirit be rather glorious? For if the ministration of condemnation be glory, much more doth the ministration of righteous-

---

*Both these long passages quoted again here.

ness exceed in glory. For even that which was made glorious had no glory in this respect, by reason of the glory that excelleth. For if that which is done away was glorious, much more that which remaineth is glorious. Seeing then that we have such hope, we use great plainness of speech: and not as Moses, which put a veil over his face, that the children of Israel could not stedfastly look to the end of that which is abolished: but their minds were blinded: for until this day remaineth the same veil untaken away in the reading of the old testament, which veil is done away in Christ. But even unto this day, when Moses is read, the veil is upon their heart. Nevertheless when it shall turn to the Lord, the veil shall be taken away.

Here we have the two covenants beautifully contrasted by the Apostle—the Old as working *spiritual death* and ending in *eternal death;* the New as consisting in *righteousness and eternal life.*

12. The Old Covenant was only a schoolmaster to bring us to Christ. Gal. 3:24: "Wherefore the law was our schoolmaster to bring us unto Christ, that we might be justified by faith." But the New Covenant is the reign of Christ in the heart. Jer. 31:31-34:

Behold, the days come, saith the Lord, that I will make a new covenant with the house of Israel, and with the house of Judah: not according to the covenant that I made with their fathers in the day that I took them by the hand to bring them out of the land of Egypt which my covenant they brake, although I was an husband unto them, saith the Lord: but this shall be the covenant that I will make with the house of Israel; After those days, saith the Lord, I will put my law in their inward parts, and write it in their hearts; and will be their God, and they shall be my people: and they shall teach no more every man his neighbour, and every man his brother, saying, Know the Lord: for they shall all know me, from the least of them unto the greatest of them, saith the Lord: for I will forgive their iniquity, and I will remember their sin no more.

Jer. 32:39-40: "And I will give them one heart, and one way, that they may fear me for ever, for the good of them, and of their children after them: and I will make an everlasting covenant with them, that I will not turn away from them, to do them good; but I will put my fear in their hearts, that they shall not depart from me." Ezek. 36:25-27: "Then will I sprinkle clean water upon you, and ye shall be clean: from all your filthiness, and from all your idols, will I cleanse you. A new heart also will I give you, and a new spirit will I put within you; and I will take away the stony heart out of your flesh, and I will give you an heart of flesh. And I will put my Spirit within you, and cause you to walk in my statutes, and ye shall keep my judgments, and do them." Col. 1:27: "To whom God would make known what is the riches of the glory of this mystery among the Gentiles; which is Christ in you, the hope of glory." 1 John 4:4: "Ye are of God, little children, and have overcome them: because greater is he that is in you, than he that is in the world." Rom. 8:9: "But ye are not in the flesh, but in the Spirit, if so be that the Spirit of God dwell in you. Now if any man have not the Spirit of Christ, he is none of his." Gal. 4:6: "And because ye are sons, God hath sent forth the Spirit of his Son into your hearts, crying, Abba, Father." Gal.

2:20: "I am crucified with Christ: nevertheless I live; yet not I, but Christ liveth in me: and the life which I now live in the flesh, I live by the faith of the Son of God, who loved me, and gave himself for me." Rom. 8:10-11, 16: "And if Christ be in you, the body is dead because of sin; but the Spirit is life because of righteousness. But if the Spirit of him that raised up Jesus from the dead dwell in you, he that raised up Christ from the dead shall also quicken your mortal bodies by his Spirit that dwelleth in you." "The Spirit itself beareth witness with our spirit, that we are the children of God." Phil. 1:19: "For I know that this shall turn to my salvation through your prayer, and the supply of the Spirit of Jesus Christ."

Here observe that the Old Covenant was designed to strip us of self-righteousness and show us our need of Christ, to develop our selfishness and enmity and our entire helplessness and dependence upon a foreign influence to incline us to holiness. . . , and thus preparing the way for our acceptance of Christ as an indwelling and reigning Savior. Then when the Old Covenant, as a schoolmaster, has brought us to Christ, the New enters. In other words Christ enters the soul, takes up His residence there, *writes the law of love in the heart*, takes away the stony heart of flesh, makes the New Covenant with the soul, and sheds His divine influence over the *entire moral being*. Now if as much as this is not taught in these scriptures and in various other parts of the Bible, what is taught? And if these texts are to be set aside and explained away after the common manner of disposing of Scripture testimony on this subject, what doctrine or truth may not be expunged from the Bible?

LECTURE 14

The Promises, No. 4

2 Pet. 1:4: "Whereby are given unto us exceeding great and precious promises: that by these ye might be partakers of the divine nature, having escaped the corruption that is in the world through lust."

In resuming the subject of the contrast between the Old and New Covenants, I remark:

13. The Old Covenant was the *strength of sin*. 1 Cor. 15:56: "THE STRENGTH OF SIN IS THE LAW." In this passage and in others, the Apostle plainly teaches that the Old Covenant, or law, strengthened depravity instead of annihilating it. But the New is represented as the *death of sin*. Ezek. 36:25-29: "Then will I sprinkle clean water upon you, and ye shall be clean: from all your filthiness, and from all your idols, will I cleanse

you. A new heart also will I give you, and a new spirit will I put within you: and I will take away the stony heart out of your flesh, and I will give you an heart of flesh. And I will put my Spirit within you, and cause you to walk in my statutes, and ye shall keep my judgments, and do them. And ye shall dwell in the land that I gave to your fathers; and ye shall be my people, and I will be your God. I will also save you from ALL YOUR UNCLEAN-NESS." Rom. 6:1-14:

What shall we say then? Shall we continue in sin, that grace may abound? God forbid. How shall we, that are DEAD to sin, LIVE any longer therein? Know ye not, that so many of us as were baptized into Jesus Christ were baptized into his DEATH? Therefore we are buried with him by baptism into DEATH: that like as Christ was raised up from the dead by the glory of the Father, even so we also should WALK IN NEWNESS OF LIFE. For if we have been planted together in the likness of his death, we shall be also in the likeness of his resurrection: knowing this, that our OLD MAN IS CRU-CIFIED with him, that the body of SIN MIGHT BE DESTROYED, that henceforth we should not serve sin. For he that IS DEAD IS FREED FROM SIN. Now if we be dead with Christ, we believe that we shall also live with him: knowing that Christ being raised from the dead dieth no more; death hath no more dominion over him. For in that he died, he DIED UNTO SIN once; but in that he liveth, he liveth unto God. Likewise reckon ye your-selves to be DEAD indeed unto sin, but alive unto God through Jesus Christ our Lord. Let not sin therefore reign in your mortal body, that ye should obey it in the lusts thereof. Neither yield ye your members as instruments of unrighteousness unto sin: but yield yourselves unto God, as those that are alive from the dead, and your members as instruments of righteousness unto God. For SIN SHALL NOT HAVE DOMINION OVER YOU: FOR YE ARE NOT UNDER THE LAW, BUT UNDER GRACE.

Rom. 7:4-6: "Wherefore, my brethren, ye are also become DEAD to the law by the body of Christ; that ye should be married to another even to him who is raised from the dead, that we should bring forth fruit unto God. For when we were in the flesh, the motions of sins, which were by the law, did work in our members to bring forth fruit UNTO DEATH. But now we are delivered from the law, that being DEAD wherein we were held; that we should serve in NEWNESS OF SPIRIT, and not in the oldness of the let-ter." Gal. 5:16-18: "This I say then, Walk in the Spirit, and ye shall not ful-fil the lust of the flesh. For the flesh lusteth against the Spirit, and the Spir-it against the flesh: and these are contrary the one to the other: so that ye cannot do the things that ye would. But if ye be led of the Spirit, YE ARE NOT UNDER THE LAW."

Now as I have before remarked, if to be dead *to* sin be not *entire holi-ness,* then to be dead *in* sin is not *entire* depravity.

14. The Old Covenant made nothing perfect. Heb. 7:19: "For the LAW MADE NOTHING PERFECT, but the bringing in of a better hope did, by the which we draw nigh unto God." Heb. 9:9: "Which WAS a figure for the time then present, in which were offered both gifts and sacrifices that COULD NOT make him that did the service PERFECT, as pertaining to the conscience." Heb. 10:11: "And every priest standeth daily ministering,

and offering oftentimes the same sacrifices, which CAN NEVER TAKE AWAY SINS."

It is abundantly taught in this epistle that Abraham and the other Old Testament saints did not receive the promises, that is, they did [not] receive the fulfillment of the promises. The promises were made to them, or rather through them, to the Christian church. But it is expressly said that they did not receive the fulfillment of the promises. Of the long list of saints mentioned in chapter 11 of this epistle, it is said, verse 13, "These all died in faith, NOT HAVING RECEIVED THE PROMISES." And in verses 39-40 it is said, "And these all having obtained a good report through faith RECEIVED NOT THE PROMISE, God having provided some better thing for us, that they without us should not be made perfect."

The New Covenant is perfection itself. Lest this should be doubted, it may be well to inquire what we understand by Christian Perfection. Has God anywhere required perfection in the Bible? If so, where? Does His law require perfection? If not, what part of the Bible does? And if His law does not require perfection, why does it not? Is it not manifestly an imperfect law? And how can it be said that the "law is HOLY, JUST and GOOD"? But it probably will not be doubted that God's law is perfect and that entire conformity to it is perfection itself. Now what does this law require?

(1) Not that we should love God as much as we should be under obligation to love Him, had we a perfect knowledge of all our relations. If the law required this, it would be more than any saint on earth or in heaven, or any angel in heaven could perform. None but an infinite mind can perceive all the relations that exist between God and ourselves and between ourselves and our fellowmen.

(2) It does not require the same degree of love that we might have rendered had we never abused our powers by sin. If it did there is not a saint on earth or in heaven that could obey the law. The law is directed to us as we are, and it says to every individual *as he is,* "Thou shalt love the Lord thy God with all THY heart, and with all THY soul, and with all THY strength," not with all the strength thou mightest have had, hadst thou never sinned. Perfection would be as impossible to saints in heaven as to saints on earth, did God require the same strength of affection that might have been rendered had our powers never been debilitated by sin.

(3) Nor does the law require the same love that might be rendered had we as much knowledge of God as we might have gained if we had always improved our time in the acquisition of knowledge. If this were required of the saints, there is not a saint in heaven that is or ever will be perfect; for there is not one that has as much knowledge as he might have possessed had he always improved his time and talents in its acquisition. What is lost in these respects is lost forever. And God no more requires us to make up the deficiency than He requires us to recall past time. Repentance for all the past and perfect obedience in the future, with such powers as we have, is all that the law or the gospel requires. "THOU shalt love the Lord thy God with all THY heart, and with all THY soul, and with all THY strength." This is the Old Covenant. I have before said that it made nothing perfect.

I now add that the New Covenant is perfection itself. Jer. 31:31-34:

> Behold, the days come, saith the Lord, that I will make a new covenant with the house of Israel, and with the house of Judah: not according to the covenant that I made with their fathers in the day that I took them by the hand to bring them out of the land of Egypt; which my covenant they brake, although I was an husband unto them saith the Lord: but this shall be the covenant that I will make with the house of Israel. After those days, saith the Lord, I will put my law in their inward parts, and write it in their hearts: and will be their God, and they shall be my people. And they shall teach no more every man his neighbour, and every man his brother, saying, Know the Lord: for they shall all know me, from the least of them unto the greatest of them, saith the Lord: for I will forgive their iniquity, and I will remember their sin no more.

Heb. 8:8-12:

> Behold, the days come, saith the Lord, when I will make a new covenant with the house of Israel and with the house of Judah: not according to the covenant that I made with their fathers in the day when I took them by the hand to lead them out of the land of Egypt; because they continued not in my covenant, and I regarded them not, saith the Lord. For this is the covenant that I will make with the house of Israel after those days, saith the Lord; I will put my laws in their mind, and write them in their hearts: and I will be to them a God, and they shall be to me a people: and they shall not teach every man his neighbour, and every man his brother, saying, Know the Lord: for all shall know me, from the least to the greatest. For I will be merciful to their unrighteousness, and their iniquities will I remember no more.

Ezek. 36:25-27: "Then will I sprinkle clean water upon you, and ye shall be clean: from all your filthiness, and from all your idols, will I cleanse you. A new heart also will I give you and a new spirit will I put within you: and I will take away the stony heart out of your flesh, and I will give you an heart of flesh. And I will put my Spirit within you, and cause you to walk in my statutes, and ye shall keep my judgments, and do them." Deut. 30:6: "And the Lord thy God will circumcise thine heart, and the heart of thy seed, to love the Lord thy God WITH ALL THINE HEART, and WITH ALL THY SOUL, that thou mayest live." Rom. 8:1-4: "There is therefore now no condemnation to them which are in Christ Jesus, who walk not after the flesh, but after the Spirit. For the law of the Spirit of life in Christ Jesus hath made me FREE from the law of sin and death. For what the law could not do, in that it was weak through the flesh, God sending his own Son in the likeness of sinful flesh, and for sin, condemned sin in the flesh: that the righteousness of the law MIGHT BE FULFILLED IN US, who walk not after the flesh, but after the Spirit."

Now if you look into the promise of the covenant in Jeremiah, you will see that it is just this: a promise to write the Old Covenant in the heart. It should be remembered that the words old covenant and law are synonymous terms. And when God promises to write the law in the heart, He promises that the Old Covenant shall be written in the heart.

Now if the Old Covenant or Law required perfection (and if it did not there is no requirement of perfection in the Bible), the promise in Jeremiah is that this same perfection shall exist in the soul. And in the quotation from Rom. 8:4 it is expressly asserted that this was the object of the atonement of Christ. Now it does appear to me that the argument in favor of entire sanctification may be settled to a demonstration, by looking at what the Old Covenant required and recognizing *that* as the highest perfection that God requires of man, and then seeing that this Old Covenant is to be written in the heart by the Spirit of God. If, when the Old is fulfilled in the heart, men are not perfect in the Bible sense of that term, we may hope in vain to understand what perfection is.

15. The Old Covenant gendered to *bondage*. Gal. 4:21-31:

> Tell me, ye that desire to be under the law, do ye not hear the law? For it is written, that Abraham had two sons, the one by a bondmaid, the other by a freewoman. But he who was of the bondwoman was born after the flesh; but he of the freewoman was by promise. Which things are an allegory: for these are the two covenants; the one from the mount Sinai, which GENDERETH TO BONDAGE, which is Agar. For this Agar is mount Sinai in Arabia, and answereth to Jerusalem which now is, and is in bondage with her children. But Jerusalem which is above is free, which is the mother of us all. For it is written, Rejoice, thou barren that barest not; break forth and cry, thou that travailest not; for the desolate hath many more children than she which hath an husband. Now we, brethren, as Isaac was, are the children of promise. But as then he that was born after the flesh persecuted him that was born after the Spirit, even so it is now. Nevertheless what saith the scripture? Cast out the bondwoman and her son: for the son of the bondwoman shall not be heir with the son of the freewoman. So then, brethren, we are not children of the bondwoman, but of the free.

Here the Apostle represents all men under the law as being in a state of *slavery* and rendering merely the service of fear.

But the New Testament is *liberty itself*. Gal. 5:1: "Stand fast therefore in the LIBERTY wherewith Christ hath made us free, and be not entangled again with the yoke of bondage." John 8:32-36: "And ye shall know the truth, and the truth shall make you FREE. They answered him, We be Abraham's seed and were never in bondage to any man; how sayest thou, Ye shall be made free? Jesus answered them, Verily, verily, I say unto you, Whosoever committeth sin is the servant of sin. And the servant abideth not in the house for ever: but the son abideth ever. If the Son therefore shall make you FREE, ye shall be FREE indeed." Rom. 6:14: "For SIN SHALL NOT HAVE DOMINION OVER YOU; FOR YE ARE NOT UNDER THE LAW, BUT UNDER GRACE." Gal. 4:2-6: "But is under tutors and governors until the time appointed of the father. Even so we, when we were children, were in BONDAGE under the elements of the world: but when the fulness of the time was come, God sent forth his Son, made of a woman, made under the law, to REDEEM THEM that were under the law, that we might receive the ADOPTION OF SONS. And because ye are sons, God hath sent forth the Spirit of his Son into your hearts, crying Abba, Father." Isa. 61:1: "The spirit of the Lord God is upon me; because the Lord hath anointed me to preach good tidings unto the meek; he hath sent me to bind up the broken-hearted, to PROCLAIM LIBERTY to the captives, and the opening of the prison to them that are bound." Rom. 8:21: "Because the creature itself also shall be delivered from the bondage of corruption into the GLORIOUS LIBERTY of the children of God." 1 Cor. 8:9: "But take heed, lest by any means this LIBERTY of yours become a stumblingblock to them that are weak." 2 Cor. 3:17: "Now the Lord is that Spirit; and where the Spirit of the Lord is, there is LIBERTY." Gal. 5:13: "For, brethren, ye have been called unto LIBERTY; only use not liberty for an occasion to the flesh, but by love serve one another."

16. The Old Covenant produced only *outward morality,* while it *aggravated the sin of the heart.* Matt. 23:25: "Woe unto you, scribes and Pharisees, hypocrites! for ye make clean the OUTSIDE of the cup and of the platter, but WITHIN THEY ARE FULL OF EXTORTION AND EXCESS." Rom. 7:8: "But sin, taking occasion by the commandment, WROUGHT IN ME ALL MANNER OF CONCUPISCENSE."

The New Covenant is the purifying of the heart. Jer. 31:31-34:

Behold, the days come, saith the Lord, that I will make a new covenant with the house of Israel, and with the house of Judah: not according to the covenant that I made with their fathers in the day that I took them by the hand to bring them out of the land of Egypt; which my covenant they brake, although I was an husband unto them, saith the Lord: but this shall be the covenant that I will make with the house of Israel. After those days, saith the Lord, I will put my law in their inward parts, and write it in their hearts; and will be their God, and they shall be my people. And they shall teach no more every man his neighbour, and every man his brother, saying, Know the Lord: for they shall all know me, from the least of them unto the greatest of them, saith the Lord: for I will forgive their iniquity, and I will remember their sin no more.

Ezek. 36:25-27: "Then will I sprinkle clean water upon you, and ye shall be clean: from all your filthiness, and from all your idols, will I cleanse you. A new heart also will I give you, and a new spirit will I put within you: and I will take away the stony heart out of your flesh, and I will give you an heart of flesh. And I will put my Spirit within you, and cause you to walk in my statutes, and ye shall keep my judgments, and do them." Deut. 30:6: "And the Lord thy God will circumcise thine heart, and the heart of thy seed, to love the Lord thy God with all thine heart, and with all thy soul, that thou mayest live."

17. The Old Covenant had only a *shadow* of the Gospel. Heb. 10:1: "For the law having a SHADOW of good things to come and not the very image of the things, can never with those sacrifices which they offered year by year continually make the comers thereunto perfect." The New is the *inwrought effect of the gospel.*

Let it be understood that the New Testament is not the gospel itself, but is that which is to be effected by the gospel. The New Testament and the gospel are by no means to be confounded the one with the other. The New Testament or Covenant is that work in the heart which is wrought by the Holy Ghost, by the instrumentality of the gospel. Most professors of religion, in speaking of the New Testament, mean by it the book containing the Gospels, the Acts of the Apostles, the Epistles and the Apocalypse. Now these are not the New Testament; for the New Testament and Covenant, you understand, are the same thing. These books are the gospel. And, as I have said, the gospel is only the means by which God makes the New Covenant with the soul, or by which He inclines the soul to close in with and obey the Old Covenant. Now the whole object of God in the gospel is not to abrogate the Old Covenant but to bring men into obedience to it, that is, to be perfectly conformed to the law of love. The gospel is as distinct from the New Covenant as the means are distinct from the end.

And for an individual to suppose he has received the New Covenant because he has the gospel in his hands, or because he lives under the gospel dispensation, is a dangerous and fatal error. A man may live under the gospel, may understand and believe many of its truths, and yet the gospel may never have been so fully received by him, as effectually and permanently to have written the Old Covenant or law in his heart.

It has been said that *regeneration* is all that is included in the promise of the New Covenant and that every real Christian has received this New Covenant. Now if this be so, in what sense did not Abraham and the Old Testament saints receive the promises and their fulfillment? Were they not regenerated? See Heb. 11:13: "These all died in faith, NOT HAVING RECEIVED THE PROMISES." Also verses 39-40: "And these all, having obtained a good report through faith, RECEIVED NOT THE PROMISE: God having provided some better thing for us, that they without us should not be made perfect." Now here many of the most distinguished saints under the Old Testament dispensation are mentioned by name, and it is expressly said of every one of them that they "died in faith" but "had not received the promises." It is not meant that they had not heard the promises, for to them the promises were given. It must therefore mean that they did not receive their fulfillment. But who will doubt that they were regenerated?

Now I cannot resist the conviction that to suppose regeneration to be the receiving of the New Covenant or New Testament, in the sense in which it is promised in the passages [I have] so often quoted, is a great and dangerous error. It appears to me that the Bible abundantly teaches that these promises are made to believers and not to unbelievers, that they are made to the church and not to the world, and that it is after we believe that we are to be sealed with the Holy Spirit of promise. Eph. 1:13: "In whom ye also trusted, after that ye heard the word of truth, the gospel of your salvation: in whom also AFTER THAT YE BELIEVED, YE WERE SEALED WITH THAT HOLY SPIRIT OF PROMISE." I have been ready sometimes to ask, can it be possible that those who maintain that the promise in Jeremiah means nothing more than regeneration have thoroughly considered what they say and whereof they affirm?

18. The condition of the Old Covenant was *perfect obedience to law.* I have so often quoted the passages to prove this that I need not here repeat

them. The condition of the New Covenant is *faith in Christ.* Gal. 3:14: "That the blessing of Abraham might come on the Gentiles through Jesus Christ, that we might receive the promise of the Spirit THROUGH FAITH." Now it is naturally impossible that the New Covenant should be received or the Old written in the heart upon any other condition than faith. Without confidence or faith there can be no love; and there cannot be genuine faith that does not produce love.

These are only a few of the exceeding great and precious promises of which the Apostle speaks in the text. Every student of the Bible knows that I might extend this examination indefinitely, and write a volume as large as the Bible itself, should I quote all the promises and remark upon them only to a limited extent. Some of them I have quoted over and over again for the purpose of showing their particular bearing upon the different propositions I have laid down. Those which I have quoted are only specimens of the promises, and designed only as illustrations of the truth that the promises are sufficient to accomplish the great work of making us partakers of the divine nature. The Lord willing, I design ere long to take up a more direct examination of the question whether entire sanctification is attainable in this life, and enter more into detail than would be proper in these discourses on the promises. In my next, I design to present some reasons why the promises are not fulfilled in and to us.

In the meantime, I wish to call your attention to what I regard as a settled truth, namely, that the doctrine of sanctification is so spiritual a subject that no mind will understand it that is not in a truly and highly spiritual state. No man ever understood discourses on regeneration, and especially on the evidences of regeneration and the exercises of a regenerated heart, who had not himself been regenerated. Nor will a man understand any course of reasoning on the subject of sanctification who has not experience on that subject. By this I do not mean that he may not have sufficient intellectual perception to understand some things about it. But I do mean that he will not understand the fullness with which the Bible teaches that doctrine until his spiritual perceptions are made clear and penetrating. For example, no man ever believed that Jesus was the Christ who was not born of God. It is expressly asserted in the Bible that "whosoever believeth that Jesus is the Christ is born of God" and that "no man can say that Jesus is the Lord but by the Holy Ghost." Now it is not intended in this passage that a man may not settle the abstract question to some extent, as a matter of science and evidence respecting the divinity of Christ. But it is intended that none but a spiritual mind can have any knowledge of Christ as God. And to me it seems plain that the more spiritual any truth is the more certainly it will be misunderstood by any but a spiritual mind; for the natural man discerneth not the things of the Spirit of God, neither can he know them because they are spiritually discerned. The utmost that I expect to do by anything that I can say and by any scriptures that can be quoted, with minds not in a truly spiritual state, is so far to convince their understanding as to convict their heart of being wrong, and thus to bring them to search after the true light.

LECTURE 15

The Promises, No. 5

2 Pet. 1:4: "Whereby are given unto us exceeding great and precious promises, that by these ye might be partakers of the divine nature, having escaped the corruption that is in the world through lust."

In some of my last lectures, I examined a few of the promises with the design of showing that they are sufficiently full and explicit to cover the whole ground of our necessities and that they afford us abundant means of entire conformity to the divine nature or image—that we have only to realize in our own experience the fullness of the promised blessing and to believe and receive all that is actually promised, in order to know by our own blessed experience what it is to be made partakers of the divine nature. I might extend this examination of the promises to almost any length, as every attentive reader of the Bible knows. I have only quoted such specimens of the different classes of promises as seem to me to afford a fair illustration of the extent and fullness of the salvation promised in the gospel.

According to my plan, I am now to show:

IV. *Some of the reasons why the promises are not fulfilled in and to us.*

1. They are overlooked in a great measure by the church. They seem as a body not to know that there are any such promises as these in the Bible. Now as the fulfillment of a promise must depend upon our knowing, understanding and believing it, there is a very obvious reason why to multitudes the promises are never fulfilled.

2. Many who know that such promises are in the Bible do not at all understand their application. I was amazed, not long since, to hear a minister contend that the promise of the New Covenant, which I have so often quoted, was made to the Jews—that inasmuch as Israel and Judah are mentioned we had no right to apply the promise to any but the Jews. He seemed entirely to overlook the fact that these promises were made to the Israel of God, and more especially to the Christian church than to the Jewish church. Now it is perfectly manifest that where such ignorance as this prevails (and it does very extensively prevail in the Christian church) that there is a natural reason why the promises are not fulfilled—are not pleaded, believed and applied by the church to their own case. Therefore they are as ineffectual to them as the gospel provisions are to sinners who starve to death with the gospel feast before them.

3. Another reason why they are not fulfilled to many is, they will not believe the promises mean all they say. They reason thus. As a matter of fact,

say they, the Christian church is not wholly sanctified and never has been—that very few, if any, believers in Christ have ever been wholly sanctified in this life. Therefore, as a matter of fact either they do not mean to promise entire sanctification or God has not kept His word. They therefore suffer themselves to fritter away the meaning of the promises. Now if the objection that the promise cannot mean entire sanctification because, as a matter of fact, entire sanctification has not taken place in the church be good for anything, it must amount to this, that nothing more is promised in the New Covenant than the church have actually realized. For the whole force of the objection lies in this, that if God has not fulfilled all that He promised, then He has forfeited His word. Therefore, the New Covenant does not mean entire sanctification, but these promises of the New Covenant and all the promises which I have quoted mean nothing more than the church has actually realized. Now if this objection amounts to anything, it is this, that nothing more is promised than has been fulfilled; that the gospel has done for the church all that it can do in this world; and that every Christian has actually been at every moment just as holy as there was any provision for him to be.

Now the first absurdity involved in this objection is that it would make the promises mean more or less to different individuals, just according to the measure of grace which each one has had. For according to the objection, if the promise has not been fulfilled, then God has broken His word. And if one Christian has had more holiness than another, it must be because God has promised more to one than to another. For in this objection, let it be remembered, it is contended that He has fulfilled all His promises.

A second absurdity is, it assumes that these promises are without any condition or that the condition has been complied with by every Christian. For certainly it would not be assumed that God had violated His promises, if He intended to promise entire sanctification, unless it were assumed either that they are without condition, expressed or implied, or that the condition had been complied with. But these promises are all made on conditions, either expressed or implied. They are to be recognized and pleaded and believed. The conditions are often expressed along with the promises, and when not expressed are always implied. The conditions are not arbitrary, but there is a natural necessity that they should be understood and believed and a personal application made of them, as the indispensable means of getting that state of mind that constitutes the divine image or nature in man.

It is indeed a shorthand method of frittering away the promises of God, to overlook the conditions upon which they are made and contend that they can mean no more than has been actually realized by the church; because on any other supposition, God has not performed His word. Now the reason, and a sufficient reason, why entire sanctification has not been realized by the church is that she has not believed and applied these promises according to their real import.

I don't know how to leave this objection without saying it is truly ridiculous. Upon the principle assumed in the objection there is no promise in the Bible that has become due that can be or ought to be pleaded by Christians, inasmuch as the promises must be already fulfilled, else God has violated His word.

But to what I have said, it may be objected that the New Testament times have really come, that the New Covenant has been actually made with the church, and that those who have actually received it have not been entirely sanctified. To this I reply that the church may have received more or less of the New Covenant precisely according to their understanding of the fullness of the promised blessings and their faith in the promises. When God had promised the New Covenant He said, "Nevertheless I will be inquired of by the house of Israel to do it for them." Now it is nowhere asserted in the Bible that the New Testament, or Covenant, has been fully received, although the time has come when it is offered to the church. Under the New Covenant dispensation it is promised that the fullness of the Gentiles shall turn to the Lord and that the Jews themselves shall be converted and receive this covenant. Now the fact that the church has not actually received the blessing of sanctification no more proves that that blessing is not fully promised in the New Covenant, than the fact that the Jews and Gentiles have not been converted proves that no such thing is promised. It is certain that the promises are not fulfilled in regard to the world's conversion, for the very reason that the church and the world have not believed and applied these promises. The same is true of the New Covenant blessing of sanctification. This blessing has been received to a very limited extent by the church because she has neglected to believe and apply the promise.

4. Another reason why the promises are not fulfilled in us is that we often fail to search out the one that is applicable to our circumstances. There are promises adapted to all our circumstances and states of mind, as I have before shown. No one will answer our purpose for the time being but the one that is applicable to our state of mind.

I have often been struck with this, in endeavoring to help anxious souls out of their difficulties. After inquiring as clearly as I was able into their state of mind, I have presented one and another and another of the promises and found that they would instantly perceive that these promises did not exactly meet their case. But when the Spirit of the Lord directed to the selection of the right promise, I have often been amazed and delighted to see how instantly they would recognize it as exactly suited to their case, as made to one exactly in their state of mind, as meeting them where they are and affording them just the aid they needed. It is often most refreshing to see with what a grasp the mind in such a state will lay hold upon such a promise and how, in a moment, it becomes as an "anchor to the soul, sure and stedfast" and how easily the mind when anchored down upon such a promise can look out upon the storm that rages without and smile through tears of joy.

It is one of the great and sweet employments of the ministry to search out and apply the blessed promises to the different states of mind in which their people are, to feed the lambs and sheep with food suited to their age and spiritual health. And he is surely but ill-instructed in the oracles of God who has not sufficient spiritual discernment, experience and knowledge of the Bible and of the laws of the human mind to know how to search out the real state of different persons and apply the promises that belong to them. It is a most divine employment; and if ministers were much better fitted for it than they are, the weak ones of the flock would soon be strong.

5. Another reason is that we do not anchor down in naked faith upon the promises. We are waiting for some state of mind to precede the exercise of faith, which we suppose must be had before we are at liberty to lay hold on the promise. And often the very state of mind which we suppose must precede the exercise of faith is to be the effect of faith and can only be produced by it. When I speak of anchoring down upon a promise in naked faith, I mean that we should take the promise and believe it as a matter of fact, as the word of God, as infallible truth, entirely irrespective of any state of mind in which we may be at the time.

Take an illustration of what I mean. A young man not long since had been for a long time anxious and going to one and another and inquiring into their experience and how they obtained the blessing. When one had told him, he would think, now I must get just into that state of mind and then I shall have the blessing. And when another had related his experience, he would strive to imitate that; and so he went from one to another, but all in vain. Finally he came to this conclusion that what the Bible said about Christ Jesus were matters of fact, that there he would begin by taking these things as facts—that he would not inquire about this or that man's experience but would take the facts about Christ Jesus and the promise as certain truths. Now this is what I call naked faith. This immediately brought him into the state of mind after which he had been seeking and which, it seems, he expected in some degree at least to realize before he exercised faith in the promises. Now if we ever expect to receive the fulfillment of the promises, we must not wait for appearances or any indications that God is about to fulfill His promises, but must anchor right down upon them in naked faith because they are the word of God.

6. Again, we do not receive them as belonging to us, as in the case that I have mentioned, where one supposed that the promise of the New Testament was made only to the Jews. Now multitudes seem never to have understood the promises made to individuals and to the church under the Old Covenant as belonging still more emphatically to the church and to individuals under the Christian dispensation. They seem entirely to have overlooked the fact that Christ and His apostles always treated the promises of the Old Testament as more emphatically belonging to Christians under the new dispensation. Now here is a sufficient reason for their not receiving the fulfillment of the promises, that they do not understand them as made to themselves. Consequently they do not believe nor apply them.

7. It does not seem to be generally understood that the promises mean all that they say, that they are to be interpreted by the same rules by which

the commandments and other parts of Scripture are to be interpreted. For example, the promise "The Lord thy God will circumcise thine heart, and the heart of thy seed, to love the Lord thy God with all thine heart, and with all thy soul," does not seem to be understood to mean as much as the command "Thou shalt love the Lord thy God with all thy heart, and with all thy soul, and with all thy strength." It is a matter of amazement and grief that so many individuals who will contend for the literal meaning of the commandments will fritter away the promises (when the same terms are used) as meaning infinitely less than the language in the commandments means, just as if an infinitely bountiful God meant less by the promises of grace than by the requirements of justice. If that man is to be accounted least in the kingdom of God who shall teach men to cast away one of the least of the commandments of God, what shall be said of him who not only casts away himself but teaches others to cast away the promises of God? Were this the place, it could be easily shown that it has been a common thing, with those who have written against the doctrine of entire sanctification in this life, to interpret the promises by a very different rule from that which they applied to the commandments. Now I would humbly ask, where is their authority for doing this? Is not such a course manifestly a violation of the Word of God?

8. Another reason is, we are so prone to limit their meaning to our own experience or to the experience of others whom we esteem to be eminent saints. How common is it for persons to inquire, if these promises mean this, why did not President Edwards or his wife or Mrs. Isabella Graham or Dr. Payson understand them and experience their fulfillment? Now we are apt to suffer such cases as these to stumble us, by assuming that they understood and applied the promises in all their length and breadth. It should be understood that no man's experience is the standard of truth. We are not to interpret the Bible by the experience of any man, but bring the experience of every man into the light of the Bible. The plain meaning of the Bible as it reads is the standard, whatever we may have experienced to the contrary notwithstanding. It is the practice of some men in these days, when the full meaning of the promises of the gospel is contended for, to reply by demanding an example. They say, show us an example of a perfect man. To this I reply,

(1) That should such an example be produced its perfection would not be acknowledged. Christ claimed and really possessed perfection. But His claim was set aside by the religious teachers of His day, and He was considered as a blasphemer and as one possessed with a devil. I verily believe that examples have been produced, and that some have all along existed in the church and now exist who enjoy the blessing of entire sanctification, as I understand that term, and who nevertheless have been and still are looked upon, even by the mass of professors of religion, as being so far from a sanctified state as to render it very doubtful whether they have any religion at all. Certainly the most holy persons that I have ever seen have been the most maligned and persecuted and denounced, even by many of the church, as being almost anything else than what they ought to be. And this

is exactly according to the Word of God: "If any man will live godly in Christ Jesus, he shall suffer persecution."

(2) But another answer to this call for an example is that if no such example were known to us, this would no more prove that they did not exist than the fact that Elijah did not know that God had reserved seven thousand men that had not bowed the knee to Baal proved that they did not exist.

(3) If no such example did exist or ever has existed, it would prove nothing more than that the gospel has not yet done all for the world and the church which it was designed to accomplish. And who, I would humbly ask, believes that it has? Who believes that either the church or the world has experienced all that the gospel is designed to effect? If no case can indeed be found where entire sanctification is enjoyed by any saint, it certainly does not prove that the promises mean no more than is enjoyed, but only that they are not believed and the fullness of their meaning realized in the experience of the church.

9. Another reason why the promises are not fulfilled in us is a want of perseverance. The Bible insists largely upon the importance of perseverance in prayer. The case of the "woman of Canaan" is recorded in the 15th of Matthew, and that of the unjust judge in the 18th of Luke; and many other instances recorded in the Bible set the importance of perseverance in prayer in a strong light. It is often the case that individuals will pray with confidence for blessings for a short time, but becoming discouraged because the blessing does not come, or supposing perseverance to be unnecessary and that the blessing will come in its time without it, they cease their efforts and wrestling and, in this respect, restrain prayer before God. Now it is very often the case that perseverance is naturally indispensable to our obtaining the blessing, that nothing else can prepare our minds to receive it; and it is often the case that it cannot be granted but through our own agency and protracted and agonizing efforts. Some obstacle may be to be overcome, either within or without ourselves, that can be overcome in no other way. As Christ said on a certain occasion, "This kind goeth not out but by prayer and fasting."

10. Again, we hold on too long, that is, we do not go from promise to promise, taking hold on them as they rise one above the other. Now it is manifest to those who have experience on the subject that the promises are adapted to all possible states of mind, from the lowest degree of grace and from the lowest depths of despondency, step by step, up to the highest degrees of holy confidence and triumph of which the human mind is capable. It often comes to pass that when individuals have taken hold on some of those promises designed to reach the Christian in his most languid state—such as "he giveth power to the faint, and to him that hath no might he increaseth strength," [or] "the bruised reed shall he not break, and the smoking flax shall he not quench till he bring forth judgment unto victory"—that here he rests. And being comforted by these promises he does not proceed to take hold on promises suited to his state of mind as he rises, and thus rise quite out of the murky regions of his unbelief and selfishness, but

contents himself with hanging upon that one, or those of that class, without rising any higher. It is impossible that a believer should remain stationary. He must go from strength to strength or he will certainly insensibly decline. The promises are like a ladder that reaches from earth to heaven, and the cry continually is, come up higher, *come up higher*. And unless the mind is taken up with viewing the heights still above, and what is still to be attained, it is apt to become giddy with looking down upon those below and, dwelling upon its own attainments and being lifted up with pride, falls into the condemnation of the devil.

11. We do not duly consider how intimately God's glory is connected with our receiving all that the promises mean. We are apt to be taken up with a sense of our unworthiness and be discouraged by a consideration of it, and not duly to consider that this very unworthiness would render it exceedingly honorable to God to give us the fullness of His grace and wholly to transform us into His own image. I love to contemplate the grace of God as manifested in Paul—once a Saul, a raging persecutor breathing out threatenings and slaughter against the infant church, afterwards so changed by the grace of God as to become the wonder of the world in his remarkable resemblance of the Son of God.

God's glory is His reputation or renown. And if to bestow great and transforming grace upon the children of men who are in the image of hell is calculated to convey a high idea of the patience, forbearance, goodness and moral omnipotence of God, then certainly His glory is intimately connected with our receiving the full meaning and power of His promises.

12. We do not sufficiently consider the importance of our becoming living illustrations of the power and grace of God. There should be among Christians a holy ambition, each one to become a living, standing illustration of the full meaning of the promises and of the provisions of the gospel to transform the soul into the divine image and make it a partaker of the divine nature. Who that has read the life of Mrs. President Edwards has not been encouraged and edified and strengthened to press after higher attainments in holiness when they have seen what grace can do and what it actually has done, even in modern times, to transform and elevate the soul. Now as we prize the glory of God, as we desire to do good to the church, instead of being satisfied with small attainments we should reach after the highest measure of grace, and try the full strength and intent of the promises, and ask God to give us for His own glory all that He meant to promise—that the unbelief of the church may be rebuked and that we might so illustrate in our own experience the fullness of gospel salvation that the frittering away of the promises and paring them down to the legal experience of the church in her present state may be done away forever.

13. Another reason is the concealing the grace of God which we actually have received, either through the suggestion of Satan that we shall lose the present blessing or through fear that we shall be thought egotistical and proud if we declare what God has done for our souls. Says the Psalmist, "I have not hid thy righteousness within my heart. I have declared thy faithfulness and thy salvation. I have not concealed thy loving-kindness and thy

truth from the great congregation." And when he had been brought up from the horrible pit of miry clay and his feet set upon a rock, his goings established and a new song put into his mouth, he said, "Many shall see it and shall fear, and shall trust in the Lord." Christ has said that "men do not light a candle and put it under a bushel, but on a candlestick, that it may give light to all that are in the house." Even so, he adds, "let your light so shine that men may see your good works and glorify your Father in heaven."

Now it is not enough that we should merely behave ourselves aright, but we should be prompt and plain and simple-hearted in ascribing all our good works to the grace of God within us, else ourselves and not God will have the glory in the estimation of men. If we conceal the loving-kindness of the Lord, if we are ashamed or afraid or for any cause neglect to give Him glory and tell what the Spirit hath done for our souls, we may expect that to overtake us which was spoken by the prophet, "If ye will not hear and if ye will not lay it to heart to give glory unto my name, saith the Lord of hosts, I will even send a curse upon you and I will curse your blessings."

14. A voluntary humility may prevent us from receiving the fulfillment of the promises. Many individuals seem afraid to hope or expect to attain to any but the lowest measures of grace, on account of their great unworthiness. They feel as if it would be aspiring and getting out of their place to ask for the children's bread, and therefore suppose themselves to be doing God service in consenting to live upon the crumbs under the table. They read of the attainments of others, but ah! they think, these are not such great sinners as themselves. They thus dishonor the grace of God by somehow imagining that it was because they were not so great sinners that they have been so highly exalted. In other words, they insult the grace of God by accounting for the attainments of those of whom they read upon the score of justice rather than grace, supposing that it was because they were not so ill-deserving as themselves. Now what is this but wicked and shocking unbelief—depreciating the grace of God and ascribing that to justice which is only the result of infinite grace—and besides, a most self-righteous keeping down in the dust by a most God-dishonoring idea that our worthiness and not unworthiness is to recommend us to the grace of God?

Now it should be forever understood that worthiness recommends us to the justice and not to the grace of God and that our deep unworthiness, while it lays us under the condemning sentence of justice, recommends us to the grace of God. Let no one therefore suppose himself to be pleasing God when he voluntarily consents to grovel in the lowest attainments, when he ought to rise into the full sunlight of God's countenance and to be filled with all the fullness of God.

15. Another reason is a God-dishonoring unbelief, and a blasphemous putting in of "but and if" when pleading the promises of God, which imply insincerity on the part of God in making the promises. For example, Christ has said God is more willing to give the Holy Spirit to them that ask Him than parents are to give good gifts to their children. Suppose we pray for the Holy Ghost and preface and conclude the petition by saying, "if it be thy

will," &c. Now wherever there is an express promise, to put in an "if" in this way is to call in question the sincerity of God. Where He has made no conditions we are to make none, unless we would be guilty of adding to or subtracting from His Word.

16. Another difficulty is, very few have ever learned how to use the promises. They have so little faith in them as not to select them, nor have [they] committed them to memory nor arranged them in any order in their own minds. And to them, the weapons of their spiritual warfare are about as useless as if they were locked up in an armory. Now the promises of God should be so pondered, selected, arranged and remembered as to be ever ready at hand, that the one that is needed may be presented at any time to quench the fiery darts of the wicked. To understand how to use the promises of God is a science of vast extent, and it requires the highest exercise of the human faculties always to be able to seize upon the one we need for our own or for others' edification and support. I regard this as one of the principal qualifications of ministers. We need to know how so to apply the promises of grace as to bring the church from her low estate to those heights to which the promises were designed to elevate her.

17. Another reason is that the ministry to a great extent are frittering away instead of applying the promises of God to the help and edification of the church. My soul is often sick to see how the promises are understood and how they are explained away, and the church robbed of its heritage and the sheep starved to death by those who are set to feed the flock of God.

18. Another reason is, we regard iniquity in our hearts. If any sin is cherished there, if any lust is spared, if any unholy indulgence is pleaded for or defended, or pride or sin of any kind, the Lord will not hear us. "If I regard iniquity in my heart, the Lord will not hear me."

19. Another reason is, a disposition to defer the fulfillment of the promises to the millennium. In my apprehension, this is the very reason why the millennium has not already come: because the church are waiting for the effect to precede the cause. The millennium will be the fulfillment of these promises. Before they can be fulfilled they must be believed and pleaded. But the church seems to be waiting for the millennium first to come, and then they will lay hold of the promises. How long shall the church thus act? How long shall the promises that are conditioned in their very nature upon our faith remain a dead letter in the Bible because the church is waiting for their fulfillment before they are believed?

20. Many are doubting whether these promises are to be fulfilled until we get into eternity. For example, of the promise of the New Covenant it is said by some that no time is specified when it shall be fulfilled, and consequently we know not that we have a right to expect the blessing until we arrive at heaven. Now to this a multitude of answers might be given. But at present I will only say,

(1) That a promise in which no time for its fulfillment is either expressed or implied is void and a ridiculous mockery. Should I promise to pay A. B. twenty-five dollars without saying anything at all of the time, then he may call upon me at any time, for my obligation is considered as on

demand. But if I should say *at some* FUTURE time, without specifying when, it would be void, as the time would never come when it would be considered as due. This is true of the promises of God. When a promise is made in the present tense it is always due or may at any time be pleaded; if at a future time, it is not due until that time arrives. If a promise should be found (of which there is no instance in the Bible) in which no particular future time is expressed or implied, that promise must from its nature be a mere nullity. For faith being the condition, it is plain that the condition can never be fulfilled because there is nothing on which it can rest, it being impossible to ascertain whether the time is come or when it will come that the promise was intended to be fulfilled. If it be said, as in the promise of the New Covenant, that "after those days," "at that time," &c.—evidently referring to some particular future time when the promise should be fulfilled—at that time it becomes due; and ever after that time it may be pleaded as a promise in the present tense. The particular time referred to in such cases may be learned in general by the connection in which the promise stands or by reference to other parts of Scripture.

For example, many things are promised to be fulfilled "in the latter day," "at the end of the world or Jewish age," &c. From the Bible, it is abundantly evident that the latter day is the gospel day; that the end of the world, when by the phrase is meant the end of the Jewish state, is also the commencement of the Christian dispensation; and that all the promises of blessings to be bestowed "in the last days" are now to be regarded as in the present tense, to be fulfilled at any time and to anyone who will believe them. This is undeniably the understanding of the Apostle when, in Hebrews, he quotes the promise of the New Covenant from Jeremiah, as a promise to be fulfilled at the coming of Christ, who was the mediator of the New Covenant. Now the coming of Christ was the particular time at which the promise made by Jeremiah, and so often repeated in the prophets, was to be considered as due and forever after treated as a promise in the present tense. Christ's coming did not of itself secure the fulfillment of the promise, irrespective of our own faith and agency; but it pointed out the time when the church was to look for its fulfillment and when its fulfillment should depend upon their pleading it in faith.

(2) If there be no particular time in which the promises of God are to be fulfilled, I mean those of them that are in the future tense, then we can no more receive their fulfillment in heaven than we can here. For without a new revelation informing us that the time has come, we can never lay hold on them as due, we cannot believe and receive their fulfillment. If the promise is evidently future and no time is expressed or implied when it shall be fulfilled, when we have been in heaven myriads of ages we shall no more be able to lay hold on the promise as due nor, so far as I can see, be any more certain that the time for its fulfillment is not yet future than we are now.

21. Another reason why the promises are not fulfilled in us is, we are unwilling on some accounts to have them fulfilled—such as a fear of disgrace, being called fanatics, perfectionists or something else of the kind

that we dread, [or] lest we should have to abandon some particular indulgence, lust or favorite pursuit. Now it often happens that we would be very willing to have the blessing of sanctification if it did not imply the actual giving up of sin under every form. Many are praying for that blessing who are after all holding on to some form of sin.

22. Selfishness in our motives. Under one form and another, selfishness is often lurking in our applications to the throne of grace for promised blessings. God cannot be deceived in this. And unless our eye be single our whole body cannot be full of light.

23. Our experience of the inefficacy of prayer, such as we have so often offered in selfishness, operates as a discouragement, and we come to God in the peevishness of unbelief. We have so often come to God in our selfishness and pleaded His promises, overlooking the wickedness of our motives, that we are ready to conclude either that we have misunderstood the promises altogether, that the time has not come for their fulfillment, or [that] for some reason our prayers cannot prevail; and therefore we do not expect to receive the blessing. We are straitened by our wants and cry to God; but it is in the anguish of unbelief and we are of course denied.

24. Presumptuous misapplication of a promise. For example the promise, "I will never leave thee nor forsake thee" is so misapplied and misunderstood that we become presumptuous and depart from Him instead of His departing from us. So the promise in James, "If a man lack wisdom let him ask of God and it shall be given him," is sometimes so misunderstood as to lead persons to expect wisdom without research.

25. Persons often tempt God in asking the fulfillment of a promise without performing its conditions.

I might mention a great many other reasons, but these must suffice. And now I must close this discourse by saying that I cannot tell you how much I felt shocked when the question came fully up whether the grace of God was sufficient *as a matter of fact* for the entire sanctification of Christians in this life, and it was flatly denied. The question in this shape had never come fairly and fully before my mind as a subject of distinct consideration till the last winter of my residence in New York. And I can never express my astonishment and grief when I found that men standing high in the church of God flatly denied it. I have often asked myself, is it possible that these brethren can be of the opinion that if a man should believe and realize in his own experience the full meaning of the promises and all that the gospel and the grace of God can do for a man in this world, that he would not be entirely sanctified? I would humbly ask, where is there one among them that has tried the experiment? It is no answer to this to turn around and inquire, have you received the fullness of the promise? Are you sanctified? For if I have not, and if there were not a man on earth that has, that does not at all change the meaning of the promises nor prove that they are not sufficient to produce entire sanctification, so long as it is true that every one of them must confess that they have never received or hardly begun to receive all that they themselves admit the promises mean.

LECTURE 16

Being in Debt

Rom. 13:8: "Owe no man anything."

In discussing this subject I design to show:

I. The meaning of the text.
II. That to be in debt is sin.
III. The duty of those who are in debt.

I. *I am to show the meaning of the text.*

The meaning of this text, like most others, is to be learned from a careful examination of the verses in its connection. The Apostle begins the chapter by enforcing the duty of obedience to civil magistrates.

> Let every soul be subject unto the higher powers. For there is no power but of God: the powers that be are ordained of God. Whosoever therefore resisteth the power, resisteth the ordinance of God: and they that resist shall receive unto themselves damnation. For rulers are not a terror to good works, but to the evil. Wilt thou then not be afraid of the power? do that which is good, and thou shalt have praise of the same: for he is the minister of God unto thee for good. But if thou do that which is evil, be afraid; for he beareth not the sword in vain: for he is the minister of God, a revenger to execute wrath upon him that doeth evil. Wherefore ye must be subject, not only for wrath, but also for conscience sake. For for this cause pay ye tribute also: for they are God's ministers, attending continually upon this very thing.

They are the servants of God, employed for your benefit. You are therefore to pay them tribute, that is, give them the support which their circumstances require.

In the light of this and various other passages of scripture, I have often wondered how it was possible that any person could call in question the duty of obeying civil magistrates, or how they could call in question the right and duty of magistrates to inflict civil penalties, and even capital punishment where the nature of the case demands it. Certainly this passage recognizes their right and their duty "to execute wrath" upon transgressors, as the servants and executioners of God's vengeance.

> Render therefore to all their dues: tribute to whom tribute is due; custom to whom custom; fear to whom fear; honour to whom honour. Owe no man any thing, but to love one another; for he that loveth another hath fulfilled the law. For this, Thou shalt not commit adultery, Thou shalt not kill, Thou shalt not bear false witness, Thou shalt not covet; and if there be any other commandment, it is briefly comprehended in this saying, namely, Thou shalt love thy neighbour as thyself. Love worketh no ill to his neighbour: therefore love is the fulfilling of the law.

From this connection it is evident that the Apostle designed to teach that whenever we come to owe a man, we should immediately pay him and not suffer any debt or obligation to rest upon us undischarged. "Owe no man any thing, but to love one another." Here the Apostle recognizes the truth that love is of perpetual obligation, and that this obligation can never be so canceled or discharged as to be no longer binding. He recognizes no other obligation except love with its natural fruits as being, in its own nature, of perpetual obligation. In respect to this obligation, all that we can do is to fulfill it every moment, without the possibility of so fulfilling it as to set aside the continued obligation to love.

But we are to owe no man anything else but love. We are to "render to all their dues, tribute to whom tribute is due, honour to whom honour." I understand the text then simply to mean, let no obligation but that of love with its natural fruits, which is from its very nature a perpetual obligation, rest upon you undischarged. I am aware that some modern critics maintain that this passage should have been rendered indicatively. But such men as Doddridge and Henry, Barnes and Prof. Stuart, are of the opinion that its imperative rendering is correct. And all are agreed that the doctrine of this text, as it stands, is plainly a doctrine of the Bible.

Here the question arises, what is it to owe a man in the sense of this text? I answer,

1. If you *employ* a laborer and do not stipulate the time and terms of payment, it is taken for granted that he is to be paid when his work is done and to have the money. If you hire him for a day and nothing is said to the contrary, he cannot demand his pay till his day's work is done; till then you owe him nothing. The same is true if you hire him for a week or a month or a year. When the time which he is to labor is stipulated and nothing is said about the time and terms of payment, you owe him nothing, that is, nothing is due till his time has expired. But if the time was not specified which he was to labor, he may break off at any time and demand pay for what he has done. Or if the time of payment was expressed or understood, whenever it arrives you then owe him and are bound to pay him agreeably to the un-

derstanding.

2. The same is true if you hire a horse or any other piece of property. If you hire it for a specified time and nothing is said of the conditions of payment, the understanding is that you are to pay when the time for which the property was hired has expired. It then becomes a debt. Then you are to pay, and pay the money. If there were any other understanding fixing the time and terms of payment, you do not owe the man until the specified conditions are complied with.

3. The same is true if you *purchase* any piece of property. If nothing is stipulated to the contrary, the understanding is that you are to pay the cash at the time you receive the property. At that time, and neither before nor after, you are expected to pay the purchase money.

We do not properly owe an individual until we are under an obligation to pay him. Whenever he has a right to demand the pay we have no right to withhold it. There may be such a thing as contracting a prospective debt, giving your obligation to become due at a certain time. But then you do not properly owe because you are under no obligation to pay till it becomes due. But whenever it becomes due you are bound immediately to pay it.

II. *I am to show that it is a sin to be in debt.*

1. Because it is a *direct violation of the command of God*. This text is just as binding as any command of the decalogue. And a violation of it is a setting aside [of] the command of Jehovah, as much as to commit adultery or murder. It is not to be regarded merely as a piece of advice given by the Apostle but as a direct and positive and authoritative command of God.

2. It is *unjust to be in debt*. If your creditor has a right to demand payment, you certainly have no right to withhold it. If it is due it is a contradiction to say that it is not unjust for you not to pay. It is a contradiction, both in *terms* and in *fact*, to say that you owe a man, and at the same time are guilty of no injustice in refusing or neglecting to pay him. It is as much injustice as *stealing* and involves the same principle. The *sin* of stealing consists in the appropriating to ourselves that which properly belongs to another. Therefore whenever you withhold from any man his due, you are guilty of as absolute an injustice as if you stole his property.

3. It is sin *because it is falsehood*. I have already shown that you do not properly owe a man till it becomes due. It becomes due when and because there is a promise on your part expressed or implied that you will pay it at that time. Now you cannot violate this promise without being guilty of falsehood.

4. If what has just been said is true, it follows that men should *meet their contracts* as they would avoid the grossest sin. They are bound to avoid being in debt, to meet and fulfill their engagements, as much as they are bound to avoid blasphemy, idolatry, murder or any other sin. And a man who does not pay his debts is no more to be accounted an honest man than he who is guilty of any other heinous crime.

178

5. If a professor of religion is in debt, he is a *moral delinquent* and should be accounted and treated as a subject of church discipline.

OBJECTION. It may be said, I cannot avoid being in debt. I answer to this,

That if you cannot pay you could have avoided contracting the debt and were bound to do so.

Do you reply, I really needed the thing which I purchased?

I ask, were your necessities so great that you would have been justified in your estimation in lying or stealing to supply them? If not, why have you resorted to fraud? The same authority that prohibits lying or stealing prohibits your owing a man. Why then do you violate this commandment of God any more than the other? Is it not because a corrupt public sentiment has rendered the violation of this commandment less disgraceful than to violate these other commands of God? Why did you not resort to begging instead of running in debt? Better far to beg than to run in debt. Begging is not prohibited by any command of God but being in debt is prohibited. True, it is disgraceful to beg. But a God-dishonoring public sentiment has rendered it far less so to be in debt. And does not this account for your shameless violation of this command of God?

Do you say again, I have been disappointed. I expected to have had the money. I made the contract in good faith and expected to meet it at the time; but others owe me and do not pay me, therefore I am unable to pay my debts. To this I reply,

You should have contracted with that expressed condition. You should have made known your circumstances and the ground of your expectation in regard to being able to pay at the time appointed. In that case, if your creditor was willing to run the risk of your being disappointed, the fault is not yours, as you have practiced no injustice or deception. But if your contract was without condition, you have taken upon yourself the risk of disappointment and are not guiltless.

But here it may be said again, nearly the whole church are in debt, and if subject to discipline, who shall cast the first stone? I reply,

(1) If it be true that the church is so extensively in debt, no wonder that the curse of God is upon her.

(2) Again, it may be true that a church may be so generally involved in any given sin as to make that sin a difficult subject of discipline. But when this is true of any church, it is a shameless abomination for the members of that church to attempt to hide themselves under the admitted fact that nearly all the church are involved in the guilt of it. Now rest assured that when any sin becomes so prevalent that it cannot and is not made, in that church, a subject of discipline, God himself will sooner or later take up the rod and find means to discipline, and that effectually, such a church.

III. *I am to state the duty of those who are in debt.*

1. They are bound to make any *sacrifice* of property or time, and indeed *any sacrifice* that it is possible for them to make, to pay their debts.

Here it may be asked again, does the law of love permit my creditor to demand a sacrifice of me? If he loves me as he does himself, why should he require or even allow me to make a sacrifice of property to pay what I owe him? I reply:

(1) If anyone is to make a sacrifice or suffer loss, it is the debtor and not the creditor. It will almost certainly be some damage to him to be disappointed in not receiving his due. It may so disarrange his affairs and break in upon his calculations as to occasion him great damage. Of this he is to be the judge.

(2) Your sacrifice may be necessary not only to prevent his *loss* but to enable him to meet his contracts, and thus prevent his *sin*. His confidence in your veracity may have led him to contract prospective debts, and by not paying him you not only sin yourself but cause him to sin.

(3) The refusal of one to make a sacrifice to pay his debts may involve many others in both *loss* and *sin*. A owes B, B owes C and C owes D, and so on in a long chain of mutual dependencies. Now if there be a failure in the first or any other link of this chain, all below it are involved in loss and sin. Now where shall this evil be arrested?

Suppose you hold the place of C. A refuses to make a sacrifice to pay B, and B to pay you. Shall you sin because they do, and involve your creditor in loss and sin? No. Whatever others may do, you are bound to pay your debts. And unless your creditor voluntarily consents to defer the time of payment, you are bound to pay him at any sacrifice.

2. Persons that are in debt should not *contract new debts* to pay old ones. It is the practice of some, when they get involved, to keep up their credit by borrowing of one to pay another. Their meeting and canceling the last debt depends altogether upon the presumption that they shall be able to borrow the money of somebody else. When they have borrowed of one they will keep him out of his pay as long as possible without losing their credit. And then, instead of making a sacrifice of property sufficient to discharge the obligation, they borrow from B to pay A and from C to pay B and thus, perhaps, disappoint and disoblige a dozen men by not paying them exactly at the time agreed, instead of at once stopping short and parting with what they have, at any sacrifice, to pay the debt.

I do not say that a man should not in any case borrow of one man to pay another. But this I say, that as a general thing such practices are highly reprehensible. Still, if a debt becomes due and you have not the money at hand but are certain that at a given time you shall have it, I do not suppose it wrong for you to borrow and pay this debt, with the understanding that you pay this borrowed money at the time specified. But to borrow money with no other prospect of an ultimate payment than that you can borrow again, and thus keep up your credit from time to time, is wicked.

3. Those who are in debt have no right *to give away* the money which they owe. If you are in debt the money in your hands belongs to your creditor and not to you. You have no right, therefore, "to be generous till you are just." You have strictly no more right to give that money away than you have to steal money to give away.

But here it should be particularly understood what *is* and what *is not* to be accounted as giving money away; for example, it is not giving away your money to pay the current expenses of the congregation to which you are attached. Your proportion of the current expenses of the congregation or church to which you belong is impliedly if not expressly contracted by you. You cannot withhold it any more than the payment of any other debt. The same may be said of the support of ministers and foreign missionaries and all for whose support the faith of the church is pledged. It seems to be a common but erroneous understanding of professors of religion that what are more generally called their secular debts or obligations are binding and are to be discharged of course, but that their obligations, expressed or implied, to religious institutions are not so absolutely binding; and of course they can *give* nothing, as they express it, to these objects until their debts are paid.

Now beloved, you ought to know that to the support of the institutions of religion, you are pledged, both virtually and actually, by your profession, and that these are your most sacred debts and are thus to be considered and discharged by you. I beseech of you not to consider the meeting and canceling of such demands as these in the light of a *gift*, as if you were making God a present instead of discharging a solemn debt. I have been astonished to find that the pecuniary embarrassments of the few past years have so far crippled the movements of the great benevolent societies for want of funds, and that missionaries, for whose support the faith and honor of the church were pledged, should be so far cut short of their necessary supplies, under the pretense that the church must pay her secular debts before she could discharge her high and sacred obligations to them and the work in which they are engaged.

4. A person who is in debt has no right to purchase for himself or family things not absolutely essential for their subsistence. Things that might lawfully be purchased and used under other circumstances become unlawful when you are in debt. A creditor has no right to deprive you of necessary food and indispensable raiment, or of your liberty. To do so would put it out of your power ever to pay. But you have no right to indulge in any thing more than the necessaries of life while your debts are unpaid. To do so is as unlawful as it would be to steal to purchase unnecessary articles.

REMARKS

1. From what has been said it is plain that the whole credit system, if not absolutely sinful, is nevertheless so highly dangerous that no Christian should embark in it.

Since the preaching of this sermon this remark has been censured as a rash one. A rash remark! Let the present history and experience of the church say whether the credit system is not so highly dangerous that the man who will venture to embark in it is guilty of rashness and presumption. When has religion for centuries been so generally disgraced as by the bankruptcy of its professors within the last few years? And how many millions of [dollars] . . . are now due from church members to ungodly men that will never be paid? Rash! Why, this is the very plea of the church, that they can do nothing for the support of the gospel because they are so much in debt. Is there no danger of any man's getting in debt who attempts to trade upon a borrowed capital? Indeed it is highly dangerous, as universal experience shows.

And what is the necessity, I pray, for Christians to embark in so dangerous an enterprise, and one that so highly jeopardizes the honor or religion? Is it because the institutions of religion demand it? Religion sustains a greater loss through the debts and bankruptcies of Christians than it ever gains by their prosperity.

But the credit system, as it now prevails and has prevailed, is useless and worse than useless. For example, suppose the consumers of merchandise, instead of anticipating their yearly crops and yearly income and running in debt with the expectation of paying from these, were to take a little pains to reverse this order of things and be a year beforehand, paying down for what they purchase and having the income of each year beforehand, so as to contract no debts. In this case the country merchants, giving no credit but receiving ready pay, would be able to pay down on the purchase of their goods from the wholesale dealer, the wholesale dealer would pay down to the importer, the importer to the manufacturer, and the manufacturer to the producer.

Now any man can see that many millions a year would be saved to this country in this way. The manufacturer could afford an article cheaper for ready pay, and so could the importer and the wholesale dealer and each one in his turn, down to the consumer. Every one could sell cheaper for ready pay as no risk would be run, and business could be done with much greater convenience and safety. Thus an entire rejection of the credit system in its present form and an adoption of the system of ready pay would afford to the consumer every article so much cheaper as to save millions of dollars every year. And I do not apprehend that there is in reality any serious difficulty in so reversing the whole order of business.

At another time I may more particularly examine the credit system in its foundation and various ramifications, and the nature and tendencies of the prevailing system of doing business on borrowed capital. But at present I can only say, as I have said, that waiving the question whether it is absolutely sinful in itself, it is too highly dangerous to be embarked in by those who feel a tender solicitude for the honor and cause of Christ.

2. That if in any case the present payment of debts is impossible, your duty is to regard your indebtedness as a sin against God and your neighbor, to repent, and set yourself with all practicable self-denial to pay as fast as you can. And unless you are laying yourself out to pay your debts, do not imagine that you repent either of your indebtedness or any other sin. For you are impenitent and a shameless hypocrite rather than a Christian, if you suffer yourself to be in debt and are not making all practicable efforts to do justice to your creditors.

3. If payment is *possible* by any sacrifice of property on your part, sin is

upon you till you do pay. There is a wicked custom among men, and to a considerable amount in the church, of putting property out of their hands to avoid a sacrifice in the payment of their debts. As an instance take the elder whom I mentioned in a former lecture, who confessed to me that "he was avoiding the sacrifice of his property in the payment of his debts by *finesse* of law."

4. The lax notions and practices of the world and of the church upon this subject are truly abominable. It has come to pass that a man may not only be considered a respectable citizen but a respectable member of the church, who suffers himself to be in debt, who has judgments and executions against him, and who resorts not only "to *finesse* of law to avoid the payment of his debts" but who practices the most palpable frauds against both God and man by putting his property out of his hands to avoid meeting his just responsibilities. O shame on the church and on these professors of religion! Some of them will even go to an unconverted lawyer for advice in this iniquitous business and lay open before his unconverted heart their shameless iniquity. Alas, how many lawyers are thus led to call in question the whole truth of the Christian religion, and over these dishonest professors they stumble into hell. And until the church will rise up and wash her hands and cleanse her garments from this iniquity, by banishing such persons from her communion, the cause of Christ will not cease to bleed at every pore.

5. Some persons take the ground that not to meet their contracts and pay their debts when they become due is not sinful, on account of the general understanding of businessmen upon such subjects. To this I answer,

(1) There is no understanding among businessmen that debts are not to be paid when they become due. Among that class of men the nonpayment of a debt always involves a disgrace and a wrong, even in their own estimation.

(2) Let the public sentiment be what it might among businessmen, still the law of God cannot be altered; and by this unchanging law it is a sin to be in debt. And as "sin is a disgrace to any people," it is both a *sin* and a *shame* to be in debt.

6. The rule laid down in this text is applicable not only to individuals but to corporations and nations and all bodies of men assuming pecuniary responsibilities.

7. It is *dishonest* and *dishonorable* to hire or purchase an article and say nothing about payment till afterwards.

8. The violation of this law is working immense mischief in the church and in the world. It is truly shocking to see to what an extent the church is involved in debt and church members are engaged in collecting debts of each other by force of law. The heart-burnings and bitterness that exist among church members on account of the nonpayment of their debts to each other are awfully great and alarming. Besides all this, in what light does the church appear before the world—as a mass of money-makers and speculators and bankrupts, shuffling and managing through *finesse* of law to avoid the payment of their debts? I could relate facts within my own

knowledge, and many of them too, that would cause the cheek of piety to blush. Alas for the rage and madness of a speculating, money-making, fraudulent church!

9. There is great reason to believe that many young men in the course of their education involve themselves in debts that so far eat up their piety as to render them nearly useless all their days. I would sooner be twenty-five years in getting an education, and paying my way, than involve myself in debt to the Education Society or in any other way. How many young men there are who are in debt to the Education Society and who are dealing very loosely with their consciences on the subject of payment. Because the Education Society do not press them right up, they let the matter lie along from time to time [and] increase their expenditures as their income may increase, instead of practicing self-denial and honestly discharging their obligations to the Society.

10. I cannot have *confidence* in the piety of any man who is not *conscientious* in the payment of his debts. I know some men who are in debt and who spend their time and their property in a manner wholly inconsistent with their circumstances, and still make great pretensions to piety. They are active in prayer meetings, take a conspicuous place at the communion table, and even hold a responsible office in the church of Christ; and yet they seem to have no conscience about paying their debts.

I believe it is right and the duty of all churches and ministers to exclude such persons from the communion of the church. And were it generally done it would go far to wipe away the stains that have been brought by such persons upon the religion of Jesus Christ. I do not see why they should be suffered to come to the communion table any more than whoremongers or murderers or drunkards or Sabbath breakers or slaveholders.

11. There must be a great reformation in the church upon this subject before the business class of ungodly men will have much confidence in religion. This reformation should begin immediately and begin where it ought to begin, among the leading members of the church of Christ. Ministers and church judicatories should speak out upon the subject, should "cry aloud and spare not, but lift up their voice like a trumpet and show Israel his transgressions and the house of Jacob their sins."

And now, beloved, are any of you in debt? Then sin is upon you. Rise up and show yourselves clean in this matter, I beseech you. Make every effort to meet and discharge your responsibilities. And beware that in attempting to pay your debts you do not resort to means that are as highly reprehensible as to be in debt.

12. Let no one complain and say that instead of preaching the gospel I am discussing mere business transactions of the world. Religion is to regulate the business transactions of the world. Religion is a practical thing. It does not consist in austerities, prayers and masses and monkish superstitions, as Papists vainly dream. If religion does not take hold of a man's business operations, if it does not reform his daily life and habits, of what avail is it? Until in these respects your practice is right, you cannot expect to enjoy the influences of the Holy Spirit. You cannot grow in holiness any

further than you reform your practice.

The preceptive part of the gospel, therefore, is to be spread out in all its detail before you. And when you find it "convinces you of sin," I beg of you not to turn around and say that this is preaching about business and not about religion. What is business but a part of religion? A man that does not consider it so in practice has no religion at all.

And now, dearly beloved, instead of suffering your heart to rise up and resist what I have said, will you not as I have often requested go down upon your knees and spread this whole subject before the Lord? Will you not inquire wherein you have erred and sinned, and make haste to repent and reform your lives?

LECTURE 17

The Holy Spirit of Promise*

Gal. 3:14: "That the blessing of Abraham might come on the Gentiles through Jesus Christ; that we might receive the promise of the Spirit through faith."

This text teaches us:

I. That the blessing of Abraham has come on the Gentiles through Jesus Christ.
II. It teaches what this blessing is.
III. That it is to be received by faith.

Before I conclude what I wish to say upon the promises, I will notice the relation which the New Covenant sustains to the Covenant made with Abraham. And I am to show:

I. *That the blessing of Abraham has come on the Gentiles through Jesus Christ.*

In the 12th chapter of Genesis we have the first mention of the covenant which God made with Abraham. In the last clause of the third verse it is said, "In thee shall all the families of the earth be blessed." In Gen. 17:4 it is written, "As for me, behold my covenant is with thee, and thou shalt be a father of many nations," [and in] verse 7, "I will establish my covenant between me and thee and thy seed after thee in their generations, for an everlasting covenant, to be a God unto thee and to thy seed after thee." [In

---

* The title is taken from Ephesians 1:13.

Gen.] 18:18 the same promise is noticed again, [as in] 22:18, "and in thy seed shall all the nations of the earth be blessed," and 26:4, [where] the same words are repeated.

Now it should be remembered in regard to the covenant made with Abraham that there were two things promised. Temporal Canaan or Palestine was promised to the Jews or natural descendants of Abraham. There was also a blessing promised through Abraham to all the nations of the earth. This covenant was not only made with Abraham but through his seed, as we shall see, with all the nations of the earth. This was a spiritual blessing, and that which the text says has come on the Gentiles through Jesus Christ.

I will quote several other passages to show that this *spiritual blessing* was intended for and has come on the Gentiles. In Rom. 4:13 it is said, "For the promise, that he should be the heir of the world, was not to Abraham, or to his seed, through the law, but through the righteousness of faith"; and [in] verse 16, "Therefore it is of faith, that it might *be* by grace; to the end the promise might be sure to all the seed; not to that only which is of the law, but to that which is of the faith of Abraham, who is the father of us all." This epistle to the Romans was written to the Gentiles. And the Apostle here expressly affirms that the Gentiles who had *faith* are of the seed of Abraham, and that he is the father of us all.

Gal. 3:7, 9, 14, 29: "Know ye therefore that they which are of faith, the same are the children of Abraham. So then they which be of faith are blessed with faithful Abraham, that the blessing of Abraham might come on the Gentiles through Jesus Christ; that we might receive the promise of the Spirit through faith. And if ye *be* Christ's, then are ye Abraham's seed, and heirs according to the promise." Here again it is manifest that the Apostle in writing to the Gentiles expressly includes them in the covenant made with Abraham and affirms that if they are Christians, then they are "Abraham's seed, and heirs according to the promise." And [in] 4:28 he says "Now we, brethren, as Isaac was, are the children of promise." Here then he affirms that the Gentiles are as absolutely within the promise made to Abraham as Isaac was. In Eph. 2:12-22 we have it declared in full that the Gentiles inherit all the promises of spiritual blessings made to Abraham and the fathers, that there is no distinction in this respect between Jews and Gentiles, that all who have *faith* are entitled to the promises of spiritual blessings.

> That at that time ye were without Christ, being aliens from the commonwealth of Israel, and strangers from the covenants of promise, having no hope, and without God in the world. But now in Christ Jesus ye who sometime were far off are made nigh by the blood of Christ. For he is our peace, who hath made both one, and hath broken down the middle wall of partition *between us*, having abolished in his flesh the enmity, *even* the law of commandments *contained* in ordinances; for to make in himself of twain one new man, *so* making peace; and that he might reconcile both unto God in one body by the cross, having slain the enmity thereby; and came and preached peace to you which were afar off, and to them that were nigh. For

through him we both have access by one Spirit unto the Father. Now therefore ye are no more strangers and foreigners, but fellowcitizens with the saints, and of the household of God; and are built upon the foundation of the apostles and prophets, Jesus Christ himself being the chief corner *stone*; in whom all the building fitly framed together groweth unto a holy temple in the Lord: in whom ye also are builded together for an habitation of God through the Spirit.

I might quote many more passages to the same import, but these must suffice.

II. *I am to show what this blessing is.*

1. It is not merely a promise that Christ should be of his seed, for the Apostle affirms in Gal. 3:16, 19 that the promise was made to Christ through Abraham. "Now to Abraham and his seed were the promises made. He saith not, And to seeds as of many, but as of one, And to thy seed, which is Christ. Wherefore then *serveth* the law? It was added because of transgression, till the seed should come to whom the promise was made; *and it was* ordained by angels in the hand of a mediator." And in the text it is said "that the blessing might come on the Gentiles through Jesus Christ." This blessing then promised was not Christ himself but some promise to Christ, and through Christ to all the nations of the earth.

2. The text informs us that this blessing promised to Abraham and to his seed, and through Christ his seed to all the nations of the earth, is the Holy Spirit. This is the grand thing upon which the prophets and the inspired writers seem to have had their eye all along under the old dispensation. And by a careful examination of the Scriptures, it will be found that the promises are one unbroken chain from Abraham to Christ and even to the time when the canon of the Scripture was complete, everywhere pointing out this particular blessing. It was promised sometimes in figurative language, where the Spirit of God is represented as water. But in most instances the prophets have spoken without a figure and promised the Spirit by name:

Isa. 32:15, "Until the Spirit be poured upon us from on high, and the wilderness be a fruitful field, and the fruitful field be counted for a forest"; and 44:3, "For I will pour water upon him that is thirsty, and floods upon the dry ground: I will pour my Spirit upon thy seed, and my blessing upon thine offspring"; and 59:21, "As for me, this *is* my covenant with them, saith the Lord; My Spirit that *is* upon thee, and my words which I have put in thy mouth, shall not depart out of thy mouth, nor out of the mouth of thy seed, nor out of the mouth of thy seed's seed, saith the Lord, from henceforth and for ever."

Jer. 31:33, "But this *shall be* the covenant that I will make with the house of Israel; After those days, saith the Lord, I will put my law in their inward parts, and write it in their hearts; and will be their God, and they shall be my people"; and 32:40, "And I will make an everlasting covenant with them, that I will not turn away from them, to do them good; but I will put my fear in their hearts, that they shall not depart from me." Ezek.

11:19, "And I will give them one heart, and I will put a new spirit within you; and I will take the stony heart out of their flesh, and will give them an heart of flesh"; and 36:27, "And I will put my Spirit within you and cause you to walk in my statutes, and ye shall keep my judgments, and do *them.*" And the text, "That the blessing of Abraham might come on the Gentiles through Jesus Christ, that we might receive the promise of the Spirit through faith." Acts 1:4-5, "And, being assembled together with *them*, [Jesus] commanded them that they should not depart from Jerusalem, but wait for the promise of the Father, which, *saith he*, ye have heard of me. For John truly baptised with water; but ye shall be baptised with the Holy Ghost not many days hence."

John 7:38, 39, "He that believeth on me, as the scripture hath said, out of his belly shall flow rivers of living water. (But this spake he of the Spirit which they that believe on him should receive; for the Holy Ghost was not yet *given*; because that Jesus was not yet glorified.)"; and 16:7, 13, "Nevertheless I tell you the truth; It is expedient for you that I go away: for if I go not away, the Comforter will not come unto you; but if I depart, I will send him unto you." "Howbeit when he, the Spirit of truth, is come, he will guide you into all truth: for he shall not speak of himself; but whatsoever he shall hear, *that* shall he speak: and he will shew you things to come"; and 14:16, 17, "And I will pray the Father, and he shall give you another Comforter, that he may abide with you for ever; *even* the Spirit of truth; whom the world cannot receive, because it seeth him not, neither knoweth him: but ye know him; for he dwelleth with you, and shall be in you."

A careful examination of these passages will show what the great blessing under the eye of inspiration was. The great thing promised to Abraham as affirmed in the text and in these passages which I have now quoted, with numerous other passages that might be quoted, demonstrate that the great thing promised was the Holy Spirit. This was the spiritual blessing that belonged to all nations, while temporal Canaan belonged only to the Jews. In Eph. 1:13 the Holy Spirit is expressly called the "Holy Spirit of promise."

III. *This blessing is to be received by faith.*

1. This is expressly asserted in the text, "that we might receive the promise of the Spirit THROUGH FAITH." In the second verse of this same chapter the Apostle inquires, "Received ye the Spirit by the works of the law or by the hearing of FAITH?" [In] John 7:38-39 Christ says, "He that BELIEVETH ON ME, as the scripture hath said, out of his belly shall flow rivers of living water. (But this spake he of the Spirit, which they that BELIEVE ON HIM should receive.)" Other passages might be quoted to the same effect.

2. It is a natural impossibility that it should be received but by faith. This will be manifest if we inquire (1) into the nature of faith [and] (2) what it is to receive the Holy Ghost.

(1) The three elements of faith are (a) an intellectual perception of the truth, (b) a realization of the truth [and] (c) that trust or confidence of the

heart that yields all our voluntary powers up to the control of truth. These are the essential elements of faith.

(2) To receive the Holy Spirit is to take Him for our *Parakletos*, our comforter, guide, instructor. Now it is manifest on the very face of it that the Holy Spirit can only be received by the mind, by that act which constitutes faith. Perception of the truth is not itself faith. A realization of the truth is not itself faith. Though both these are indispensable to its existence, yet faith itself is an act of the will—a trust, a confiding in, a yielding up of the whole being to the influence of truth. Faith then is the yielding up of our voluntary powers to the guidance, instruction, influences and government of the Holy Spirit. This is receiving Him, and this is the only possible way in which He can be received. The mere perception of truth respecting Him is not faith, nor is it a receiving of Him. For the truth respecting Him may be perceived, and often has been perceived, and yet rejected. Nor is a realization of the truth respecting Him, however deep and intense, either faith or a receiving of Him. But when His offers of guidance are perceived and realized, faith is that act of the mind that lays hold upon these offers, that yields up the whole being to His influences and control.

REMARKS

1. The Abrahamic covenant is not abolished. Nor is it yet fulfilled to all the world. It has been supposed by some that the Abrahamic covenant was fulfilled at the coming of Christ and was then abolished. This notion arises out of the mistaken opinion that Christ was the particular blessing promised. But it has been shown that Christ was not the thing promised but that the promise was made to Him and, through Him, to all the nations of the earth. This covenant then is not abrogated nor set aside, nor can it be till all the nations of the earth are blessed by the outpouring of the Holy Ghost. And it is manifest that this covenant not only concerns all the nations of some one generation but extends its provisions to the end of time.

2. This promise made to Abraham, and all those others founded upon it and promising the same things, are now due, that is, the time has come when they are to be considered as promises in the present tense. They may now be claimed by the church for themselves and for all the nations of the earth. These promises were not due in Abraham's day. They were promises to him and to all the Old Testament saints of future good. And it is expressly said of Abraham and of the Old Testament saints that they "all died in faith not having received the promises but having seen them afar off." And again in Heb. 11:39, 40, "And these all, having obtained a good report through faith, received not the promise, God having provided some better thing for us, that they without us should not be made perfect." Here it is plainly declared that these promises are due to us and available to us in a higher sense than they were to Abraham and the Old Testament saints.

3. The New Covenant, so often quoted and so largely dwelt upon, is the fulfillment of the Abrahamic covenant to those who receive it. It consists in the Holy Spirit taking up His abode in the heart and writing His law there.

Let it be understood then that the New Covenant sustains the same relation to the Abrahamic covenant that the fulfillment of a promise does to the promise itself. The Abrahamic covenant and the New Covenant are not identical, but the one is the fulfillment of the other.

4. This blessing of the Holy Spirit is to be received at once, by faith, irrespective of all works. No work whatever performed without His influences prepares us in the least degree to receive Him or at all puts us in more favorable circumstances in respect to our salvation or sanctification.

5. All preparation on our part to receive Him and all delay, however earnest we may suppose ourselves to be in seeking and preparing to receive His influences, are only self-righteousness and rebellion—a vain and God-provoking attempt to get grace by works and to purchase by our Pharisaical efforts the gift of the Holy Ghost. It does seem to be one of the most difficult things in the world for the self-righteous spirit of man to understand the simplicity of gospel faith. He is continually seeking salvation and sanctification by works of law without being aware of it.

6. I have already said that since the seed has come to whom the promise was made, that is, Christ, that we are to regard the promise of the universal effusion of the Holy Spirit as a promise in the present tense, to be so understood and pleaded and its present fulfillment urged by the church. Until the church come to understand this as a promise actually made to all nations, and as having actually become due and now to be received and treated by them as a promise in the present tense, the millennium will never come.

When God had promised the restoration of Israel after seventy years' captivity in Babylon, it is said that Daniel learned by books, that is, by the prophets, that the captivity should continue but seventy years. At the end of the seventy years therefore he set his face, by prayer and supplication with sackcloth and ashes, to the Lord for the fulfillment of his promise. And he wrestled with God until he prevailed.

When God had expressly promised to Elijah that if he would go and show himself to Ahab he would send rain upon the earth, he regarded the promise, after he had shown himself to Ahab, as in the present tense, as he had a right to do. But he did not expect the fulfillment without prayer. But on the contrary he gave himself to mighty wrestlings with God and did not leave his knees until the cloud was seen to arise that watered all the land.

So God in the promise of the outpouring of His Spirit in Ezek. 36:25, 27 has added in the 37th verse, "I will yet for this be inquired of by the house of Israel to do it for them." Now the church are praying, and have been for a long time, for the millennium to come and for the fulfillment of this promise. But let me inquire. Do they understand these as promises now due, which they have a right to plead in faith for all the nations of the earth? It would seem as if they supposed the promise still future and do not understand that a promise which is due at some specified future time is ever after that time, to all intents and purposes, a promise in the present tense. And until it is so regarded and treated and pleaded, and the requisite means used for its accomplishment, it can never be fulfilled. Christians seem to pray as if they supposed it questionable whether God's time had come to convert the world. They ask Him to do it in His own time and way, &c. Now it should be understood that He has bound himself by a promise to give His Spirit to all the nations of the earth, when the seed to whom the promise was made had come and prepared the way for the bestowment of the blessing. Now God says He "will be inquired of by the *house of Israel.*"

It is not enough that some one or some few should understand these promises aright and plead them. A few can never use a sufficient amount of means to bring about their fulfillment. They must be understood by Christians generally, in their proper import and as being now due, and they must resolve not to hold their peace nor give God rest until He makes Jerusalem a praise in the earth. They must insist upon their fulfillment now, and not consent that it should be put off any longer. Hundreds of millions have gone to hell since these promises have become due, and should have been so regarded and pleaded and means used for their fulfillment. How long shall the church make it an act of piety and think themselves submitting to the will of God in letting these promises rot in their Bible, while God is waiting to fulfill them and commanding them not to give Him rest until He does fulfill them?

7. The Old Testament saints were saved not by works of law but by faith in the covenant made with Abraham. In other words Abraham himself together with all that were saved before and after him, under the Old Testament dispensation, were saved by faith in Christ. The ceremonial law was a shadow of the gospel, and it is expressly said in Gal. 3:8 that "the scripture, foreseeing that God would justify the heathen through faith, preached before the gospel unto Abraham, saying in thee shall all nations be blessed." Here then this covenant with Abraham is called the gospel, a preaching before or foretelling the gospel to Abraham.

The difference then between the old dispensation and the new does not lie in the fact that under the old dispensation the saints were saved by works, while under the new they are saved by grace. All that ever were saved were saved by grace through faith in Christ. But under the old dispensation the Holy Ghost was neither promised nor enjoyed to such an extent as He is promised and enjoyed under the new dispensation. The thing that Abraham and the Old Testament saints did not receive was that measure of the Holy Spirit which constitutes the New Covenant and produces the entire sanctification of the soul.

8. Finally, every individual Christian may receive and is bound to receive this gift of the Holy Ghost through faith at the present moment. It must not be supposed that every Christian has of course received the Holy Ghost in such a sense as it is promised in these passages of Scripture, or in any higher sense than He was received by the Old Testament saints who had actually been regenerated and were real saints, of whom it is said that "they all died in faith not having received the promises." Now it would seem as if there were thousands of Christians who have not received the promises on account of their ignorance and unbelief. It is said that "*after we believe we are sealed with the Holy Spirit of promise.*" Now, beloved, the

thing that we need is to understand and get hold of this promise to Abraham, and through Abraham to Christ, and through Christ and by Christ to the whole church of God. Now remember it is to be received by simple faith in these promises. "Be it unto thee according to thy *faith*." "For it is written the just shall live by *faith*."

LECTURE 18

The Covenants

Heb. 8:13: "In that he saith, A new covenant, he hath made the first old. Now that which decayeth and waxeth old is ready to vanish away."

The more experience I have in preaching the gospel, the more ripe are my convictions that ministers take it for granted their hearers are much better instructed on religious subjects than most of them really are. They therefore take many things for granted as already understood by their hearers for which in reality they are ignorant. This sometimes exposes them to misconceptions of what they hear and often throws them into an unsettled state of mind in regard to the truths they may have heard, so many things having been assumed of which they have no knowledge. From some remarks I have heard, I have thought that what I have said on the subject of the covenants has been liable to misconstruction for want of a somewhat more fundamental examination of the subject of covenants than has been contained in any of my lectures.

In this text and the context, Paul is speaking of the setting aside of the *Old* Covenant and the introduction of the *New*.

In discoursing upon the subject I design to show:

I. What is implied in a covenant.
II. The different kinds of covenants.
III. Some of the principal covenants of God with men.
IV. Which of them are set aside and in what sense they are set aside.
V. That the new covenant is the accomplishment of what was proposed by the preceding covenants.

I. *I am to show what is implied in a covenant.*

1. *A mutual promise* between two or more parties. A promise of one party not consented to by the other is not a covenant but a promise. To be a covenant the promise must be mutual.

2. The promise must be made *by lawful persons,* that is, they must be of

suitable age, of a sound mind, not lunatics or idiots, and be so circumstanced that it is lawful for them to enter into the proposed *covenant*. Persons may, in certain circumstances, contract a covenant for their heirs or those whom they represent. In all such cases, those whom they represent are equally bound with themselves. Thus parents can covenant in respect to their estates binding their heirs. And thus Abraham could covenant with God in relation to himself and his posterity.

3. A covenant is not only a mutual promise by lawful persons but it must be *to do a lawful thing.* Persons cannot covenant and bring themselves under an obligation to do a thing that is unlawful or of immoral tendency. In other words such a covenant is void and can be no covenant at all. No courts of law or equity, nor will the tribunal of God, hold such covenants as of any validity whatever.

II. *The different kinds of covenants.*

1. With respect to the covenants wherein the *parties are equal*, that is, where one party is under no special obligation to the other, but where each has an equal right to canvass and dictate the terms of the covenant, this is one kind of covenant and is called by Greek grammarians *suntheke.* No covenant of *this kind,* of course, exists between God and His creatures.

2. Where *one has the right to dictate the terms of the covenant* to the other, and where the parties sustain to each other the relation of sovereign and subject, this kind of covenant is called *diatheke* and is synonymous with the Hebrew word *berith.* Covenants of this kind are the same as laws, institutions and ordinances of government. All government implies a mutual promise between the sovereign and subjects, a promise of protection on his part and of obedience on theirs. Therefore all laws, ordinances and institutions dictated by the sovereign and consented to by the subjects are properly covenants between the parties.

3. Another important distinction which should be made in regard to covenants is,

(1) Where persons covenant to do what they were under previous obligation to do on the ground of natural right or justice. This kind of covenant can never be dissolved by the consent of parties, because they were under obligation to do what they engaged to do previously to any promise.

(2) Where parties covenant to do what was not before obligatory, but the whole obligation arises out of their mutual promise. This kind of covenant may be dissolved by the consent of all parties.

In regard to those laws and institutions which require only what is obligatory on the principles of natural justice, they cannot be repealed or set aside by either or by both parties. For example, the law of God requiring His creatures to love Him with all the heart can never be repealed by Him or its obligation in any way dispensed with, because it is plainly right in itself and a dictate of natural justice. Those laws and institutions which are of a ceremonial character and are not in their own nature obligatory may be set aside at any time, at the will of the lawgiver. Let it be understood then that in the sense of *diatheke,* all laws, institutions and ordinances are covenants and imply the mutual consent of the sovereign and subjects and mutual obligations devolve upon each. In this sense the laws and ordinances of God are covenants.

III. *I will notice some of the covenants of God with men.*

1. The Adamic covenant, or the covenant made with Adam. This must have been in substance the moral law, as epitomized by the Savior in the two great commandments. The test of this covenant was the refusing [of] the forbidden fruit. If he abstained wholly from this fruit, it was sufficient evidence that his love to God was supreme and that he regarded the authority of God above the indulgence of his constitutional appetites. But if he partook of this fruit it was conclusive evidence that his regard to God was not supreme, but that the indulgence of appetite was with him superior to the authority of God. That this was properly a covenant and consented to by Adam is manifest from the fact that for a time he obeyed it. This was strictly and properly a covenant of works and proposed to save him on the ground of his perfect and perpetual obedience to God.

2. Passing by the covenant with Noah, I notice the covenant made with Abraham, as recorded in the twelfth, fifteenth and seventeenth chapters of Genesis. This was a covenant of grace in opposition to the Adamic covenant. It proposed a new way of salvation. Salvation by works of the law had become impossible, as Adam and all his posterity had disobeyed the law. God, therefore, in the Abrahamic covenant proposed to save mankind by grace through faith. The substance of this had been intimated to Adam immediately after the Fall and was, no doubt, understood and embraced by all the saints from Adam to Abraham. We find Abel offering a sacrifice in faith, and his sacrifice was typical of the atonement of Christ. This covenant, made more fully with Abraham, is said by the Apostle in Gal. 3:8 to be the gospel: "And the scripture, foreseeing that God would justify the heathen through faith, preached before the gospel unto Abraham, saying, In thee shall all nations be blessed."

That it was a covenant of grace in opposition to a covenant of works is evident from the passage just quoted and from the sixteenth verse of the same chapter—"Now to Abraham and his seed were the promises made. He saith not, And to seeds as of many, but as of one, And to thy seed, which is Christ"—[and] also from Rom. 4:13, 16: "For the promise, that he should be the heir of the world, was not unto Abraham, or his seed, through the law, but through the righteousness of faith. Therefore it is of faith, that it might be of grace; to the end the promise might be sure to the seed; not to that only which is of the law, but to that also which is of the faith of Abraham; who is the father of us all." These and many other passages show that this covenant with Abraham was a gracious, in opposition to a legal, covenant or a covenant of works.

We have an account of the solemn ratification of this covenant according to the custom of those times, by dividing beasts and the parties passing between the pieces, in Gen. 15:8-12, 17:

> And he said, Lord God, whereby shall I know that I shall inherit it? And he said unto him, Take me an heifer of three years old, and a she-goat of three years old, and a ram of three years old, and a turtle-dove, and a young pigeon. And he took unto him all these, and divided them in the midst, and laid each piece one against another; but the birds divided he not. And when the fowls came down upon the carcasses, Abram drove them away. And when the sun was going down, a deep sleep fell upon Abram; and lo, a horror of great darkness fell upon him. And it came to pass, that, when the sun went down, and it was dark, behold a smoking furnace, and a burning lamp that passed between those pieces.

Here the lamp is the symbol of the divine presence. In the seventeenth chapter we have an account of the seal's being added to the covenant, to which Abraham fully consented on his part by circumcising himself and all the males of his household. This covenant was made with Abraham and with all believers in the God of Israel, whether Jews or Gentiles. If they would receive this covenant they were to acknowledge His authority by affixing its seal to themselves and all the males of their household. Thus the proselytes to the Jew's religion, before they were allowed to eat of the passover, were required to be circumcised with all their males. Ex. 12:48-49: "And when a stranger shall sojourn with thee, and will keep the passover to the Lord, let all his males be circumcised, and then let him come near and keep it; and he shall be as one born in the land: for no uncircumcised person shall eat thereof. One law shall be to him that is homeborn, and to the stranger who sojourneth among you."

3. The Sinai covenant, or the law given at Mount Sinai. It appears that all the laws and ordinances given at Mount Sinai taken together made up this covenant. In the following passages the Ten Commandments are called the covenant: Heb. 9:4, "Which had the golden censer, and the ark of the covenant overlaid round about with gold, wherein was the golden pot that had manna and Aaron's rod that budded, and the tables of the covenant. . . ."; Ex. 34:28, "And he was there with the Lord forty days and forty nights; he did neither eat bread nor drink water. And he wrote upon the tables the words of the covenant, the ten commandments"; [and] Deut. 9:9, 11, 15, "When I was gone up into the mount to receive the tables of stone, even the tables of the covenant which the Lord made with you, then I abode in the mount forty days and forty nights, and I neither did eat bread nor drink water: and it came to pass at the end of forty days and forty nights, that the Lord gave me the two tables of stone, even the tables of the covenant. So I turned and came down from the mount, and the mount burned with fire: and the two tables of the covenant were in my hands."

These commandments however were only a part of the covenant as other passages clearly show, [notably] Heb. 9:18-20 compared with Ex. 24:3-8:

> Whereupon neither the first testament was dedicated without blood. For when Moses had spoken every precept to all the people according to the law, he took the blood of calves and of goats, with water, and scarlet wool,

and hyssop, and sprinkled both the book, and all the people, saying, This is the blood of the testament which God hath enjoined upon you.

And Moses came and told the people all the words of the Lord, and all the judgments; and all the people answered with one voice, and said, All the words which the Lord hath said will we do. And Moses wrote all the words of the Lord, and rose up early in the morning, and builded an altar under the hill, and twelve pillars according to the twelve tribes of Israel. And he sent young men of the children of Israel, who offered burnt offerings, and sacrificed peace-offerings of oxen unto the Lord. And Moses took half of the blood, and put it in basins; and half the blood he sprinkled on the altar. And he took the book of the covenant, and read in the audience of the people; and they said, All that the Lord hath said will we do, and be obedient. And Moses took the blood, and sprinkled it on the people, and said, Behold the blood of the covenant, which the Lord hath made with you concerning all these words.

In these passages we learn that every precept of the law was included in the Sinai covenant. In the passage quoted above from Exodus we have a solemn ratification of this covenant, which is mentioned also in the passage quoted from Hebrews. As these are nowhere called two covenants, and as the law upon the two tables had already been given and was so important in its nature and is so often itself called the covenant, I conclude that all the laws given at Mt. Sinai were included in this covenant. Upon this covenant I remark,

(1) That it did not set aside the Abrahamic covenant and introduce again the covenant of works. This is asserted and fully argued by Paul in Gal. 3:17-19: "And this I say, that the covenant, that was confirmed before of God in Christ, the law, which was four hundred years after, cannot disannul, that it should become of none effect. For if the inheritance be of the law, it is no more of promise: but God gave it to Abraham by promise. Wherefore then serveth the law? It was added because of transgressions, till the seed should come to whom the promise was made; and it was ordained by angels in the hand of a mediator."

Some have understood the Sinai covenant as united with the covenant of Abraham in such a sense as to make the whole a covenant of works. Now there can be no greater mistake than this, as is evident from the whole drift of the Apostle's reasoning in the fourth chapter of Romans and the third chapter of Galatians.

(2) This covenant or dispensation was a schoolmaster to bring us to Christ, instead of being a covenant of works; Gal. 3:24, "Wherefore the law was our schoolmaster to bring us unto Christ, that we might be justified by faith." The moral precepts were to convict us of sin and cut us off from self-righteous efforts and expectations; and the whole system of sacrifices and types were a shadow of the gospel, or a typical representation of good things to come, that is, of the great blessings of the gospel of Christ. All those who were saved under this dispensation were saved by faith in the atonement of Christ, as dimly shadowed forth in this typical dispensation. That all the ancient patriarchs were saved by faith is perfectly certain from the whole Bible, and is particularly declared in the eleventh chapter of Hebrews.

(3) This covenant became a stumbling block to the Jews by being mistaken by the great mass of them for a covenant of works. They were so earthly and sensual as to overlook the spiritual truth taught by those ordinances, and to understand conformity to them to entitle them to salvation on the ground of their own works.

(4) Thus failing to secure the sanctification and consequently the salvation of the people, God foretold and published at various times, and expressly by Jeremiah, that at a certain future time he would make a New Covenant with the house of Israel and Judah, that is, with the whole church of God.

4. Which brings me to remark that the New Covenant mentioned in Jeremiah was according to the words and tenor of it to consist in *writing the moral law in the hearts of His people*. By the moral law I mean the moral precepts, as comprised and summed up by our Savior in the two great precepts on which, He affirms, hang all the law and the prophets. Jer. 31:31-34: "Behold, the days come, saith the Lord, that I will make a new covenant with the house of Israel, and with the house of Judah: not according to the covenant that I made with their fathers in the day that I took them by the hand to bring them out of the land of Egypt; which my covenant they brake, although I was an husband unto them, saith the Lord: but this shall be the covenant that I will make with the house of Israel; After those days, saith the Lord, I will put my laws in their inward parts, and write them in their hearts; and will be their God, and they shall be my people. And they shall teach no more every man his neighbour, and every man his brother, saying, Know the Lord: for they shall all know me, from the least of them to the greatest of them, saith the Lord: for I will forgive their iniquity, and I will remember their sins no more." On this I remark:

(1) This covenant implied (*a*) so full a revelation of God, (*b*) so much of the Holy Spirit [and] (*c*) such an efficacious dispensation, as to beget true holiness of heart in the people of God. The substance of this promise of the New Covenant is to be found in a great many places in the Old Testament; and from the quotation of it by the Apostle in his epistle to the Hebrews, we learn when this promise of the New Covenant became due, and that the New Covenant dispensation was actually introduced by the first publishers of the gospel. To my mind, it seems plain that the day of Pentecost was regarded by Christ and the apostles as the commencement of the new dispensation. Christ seems to intimate to His disciples that that was the occasion on which the promise of His Father, so often repeated and which they had heard of Him, should be fulfilled.

(2) This writing the law in the heart is called a covenant because it implies in the fullest manner the consent of him who enters into this covenant with God. As the writing this law in the heart consists in begetting the spirit and temper required by the law, it implies of course the fullest consent on the part of him who receives it.

(3) I have said the promise of this covenant became due at the day of Pentecost. The extent to which it has been fulfilled and will be fulfilled has depended and will continue to depend upon the extent to which it is under-

stood, believed and embraced by the church. From the nature of the case, it is a covenant to be made with individuals. No one can receive it but by faith. And as the promise is now due, it is the privilege and duty of every soul to lay hold on full salvation.

IV. *I am to show which of the covenants are set aside, and in what sense.*

1. The Adamic, or covenant of works, *is set aside as a method or condition of salvation.* As a rule of duty it is not and cannot be set aside. The particular test of the forbidden fruit given to Adam is of course nothing to us. But the substance of the covenant, the requisition—that is, perfect love to God and men—is not and cannot be set aside; because it is a covenant of that kind where the thing to be performed is right in itself, and obligatory on the ground of natural justice.

2. *The Abrahamic covenant is not done away.* I waive the question in respect to that part of it that promised the temporal blessing or the land of Canaan to the Jews and speak of infinitely the most important part of the covenant, which promised a spiritual blessing through Abraham and his seed to all the nations of the earth, and of which particular blessing or rest temporal Canaan was only a type. That this part of the covenant is not abolished is evident.

(1) From the reasonings of the Apostle in the fourth chapter of Romans and third chapter of Galatians. He shows most fully that the promise made to Abraham is yet to be fulfilled both to Jews and Gentiles. And there are a great many other passages that teach the same truth.

(2) Because it is not yet fulfilled. It was actually made through Abraham and his seed, that is, Christ, with all the nations of the earth. And from the very nature of it, it cannot be fulfilled until the end of time. In my last lecture I said it was never fulfilled in its fullest sense to Abraham, but is to be fulfilled in a fuller sense to Christians under the present dispensation.

(3) Because the New Covenant spoken of in Jeremiah is only the carrying out and fulfillment of the covenant made with Abraham, as the Apostle asserts in Gal. 3:14: "That the blessing of Abraham might come on the Gentiles through Jesus Christ, that we might receive the promise of the Spirit through faith."

3. The covenant of Sinai is in one sense abolished; in another sense it still remains.

It should be understood that the covenant of Sinai was a collection of statutes and ordinances, making up as a whole the means of salvation by grace through faith, as the Apostle says in Heb. 10:1: "For the law having a shadow of good things to come," &c. From this and other passages, as well as from the nature of the case, it is manifest that the old or Sinai covenant is to be regarded as a peculiar method of teaching the substantial truths of the gospel—a still further and more perfect foretelling of the gospel than had been made to Abraham.

Now this covenant as a dispensation—as a method of teaching the gospel, as the means of sanctification and salvation—is set aside to give place to the reality or anti-type, the fuller and more perfect revelation by Jesus Christ and His apostles, of which truth the typical dispensation was only a shadow. But the moral precepts of this covenant, that is, those precepts that require what is right in itself and are obligatory in the nature of things, remain still as a rule of duty in full force. This must be, of course, as the precepts are of the nature of that kind of covenants that cannot be abolished at the pleasure of either or both parties. Nothing is of more importance than that we should clearly understand in what sense the Old Covenant is done away, and in what sense it is not done away. Those precepts that are typical and ceremonial are now of course not to be observed at all, as the revelation of Jesus Christ and the coming of the great Anti-type has rendered their observance useless and worse than useless.

But that the whole substance of the moral precepts and those that are obligatory on the ground of natural justice are still binding and of full force and authority, is manifest:

(1) From the nature of the case. It is impossible that these should cease to be binding, for God has no right to dispense with their obligation. These precepts, whether found among the Ten Commandments or among the precepts recorded by Moses, are of perpetual obligation because they belong to the race and are obligatory in the nature of things. Their obligation grows out of and rests upon the unalterable nature and relations of moral beings.

Were this the place, it would be easy to take up these commands, one by one, and show that they have their foundation in the nature and necessities of man and can never be dispensed with while the world stands. Especially should I like to show this in respect to the two commands respecting the Sabbath and marriage. I mention these two merely because some have doubted whether these were of perpetual obligation. But to me it seems that this subject may be made as clear as sunlight, that these together with all the other commands of the Decalogue and some other precepts of the Old Covenant are of perpetual obligation, for example, such as this, "Thou shalt not deliver unto his master him that is escaped from his master unto thee," &c. I must not however enter into this subject in this place, but content myself with saying,

(2) That the Bible and especially the New Testament everywhere recognizes all the moral precepts as of perpetual obligation. Hear what the Apostle says in Rom. 13:9: "For this, Thou shalt not commit adultery, Thou shalt not kill, Thou shalt not steal, Thou shalt not bear false witness, Thou shalt not covet; and if there be any other commandment, it is briefly comprehended in this saying, namely, Thou shalt love thy neighbour as thyself." Here he recognizes the eternal obligation of the moral precepts. This together with the whole of the New Testament proves conclusively that the moral precepts are as a rule of duty by no means done away, but the strictest obedience to them is everywhere insisted upon.

(3) If they were repealed, neither sin nor holiness could exist at all. Without a rule of duty no obedience can of course exist. Consequently if the moral law is abolished there is no sin or holiness in the universe.

V. *The New Covenant is the accomplishment of what was proposed by the preceding covenants.*

The thing proposed by the preceding covenants was the sanctification and salvation of man. Now that the New Covenant consists in the accomplishment of this end is evident from the words of the covenant itself, Jer. 31:31-34:

> Behold, the days come, saith the Lord, that I will make a new covenant with the house of Israel, and with the house of Judah: not according to the covenant that I made with their fathers in the day that I took them by the hand to bring them out of the land of Egypt; which my covenant they brake, although I was a husband unto them, saith the Lord: but this shall be the covenant that I will make with the house of Israel; After those days, saith the Lord, I will put my law in their inward parts, and write it in their hearts; and will be their God, and they shall be my people. And they shall teach no more every man his neighbour, and every man his brother, saying, Know the Lord: for they shall all know me, from the least of them unto the greatest of them, saith the Lord: for I will forgive their iniquity, and I will remember their sin no more.

The thing here promised is sanctification or the writing of the law in the heart. If therefore obedience to law be sanctification, then this is the blessing proposed in this promise of the New Covenant. So far then from the moral law being done away, the New Covenant is nothing else than real obedience to the law. This exactly accords with what the Apostle says in Rom. 8:3-4: "For what the law could not do, in that it was weak through the flesh, God sending his own Son in the likeness of sinful flesh, and for sin, condemned sin in the flesh; that the righteousness of the law might be fulfilled in us, who walk not after the flesh, but after the Spirit."

REMARKS

1. The two covenants contrasted by the Apostle in his epistle to the Hebrews as the Old and New Covenants, the first and second covenants, &c., are the Sinai covenant and the one promised in Jeremiah. The Apostle does not here allude to the covenant with Adam or with Abraham. By reading the covenant it will be evident that the covenants contrasted are the Sinai covenant, or that which was made with the people when God led them out of the land of Egypt, and the covenant in Jer. 31:31-34 and Heb. 8:7-13 . . . [which Finney quotes here]. In Heb. 9:18-20, he speaks expressly of this covenant, and so refers to the Old Testament as to render it certain that it was the law given at Sinai and not the covenant of Abraham of which he was speaking.

2. The New Covenant and the Abrahamic covenant sustain to each other the relation of a promise to its fulfillment. As I said in my last and have repeated in this lecture, the New Covenant is nothing more or less than the carrying out and fulfilling [of] the covenant made with Abraham.

3. In the light of this subject the mistake into which those have fallen who maintain that the Abrahamic covenant is repealed may be seen. They confound the Abrahamic with the Sinai covenant and suppose that the new dispensation abolishes both together. This appears to me to be a sad mistake.

4. From this subject may be seen the error of some of the modern perfectionists who seem to suppose that the old dispensation, or Sinai covenant, was a covenant of works. They do not seem to understand that it was only a method of carrying out and accomplishing the promises of grace first intimated to Adam immediately after the Fall and more fully afterwards confirmed to Abraham. This, as a system of means for the sanctification and salvation of men, has been set aside to give place to a fuller revelation and to the dispensation of the Holy Ghost under the gospel, retaining at the same time in all its strength, as a rule of duty, the obligation of all the moral precepts. The persons to whom I allude have manifestly mistaken the sense in which the Old Covenant is done away and understood even the moral precepts to be so abrogated as to be no longer binding. And they seem to be very happy in the idea of being wholly discharged from the obligation of the moral law. Before them the door of licentiousness is fully open, and imagining themselves, as some of them do, to be led by the Spirit to trample upon the great commands of the Decalogue, they most richly deserve and are likely to receive the execration of God and man.

5. The gospel dispensation is not itself the New Covenant but simply the means of it. The New Covenant, as I have fully shown in my past lectures, consists in the writing of the law in the heart. This is done by the Spirit through the instrumentality of the gospel.

The design of this lecture is merely to guard against the impression that the moral law only is to be regarded as the Old Covenant, as in quoting passages in my former lectures to show what the Old Covenant was I confined myself, if I mistake not, to those that spoke of the Ten Commandments as constituting that covenant, without particularly noticing the other parts of the covenant. This I did because my main design in those lectures was to dwell upon that part of the Old Covenant which was to be written by the New Covenant in the heart.

Nothing is more important than that the church should have just and comprehensive views of the covenant dealings of God with his people. It cannot be too distinctly understood that the Adamic covenant, or covenant of works, is still binding as a rule of duty, but is not the condition of salvation. Also that all the covenants of God with the church have had for their grand object the bringing of man into a state of complete conformity to the law, under which man was originally placed and under which he must be placed to all eternity.

With respect to this New Covenant, I remark in a word that the promise of it has been due for more than eighteen hundred years. And I would solemnly ask, shall it lie in your Bibles till they rot and your souls sink down to hell before you lay hold on the salvation from sin which it promises?

LECTURE 19

The Rest of Faith, No. 1

Heb. 3:19 and 4:1: "So we see that they could not enter in because of unbelief. Let us therefore fear, lest a promise being left us of entering into his rest, any of you should seem to come short of it."

The following is the order in which I will direct your attention.

  I. Inquire of whom the Apostle is speaking in this text and into what it is said they could not enter.
 II. Why they could not enter in.
III. Show that temporal Canaan was typical of the rest of faith.
IV. What is implied in this rest.
 V. How we may seem to come short of it.
VI. How we may take possession of it.

I. *I am to inquire of whom the Apostle is speaking and into what they could not enter.*

In this connection the Apostle is speaking of the Jews, and that into which they could not enter was temporal Canaan, as is evident from the context.

II. *Why they could not enter in.*

It is asserted in the text that they could not enter into Canaan because of unbelief. The Jews had arrived upon the borders of the promised land. And Moses deputed a number of individuals as spies and sent them to spy out the land. They went up and surveyed the land and returned bringing some of the fruits of the land, and represented to the children of Israel that it was an exceeding good land but that it was impossible for them to take possession of it—that the towns and cities were walled up to heaven, that the country was inhabited by giants, and that therefore they were utterly unable to take possession of the land.

In this testimony all the spies agreed except Caleb and Joshua. This discouraged the people and produced a rebellion that prevented that generation from taking possession of Canaan. Their confidence in divine assistance was utterly shaken, and their unbelief prevented any such attempt to take possession of the land as would otherwise have been made with complete success. The bringing up of the evil report by those who were sent out to reconnoiter and their failing to encourage and lead forward the people were the means of that generation being turned back and utterly wasted in the wilderness. God was so incensed against them for their want of confidence in His help, and of His ability and willingness to give them possession, that He "swore in his wrath that they should not enter into his rest."

III. *Show that temporal Canaan was typical of the rest of faith.*

It is plain from the context that the Apostle supposes the land of Canaan to have been typical of the rest of faith. The land of Canaan was to have been their rest after their perilous journey from Egypt. In this land they were to have been secure from the power of all their enemies round about. He concludes the third chapter of this epistle by asserting that "they could not enter into this rest because of unbelief." And he begins the fourth chapter by exhorting the Jews to whom he was writing "to fear lest a promise being left them of entering into rest [the rest of faith],* any should seem to come short of it." And in the third verse he affirms that "we who have believed do enter into rest."

IV. *What is implied in this rest.*

1. Not a state of *spiritual indolence.*

2. Not *waiting for God to do His own work and ours too.* Some people seem to be waiting for God and to have such an idea of His sovereignty as to throw upon Him the responsibility of doing not only that which belongs to Him but that also which belongs to themselves. They seem to forget that holiness in man is his own act and talk as if God would make men holy without the proper and diligent exercise of their own powers. Others are waiting for God to convert their children and their neighbors and the world without any instrumentality of theirs, affirming that God can and will do His own work in His own way and in His own time, thus entirely overlooking the fact that when God works He works by means. This is anything but a right view of the subject, and that is anything but faith which leads to these views, and to this course of conduct; and this state of spiritual indolence and this waiting for God are anything but gospel rest. Faith always implies a diligent and constant use of means. Faith respects not only the fact that God will do thus and thus, but also recognizes the fact that He will do it by the appointed means. Consequently true faith in God leads to anything but the neglect of employing the suitable instrumentality to effect the desired object.

3. The rest of faith does not imply that the church is to be sanctified and the world converted *without the diligent and effectual co-operation* of those who are co-workers with God.

4. Nor *rest from labors of love.*

5. Nor *rest from watchfulness,* nor from any of those holy exertions that are indispensable to guard against our enemies in this state of trial, and while in an enemy's country. Nor does it imply any cessation from a diligent use of all the means of instruction and of grace, both for our own and others' edification and salvation.

6. Nor *the casting off responsibility* and the giving ourselves up to be drifted in any direction by the tides of influence which surround us.

7. Nor does it imply an exemption from temptation. Christ was tempted in all points like as we are. And from our circumstances in this world, it

---
*The brackets and the words they contain are Finney's.

is impossible that we should not continue to be the constant subjects of temptation from the world, the flesh and the devil. Nor does it imply exemption from all heaviness and distress of mind. Christ was in heaviness. Paul had great heaviness and continual sorrow of heart on account of his brethren. And Peter in his general epistle to the saints says, "Now are we in heaviness through manifold temptations." Nor does it imply exemption from severe trials and mental conflicts, for these things may always be expected while we are in the flesh. And the gospel plainly teaches that to us it is given not only to believe in Christ, but also to suffer for His sake.

But gospel rest does imply,

1. A *complete cessation from all our own selfish works*, the end of which is to promote our own interests, temporal or eternal.

2. It implies *a cessation from all self-righteous efforts*. By self-righteous efforts, I mean (1) all attempts to recommend ourselves to God by our own works; (2) all efforts to avoid punishment or escape from the wrath of God by any efforts of our own; [and] (3) all those things which originate in our own convictions and are performed in the strength of our own resolutions without being influenced thereto by the love of God in our heart.

3. This rest implies a state of mind that feels *no necessity for attempting anything in our own strength*. There is a state of mind, which perhaps is better known by experience than described by words, in which an individual feels pressed with a necessity of doing something, and everything, in a manner which shall be acceptable to God. And yet on account of his unbelief, he feels agonized with the thought that he is in no such sense strengthened by the Spirit of God as shall, as a matter of fact, enable him and cause him to do that which his convictions of duty demand of him. This is a distracting, restless state of mind and the exact opposite of the rest of faith. Faith so leans upon God as to bring the mind into a state of sweet repose and confidence that God will help and that there is no necessity for making any efforts in our own strength.

4. It implies exemption from all the carefulness induced by unbelief on every subject. Faith reposes in God, for time and for eternity, for direction and help and provisions in temporal as well as spiritual matters. It excludes all carefulness, in the proper sense of that term, on every subject.

5. It implies exemption from the fear of death and hell. Faith produces that perfect love that casteth out fear—the fear of future want, of the judgments of God, that we shall be overcome by our enemies spiritual or temporal, and of all that fear that hath torment.

6. It implies an *exemption from a sense of condemnation*. "There is no condemnation to them who are in Christ Jesus, who walk not after the flesh but after the Spirit."

7. A *rest from the reproaches of conscience*. In a state of unbelief, conscience often inflicts grievous wounds upon the peace of the soul. But when we take possession of the rest of faith the conscience is as quiet as a lamb.

8. It implies *an exemption from being afflicted or distressed with the occurrences of life*. The soul is able to meet with calmness and sweetness that which would otherwise throw the mind into a state of the utmost agita-

tion and distress. By this I do not mean, as I have said above, that individuals will have no trials, but that this state of mind will enable them to pass through their trials with a composed and heavenly temper.

Mrs. President Edwards says of herself that for some years there were two trials which she thought she should be unable to bear. One was the loss of her husband's confidence and ill treatment from him; the other was the loss of the confidence and respect of the people of the town in which they lived. But when she entered fully into the rest of faith, she declares that it did not appear to her as if those things could, in the least, affect her happiness or disturb the repose of her mind. It appeared to her as if she were as far above being discomposed by anything that could occur in the providence of God as the sun is high above the earth—that to be treated with the utmost disrespect by her husband, to be cast out by the people of the town to perish in the snow, would not break up the deep tranquillity and repose of her mind in God.

9. It implies *exemption from the dominion of temptation.* I have said that in this life we may always as a thing of course expect more or less temptation. But this rest is a state of mind in which temptation will not prevail. It will assail us and make a greater or less impression upon our minds, that is, it will in a greater or less degree agitate and ruffle our feelings in proportion to the strength of our faith.

10. Finally, and in a word, it implies *exemption from the strength and dominion of sin in all its forms.* The case supposed by the Apostle in the seventh chapter of Romans, to illustrate the influence of law over one who is carnal and sold under sin, is a striking exemplification of that state of slavery to lust and passion in which great multitudes, both in and out of the church, are. And the striking transition from that state of mind into that described in the eighth chapter exactly illustrates what I mean by an individual passing from a state of slavery and sin into a state of liberty and rest.

V. *How we may seem to come short of it.*

The word rendered *seem* here does not imply what is commonly meant by the English term seem, as if the coming short were only in appearance and not in fact. But from the manner in which it is rendered in other passages it is manifest that it means to express the actual coming short, as if the Apostle had said "lest any of you should *be seen* to come short of it."

1. We may fail of entering into this rest *by mistaking its nature* and thinking we have it while we have not. Many have seemed to suppose that it consists in spiritual indolence, or in such an exemption from responsibility as would give the mind up to be drifted without resistance in any direction in which the corrupt currents of this world might drive it. They seem to get the idea that all things are lawful to them in such a sense that almost any kind of indulgence is consistent with spiritual purity and the love of God. Gospel rest, to them, is the mere casting off of responsibility, a lolling and wallowing in their own filthy indulgences.

2. Many fail to enter into this rest *by not realizing that there is any*

such state. They seem not to know anything about the tranquilizing effects of faith and that state of deep repose in God which those enjoy who have taken possession of the promised rest. They seem to suppose that the Christian warfare consists in that mental conflict which they are conscious is going on within themselves, with their hearts and consciences. They are conscious of a continual mutiny being kept up between the conflicting powers of their own minds, which they express by saying they are constantly sinning and repenting; by which nothing more can be meant than that their hearts and consciences are at fearful war with each other. They appear to be utter strangers to the sweet peace and repose of mind which results from a harmony of the powers of their own mind, where their conscience and their heart are at one. Understanding from the Bible that their warfare is to continue through this life and mistaking their inward conflicts for the Christian warfare, they take it for granted that no such rest as that of which I have spoken exists.

3. Many fail to enter into this rest because *they think it belongs exclusively to heaven.* Now that this rest will be more perfect in heaven than it is on earth is undeniably true. But it is the same in kind on earth as in heaven, just as holiness is. Now if persons do not become holy on earth, how should they hope to be holy in heaven? And if this rest be not begun on earth it will never be enjoyed in heaven.

4. Many come short of this rest by *supposing that the world, the flesh and Satan put the attainment of it utterly out of the question.* It is amazing to see how little of the gospel is understood and received by the church. It would seem that in the estimation of the great mass of the church, the gospel itself has made no adequate provision for the entire sanctification of men in this world of temptation. Just as if God were unable to overcome these enemies in any other way than by snatching His children out of their reach, and that Christ came not so much to destroy the works of the devil in this world as to drive His people out of it and get them off from His ground—that He destroys the flesh because He is unable to overcome it, and that He will burn up the world because He is unable to prevent its leading His people into sin. Now it does appear to me that God's glory demands that the battle should be fought and the victory won in this world. The Apostle plainly represents us, under the grace of God, as not only conquerors but "more than conquerors." And he certainly has but a very limited knowledge of the Bible or of the grace of God who can assume that the world, the flesh and Satan are too strong for Christ, so that He cannot save His people from their sins.

5. *Ignorance of the power of faith* is another reason why persons do not enter into this rest. They do not understand that as a matter of fact faith in the existence, power, goodness, providence and grace of God—that unwavering confidence in all He does and says—would in its own nature, as a thing of course, bring them into the rest of which I am speaking.

Suppose a ship should be bestormed at sea, that all on board is confusion, dismay, and almost despair; the ship is driven by a fierce tempest upon a lee shore. Now suppose that in the midst of all the uncertainty, racking, and almost distracting anxiety of the passengers and crew, a voice should be heard from heaven, they knowing it to be the voice of the eternal God, assuring them that the ship should be safe, that not a hair of their heads should perish, and that they should ride out the storm in perfect safety. It is easy to see that the effect of this announcement upon different minds would be in precise proportion to their confidence in its truth. If they believed it, they would by no means throw up the helm and give themselves up to indolence and let the ship drive before the waves, but standing every man at his place and managing the ship in the best manner possible, they would enjoy a quiet and composed mind in proportion to their confidence that all would be well. If any did not believe it, their anxiety and trouble would continue, of course; and they might wonder at the calmness of those who did, and even reproach them for not being as anxious as themselves. You might see among them every degree of feeling from the despair and deep forebodings of utter unbelief up to the full measure of the entire consolation of perfect faith. Now the design of this illustration is to show the nature of faith and to demonstrate that entire confidence in God naturally hushes all the tumults of the mind and settles it into a state of deep repose; that it does not beget inaction, presumption or spiritual indolence, any more than the revelation of which I have spoken would beget inattention to its management on board the ship.

6. Another reason is, many are *discouraged by the misrepresentations of the spies who have been sent to spy out the land.* It is a painful and really an alarming consideration that so many of those who are leaders in Israel, and who are supposed by the church to have gone up and reconnoitered the whole land of spiritual experience—that almost with united voice they should return to the church and represent that we are unable to go up and possess the land. Of all those that were sent by Moses to spy out the land only two had any faith in the promise of God, whereas all the rest united in their testimony that they were unable to possess the land, and that rest was unattainable to them in this life. So it appears to me in these days. Those that are appointed to direct and encourage the people—by first acquainting themselves thoroughly with the ground to be possessed and then carrying to the people the confidence of faith, encouraging them not only by the promises of God but by their own experience and observation that the land may be possessed—instead of this they bring up an evil report; discourage the hearts of the people of God; maintain that the grace of God has made no sufficient provisions for their taking possession of the land of holiness in this life; that the world, the flesh and the devil are such mighty Anakims as that to overcome them is utterly out of the question; and that no hope remains, only as we flee from their territories and get out of the world the best way we can.

Now I greatly fear that will happen to them which came upon the spies in the days of Moses. They were driven back and their carcases fell in the wilderness. God swore in His wrath that they should not enter into His rest. And not only they but that entire generation who were deceived by them and who could not enter in because of unbelief were wasted away and died without rest in the wilderness of sin! How long will generation after generation of spies continue to bring up their evil report, discouraging the hearts and confirming the unbelief of the people, and effectually preventing their taking possession of that rest which remains for the people of God!

7. Many are discouraged *by the present and past attainments of Christians.* They are constantly stumbled by the consideration that holy men of former and present times have known so little of full gospel salvation. They might just as reasonably let the past and present state of the world shake their confidence in the fact that the world will ever be converted. And indeed, whether they are aware of it or not, I suppose they have as much confidence in the one as in the other. They seem not to be aware of the fact that they are full of unbelief in regard to the world's conversion, while they are sensible that they have no confidence in the attainableness of rest from all their sins in this life. The reason why they are sensible of unbelief in the one case and not in the other is: the one is placed before them as a present duty, in attempting to perform which they experience the chilling influence of unbelief, while the other is a thing which they have never tried to do and which they do not understand to be their duty to do. Consequently a want of confidence in respect to this is not the object of the mind's attention. Certainly a state of mind that can be discouraged by the past or present history of the church would of course feel the same discouragement, and have the same reason for discouragement, in regard to the world's conversion.

8. Others fail to take possession of this rest on account of the *ignorance of the real attainments of the ancient and modern saints.* They have taken but little pains to examine carefully into the history of eminent saints either ancient or modern, and of course do not know what the grace of God has actually done for men.

9. Many fail *from a regard to their reputation.* They have so much fear of being called heretics, fanatics, perfectionists or some other opprobrious name that they resist the Spirit and truth of God.

10. *Pride and prejudice* prevent a careful and honest examination of the subject. I have been amazed, and I might add ashamed, to witness the great ignorance of the Bible and of the real merits of this question in the articles that have appeared in the different periodicals of the present day. They have reminded me of the conduct of Dr. Hill in the late General Assembly, when the discussion of the question of slavery came up. He arose and read certain passages of Scripture, with as much assurance as if he supposed they had been overlooked by the abolitionists—as if he supposed it would be entirely manifest that these scriptures were a "Thus saith the Lord" in the face of all abolitionism. He afterwards intimated that he was master of the subject, and seemed not to understand that all his arguments and scriptures and grounds of objection had often been weighed in the balance and found wanting. Now just so it has appeared to me when I have read the various articles that have appeared of late against the attainableness of entire sanctification in this life. The least I could say would be in the words of President Edwards, that "they have not well considered the mat-

ter."

11. Many fail because *they are too proud to confess their ignorance and want of spirituality and put themselves in the attitude of inquirers.* A vast many individuals are not aware of their own ignorance and want of spirituality, and many who are convinced of their ignorance and their destitution of spirituality seem to think it indispensable to their usefulness to conceal their defects and to keep up the appearance, at least, of sound knowledge and sound piety. And some, how many I cannot say, have adopted it as a principle not to speak much of their own experience in the divine life.

12. Many *are ashamed to be taught* by the ignorant through spiritual Christians. There are perhaps but few among ministers and church officers who might not take some most useful and salutary lessons from some obscure female or other unnoticed person in the church. Unless a man is willing to sit at the feet of any spiritual child of God, he is never likely to know what that rest is that remaineth for the people of God.

13. *Pride of learning and dependence upon their own powers of criticism* have done and are doing much to shut the learned world out of faith. There is a great tendency in a certain class of minds to substitute their own reasonings for faith, to believe what they can establish by reasoning and argument, and to hold as fanatical or doubtful any depth of spirituality that they cannot fathom by their "inch of line." Nor do they seem aware that the confidence which they have in those things which they cannot establish by reason is not faith in the truth of God but a leaning to their own understanding. God's testimony is to be set aside unless it is backed up and established by their own profound reasonings and criticisms.

14. Another reason is, many *settle down into a stereotyped orthodoxy* and are opposed to all advances in religious knowledge and experience.

15. Others fail because they are *waiting and struggling for some preparation* before they go up and take possession of the land. They do not understand that they are immediately to enter into this rest by faith. They are waiting for certain feelings and views to prepare them to exercise faith, not knowing that these very views and feelings are the effects of faith. Thus they expect the effect to precede the cause.

16. Others fail *through sheer carelessness.* The Apostle exhorts the church to take heed in this matter, and certainly without attention and inquiry this rest will not be attained.

VI. *How we may take possession of it.*

This rest is to be possessed at once by anchoring down in naked faith upon the promises of God. Take the illustration which I have already given, namely, the ship at sea. Suppose she were dashing upon the rocks and a voice from heaven should cry out, "Let go your sheet anchor and all shall be safe." Suppose they believed that. With what confidence and composure would they let go the anchor, understanding it to be certain that it would bring them up and that they should ride out the storm. Now this composure of mind, anyone may see, might and would be entered upon at once by an act of naked faith.

Just so there are no circumstances in which men are ever placed, where they may not enter into rest at once by anchoring down in naked faith upon the promises of God. Let the first six verses of the thirty-seventh Psalm be an illustration of what I mean:

> Fret not thyself because of evil-doers, neither be thou envious against the workers of iniquity. For they shall soon be cut down like the grass, and wither as the green herb. Trust in the Lord, and do good; so shalt thou dwell in the land, and verily thou shalt be fed. Delight thyself also in the Lord: and he shall give thee the desires of thine heart. Commit thy way unto the Lord; trust also in him; and he shall bring it to pass. And he shall bring forth thy righteousness as the light, and thy judgment as the noonday.

Now suppose an individual to be borne down by the persecution of his enemies, or to be so situated in his temporal circumstances as not to know what he should do for bread. Let him take hold upon these promises and peace and rest would flow in upon his mind; and light and joy would spring up like the sun breaking through an ocean of storm.

Take the promise in Isa. 42:16. Suppose the soul to be surrounded with darkness, perplexity and doubt, with regard to the path of duty or with regard to any other matter—borne down under a weight of ignorance and crushed with a sense of responsibility, however deep his agony and his trials may be. Hark! Hear Jehovah saying, "I will bring the blind by a way that they know not; I will lead them in paths that they have not known. I will make darkness light before them, and crooked things straight. These things will I do unto them and not forsake them." Now who does not see that faith in this promise would make the soul in a moment as quiet as a weaned child. It would at once become as calm as an ocean of love.

Take Isa. 41:10-14. Suppose a soul to be under circumstances of great temptation from the world, the flesh and the devil and ready to exclaim, "My feet are slipping, and I shall fall into the hand of my enemies; I have no might against this host. All my strength is weakness, and I shall dishonor my God." Hark again! Hear the word of the Lord.

> Fear thou not; for I am with thee: be not dismayed; for I am thy God: I will strengthen thee; yea, I will help thee; yea, I will uphold thee with the right hand of my righteousness. Behold, all they that were incensed against thee shall be ashamed and confounded; they shall be as nothing; and they that strive with thee shall perish. Thou shalt seek them, and shalt not find them, even them that contended with thee: they that war against thee shall be as nothing, and as a thing of nought. For I the Lord thy God will hold thy right hand, saying unto thee, Fear not; I will help thee. Fear not, thou worm Jacob, and ye men of Israel; I will help thee, saith the Lord, and thy redeemer, the Holy One of Israel.

What is here but an ocean of consolation to a mind that has faith?

Now what wait ye for. Anchor right down upon these promises. They can give you instant rest. Nothing but faith is wanting to put you in possession of it. And nothing else than faith can do you any good. There is no need of going around or waiting to come at this rest by degrees. It is to be entered upon at once. The land may be possessed now in the twinkling of an eye.

I designed to have added several remarks, but as I intend to pursue this subject at another time, I will defer them till then.

LECTURE 20

The Rest of Faith, No. 2

Heb. 3:19 and 4:1. "So we see that they could not enter in because of unbelief. Let us therefore fear, lest a promise being left us of entering into his rest, any of you should seem to come short of it."

Upon these words I remark:

1. That this rest into which they could not enter had been expressly promised to them.

2. That though no condition was expressly annexed to this promise, yet faith as a condition was necessarily implied; for if they had no confidence in the promise, they would of course neglect the necessary means to gain possession of the promised land.

3. Unbelief rendered the fulfillment of the promise impossible, inasmuch as it prevented their going up and taking possession when commanded to do so.

4. In my last, I showed that the land of Canaan was typical of spiritual rest or the rest of faith.

5. This spiritual rest is expressly promised and it is said that some must enter therein, yet faith is an indispensable condition to its fulfillment.

These remarks prepare the way for the discussion of the two following propositions:

I. That faith instantly introduces the soul into a state of rest.

II. That unbelief renders the rest of the soul impossible.

I. *Faith instantly introduces the soul into a state of rest.*

1. This is evident *from the nature of faith.* Faith is the confidence of the heart in the truth of God. It is a resting, a repose of the mind in God. Faith is that state of mind in which everything is confidently committed to the wisdom and goodness of God. Faith is either satisfied with what we at present have, and is a confidence that this is best for us and most for God's glory, or it trusts in God to make such changes in our circumstances and in our allotments as shall be most for His glory and our interest.

2. Faith implies *such a confidence as to exclude all anxiety* about our

own interest for time or eternity. It is a confidence that God both knows and is concerned to supply all our wants, that He is both able and willing to be and do to us and for us all that our souls and bodies need. It therefore excludes all anxiety in regard to our present or future interests whether for time or for eternity.

3. Faith is that confidence in God's wisdom and goodness that prefers to have and to be denied whatever seems good in His sight. It chooses by all means that God should mete out our changes, order our affairs and dispose of everything concerning us. Faith would by no means consent to have anything otherwise than according to the good and acceptable and perfect will of God.

4. Faith finds in Christ all the necessities of soul and body amply provided for. It takes right hold on Christ as "our wisdom, our righteousness, our sanctification and our redemption." Faith sees the meaning of such expressions as these in the gospel and lays fast hold on them, and so appropriates them to its own circumstances and necessities as to feel no more trouble about its own destiny than a man who stands on everlasting rock will doubt its strength to support him. Thus faith, from its own nature, puts carefulness and disquietude entirely out of the question.

II. *Unbelief renders the rest of the soul impossible.*

1. This is evident *from the nature* of unbelief. Unbelief is not the mere absence of faith. It is distrust—the refusal of the heart to trust in the truth, wisdom, providence and grace of God. Consequently, in unbelief the soul can find nothing on which to rest for a moment. It is not satisfied with its present circumstances because there is no confidence in the wisdom and goodness of Him who appointed them.

2. Unbelief *renders it impossible for the mind to feel any security against future ills*, temporal or spiritual.

3. There is nothing in a state of unbelief *that can support the mind amid the necessary vicissitudes of life.* God's government is moving on upon a vast scale and extends not only through immensity, but throughout eternity. Now it is self-evident that in the administration of such a vast system of providences, innumerable things will occur that minds like ours cannot understand at present, and the design of which we are utterly unable to see. Nor would it be possible for God, in our present state and with our present knowledge, to explain things so as to possess our minds with all the reasons for His conduct. With infinitely more ease could a parent engaged in the most extensive worldly business in which any man was ever engaged explain to a child two years old the reason of his movements. The child has such confidence in his parent that he needs not to know the reason of anything he does. But suppose the child had no confidence in the wisdom and goodness of his parent and still had knowledge enough to understand that in ten thousand ways his own inclination might be thwarted by the administration of his father's providence. This would naturally and certainly keep his mind in a state of continual vexation. So, under the government of God,

it is impossible that we should not pass through a constant series of vicissitudes and changes which will continue to vex and fret the mind that is in the exercise of unbelief. Suppose the holy angels had not confidence in God. What think you would be the state of mind into which they would be thrown by all the sin and misery they behold in this world?

4. In unbelief the soul *finds nothing to satisfy its desires.* Having no communion with or resting in God, its very nature is such that nothing in the universe can satisfy it. It has no such friend as it feels itself to need. The soul naturally feels that it needs a friend with the attributes of a God. It knows full well that all earthly friends, however faithful, are yet frail and utterly unable to be to them all they need. There is no portion but God that can satisfy the soul. The experience and observation of every day teach that, multiply earthly goods without end, and the soul is as far and even farther from being satisfied than at the first. The more of any finite good the soul obtains the more does it realize its wants, and either grasps and heaves with convulsive longings after more or, feeling the utter insufficiency of any finite good, it loathes them all. God is the only possible satisfying portion of the soul; and it is as impossible that the soul should find a resting place except in God as that a dove should rest in mid-heaven with weary wing, without a place upon which to rest the sole of her foot. Unbelief then is the soul's refusal to settle down and rest upon the infinite wisdom, goodness, truth and grace of God. It is the soul's refusal to bathe in the ocean of His love, to bask in the sunlight of His countenance, to rest sweetly and composedly in His hand, and hide under the cover of His wing.

5. Consequently, the soul in unbelief has *no sufficient barrier against the power of temptation.* Lust rages and of course reigns while unbelief is in the heart. The soul without faith has no perception of those higher motives that lift its desires and affections above sensible objects. And in this state the mind is given over to the reigning power of the flesh, and the gratification of sense becomes the soul's supreme object of pursuit. Thus the soul becomes the slave of the body. The spiritual eye being shut and the bodily eye open, the whole being grovels in the dust like a brute. While the soul is chained down to this miserable earth it languishes and groans and hopes and ever hopes in vain for future or present good to satisfy its immortal cravings. Being thus delivered up to the power of temptation, it wallows in its own filth and is even ashamed of its own deformity. It loathes itself and abhors everything else. A universal feeling of distrust and enmity and hell keep it continually on the rack.

6. I said *that in unbelief the soul was, of course, delivered over to the reigning power of lust.* The mind must be under the influence of motives of some kind. If unbelief prevails, no motive from eternity, from heaven, no voice or truth of God, no spiritual or elevating considerations will call the attention of the mind and elevate its aims and hopes and efforts. The whole spiritual world being annihilated in the estimation of such a mind and the world of sense being that alone from which such a mind receives impressions, all the motives under which it acts or in such a case can act being those derived from sensible objects, it will be influenced by such considera-

tions as might affect the beasts.

7. Another reason why unbelief renders the rest of the soul impossible is this. Where there is any degree of spiritual light, *the conscience is quickened to keep the distrustful mind in a state of perpetual disquietude.*

8. Unbelief delivers the soul over to a train of emotions, exercises and affections *which constitute essential misery.* The soul that distrusts the wisdom, goodness and providence of God will, as a thing of course, be greatly soured by the providences of God and misanthropized by the conduct of men. To such a mind everything goes wrong. Understanding and believing nothing of God's great plan of government, the universe seems to such a mind as little else than a general chaos or ocean of confusion and misery. And being supremely selfish, it is continually rasped and outraged by the selfish collisions of clashing interests with which it is surrounded. To trust in man it cannot, and feels that it has no reason. To trust in God it will not, and consequently it has no place of repose in the world.

9. Unbelief therefore plunges the mind into an ocean of storms and keeps it there. Ignorant of the past, uncertain of the future, a prey to lust and passion, without hope and without God—to rest is impossible.

REMARKS

1. Both faith and unbelief are volitions and are, therefore, in the highest sense within our reach, that is, we are in the highest and most absolute sense voluntary in their exercise. It is utterly absurd to say that we are unable to exercise either faith or unbelief. Faith is the mind's acceptance of the truth of God. Unbelief is the mind's rejection of that truth.

2. Faith is indispensable, in moral beings, to all virtue and all holiness in all worlds. Were it not for their confidence in God, how soon would the angels be stumbled at His providence and fall into rebellion. How many myriads of things does God find it necessary to do, the reasons and wisdom of which they cannot at present understand. Faith therefore is as indispensable to their virtue and happiness as to ours.

3. We can see why God has taken so much pains to inspire faith. The great object of all His dispensations and all His works and ways is to make himself known, and thereby secure the confidence of intelligent creatures. Knowing that their virtue and eternal happiness depend on this, He spares no pains, nay He did not hesitate to give His only begotten and well-beloved Son, to secure the confidence of His creatures in His love.

4. We see that unbelief is the most shocking and abhorrent wickedness. Suppose that children should refuse to trust their parents and, casting off all confidence in their goodness and providence, they should refuse all obedience except the reasons for everything were satisfactorily explained; that neither the wisdom or justice of any requirement or prohibition could be admitted without being made plain in all their relations to their comprehension; that the parent could be trusted for nothing, but that all was distrust and of course murmuring, uncertainty and discontent. Who does not see that any family under the influence of unbelief would present an image

of bedlam and would be an epitome of hell? What parent would not consider himself insulted in the highest degree and feel the utmost certainty that his family were ruined, if unbelief should come to be the prevailing principle of action?

We naturally feel in the highest degree insulted and outraged whenever our veracity is called in question. And you can scarcely anger men sooner than to suffer even an incredulous look to advertise them that you doubt their word. And what is there more shocking and offensive among dearest friends than to discover among those we love a want of confidence in us? Let every husband and wife, let every parent and child, every friend that is susceptible of the feelings of humanity rise up and bear witness. Say, is there anything within the whole circle of disgusting and agonizing considerations that is capable of inflicting a deeper wound upon your peace than a discovery of a want of confidence in those you love? It is an arrow dipped in deadly poison. It is unmingled gall.

Now how infinitely abominable must unbelief be in the sight of God. What! His own offspring cast off confidence in their heavenly Father! Virtually accusing Him of lying and hypocrisy—and proudly disdaining all comfort and impiously and ridiculously insisting upon everything being made plain to their understanding, so that they can see with their eyes and hear with their ears and thrust their hand into the wound in their Savior's side, or they will not believe. How must it grieve the heart of God to see such a state of things as this existing in His family? Distrust and consequent confusion reigning all around—and no pains-taking on his part prevails to secure confidence and hush the tumultuous elements of conflicting mind to rest.

5. You can see why unbelief is so anathematized in the Bible as that awful sin against which God has unmasked all the batteries of heaven. The reason is, it is at once the foundation and implies the whole aggregate of all abominations. It breaks the power of moral government, shuts out the peace of God, [and] lets in the infernal brood of all the abominable passions of earth and hell upon the soul.

6. You who do not enter into the rest of faith may understand your present character and your prospects. Remember that you are in the exercise of this greatest of all infernal sins. Unbelief is the sin and the misery of hell. It is the sin and misery of earth. Why do you harbor such an infernal monster in your bosom? It is as hideous and frightful as the apocalyptic beast with seven heads and ten horns, and as full of curses as the seven last plagues.

7. How strange that unbelief is so seldom reckoned as sin. When professors of religion and impenitent men are enumerating their sins, they almost never consider unbelief as the foundation and cause of all their other sins. In confessing their sins to God, if at all sensible of unbelief they seem to whine over it as a calamity rather than confess and mourn over it as a crime. While this is so, and unbelief is neither understood nor repented of as a sin, there is no prospect of a reconciliation between God and the soul.

8. Faith is the most simple and easy exercise of the mind conceivable. It is one of the earliest and most frequent exercises of the human mind. It is

one of the first exercises that we witness in little children. Confidence in those around them seems to be as natural to them as their breath. The admirable simplicity, sincerity and confidence of little children in their parents and those around them are truly affecting and afford a beautiful illustration of the wisdom and goodness of God. This confidence which is so natural to them is indispensable to their well-being in almost every respect.

Now confidence in God differs nothing in kind, so far as the philosophy of mind is concerned, from confidence in parents. While the little child knows nothing of its wants, present or future, nothing of its dangers, and has no idea of any other wants than what its parents can supply, it rests in peace, confiding in its earthly friends for all its necessities. But as soon as he learns how little confidence can be placed in men and that its necessities are far-reaching beyond the power of any human arm, its confidence in its parents can no longer keep the soul at rest.

9. Hence for those who will not believe there can be no remedy. Salvation to them is a natural impossibility. Under the wings of unbelief are congregated and sheltered the whole brood and catalogue of the miseries of earth and hell. Nothing but faith can be a remedy for their accumulated evils. At the bidding of faith the whole congregation of abominations break up and are scattered to the winds of heaven. But to the influence of nothing else can the mind yield itself up, that will relieve its anxieties, dissipate its forebodings and lull it into sweet repose upon the bosom of the blessed God.

10. How few have faith enough to enter into rest. In my last I assigned several reasons why the church does not enter into the rest of faith. It is perfectly obvious upon the very face of the church that very few of her members have entered into rest. They are filled with nearly the same cares and anxieties as other men. This is a great stumbling block to the world, and they often inquire what is religion worth? They see their professedly Christian friends as restless and fretful and uneasy as themselves. What then, they inquire, can religion be?

11. The great mass of the church have just conviction enough to make them even more miserable than worldly men. They have so much conviction of sin and of the reality of eternal things as to render it impossible for them to enjoy the world and, having no faith, they do not enjoy God. Consequently they are really destitute of all enjoyment and are the most miserable of all the inhabitants of earth; their inward unhappiness is great, often beyond expression or endurance. They are so miserable themselves as to make all around them unhappy. I know a woman who is little else than a bundle of disquietudes. I scarcely ever saw her five minutes in my life without her falling into a complaining strain of herself or somebody else. Everything and everybody are wrong. And whenever anyone thinks she is wrong it is because they do not understand her. I have several times thought it might well be said of her, she is of all women most miserable. It would seem that she cannot be made to see that the whole difficulty lies in her unbelief; but full of uneasiness about the present and forebodings as to the future, blaming everybody and blamed by everybody, she seems to be afloat upon an ocean of darkness and storms.

12. It seems almost impossible to make those who are filled with unbelief understand what is the nature of their difficulty. They often have so much conviction as to think that they believe. You tell them to believe, they tell you they do believe. They seem not to discriminate at all between intellectual conviction and the repose of the heart in the truth.

13. You can see the desperate folly, wickedness and madness of infidelity. Infidels seem to imagine that if they can get rid of the impression of the truths of Christianity, can persuade themselves that the Bible is not true and thus shake off their fears and sense of responsibility, they shall be happy. O fools and blind. What utter madness is in such conclusions as these! For in exact proportion to their unbelief is their desperate and incurable misery: an immortal mind with all its immortal wants and desires, launched upon the ocean of life and crowded forward without the possibility of annihilation; covered with complete ignorance and darkness with regard to the past, a veil of impenetrable midnight stretched over all the future; winds and waves roaring around him, rocks and breakers just before him, no helm, no compass, no star of hope, no voice of mercy; nowhere to rest, no prospect of safety, not a point in the wide universe on which the mind can repose for a moment. Considered in every point of view, infidelity is the consummation of madness, of folly and of desperate wickedness.

14. If you to whom this rest is preached fail to enter in because of unbelief, a future generation will enter in. The Apostle says, "It remains that some must enter in." The promise in regard to the church that some generation shall enter in is absolute. As it respects individuals, whether you or your children or some future generation shall enter in must depend upon your or their exercise of faith. The contemporaries of Moses did not enter into temporal Canaan because of their unbelief, but the next generation took possession of it through faith.

LECTURE 21

Affections and Emotions of God

Hosea, 11:8: "How shall I give thee up, Ephraim? how shall I deliver thee, Israel? how shall I make thee as Admah? how shall I set thee as Zeboim? my heart is turned within me, my repentings are kindled together."

In discoursing upon this text I design to show:

I. That God is a moral agent.
II. That He really exercises all the affections and emotions ascribed to Him in the Bible.

III. That it is a real and great grief to Him to abandon sinners to death.

IV. That they really compel Him to do so.

I. *I am to show that God is a moral agent*, that is, that He possesses and exercises the powers of moral agency—intelligence, will, conscience and all those susceptibilities that lay the mind open to the full force of motives.

1. That he is such an agent, I infer from the fact that man was created in His image; and we know from consciousness that *we* possess and exercise the powers of moral agency. The image of God in which man was created could not possibly have related to his moral character, for moral character is not a subject of creation. If by moral character is intended anything that is praise or blameworthy, it is absurd nonsense to say that it can be the subject of creation. It may be induced by moral means or moral considerations, as I suppose moral character always is produced in man whenever there is any holiness in him; and in this sense man's character may be the subject of creation. But that it should be the subject of creation in the same sense in which the nature of man is created is certainly impossible.

2. If God be not a moral agent He can have no moral character. In other words, He could be neither praise nor blameworthy. For certainly none but a moral agent can have moral character, can deserve praise or blame.

3. If God be not a moral agent He cannot possess a rational happiness, that is, He could possess none of that happiness which arises out of a virtuous character.

4. If not, He is not a proper object of love or worship or obedience. And certainly a moral agent like man has no right to obey or worship any but a moral being.

5. If not, it is impossible that moral agents like men should love or worship or obey Him, when they come to know Him.

6. The works of creation afford incontestible evidence that God not only possesses and exercises the attributes of a moral agent but that these attributes are absolutely infinite in extent.

7. Both the moral and providential governments of God prove unanswerably the same truth.

8. The Scriptures everywhere, in every variety of form, represent God as a moral agent. And scarcely a single thing asserted of Him in the Scriptures could be true unless He is a moral agent.

II. *God really exercises all the affections ascribed to Him in the Bible.*

1. This must be so from the very laws of His being.

2. The Bible ascribes love, hatred, anger, repentance, grief, compassion, indignation, abhorrence, patience, longsuffering, joy and every other affection and emotion of a moral being to God. Upon these Scriptures, I remark,

(1) He must *feel* or He is not virtuous. Virtue cannot consist in the mere abstractions of the intellect but belongs to the heart. And an intellect with-

out moral feeling cannot be virtuous.

(2) He must feel towards everything according to its nature or character or He is not virtuous.

(3) He is able to consider at one and the same time the nature and character of all events and, being infinite, is able to feel towards everything in existence precisely according to its nature, character and relations.

(4) It is His duty to exercise these feelings in kind and degree just suited to everything that exists.

(5) His holiness consists in this and in nothing else, in regarding everything according to its real nature and character. Were it otherwise, instead of being holy and an object of praise and love He would be wicked and not worthy of our praise or love.

(6) All these states ascribed to Him in the Bible must be the real exercises of His mind, as they are only the natural and necessary modifications of love that must certainly exist under the circumstances in which He is placed. There really are in the universe objects that ought to excite all the affections and emotions ascribed to Him.

III. *It is a real and great grief to God to abandon sinners to death.*

1. This is evident from the fact that it really *ought* to be a great grief to God to give the wicked up to eternal death. It is really a great evil. And it is impossible that benevolence should not regard it as such. And if there really exist a necessity for it, it must notwithstanding be regarded as a great evil.

2. It really must be a great grief to God if He is love. It is impossible that it should not be. And it is a contradiction to affirm that God is love and yet that He is not grieved with the necessity of taking such a course with sinners.

3. The Bible declares it in many ways. See the text, "How shall I give thee up, Ephraim? how shall I deliver thee, Israel? how shall I make thee as Admah? how shall I set thee as Zeboim? my heart is turned within me, my repentings are kindled together." Here the language is plainly that of a father who finds himself under the necessity of giving up and expelling from his family a froward son as less evil than to suffer him, by his example, to ruin all the rest. In this text God expresses himself as not only exercising the feelings of a father but as exercising the feelings of intense grief, as if He had said, "I have done all that in me lies to reclaim and save you, and oh, how shall I give you up? My heart is turned within me, my repentings are kindled together!" As if God were standing before the sinner in the attitude of a father and really overcome with excessive grief. There are many other passages of scripture that plainly declare the same truth.

4. All His works imply it. Everything that God has made in the universe demonstrates His intense desire to promote the happiness of His creatures. And so much pains certainly could not be taken by any mind to promote the happiness of others without being grieved with the necessity of giving them up to ruin.

5. His grace manifested in the atonement is the highest possible demonstration that He has all the feelings ascribed to Him in the Bible, and in an infinite degree. Did He not really love sinners, could He make so great a sacrifice to save them? Were He not angry at sin, were He not infinitely just and inflexible in maintaining the principles of His government, could He have given His Son to die as their substitute rather than pardon them without an atonement? We certainly should consider it the highest possible evidence of love in a human being to give himself or his son to die for us.

IV. *Sinners really compel God to give them up.*

I know that this statement is very diverse from the common opinions of men; for they argue merely from the omnipotence of God that He can save them if He will. And they never ask the question whether under all the circumstances of the case He can wisely *will* to save them. Under this head, I remark,

1. That since God has created you moral agents and placed you under a moral government, making you responsible for the right exercise of your powers of moral agency, He has no right to set aside your liberty and treat you inconsistently with the nature He has given you.

2. If He had a right and should actually set aside your liberty, in doing this He would render your salvation naturally impossible; for salvation without virtue is absurd, and virtue without free-agency is a contradiction. So that you cannot possibly be saved unless you can be induced by the considerations of the gospel to love and serve God.

Here it may be objected that in the parable of the marriage the king is represented as ordering his servants to go out and *compel* people to come in. But this is only a *moral* compulsion, such a degree of argument and persuasion that, as it were, constrains the sinner to come without at all interfering with his freedom.

3. There certainly is a point beyond which forbearance in God would be no virtue, and where further arguments and persuasions and efforts to save them would be entirely inconsistent with the honor and dignity and glory of God and, consequently, with the rights and well-being of the universe. Beyond this point, then, God cannot and ought not to go. If He sacrifices His own character He sacrifices with it the holiness and happiness of all other beings, as their holiness and happiness must depend upon their confidence in Him. It is easy to see, therefore, that the conduct of sinners imposes the necessity upon God of giving them up to damnation as the least of two evils. If they take such an attitude, as they often do, as to render it unwise in Him to pursue them any further with offers of grace, He must either give them up and save the universe of holy beings, or He must give up His character and thereby abandon the entire universe to ruin.

REMARKS

1. It is a great and ruinous error to suppose that the declarations of

Scripture with regard to the moral feelings of God are mere accommodations to human weakness, because (1) it is denying the nature of God, (2) it is denying His whole moral character, [and] (3) it is representing Him as a hypocrite. He *professes* such feelings, and what shall we say if He does not possess them? When He professes to love His creatures, are we to understand that He does not really love them but that He merely *acts* as we do when we love? But why does He act so? How are we to understand Him as feeling? If this language does not mean what it says, what does it mean? He really ought to exercise benevolence and He professes to exercise it; and are we to be told that His professions are a mere empty boast, an accommodation to human weakness?

But it probably will not be denied that He really loves.

If this be admitted, then all the other affections and emotions ascribed to Him must necessarily be exercised by Him. They are the very modifications that ought and must exist in view of the objects presented to the mind of God. So that if God does not really exercise these affections and emotions, He is not only a hypocrite but is in all other respects infinitely far from His duty. If therefore it be maintained that the moral feelings ascribed to God are mere accommodations to human weakness, it must also be denied that God is love or benevolence. And that to deny this is a ruinous and damning error needs no proof.

2. To maintain that the representations of the moral feelings of God in the Bible are only accommodations to human weakness is to represent Him as a mere intellect or abstraction, and consequently destitute of everything that ought to or can engage our love.

3. It is cutting off all possible sympathy between us as moral beings and God. If God be not a moral being with moral attributes and feelings we can have no sympathy with Him, can neither know nor love nor worship Him any more than we could Juggernaut.

4. It is to render all true religion impossible. The man that has an idea that these declarations are mere accommodations to human weakness can certainly have no true knowledge of God and consequently no true religion. If God be not what the Bible represents Him to be, then what is He, and who knows Him? If these are not His real feelings, then we are infinitely mistaken about His character. If these are not His' feelings and this His character, then we know not what they are.

5. If these are not the real feelings of God, then we have no true revelation of God. If these passages of Scripture do not mean what they say, it is impossible for us to tell what they do mean. And if God has not, in these passages, discovered to us the real state of His heart, we know nothing of His heart. But the truth is that these passages speak the same language with all His works. It is plain that His works and word are one continuous and complete system of revelation. And the same great gushing heart of love is everywhere manifest. And to maintain that the Bible declarations instead of meaning what they say are mere accommodations to human weakness amounts to the affirmation that all God's ways and works and word are a stupendous system of hypocrisy and deception.

6. The representing of the Scriptures as an accommodation to human weakness is an overlooking and denying a principal design of the incarnation of Christ. One of the grand objects Christ had in view was to reveal to us the heart of God. Now that which we see in Christ are the very feelings of the mind of God. Did Christ exercise these feelings in reality, then God exercises them; and so does every other holy mind that has a knowledge of the same facts.

7. But it may be objected that we ought not to ascribe human feelings to God. I answer, we ought to ascribe feelings the same in kind to God that holy men have. Wicked human feelings are by no means to be ascribed to God. But holiness in men is just what it is in God.

8. But again it is objected that God is not man that He should repent. I reply that repentance may mean emotions of sorrow or it may mean a change of mind. God never changes His mind but often, nay always, exercises emotions of sorrow; for objects that ought and must excite these emotions in a holy mind are always present before Him.

9. Again it is objected that if these things are so, God cannot be happy. I answer that all these feelings ascribed to God when combined are perfect happiness. I don't know how to make this plainer than by borrowing an illustration from the prismatic colors produced by the sun's rays. Let a pencil of the sun's rays be thrown upon a prism and, as you doubtless know, the rays will be so refracted as to exhibit all the colors that exist in nature. Now when these rays are separated it is found that none of them are white, yet when combined their brightness is eneffable. Just so with the feelings of God. Separate His moral feelings, and no class of them would be unmingled happiness; yet when combined they are infinite happiness.

10. Again it is objected that this view of the subject really implies change in God. I answer, No. For God has always known and felt what He now knows and feels. He has no new knowledge. All events have been eternally present to Him. He has always known, and feels and enjoys.

11. God enters fully into all the relations between himself and His creatures. I mean that He enters into these relations with all His heart and all His soul. He is feelingly alive to them all. It should ever be remembered that He is not a mere abstraction, an intellect without volition, emotion or sympathy. But His feelings are infinitely intense. So that every object in the universe, every creature, every want, every woe, every sorrow and every joy enkindle in His mind just that feeling in kind and degree which the nature of the thing is calculated to excite.

12. In Christ He has the most perfect sympathy with us. From many parts of Scripture it is manifest that one great design of the incarnation was to create a sympathy between God and men. Having been in the flesh, Christ has been "tempted in all points like as we are." He was made perfect by suffering and temptation, so as to be able to succor all those that suffer and are tempted.

13. It is objected that if God really exercises anger, He is wicked. I answer, No. His anger is a benevolent anger. It is not selfish or malicious or a disposition unjustly to inflict pain. But it is the holy indignation of a good

and gracious sovereign against those who would injure the interests, disturb the tranquillity and mar the happiness of his obedient subjects.

14. This view of God's character is that which renders God acceptable to creatures like us. We have the advantage of approaching Him knowing that He has the feelings and heart of a father. A guilty son knows that a *father's* heart can be reached when the bosom of a stranger could not be approached or moved by his tale of woe. And however guilty this son may be, if he knows that his father is good he is assured that in his heart he shall find a powerful advocate to plead his cause. So a wandering rebellious sinner may, like a returning prodigal, approach God with the certainty that a father's heart and a father's love will yearn over him and, if it be within the reach of possibilities, will save him from deserved destruction.

15. They don't know God who don't conceive of Him as a moral being, exercising in reality those feelings ascribed to Him in the Bible. Indeed if they conceive anything else of God, they are as far as possible from knowing the true God and might as well worship Juggernaut as the being whom they call God. He is a moral agent to all intents and purposes, exercising perfectly in kind and infinitely in degree all the affections and emotions of a moral being. As such we can form rational though inadequate conceptions of Him, can approach Him with confidence, can sympathize with Him in His efforts of benevolence. Our minds can commune with His mind and our hearts beat in unison with His heart. We can enter into His desires and purposes and efforts, and in short we can be assimilated to Him. But make anything else of God and we do not, cannot, ought not to love or worship or obey Him.

16. How aggravated in God's sight must sin appear, to induce Him with such feelings as He has to give His own offspring up to eternal death. We can conceive of a father banishing forever a beloved son because his depravity has become so great that his banishment from the family becomes indispensable. Yet the conduct of that son must be very aggravated to induce a father to do this and to justify in the estimation of the other members of the family such a course. So sin, in its tendency and in its contagious nature, must be an abominable thing to induce a God who could give His own son to die for sinners after all to give them up to go to hell.

17. The depravity that can wear out such love as this, and actually carry matters so far as to compel God to send the very sinners for whom Christ died to hell in order to preserve the universe of moral beings from destruction, must be horribly great. Sinners, think what you do. God has made you voluntary agents and made it an unalterable law of your being that you shall be free and responsible for the use of your freedom. And now, in the exercise of this liberty, you place God under circumstances where with all His love He is obliged to send you to hell as a less evil than to let you go unpunished.

18. How strongly will the universe approve of the dealings of God in destroying sinners forever. When all that He has done and suffered for them shall pass in full review in the solemn judgment before the assembled universe—His providential kindness, the giving of His Son, the influences of

His distinct consideration—what a spirit of most deep and perfect acquiescence will be felt by all the holy when the Judge pronounces the sentence: "Depart, ye cursed, into everlasting fire prepared for the devil and his angels."

19. It will be a delightful consideration to God and all the saints that God has done all the nature of the case admitted to save sinners, and they would not be saved.

20. From this and many other texts it appears that God feels compelled, and actually does give sinners up. And now remember that when He feels constrained to do this by you, your case is as hopeless as if you were already in hell. And remember that you are in danger of it every moment that you persist in impenitence. Nay, perhaps some of you are already given up. If so I have no expectation that either this or any other sermon that I could preach to you would do you any good.

Finally. Let all who have sinned and who are sensible of their guilt return immediately to God. Take the parable of the prodigal son and consider well the thrilling truths there communicated.

And now I conjure you to conceive of God as He really is, a being who not only knows but pities and deeply yearns over you with all the feelings of a heart of infinite sensibility. Go pour out your tears, your prayers, your confessions, your souls before Him; and His heart shall rejoice over you and His soul be moved for you to do you infinite good.

LECTURE 22

Legal and Gospel Experience

Ps. 40:1-3: "I waited patiently for the Lord; and he inclined unto me, and heard my cry. He brought me up also out of an horrible pit, out of the miry clay, and set my feet upon a rock and established my goings. And he hath put a new song in my mouth, even praise unto our God: many shall see it, and fear, and shall trust in the Lord."

Many of the Psalms should be regarded as inspired diaries, and as such they are most important way-marks to the Christian. The diaries of other men may mislead us. But when we find our experience to accord with that of inspired men, and with those parts of their experience which were recorded by the Spirit of God, we may be sure that we are in the same path in which they traveled to heaven. Psalm 119 together with many others are manifestly of this character. They are as if the psalmist had set up way-marks all along the pathway to heaven and, by recording his own experiences as on the milestones along the way, had given us the advantage of being certain whether or not we are in the way that inspired men have trodden.

I regard the text as an instance of this kind, wherein the psalmist, after having passed through severe trials of mind, records both his trials and deliverance for the benefit of all succeeding ages.

I will discuss this subject in the following order:

I. Inquire what we are to understand by the horrible pit of miry clay.
II. Show what is implied in waiting patiently for the Lord.
III. Show what is implied in being brought up out of the horrible pit of miry clay.
IV. What is implied in having his goings established.
V. Notice the consequences of this experience.

I. *What we are to understand by the horrible pit of miry clay.*

It should be observed that this is certainly figurative language. It cannot be supposed that the psalmist had literally fallen into a pit of clay. But he had been in circumstances that might be aptly represented by this analogy. Although language is figurative, it must have a meaning. And generally it is not at all difficult but exceedingly easy to understand figurative language. The figure here used implies,

1. That he had been placed in circumstances of extreme difficulty and danger from which he could not extricate himself.

2. That his efforts to help himself only increased his distress and danger. This is certainly implied in the figure he uses, "a horrible pit of miry clay." Now everyone knows that if a man were thrown into a pit of miry clay, his struggles to extricate himself would only sink him deeper in the mire and render his circumstances more and more desperate. Whatever else this figure teaches, we must not overlook the fact that the psalmist had been placed in circumstances where all his struggles and efforts to extricate himself had but made the matter worse.

3. It implies that his condition was desperate and horrible, like that of a man who, wandering in a solitary desert, had fallen into a deep pit of miry clay, beyond the reach and almost beyond the hope or possibility of aid.

Commentators have had numerous conjectures with regard to the psalmist's meaning in these verses. It were worse than useless to recapitulate them. It is possible that something connected with his worldly circumstances might have been under his eye when the psalmist wrote these verses. But to me it appears plain that he designed to describe his own experience, first in a state of legal bondage and then his passage from that state into the liberty of the gospel. This language is so perfectly suited to such an experience that probably no one who has had this experience will doubt that this was his design. This experience is familiar to all those, and only to those, who have passed from legal bondage to the liberty of faith. It appears to me to describe the same experience in a more condensed form as that in the seventh chapter of Romans. The latter part of the seventh contrasted with some of the first verses in the eighth chapter appear to me to exhibit an experience similar to the one before us.

A selfish soul, whether a backslider or an impenitent sinner, when attempting to serve God is really guilty, and is condemned for every act and every attempt to serve God while in a wrong state of heart. The law requires pure and perfect love, and every selfish act and effort is the direct opposite of the requirements of the law. Whether from hope or fear, whether from the lashings of conscience or any other consideration than love, [when] he attempts obedience he is condemned; and the law utters its thunders, and holds him guilty and worthy of eternal death.

Now it often comes to pass that backsliders and the unconverted (for they are both actuated by the same motives and are equally under condemnation)—it often comes to pass, I say, that they have too much conviction to be at all satisfied with anything they do; and yet they are too much distressed to do nothing. They see and feel themselves condemned even for their prayers, and yet they will cry for mercy. They drive in this and that direction and lay hold on every shrub or bush within their reach to pull themselves out of the pit, and yet their guilt and condemnation is increasing every moment they live. They read and pray, and go to meeting and stay at home, and think and meditate and seek and strive; and yet they see and feel themselves condemned for all their striving and efforts because supreme selfishness is at the bottom of them all. Such a soul finds itself ready to resolve and re-resolve, and heap up resolutions almost without end; but his resolutions are yielding as air before every breath of temptation because they are made in the face of an antagonist principle. And selfishness is found to sweep away as a dam of sand all those resolutions and efforts by which an attempt is made to withstand its influence. The truth is that in all such cases selfishness is at the foundation of all those resolutions and efforts; and while the heart is in this state nothing but a dreadful delusion can keep the mind from seeing that it is in a horrible pit of miry clay—that turn which way it will, that do what it may, while selfishness remains, the guilt is increased by every act and the soul is sinking more and more deeply under condemnation and wrath at every step.

This is truly a desperate situation. To give up effort, the soul in this state will not; and to make such kinds of efforts is worse than useless, inasmuch as every one of them is sin, and increasing his condemnation. In this state of mind, for an individual to praise the Lord is entirely out of the question. It appears to me that no figure could more perfectly describe a state of total bondage than this: convicted of sin, yet having no love to God; influenced by fear, and not by faith or love; struggling and agonizing, yet sinking deeper in guilt and condemnation every moment. This is indeed a horrible pit of miry clay.

II. *What is implied in waiting patiently for the Lord.*

1. Not an indolent sitting still. A man under these circumstances will do anything but sit still.

2. Not such a waiting as is consistent with leaving the matter and employing the time and thoughts about something else. This certainly will not, cannot be. Nor is any such thing intended in this text.

3. Not a consenting to a postponement of an answer to our requests. A soul in this state is in too much trouble and feels that it cannot and has no right to be willing to remain for one hour longer in that situation.

I have often thought that the translation of this passage was calculated to make, and had actually made in many instances, an impression directly contrary to the truth. By waiting patiently many seem to understand a kind of indifference and carelessness about the result. Now the original expresses a state of mind the exact opposite of this, and implies: (1) a *constant looking to God*—*waiting* on the Lord as a criminal condemned to die would *wait anxiously and constantly* at the door of one who had the power of pardon; [and] (2) an *earnest, agonizing* and *intense* looking or waiting upon the Lord. The translation would exactly have expressed the idea had it said "I waited *agonizingly* or *intensely* for the Lord." In the original it reads *in waiting I waited*, which is one of the forms of expressing a superlative and implies in this connection a steady yet vehement attitude of supplication.

4. Waiting patiently for the Lord implies a holding on and a refusing to be denied, like that of Jacob when he said, "I will not let thee go except thou bless me." This state of mind is frequently described in the Bible. In the parable of the loaves and the importunate widow, the necessity and power of a *persevering* state of mind are set in a striking light.

5. It implies a sense of being shut up to God for help—a full and ripe conviction of the mind that our circumstances are desperate unless God undertake our case. The psalmist seems to have waited *only* upon God.

6. It implies a ripe conviction of the voluntariness of his sin, and consequently the horribleness of his situation. He did not look upon his circumstances as calamitous and a misfortune but as desperate wickedness. A man never sees the truly horrible nature and desperateness of his circumstances until he sees that his voluntary selfishness is the only reason why he does not yield full and instantaneous obedience to God—and that this selfishness, having grown with his growth and strengthened with his strength, is sinking him every instant in the horrible pit of miry clay, and despite his resolutions is sweeping him as with a flood to the depths of hell.

7. It implies so much hope that he should be heard as to encourage prayer. Like a man that had fallen into a pit lifting up his voice again and again, if peradventure some passer-by might hear his wailing and be attracted to the spot to afford him help.

I do not think this waiting upon the Lord implies an anchoring down in faith upon the promises of God, for this would at once remove the anguish of the mind. But it means rather the cry of distress almost despairing, and yet so much hope remaining as to encourage a vehement crying to the Lord.

If it be objected that God answers none but the prayer of faith, it should be remembered that there is a sense in which He hears and answers other prayers than these. He hears the cry of the little ravens and the young lions when they lack for food. And Christ, when on earth, heard and answered the prayer of devils when they pleaded that they might not be sent out of the country but might be suffered to go into the herd of swine. God's ear is always open to the cry of distress; and where there is no good reason why He should not, He may and doubtless does often hear and in some sense answer the prayer of those whose moral character He abhors. I do not believe that God has anywhere laid himself under an obligation to answer any but the prayer of faith. And yet I cannot doubt that He often hears the cry of souls in distress and brings deliverance to those in legal bondage.

III. *Show what is implied in being brought up out of the horrible pit.*

This is an affecting figure. The language is peculiar. God is here represented as having His attention arrested by some distant cry of distress. A soul has fallen into a horrible pit and lifts up his voice and cries. "Help! O God, help!" But receiving no answer he cries again. "Help! O my God, help!" Here God's attention is arrested. The cry comes into His ear. He is represented as stooping down: "he inclined unto me." He is represented as inclining in the direction of the cry and holding himself in the attitude of intense listening. Again the cry breaks upon His ear, "Help! O my God, help!" And then hastening as upon the wings of the wind, He bows the heavens and comes down and lifts the soul up from the horrible pit of miry clay.

1. This language implies deliverance from that state of mind in which all his efforts were selfish and sinful—a breaking up of the influence of self upon the mind and filling it with love, so as to give it the consciousness that it really rendered acceptable service to God. While under legal influence, he felt continually that his services were not accepted or acceptable, that they could not and ought not to be accepted by a holy God, that his best services were selfishness and rendered it more and more impossible for God to justify and save him.

2. It implies being placed upon firm footing, where he could serve God with a conscious soundness and firmness of heart, being conscious that he was influenced by love and not by fear and that his heart was fixed and sincere and full of the love of God. Thus the power of legal considerations over the mind was broken.

3. This expresses the experience of a soul who is led to lay hold on Christ by faith. His feet are set upon the rock, Christ. Faith that produces love breaks the yoke of bondage, of selfishness, of death, and admits the soul at once into the rest and liberty of joy and faith and love. If any of you have passed through this state of mind, you do not need that I should say anything to make you understand it; and if you have not, say what I would, you would understand but very little about it.

IV. *What is meant by having his goings established.*

This is also a figure. He is represented as being set upon a rock, not to slip immediately off or to be swept off by the first wave of temptation but as having his footsteps established upon the rock.

1. This implies that his faith had a permanency and stability that worked by love and prevented his falling again under condemnation. I know that he says in the latter part of this same psalm, "Mine iniquities have taken hold upon me so that I am not able to look up." But this does not imply that he had really fallen into sin again, but that a sense of his old sin had laid him exceedingly low before God. This is a familiar occurrence to all those whose feet are so established as to abide in the faith of the gospel. They often have so great a sense of their former guilt as to produce the greatest loathing and make them cry out, "Mine iniquities have taken hold upon me so that I am not able to look up." This does not however imply that they have present doubts of their acceptance with God, or feel a sense of present condemnation, or that their hearts are not right with God. It implies rather the contrary state of mind. When their former sin is the object of their thoughts they are almost overcome with a sense of their exceeding vileness. But as soon as their thoughts return and God becomes the object of contemplation their hearts are full of love and joy and peace.

2. It implies that he was so upheld by grace that he found himself able to go forward in the service of God, without being brought under the influence of fear and legal motives and thus again entangled with the clay.

V. *The consequences of this experience.*

1. A new song was put into his mouth. He could now praise God. I have said that a man under legal influences cannot praise God. The attempt is mockery, as everyone knows who has been in this state. Praise is therefore a new song to the soul who has passed into gospel liberty.

2. Another consequence of this change was manifest. "Many," he says, "shall see it." Yes, the very countenance of such a soul is changed, so that at first flush you would see that he was out of the pit. Instead of that despondency and anguish and guilt which overspread the whole mind there is a sweet calm, a glow, a joy, a peace, a heaven in the very countenance. Everyone can see it.

I once knew an infidel whose only and beloved daughter was in great distress of mind. He observed it and became exceedingly anxious about her, and was proposing to send her out of the city to divert her mind and restore her former gaiety of disposition. At this crisis he was prevailed upon by a pious lady in his family to let his daughter attend an anxious meeting. She came, gave her heart to God and returned in great peace. As soon as her father saw her the next morning, he was struck with the change in her countenance. It was so manifest as almost to overcome him. He said to his wife that their daughter was greatly altered, and cried out to his daughter with tears, "Oh, you cannot love me anymore if you have given your heart to Christ." I have seen many cases where the change was so great in the very countenance as to tell the whole story more forcibly than any words could do, and it might well be said "they looked unutterable things."

3. Others "shall fear." When such a great change occurs in any soul, backsliders and impenitent sinners are alarmed. It brings God and eternity near to them. It produces an awe that no preaching could do. It is a matter of fact, a real living illustration of the power of the gospel and of God. How many times have I known such a change to alarm a whole household and in some instances a whole neighborhood.

It results in their trusting in the Lord. This is a common case. When one passes through this great change it first alarms then encourages, and brings many to fear and trust in the Lord.

REMARKS

1. Great multitudes of souls are in the horrible pit of miry clay. From my own observation, I am convinced that the great mass even of those who are called the most pious in the churches are in a state of legal bondage and have gone no further in religion than to find themselves in a state of almost continual condemnation. They have conviction enough to make them miserable. They are driven and dragged by their consciences and the law of God, are struggling and resolving, but are under the influence of so much selfishness as to be continually crying out, as in the case supposed by the Apostle in the seventh of Romans, "When I would do good, evil is present with me." "I find a law in my members warring against the law of my mind and bringing me into captivity." "O wretched man that I am, who shall deliver me from the body of this death?"

2. They seem not to expect to get out of this state. The seventh of Romans has been so perverted as to be a great stumbling block to many souls in this state of mind. They seem to understand the Apostle as speaking of himself as he was at the time he wrote the epistle. And thinking it not to be expected that they should advance further than an inspired Apostle did, they get the idea that they must and shall live and die in that state. I have often thought it was most unhappy that the seventh and eighth chapters were separated. If persons would read attentively the whole of the seventh and eighth chapters in their connection, they might see the drift of the Apostle's reasoning. I apprehend he merely supposed a case for the purpose of contrasting the influence of the law and of the gospel upon the mind. Now whether this is so or whether he spoke of his own experience, it is certain that the same individual who in the seventh chapter is represented as being under the bondage of law, of sin and death, is in the beginning of the eighth chapter represented as being brought into an entirely different and opposite state of mind. The same individual who could complain in the seventh chapter as being in such horrible bondage, as being a slave sold under sin, could break forth in the beginning of the eighth chapter and say,

There is therefore now no condemnation to them which are in Christ Jesus, who walk not after the flesh, but after the Spirit. For the law of the Spirit of life in Christ Jesus hath made me free from the law of sin and death. For what the law could not do, in that it was weak through the flesh, God sending his own Son in the likeness of sinful flesh, and for sin, condemned sin in the flesh: that the righteousness of the law might be fulfilled in us, who walk not after the flesh, but after the Spirit.

3. They do not take a course that can ever bring them out. They are striving to get grace by works of law, instead of taking hold at once by naked faith upon the promises of God.

4. They form no right conception of the state of mind in which they may be when the power of lust and every temptation shall be broken. They expect therefore to live and die in the pit of their own filthy lusts. And if they do so die, they are sure to go to hell.

5. Many are in the horrible pit but are fast asleep. They are dreaming that they are awake and they are fancying themselves upon the rock, while they are almost suffocated in the mire of their own filth and are ready to sink down to hell.

6. Will you consider how much more inexcusable you are for remaining in this pit one moment than the psalmist was? There are thousands of promises now that had never been written in those days. It is now also the dispensation of the Spirit. You are surrounded with so much more light, have such a full and perfect revelation, and indeed are so circumstanced in every respect as to render you infinitely guilty for remaining there one moment.

7. Those who are delivered will abound in praise. Their hearts and lips are full of praise. It is a new song. Praise is as natural as their breath. That has happened to them which is foretold in the prophet, "He shall appoint unto them that mourn in Zion to give unto them beauty for ashes, the oil of joy for mourning, the garment of praise for the spirit of heaviness; that they might be called trees of righteousness, the planting of the Lord, that he might be glorified."

Sometimes I have known those under legal bondage, [to] rebuke those who were full of praise, reminding them that they had something else to do, that they had better be praying for sinners than praising and rejoicing. But let all such persons remember that this new song of praise often does more on the one hand to rouse the careless to fear, and on the other to encourage the desponding to hope, than could be effected by any other means.

8. From this subject we can see how it may be known who are delivered: they who have "the new song in their mouth, even praise to our God."

9. You can see the importance and the effect of testifying your joy before the church and the world. The psalmist says, "I have not hid thy righteousness within my heart; I have declared thy faithfulness and thy salvation; I have not concealed thy loving-kindness and thy truth from the great congregation."

10. Many may wonder and despise, and perish. Nevertheless let all who have experienced the loving-kindness of the Lord say with the psalmist in another place, "Come, all ye that fear the Lord, and I will tell you what he has done for my soul."

LECTURE 23

How to Prevent Our Employments from Injuring Our Souls

Rom. 12:11: "Not slothful in business; fervent in spirit; serving the Lord."

In remarking upon this subject, I design to show:

I. That idleness is inconsistent with religion.
II. That all persons are bound to pursue some lawful employment.
III. That they are to be diligent in their calling whatever it is.
IV. How to prevent employments, either secular or spiritual, from becoming a snare to the soul.

I. *Idleness is inconsistent with religion.*

1. Because it is wholly inconsistent with love to God. Whoever loves God with all his heart will certainly set himself to do the will of God and will no more be idle than God will be idle.

2. It is wholly inconsistent with love to man. The love of our race will certainly lead us to exert ourselves to promote their happiness.

3. Idleness can result only from selfishness. A man must love his own ease supremely to be idle in a world like this.

4. Idleness is sponging out of the community in which we live. A man that does not earn his bread, who does not contribute as much to the happiness and good things of the world as he consumes, who lives upon the common stock without contributing his share, is a drone. If he is not engaged in some employment that promotes the well-being of man, he is subtracting continually from the common stock of blessings and sponging from the universe of God.

5. Idleness is injustice. This follows from what has just been said. A man has no more right to live by sponging than he has to live by stealing. Indeed it involves the same principle.

6. It is absolute and downright disobedience to God. God as much forbids idleness as He does theft or murder; and a man or a woman can no more be religious without pursuing some employment by which God may be glorified and the world benefited than a habitual drunkard can be religious.

II. *All persons are bound to pursue some lawful employment.*

This is a plain inference from what has already been said. But what is a lawful employment? This is an all-important question, in answer to which I observe,

1. To be lawful, an employment must not be injurious to our own best interests or the best interests of mankind.

2. Speculation is not a lawful employment. To embark in uncertain speculations involves in it the principle of gambling and is eminently *the spirit* of gambling. It is a game of chance, where one of the parties must gain and the other lose and where selfishness stalks abroad naked, to grasp every man's wealth without blushing.

3. To be lawful, an employment must not be selfish. All selfishness is sin. And every employment, however lawful it may be in itself, is rendered unlawful by being selfishly pursued.

4. To be lawful there must not be too much or too little of it. A business lawful in itself may become unlawful when too much is undertaken or too little is performed, so that on the one hand a man is crushed or on the other he is idle; but,

5. To be lawful a business must be useful, that is, it must be such an employment as is calculated in its nature to benefit mankind.

6. To be lawful a business must be suited to your capacity. You cannot lawfully employ yourself in that for which you are not fitted. By this I do not mean that you are to be perfectly qualified for the transaction of any business before you can lawfully engage in it, but that you should be as well or better fitted for that particular employment than any other.

7. To be lawful, it must be that employment to which you are called of God. You are to be wholly the Lord's and to consult His will in all things, and never to be engaged in any employment to please yourself or promote your own separate or private interest. You are bound therefore to submit yourself to the direction of the Lord in all things and to select no employment for life or for any length of time but under the direction of God.

It is generally admitted that ministers are to be specially called of God to the work of the ministry. But all men are to be equally devoted to God and all employments are to be pursued equally for the glory of God. Every faculty [and] every day and moment of all men are to be devoted to the Lord. And all men are equally bound to consult the will of God in the selection and pursuit of their employments. And no man can give himself up to employments to which he is not called of God, or to which he does not really believe himself to be called of God, without thereby apostatizing from the service of God. Now every one of you would say that if a minister should select the ministry to please himself he would lose his soul. This is equally true of every other employment.

8. To be lawfully employed you must engage in that in which you can be most useful. It is not enough that you render yourself useful in some degree; you are bound to be engaged in that employment in which you can, all things considered, do the most good. A man might render himself useful as a peddler, but if he can be more useful in some other employment he is bound to prefer it.

9. That only is a lawful employment which can honestly and reasonably be pursued for the glory of God. Every kind and degree of business that cannot, with an enlightened conscience, be solemnly engaged in and transacted for the glory of God carries its own condemnation on its very front.

10. No business is lawful that is not, *as a matter of fact*, engaged in and pursued with the supreme desire to know and glorify God therein.

11. No business is lawful which is inconsistent with the highest degree of spirituality. I mean that only which consists with entire holiness of heart and life is a lawful employment. Anything that Jesus Christ or an apostle would not engage in under the circumstances is really unlawful for everybody else.

III. *Men are to be diligent in their calling.*

1. This is implied in the text. The text is commonly quoted as if it read, "Be diligent in business." This is not the way in which it reads, though this is plainly implied in it and its real meaning.

2. It is also plainly implied in the law of God.

3. The necessities of the world require it. There is enough for every man to do. And no man has any right to be idle or dilatory in his calling.

4. Every degree of slothfulness is injurious to yourself in many ways.

5. It is also injurious to those with whom you are immediately connected. They have a right to expect the diligent use of your powers in promoting their common interests.

6. Every degree of slothfulness in you is injurious to the world at large and to the universe, inasmuch as there is just so much less of real good in the universe for every moment's idleness in which you indulge.

7. It is a bad example in you to be idle for a day or an hour or to be in any manner negligent or slothful in your employment. Its tendency is to produce universal idleness which would ruin the universe.

8. You are bound to do all the good you can in every way, both to the bodies and souls of men; and this obligation is entirely inconsistent with any degree of slothfulness.

IV. *How to prevent secular or spiritual employments from being a snare to the soul.*

It has come to be a subject of almost universal complaint that our employments lead us away from God. Men complain of their cares and [of] having so much business on their hands as to secularize their spirit, blunt the edge of devotional feeling, and more or less insensibly but certainly to draw off their hearts from God. And those who are engaged in intellectual and even spiritual occupations, such as teachers of science and teachers of religion, are by their employments apt to fall into an intellectual and hardened frame of mind and to wander far from God. It seems to be understood that there is a kind of necessity in the case, and that we are naturally unable to attend to the various duties and callings incidental to our relations in this world, without secularizing our spirit and annihilating a devotional state of mind. Now to suppose there is any necessity for this result is to charge God foolishly. He has never placed us here surrounded with these necessities to be a snare and a curse to us. On the contrary, all the employments that are strictly lawful, instead of being a snare, are indispensable to the highest development of our powers and to the growth and consummation of our piety.

The whole difficulty lies in the abuse of a thing eminently wise and good. That the facts are according to the general complaint cannot be doubted. Men really are ensnared by their employments. But why? Many seem to suppose that the only way to maintain a spiritual frame of mind is by a total abstraction from those employments in which it seems to be necessary for men to engage in this world. It was this conceit that led to the establishment of nunneries and monasteries and to all those fanatical and odious seclusions from society that have abounded among the Papists.

The truth is that the right discharge of our duties to God and man, as things are, is indispensable to holiness. And voluntary seclusion from human society and abstracting ourselves from those employments by which man may be benefited are wholly inconsistent with the principles and spirit of the Christian religion. So did not Christ nor the apostles. They were eminently active, zealous and useful in promoting the glory of God and the good of man, in every way in their power. It is a desideratum, therefore, in religion to understand the secret of making our employments, whatever they are, the means of increasing instead of destroying our spirituality. A great deal needs to be said upon this subject. I can now only say the following things and may at a future time, if God permit, resume the subject.

1. If you would not that your employment should be a snare to your soul, see to it that it is not unlawful, that is, see to it that it is not an injurious employment, that you are not engaged in that, the natural tendency of which is to injure yourself or your fellowmen.

2. See to it that you do not introduce some unlawful ingredient into a business otherwise lawful, and thus vitiate the whole and render it a curse to you and those around you. For example, [consider] a man who is an innkeeper. To keep a house of public entertainment is, in itself, lawful and useful. But if a man to increase his profits or to please all classes of people will sell ardent spirits, this is absolutely unlawful and an abomination in the sight of God, and it introduces an element into his business which vitiates the whole and renders his business a curse to mankind.

A merchant perhaps does the same thing. In order to increase his profits or please his customers, he sells tobacco and other fashionable but injurious narcotics. And while he deals in many things that are useful and important, he does not hesitate to buy and sell almost anything upon which he can make a profit. Now if he admits into his business any ingredient that is injurious to the interests of mankind he renders the whole an unlawful business. It demonstrates that he is not and cannot be pursuing his employment from right motives. And it is impossible that he should pursue a business of this kind in a manner that shall be acceptable to God. In other words his business itself is an apostasy from God. God has said, "Whosoever shall keep the whole law, and yet offend in one point, he is guilty of all."

Now the principle involved here is that while a man admits any form of sin whatever to be habitual in his employment, it is rendering all obedience for the time being wholly impossible. He is in the exercise of a spirit which is in itself disobedience to the whole law and a setting aside [of] the authority of God.

3. Be sure that you do nothing selfishly. If you allow selfishness in any of its forms to come in and to have a place in your employments, you are already departed from God, and your business, whether spiritual, intellectual or whatever it may be, has become an abomination to God.

4. See that your business is strictly and properly a lawful one. If it be not in the most proper sense a lawful employment it will, if persevered in, certainly ruin your soul. To be lawful, I have already said that it must be some employment that is useful, suited to your capacity, that to which you are called of God, that in which you can become useful, that which can be truly and honestly and solemnly dedicated to God and performed for Him, that which as a matter of fact is thus dedicated to and performed for God, that which is consistent with the highest degree of spirituality (with perfect holiness of heart and life), and such as Christ and the apostles would engage in under the same circumstances.

5. See that your eye is single, that you have but one great leading motive, and that to glorify God and serve your generation.

6. Consult God at every step of your employment. Do everything with prayer. Let every day and every hour bear witness that you are transacting everything for God and consulting Him at every step of your progress. You would no doubt feel shocked should you know that a minister went about his preparation for the pulpit without prayer to God. Should he not, on going out to visit his people, pray for divine direction, and when he returned from such visits should he not spread the whole matter and what he had done before the Lord—in short should he not take counsel of God in all the departments of his employment—you would feel shocked. And should he become exceedingly hardened and reprobate in his work and should his employment be the snare and ruin of his soul, you would not wonder; for this would be the very result that under the circumstances you would anticipate. And it is to be feared that this is the very course and the very result with multitudes of ministers. Now as everything is God's and every man is His and every employment is to be pursued as much for His glory as the employment of a minister, it follows of course that every person is bound to have as single an eye to consult God at every step, and to make His employment a subject of daily prayer, as a minister is. And if he does not, he will surely apostatize from God.

7. Be sure to do everything in a spirit of entire consecration to God. Maintain perpetually, in everything, a spirit of as entire consecration as you know and feel that you ought to maintain in the exercises of the Sabbath day. It is impossible that men should ever pursue their employment without ensnaring their souls, until they understand that the business of every day is to be as sacredly devoted to God and performed in a spirit of as entire consecration to His service as the holy exercises of the Sabbath. This must not only be understood in theory but must be reduced to practice. The Sabbath must be distinguished from other days only in the peculiarity of its employments. You must cease to suppose that the Sabbath is God's day and that the week days are yours, that you may serve God one day and

yourself six days in the week. The Sabbath has its specific and appropriate duties. And so have other days. But every day and every hour, and every employment and thought, are to be wholly consecrated to God. And until you have habituated yourself to go to your farms, to your shops or to your merchandise as to a business that belongs wholly to God and is to be performed in a spirit of as true devotion as are the duties of your closet or of the sanctuary, your whole employment will be an everlasting snare and the final ruin of your souls.

8. In short, do nothing, be nothing, buy nothing, sell nothing, possess nothing, do not marry nor decline marriage, do not study nor refrain from study, but in a spirit of entire devotion to God. Consecrate your sleep, your rest, your exercise, your all to God. Learn to do this, *practice this*, or your employment, whatever it may be, will be the snare and ruin of your soul.

9. But that without which all else will be in vain is yet to be mentioned. And mark what I say. You must abide in Christ. "Without me," says Christ, "ye can do nothing." Only as you abide in Him by faith, and He in you, will you do any one of the things that have been mentioned in a right spirit. He is your life. He is the bread and water of life. Faith in Him is the grand and universal condition of all true virtue and obedience to God.

REMARKS

1. God calls you to no employment in kind or amount that is inconsistent with entire holiness of heart and life. Whenever you find therefore that your employment really prevents your walking wholly with God, something is certainly wrong. Either your employment is unlawful in itself or, if in itself a lawful one, it is that to which you are not called, or you have taken too much upon you, or too little, or your motives have become wrong. There is utterly some fault in you. Make a solemn pause then as on the very brink of eternity and inquire after and remove the stumbling blocks out of the way. If it be a right hand or a right eye give it up in a moment, as you love the ways and dread the wrath of God.

2. God never calls you to any business and withholds the necessary grace for the perfect discharge of your obligations. If grace be sought as it ought to be and constantly will be while your motives are right, it will not be withheld.

3. But if God calls you to a business and you become selfish in it, it is no longer acceptable to Him; and your pursuing it with a selfish heart is an utter abomination to Him. I fear it is not an uncommon thing for young men who suppose themselves to be called to the gospel ministry, in the course of their preparation to become cold and ambitious and anything but holy. And yet they persevere, because they dare not go back and relinquish their course. They are sensible that they are away from God; but believing themselves to have been called to the work of the ministry, they feel as if they must go forward, partly lest they should lose their reputation with men and partly because they fear the displeasure of God, while they know that as a matter of fact their hearts are not right with Him. And thus they go through

their classical studies, hoping that when they enter upon theology their studies will be of such a character as to make them holy. But coming as they do, in such a state of heart, to the study of theology, they are only hardened more rapidly than before. But finding this to be the case does not deter them from going forward. They think that now they must make up their opinion on various points of doctrine, and that when they have settled all these things and entered upon the active duties of the ministry, then they shall be aroused to a better state of feeling. But the hardening process still goes on. So that by the time they are through their course their hearts are like the nether millstone. They are all head and no heart, all intellect and no emotion. In this state they come to the active duties of the ministry; and woe to the church that shall employ one of them. They might as well place a skeleton in their pulpit, for he is but the shadow of a minister and not the substance. He has the bones but not the marrow and life and spirit of the gospel.

4. No man has a right to undertake so much business, for any compensation whatever, as to interfere with his hours of devotion. In cases where persons labor by the day or month or year, allowance should always be made in the prices they receive for sufficient time and opportunity for devotional exercises. They have no right to exact or receive such wages as to render it necessary for them to give up all their time to labor; nor ought their employers to expect them to encroach, under any pretense whatever, upon those hours appointed to secret communion with God.

5. There is great danger of a diligence in business which is inconsistent with fervency of spirit in serving the Lord.

6. From my own observation, I am persuaded that there is a great error in requiring too much study of young men who are preparing for the ministry. There is such a great cry for a learned ministry—so much stress is laid upon a thorough education—and so much competition among colleges and seminaries as to present a great temptation to instructors to push the intellectual pursuits of young men to the utmost and even beyond the utmost limit of endurance.

Now while I am in favor of a thorough education, I do not and cannot believe, with the facts as they exist before me, that the great difference in the usefulness of ministers depends on their being learned men in the common acceptation of that term. Human science by itself never made a useful minister; and wherever human science is pushed beyond its proper limit and made to encroach upon the hours and spirit of devotion, wherever the spirit of human science instead of the Spirit of God comes to be that fountain at which a man drinks, he may become in the language of men a great man but he will never be a good minister. Until there is a great change upon this subject—until the great effort of the teachers is to make their pupils pious as well as learned, and they are more anxious and take more pains to effect the former than the latter—our seminaries can never send out efficient ministers. To require diligence in study without requiring fervency of spirit; to concern ourselves more that our students have their lessons than that they walk with God, that they commune with Cicero, Horace, and

Demosthenes, rather than with God; for us to satisfy ourselves every day in relation to their intellectual progress and pay little or no attention to the state of their hearts—is an utter abomination. And teachers who do so, whatever other qualifications they may have, are unfit to have the care of young men.

7. When you find yourselves proceeding in any employment without prayer for direction, support and guidance, you may rest assured that you are selfish; and however diligent you may be, you may know that you are not fervent in spirit serving the Lord.

8. The speculations of the last few years have so secularized the church as to annihilate her power with God. She has in reality been engaged in gambling under the pretense of making money for God. In doing this multitudes of leading church members have involved themselves and the cause of Christ in great embarrassment and disgrace. And it does seem as if they were deranged in their spasmodic efforts to enrich themselves.

9. No amount of money can save or even benefit the world in the hands of a secular church. If professors of religion had made all the money they have endeavored to make and did they possess a universe of gold, it would do nothing towards converting the world, while the very spirit and life of the church is secular, earthly, sensual and devilish.

10. No idle person can enjoy communion with God for the plain reason that his idleness is perpetual disobedience to God.

11. The Apostle has commanded that they who will not work (that is, who are idle) shall not eat. If persons are able to pursue and can find any employment by which they can benefit mankind and are idle, it is no enlightened charity to feed them.

12. If idle persons eat they cannot digest their food. It is an unalterable law of God that men shall perform some kind of labor. This is essential to the well-being of their body and mind. Idleness is as inconsistent with health as it is with good morals. So that if men will be idle they must suffer the penalty of both physical and moral law.

13. You see from this subject the great importance of training children to habits of industry and of early imbibing their minds with the spirit of continually doing something that is useful.

14. Everyone can do something to glorify God and in some way benefit mankind. He can labor with his hands or his head or his heart, he can work or teach or pray, or do something to contribute his share to the common stock of good in the universe. It is the language of a sluggard to complain that you can do no good. The truth is that if you have a spirit to do good you will certainly be trying to do good.

15. If we do what we can, however little, it is just as acceptable to God as if we could do a thousand times as much. "If there be first a willing mind, it is accepted according to what a man hath and not according to what he hath not." Christ said of the poor widow who cast in her two mites, she has cast in more than the rich, who of their abundance cast in much. It is well if you have a heart to do a great deal more than you are able to do. It is that which you really would do for which Christ gives you credit, and not

for that which you are really able to do. It is according to the largeness of your heart and not according to the weakness of your hands that God will reward you.

16. Not one of the employments that are essential to the highest good of mankind has any natural and necessary tendency to alienate the heart from God. By this, I do not mean that the perverted state of the human heart is not such that it is natural for it, being in a state of selfishness, to take occasion to depart from God in these employments. But I do mean that the real tendency of all these employments, to a mind not given up to selfishness, is to increase and perpetuate the deepest communion with God.

17. There is no excuse for a secular spirit. And, as I have already said, whenever your spirit is secular your heart is selfish.

18. If you have been called of God to any employment and have become selfish in it, it has become an abomination to God; and you are bound to abandon it instantly or to renounce your selfishness and diligently pursue your employment for God. By this, I do not mean that you would do right to abandon the employment to which God has called you but that if you will not repent and be "fervent in spirit serving the Lord," you are as far as possible from pleasing Him in pursuing your business selfishly. If God be not with you in any employment, whether it be study, the ministry, merchandise, farming or anything else, if God does not go with you in it, you are certainly out of the way, are bound to reform, to turn instantly and wholly to the Lord and go not a step forward until you have evidence of the divine acceptance.

19. Lastly, let me ask you solemnly, beloved, have you some employment in which you are endeavoring honestly and fervently to glorify God? What is your employment, in what manner do you pursue it, with what design, in what spirit, and what is its effect? Do you as a matter of fact find yourself walking with God and does the peace of God rule in your heart? Or is there some ingredient in your business that vitiates the whole? Are you dealing in some article of death, are you poisoning your fellowmen for the glory of God? Are you a Real-estate or a Multi-caulis speculator? Are you pursuing some scandalous traffic for some selfish purpose?

Oh, that the Lord may search you and pour the gaze of His eye through and through your inmost soul. And if your hands are clean, may the blessing of the Lord that maketh rich and addeth no sorrow be multiplied to you a thousandfold. But if you are out of the way, may He lay His reclaiming, sanctifying hand upon you and not suffer you to rest till all you have and are are wholly devoted to the Lord.

LECTURE 24

Grieving the Holy Spirit, No. 1

Eph. 4:30: "Grieve not the Holy Spirit of God, whereby ye are sealed unto the day of redemption."

In this discussion I shall pursue the following order:

I. Show that the Holy Spirit can be and often is grieved by men.
II. How and when He is grieved.
III. The consequences of grieving the Holy Spirit.

I. *The Holy Spirit can be and often is grieved.*

1. The Bible, in this text and in various other texts, represents him as being grieved.
2. God is a moral being and consequently He has the susceptibilities and feelings of a moral being, and must therefore be grieved with whatever is naturally grievous to a moral being.
3. His entire character is love, or benevolence, and therefore He cannot but be grieved with whatever is wrong.

But as I have recently published a sermon on the emotions of God, showing that God necessarily exercises the feelings ascribed to Him in the Bible, I need not enlarge upon the subject at this time.

II. *How and when the Holy Spirit is grieved.*

Before I enter upon this head of my discourse, I wish to make several remarks.

1. The great object of the Holy Spirit, as revealed in the Bible, is to sanctify the souls of men. Men are to be saved by "the sanctification of the Spirit through the belief of the truth."
2. He can sanctify men only with the truth. Sanctification is holiness. Holiness is voluntary obedience to God. Voluntary obedience certainly cannot be produced but by the influence of the truth. Hence Christ prays, "Sanctify them through thy truth." The Holy Spirit himself has no other means of sanctifying the soul but truth.
3. A moral agent can resist any and every truth. Moral agency implies power to resist any degree of motive that may be brought to bear upon the mind. Wherever force begins, moral agency ends. Were it possible for motive to force the mind, the forced action would have no moral character any more than the operations of the physical universe. Action must be free to be moral action. Necessary action is therefore neither virtuous nor vicious. I repeat it, then, that moral agency implies the power to resist any and every truth. Whether any man ever did or ever will as a matter of fact resist all truth is entirely another question. But certain it is that men are able to re-

sist the utmost influence that the truth can exert upon them, and therefore have ability to defeat the wisest, most benevolent and most powerful exertions which the Holy Spirit can make to effect their sanctification.

4. Every moral evil must be counteracted by truth and can be counteracted in no other way.

5. Whatever, therefore, hinders the truth from producing its sanctifying effect grieves the Holy Spirit, just in proportion to His desire to have it produce that effect.

6. In preaching this sermon, and in all my sermons, I design to be personal in what I say, so far as this is consistent with addressing so many persons at once. I am not one of those who feel as if I should be convicted of wrong, of course, if found to have adapted my discourse to the state of the audience before and around me. I never feel called upon to make an apology for being as personal as I can in "giving to each one a portion in due season." I wish, therefore, my hearers and my readers to consider me as speaking to them individually. And as I cannot call you by name I beseech you by all that you hold dear to pause at every step of this part of my discourse and solemnly ask yourselves, "Is it I?" Have I thus grieved the Holy Spirit?

With these remarks, I am prepared to notice some of the many ways in which the Holy Spirit is grieved.

1. By neglecting the truth. Men have the command of their attention and can take up any subject for contemplation they please. If they will not attend to truth they cannot be sanctified nor saved. Now how many of you are employing your thoughts about anything and everything else than that truth which is infinitely important to you and wholly indispensable to your salvation? Oh, if your neglected Bible were allowed now to speak to you, what an overwhelming testimony would it bear! And when it shall rise up in the judgment against you, of what gross and ruinous neglect will it convict you! Methinks I can almost hear it crying out to you as you go about in the neglect of it—at one time wooing and beseeching you in the melting accents of eternal love to search it, to be instructed by it and be saved; at another time it mutters, as you pass through [the] room where it is, its curses against you for neglecting it; or perhaps it cries out to you from some corner of the house, in the language of warning and expostulation—and yet you heed it not! Of what are you thinking? Would you not be grieved and afflicted if you should write letters of great importance to some beloved friend of yours and he should neglect to read and understand them? And do you think that the Holy Spirit has less susceptibility upon this subject than you have?

2. Levity of mind and conduct and conversation grieves the Holy Spirit. Levity of conduct would certainly be very unbecoming in the presence of an earthly judge or sovereign. And how much less tolerable is it in the presence of the infinitely holy God? Are you a trifler? And about what are you trifling—and in whose presence and under what circumstances? Few things in the universe can appear more shocking to one who has any faith in God than to see a human being whose eternal destiny hangs as upon a moment's point filled with levity right under the searching gaze of His omniscient

judge. Especially does this appear horrible and abominable when we consider the Holy Spirit as wooing and beseeching and following you towards the depths of hell, and pleading with constant and earnest importunity that you will turn and live! How can you, how dare you trifle? You would be shocked to see an individual, on trial for his life, trifle just as the judge was about to pronounce sentence upon him. But such conduct, and under such circumstances, would be decency and propriety when compared with the unutterable abomination of trifling in the presence of the great Jehovah, who stands and commands and exhorts and urges and threatens and expostulates and pleads and, in every way, endeavors to get your solemn attention to the subject of your soul's salvation.

3. The reading of light and trifling publications grieves the Holy Spirit. Woman, Man, dare you spend an hour in defiling your mind with some vain novel or foolish story, when so much truth of infinite weight and importance urges your investigation and instant attention? Can Jesus Christ, can eternal life and death, can the glory of God and the salvation of the souls of men, can the commandments of God, be solemnly weighed; can the blood and groans and mercy of Calvary be duly considered, when novels and plays and frivolous reading have gotten possession of your mind? Oh you poor, wicked, helpless, loathsome, miserable sinner, what do you mean? No matter whether you are a professor of religion or not; you are a miserable sinner before God and the law of your own conscience, if you spend your time in such reading. What is your name? Let me visit your chamber, your parlor or wherever you keep your books. What is here? Byron, Scott and Shakespeare, and a host of triflers and blasphemers of God and despisers of the Holy Ghost. Are these your companions, these the spirits with whom you commune, this the way in which you spend your time? And you a professor of religion? Do you not know that you are a great hypocrite to neglect your Bible and communion with the Holy Spirit and give your mind up to communion with such earthly, sensual and devilish works as these?

But do you say I do not profess to be a Christian? Then I reply, you are never likely to be a Christian in such company. You might as well expect to be weaned from habits of intoxication by sitting in the barroom with drunkards or while holding communion with a pipe of brandy, as to expect to become religious surrounded with such companions as these.

4. Vain conversation grieves the Holy Spirit. Christ says, "Let your yea be yea, and your nay, nay, for whatsoever is more than these cometh of evil." "And for every idle word that men shall speak they shall give an account thereof in the judgment." In the chapter of which the text is a part, the Apostle warns Christians not to be guilty of "vain conversation, and foolish jesting." Would you spend your time in vain and idle conversation, if you knew you had but one hour to live? And perhaps you have not. But suppose you have, are your circumstances those in which it becomes an immortal being to spend his time in vain conversation? Do you not know that God is listening to every word you say? He is pouring the blaze of His eye through your inmost soul, as if He would speak out and rebuke you.

Why are you not using your conversational powers in instructing those around you in the way of life? Perhaps those of your own household and your nearest friends need to be reproved and warned, exhorted and instructed in regard to their salvation. Professor of religion, how do you spend your time when in the midst of your impenitent friends, and what is your conversation when in the midst of professing Christians? I beg of you to answer to your own heart and to God. And if you doubt just how you appear to them, will you show them this sermon and ask them to read this paragraph and then give their candid opinion of what you ought to think of yourself and of your conversation? Now if your conversation has hitherto been vain and trifling or useless, and in any way unbecoming in a Christian, will you immediately repent and confess to those before whom you have laid a stumbling block, confess to the Holy Ghost whom you have grieved, and beseech Him to forgive you and return and take up His dwelling in your heart?

But perhaps you are not a professor of religion. Then I ask, why are you not? And I add that you probably never will be, unless you make a false profession, if you are in the habit of indulging in vain conversation. Do you expect the Holy Spirit to strive with you and wait upon you day after day, month after month and year after year, while you keep up your incessant and senseless babble, regardless of His solemn presence, His awful holiness and of His great and infinite love and desire to get your serious attention that He may save you?

5. Too much study, I mean too much mental application to those arts and sciences that have no direct reference to the sanctification of your souls, grieves the Holy Spirit. This is particularly a sin of students, into which they are sometimes betrayed by ambition, and into which at other times they are almost crowded by their teachers. Their whole mind is swallowed up from day to day in literary and scientific pursuits to the neglect of the solemn calls and warnings and strivings of the Holy Spirit. So did not James B. Taylor. With him it was the first and principal thing to obey the calls of the Holy Spirit. This was his determination, and a practical adherence to this rule was the secret of all his piety.

6. Neglect of study grieves the Holy Spirit. Where study is your employment, and you are negligent and attend to [it] less than is consistent with all your other duties, you err quite as much as if you studied too much.

7. Too much business grieves the Holy Spirit. In my last lecture, I spoke of the necessity of diligence in business and the sin of idleness, and also of the danger of engaging in too much business. Suppose your father should visit you on some most important business, and that you should suffer yourself to be so much employed as to be unable to give him any part of your time. This certainly would be entirely inexcusable. But what is this when compared with the wickedness of being too busy to converse with God?

8. Not business enough grieves the Holy Spirit. Idleness is one of the greatest of sins and wholly inconsistent, as I showed in my last, with either the spirit or duties of religion.

9. Intemperance of every kind grieves the Holy Spirit. In its largest

sense, intemperance is any violation of the laws of life and health in eating and drinking or dress or exercise—in anything and everything that is injurious to the body. Every man is bound to understand, so far as he is able, the structure and laws of his whole being, body and mind, and to conform most rigidly and conscientiously to those laws upon which his health and highest usefulness depend. And yet how many of you are neglecting and perhaps refusing to give your attention to the examination of the structure and laws of your own being, and in the indulgence of your filthy lusts are injuring your health and beclouding and stupifying your minds, and are following in the footsteps of those "whose god is their belly, whose end is destruction, and who glory in" that which ought to be "their shame."

10. Self-justification grieves the Holy Spirit. Many persons seem to be as anxious to justify their conduct as if they expected to be saved by their own works and knew that to be found guilty in anything were to insure their damnation. They are therefore continually resorting to apologies and shifts and self-justifying pleas, either in the way of entirely exculpating themselves from blame in anything or at least to bring their blameworthiness into doubt, so as to be able to say if they have done wrong they are sorry. Now it should always be understood that a spirit of self-justification is but adding insult to injury, first abusing God and then justifying yourself in it. Such a course as this renders sanctification impossible. Why do you not at once break down, confess and forsake your sin? Why do you go about to fritter away your guilt? It is unspeakably great. No human language can sufficiently describe it. No one ever has or can accuse you of half as much as you are guilty of before God. Probably you never were accused of any form of sin of which in heart and in the sight of God you are not fully guilty. But however this may be it is certain, and you ought deeply to consider it, that the thousandth part of your real guilt as it appears in the sight of God has never been named nor told nor conceived of by mortal man. Your iniquities are infinite. They are broader than the earth, they are high as heaven, they are deep as hell and black as the midnight of the second death. And why do you justify yourself or spend your time or breath in making apologies for your sins?

11. Condemning others grieves the Holy Spirit. Perhaps some of you are judging and condemning those around you instead of judging and condemning yourselves. [Matt. 7:1-5]:

> Judge not, that ye be not judged. For with what judgment ye judge, ye shall be judged; and with what measure ye mete, it shall be measured to you again. And why beholdest thou the mote that is in thy brother's eye, but considerest not the beam that is in thine own eye? Or how wilt thou say to thy brother, Let me pull out the mote out of thine eye; and, behold, a beam is in thine own eye? Thou hypocrite, first cast out the beam out of thine own eye; and then shalt thou see clearly to cast out the mote out of thy brother's eye.

12. Speaking evil of your brethren or of any human being, or even of the devil himself, grieves the Holy Spirit. By evil speaking I do not mean speaking the truth when manifestly called to speak it. But speaking false-

hood is always evil speaking; or telling truth in regard to the faults of others, when uncalled for, is also evil speaking. God is love. He exercises infinite benevolence toward all His creatures whether holy or unholy. He is infinitely far from consenting to injustice in any case. And He is infinitely opposed to all injurious treatment of His friends or His foes. He would as fully resent, as sternly rebuke and as promptly punish injustice done to the devil as to any soul on earth or in heaven. He will not, cannot, connive, nor consent to any abusive treatment of the vilest sinners in the universe. You, therefore, as greatly grieve Him when you trifle with the name, the reputation, or the feelings of the wickedest sinner on earth or even the devil in hell, as if you were guilty of the same conduct toward any of His friends. He is infinitely unlike sinful man in this respect. Wicked men will connive at the abuse of their enemies and even secretly acquiesce in it. But it is infinitely otherwise with God. There is a great and universal mistake upon this subject. There are few if any who do not consider it wicked to speak evil of a brother. But how many there are who throw up the rein when speaking of others than their brethren, and are guilty of absolute railing at and shocking abuse of the enemies of God, and perhaps also of the professed friends of God.

Now let me ask, what are your habits in this respect? Woman, when you have company, do you sit down and serve up a dish of slander? Do you dissect and mangle the character of your neighbor? Man, are you a railer? Have you forgotten that God has said, "Speak evil of no man"; "be no brawler but be gentle, showing all meekness unto all men"? Ah, but perhaps you are speaking of a political opponent or of a competitor in business or some opponent of religious views and practices. You think him very wicked—an enemy of God, of truth and righteousness—and perhaps think yourself "doing God service" in giving him over to all the curses of reprobation. Now stop! Oh stop! Pause as upon the brink of eternity! What are you saying? Of whom are you speaking? Of a man "made in the image of God." Suppose he is as bad or even immeasurably worse than you think he is; can the Holy Spirit be otherwise than grieved to hear such language as this? Remember that there is a sense in which all mankind are the children of God. Suppose they do sin and rebel; will this afford an apology, think you, in His view, for your abuse of them? I tell you nay. Infinitely far from it! And every time you do it you grieve and provoke the Holy Spirit. And it is wonderful that He does not turn away His face from you forever.

13. Evil thinking as well as evil speaking grieves the Holy Spirit. God looks at the heart. Your thoughts and the secret movements of your mind lie open before him. And your words and actions are no otherwise pleasing or offensive in His sight than as they are the expression of what passes within. You may therefore as effectually, and no doubt do more frequently, grieve the Holy Spirit by your thoughts than by your words. All your silent and most secret musings are distinctly observed and marked and pondered by the Holy Spirit. He weighs every thought of your heart in His balance. If you indulge evil and unkind and unchristian thoughts of any being in the universe, He knows it and is as truly grieved and offended with them (al-

though you may never have given utterance to them) as if they were penciled in sunbeams in every part of the universe. Are you in the habit of taking up a strict scrutiny and searching into the secret thoughts and purposes and workings of your mind? Oh, how much you may have grieved the Holy Spirit without scarcely being aware of it.

You can see that if all the thoughts you have entertained had been spoken out, both God and man might have been grieved and had a just cause of offense. Now remember that to God's ear these thoughts have been as audibly expressed as if spoken in thunder-tones. To God's eye they have been as open and as black and as grievous as if written in letters of darkness upon the very skies. Now do commune with your own heart, and be still; and take up the solemn question: what have I *thought* as well as what have I said?

14. A disposition to retaliate grieves the Holy Spirit. This temper of mind is as far as possible from the temper of Christ and is the direct opposite of a state of sanctification. The spirit of Christ would be to forgive enemies and those who have injured you, and to labor and suffer great self-denial for their good. But the spirit of retaliation is earthly, sensual, devilish.

15. Prejudice grieves the Holy Spirit. There are few things more astonishing than that prejudice should be regarded and spoken of as it often is by professors of religion. Prejudice, as the term imports, is to prejudge a case, to make up your mind without hearing both sides of a question. Now as shameful as the truth is, few things are more disgustingly common than prejudice among professors of religion—making up their minds that this or that thing is right or wrong, and setting their faces and using their influence accordingly, deaf and blind to everything on the other side. Scarcely anything is more common than to find professors of religion of all denominations, on all the most solemn subjects in regard to men and measures and doctrines, in such a state of committal on one side or the other through prejudice as to render it useless to try to approach their mind and possess them of the real truth. And thus they go blindly and often madly forward in fighting against God and the dearest interests of His kingdom. There is scarcely anything I have witnessed since I became a professor of religion at which I have been more frequently shocked and made to groan in my inmost soul, than the exhibition of this wicked spirit.

And what is worse than all the rest, this spirit is spoken of by almost all as a calamity rather than a crime. The most unreasonable conduct and the most wicked and persecuting temper seems to be sufficiently excused by saying, "Oh, the individual is under the influence of prejudice." And if peradventure a man gets his eyes open upon any question where he has been in the wrong, he speaks of his former vices and conduct as in a great measure excusable, on the ground of his having been prejudiced. The truth is that prejudice is one of the most detestable sins that disgraces the church and grieves the Holy Spirit of God.

And now are any of you under its influence? Of course you will say, no, for the very fact that you are implies that you are ignorant of it. But let me ask you if you are sure that upon every subject that at present agitates the church and the world—especially upon those great and leading topics upon which the nation and the world are so much divided: abolition, moral reform, temperance, holiness, revivals of religion, measures, doctrines, &c.—are you sure that you have attended to both sides of the question before you judge? Have you taken sufficient pains to inform yourself in regard to men and measures and the actual or probable results, to have made up an enlightened and unbiassed judgment in the case? And if not, what do you mean? Why are your feelings enlisted on one side? Why do you use your influence in the manner you do? How do you know but a view of the whole subject would entirely change your views and practice and cause you to go sorrowing down to your grave because you had been found to fight against God? Oh! how is the Holy Spirit grieved at the vast amount of prejudice which causes the jangling and misunderstanding and misrule of both the church and the world.

16. Pride grieves the Holy Spirit. Pride is undue self-esteem, and vanity is the exhibition of it. Nothing is more preposterous and marvelous than human pride; and very few things are at a greater remove from the spirit of Christ. It manifests itself in ten thousand ways; but wherever it exists, it is an effectual barrier against the exhibition or existence even of the spirit of Christ.

17. Ill will grieves the Holy Spirit. This is the direct opposite of benevolence, or the spirit and temper required by both the law and the gospel. Benevolence is good-willing. Malevolence is ill-willing. To will evil to any being under the sun is the opposite of all that is lovely. And how can it be otherwise than that a God of infinite benevolence should be grieved with the malevolence of any of His great family? How would a parent feel to see one of his children manifest ill will to others of his offspring? How this would enkindle his grief and indignation! And how must the infinite heart of God glow with grief and indignation when you are found with a spirit of retaliation or revenge rankling in your heart!

18. Every neglect of duty grieves the Holy Spirit. In reading President Edwards' account of his wife's experience, I was struck with a remark to this effect, that when she was in the highest exercise of grace she was deeply impressed with the fact that so much of religion consisted in the discharge of relative and social duties. Many people seem to overlook this part of religion and content themselves with what they call devotion to God. What they mean by devotion is praying, reading the Bible, attending on the exercises of the Sabbath, giving their money to benevolent objects and such like things, while in their temper they exhibit anything but the spirit of Christ. Now Christianity wherever it truly exists will, from its very nature, develop itself to the view of men mainly in its influence in making them discharge all their social and relative duties; and if it be not apparent here it is certain that it does not really exist. There is such a vast amount of *negligence* among professors of religion as to render it almost certain, were there nothing else forbidding in their history, that multitudes of them have no religion at all.

Some neglect to pay their debts. Not long since I published a sermon on "being in debt," since which I have seen several efforts in some of the religious periodicals to put down or set aside the principles of that sermon and to remove the pressure from the conscience of the church and the world in regard to their negligence in this respect. Some have misconceived and of course misrepresented the doctrines of the sermon. Others, by criticisms upon the text, have endeavored to show that it was not a command to abstain from being in debt.

It is not now the time or place to reply to those remarks. But I would here simply say that the doctrine of that sermon, that it is a sin to be in debt, is eternal and unalterable truth, whether that particular text prohibits it or not. To deny this is the same absurdity as to say that you may owe a man and be under no obligation to pay him, and the same contradiction as to say that you may neglect or refuse to discharge your obligation without sin. Now what is sin but the violation of an obligation, and what is an obligation but to owe a man? To what then do all such criticisms amount as these to which I have alluded? Do such editors and newspaper-writers expect to set aside the principles of eternal justice and to persuade mankind that it is not sinful to be in debt or to suffer their obligations to go uncanceled, by mere criticisms upon a text? The doctrine of that sermon is true and self-evident truth, entirely irrespective of its being taught in that or any other text in the Bible. If there were no Bible, that is a truth which must stand forever; and to deny it is a palpable absurdity.

But again let me say that many neglect to do things *when* and *as* they ought to be done. Now it is certainly a part of religion to do everything incumbent upon us at the *right time* and in the *right manner*; and any and every negligence in this respect is sin. Have you an appointment to meet a neighbor at a particular hour for the transaction of business, be there at the moment, lest you hinder him and all others associated with you in the affair. Is there an appointment for a church or any other religious meeting, for worship or the transaction of business, be there at the moment, lest you interrupt or hinder the business or devotion of others. Have you engaged to do anything for your neighbor or for any man or woman on earth, see that you do it just when and as it ought to be done. And in short no man can keep a conscience void of offense, no man can fulfill the law of love, no man can abstain from grieving the Holy Spirit, but by a most faithful and constant discharge of every duty to God or man.

19. Every form of selfishness grieves the Holy Spirit. I have often taught in my sermons that selfishness and sin are synonymous terms. By selfishness, I have often said that I do not mean the mere desire of your own happiness, for this is natural. It is self love, and not selfishness. But when even this desire becomes supreme, and leads you to sacrifice greater interests for the sake of promoting your own, this is selfishness; and in whatsoever form it is cherished or exhibited it is an utter abomination to God. How odious and detestable does selfishness appear to God, when He sees it exercised among His children in their intercourse with each other. If you are a parent, you know how you are grieved and offended if you see one of

your little ones bent upon gratifying himself at the expense of the good or happiness of the rest of your children. Now "if you being evil" are so stung and grieved with such a spirit as this, how much more shall your heavenly Father be grieved at such an exhibition of selfishness among His children?

But there are so many ways in which the Holy Spirit may be grieved that I must resume the subject, and also show the consequences of grieving the Holy Spirit, in my next.

LECTURE 25

Grieving the Holy Spirit, No. 2

Eph. 4:30: "Grieve not the Holy Spirit of God, whereby ye are sealed unto the day of redemption."

In continuing this subject, as proposed in my last, I remark,

20. Refusing or neglecting to confess your sins grieves the Holy Spirit. God has said, "He that covereth his sins shall not prosper, but whoso confesseth and forsaketh them shall find mercy." And Christ has said, "He that humbleth himself shall be exalted," and again, "If thou bring thy gift to the altar and there rememberest that thy brother hath ought against thee, leave there thy gift before the altar, first go and be reconciled to thy brother and then come and offer thy gift."

There can be no forsaking sin without confessing it. And as there can be no repentance without forsaking and no forsaking without confessing, it follows that without confession there is no salvation. It is enough to confess secret sins, or sins committed only against God and known only to Him, to God. But sins against our fellowmen must be confessed to them. And refusing or neglecting to do so is to cover sin, in which case we are expressly informed that we shall not prosper. Many people seem to be afraid to confess their sin or to have others confess, lest religion should be injured thereby. But this is so far from being true that it is doubtful whether a case ever occurred in which a full and frank confession of sin committed against a human being was not more honorable than dishonorable to Jesus Christ. The more aggravated the circumstances and the deeper the shame of him who confesses, the more striking and honorable is the contrast between the spirit of Christ and the spirit of the world.

It is said that a certain minister in New England, in the transaction of business with an infidel lawyer, was thrown off his guard and manifested a spirit of anger which led the infidel to boast in his absence that he had always believed that man to be a hypocrite. But they had been separated only a short time before the minister followed the lawyer to his house and made the most humble and heartbroken confession of his sin. This greatly moved and confounded the lawyer, insomuch that he exclaimed with great emotion as soon as the minister had left the house, "Now I know that there is something in the religion of Christ. That spirit is not of this world. It is the very opposite of anything that has its origin on earth."

I doubt not that many persons who feel as if they ought to confess are really afraid to confess, for fear they shall injure religion. I have often heard doubts expressed by wise and good men in regard to the expediency of confessing sins against our fellowmen so as to have the world or even the church come into possession of the facts. But with the express declarations of the Bible on this subject, what right have we to talk about expediency or inexpediency, as if we were wiser than God in regard to the results of doing what He requires? Human expediency would no doubt have concealed the crimes of Moses and David, the patriarchs, and the disciples and apostles of our Lord Jesus Christ. But God has recorded them to be read and known of all men. And who does not see and has not felt that this very fact of the inspired writers' recording their own and each other's faults is a most unequivocal demonstration of their honest humility and Christlike spirit?

21. Refusing to forsake your sins grieves the Holy Spirit. I have said there is no forsaking sin without confession. I now say there is no forsaking without restitution, where restitution is in your power. Certainly the man who steals your money does not forsake that sin while he keeps it in his pocket and refuses to return it. There is and can be no forsaking sin until all has been done that the nature of the case admits to repair whatever injury has been done by it to God or man. It is not enough to resolve to do it no more. And although confession is indispensable, yet confession is not the whole of your duty. You are bound to make restitution as well as confession, and until you do that God cannot and has no right to forgive you.

Many individuals abound much in confession, while they live on in their abominable course of conduct. Now remember that God has nowhere said that he who merely confesseth his sins shall find mercy, but he who "confesseth and *forsaketh* shall find mercy." And now do some of you stare at me as if I expected, as if God expected, that you would really *forsake* your sins and sin no more? Be sure this is demanded and expected of you; and your confessions, if you will not forsake, are an utter abomination. Hear that Deacon pray. Perhaps this is the nine hundred and ninety-ninth time he has confessed his lukewarmness, unbelief and worldly-mindedness, without the shadow of a reformation. What do you mean? Are you insulting God and trying to palm off your confessions upon your Maker? What shallow hypocritical confessions are those that are not followed by reformation! Suppose your neighbors and those indebted to you should attempt to satisfy you with confessing often to you, instead of walking right up to the discharge of their duty. How long, think you, would you be imposed upon or suffer yourself to be insulted by such confessions as these?

And how can you help seeing that your confessions under such circumstances are among your greatest sins? Now when you confess again suppose you should tell God the honest truth; and when you have gone through with your confessions say right out, "O God, I pray thee to accept these confessions instead of reformation, for I protest unto thee, I do not seriously intend to reform." You would be shocked at such language as this and so would those that heard you. But who does not know that this is exactly the truth, and nothing but hypocrisy prevents your seeing and saying it right out! Oh, from how many prayer meetings and closets is the Spirit of God grieved utterly away by abundant confessions, when there is no forsaking sin.

22. Every kind and degree of self-indulgence that is inconsistent with life and health and piety grieves the Holy Spirit. Some make a god of their belly; and it is astonishing and lamentable to see to what an extent the flesh is indulged to the ruin of the soul. Even professors of religion suffer themselves to be slaves to appetite and have not religion enough to keep under their bodies to mortify the flesh, or to exercise that dominion over their appetites, lusts and passions that might be expected even of a heathen philosopher. Some men use tobacco and complain that the habit is so fixed and overpowering that they cannot abstain from its use. Others use alcohol in some of its forms, and others still indulge in the use of tea and coffee and fashionable narcotics, to the permanent injury of their health—and still persuade themselves that these things are essential to their health. And if they feel languid and debilitated, and experience a temporary diminution of appetite when they have attempted to abstain from them, they imagine that they cannot do without them, not understanding as is a matter of fact that these very symptoms of which they complain are demonstration that they are permanently injuring their health. Why do you have the headache when you abstain from tea? Simply because your stomach has been greatly debilitated by its use.

It is astonishing to see the amount of self-indulgence, and that too which is greatly injurious both to body and soul, which is practiced even by professors of religion. Multitudes of families seem to be given up to the gratification of their appetites. To get something that is good to eat takes up a great part of their time, employs a great portion of their thoughts and seems to be the principal object for which they live.

23. Endeavoring to excuse your sins grieves the Holy Spirit. It is very common to see persons racking their ingenuity to find excuses for their sins. Some are pleading inability to do any better than they do, others plead their peculiar circumstances, and others still their dependence on the Spirit of God. In short there is scarcely any plea to which a proud heart can resort to evade the force of truth which is not resorted to by many, to appease their consciences and get away from breaking down their hearts before the Lord. Now it should be understood and remembered forever that a spirit that apologizes for sin is not only one of the most odious forms of iniquity in the sight of God, but is the most hardening and self-destroying process that can be pursued. And in just as far as you resort to any excuses and apologies for your sins you confirm yourselves in those sins, grieve the Holy Spirit and render your salvation impossible.

24. Procrastination grieves the Holy Spirit. God requires you now to

humble yourself before Him. And every attitude you take that defers obedience to a future time is direct disobedience and most provoking to God. It is truly wonderful to see to what extent this spirit is cherished. Many pretend to be waiting God's time, as if He, notwithstanding all His requirements, was not really ready to have them do their duty.

One of the greatest delusions under which men labor is that at some future time it will be more convenient for them to attend to the claims of God, than at the present. Could you visit hell today, and inquire among all the groaning millions of its inhabitants how they came there, the answer in almost every case would be, procrastination ruined my soul. I never intended to die in my sins but on the contrary always intended, at a future but not far distant time, to repent. Millions will tell you that they had purposed from time to time to attend to the salvation of their souls, but had continued to defer it until death plunged his arrow into their hearts and they went to hell.

25. Giving wrong instructions to those who are under conviction, and to professors of religion who are inquiring after sanctification, grieves the Holy Spirit. Multitudes give such instructions as directly to counteract the influences of the Spirit, and thus grieve Him away from themselves and from those whom they attempt to instruct. Remember that you take upon you a fearful responsibility when you attempt to aid the Holy Spirit in conducting the sinner through the labyrinth of his own delusions and bring him to an acquaintance with Christ. If you tell him one thing while the Spirit tells him another, you will probably ruin his soul, if you do not your own also.

26. Taking sides against God always, of course, grieves the Holy Spirit. "Take heed," said Gamaliel, "lest ye be found even to fight against God." I have already said that through prejudice many persons get committed on the wrong side of some important question and thereby injure their own souls and the cause of God. Many individuals, on account of personal friendship or personal dislike, will take sides against the truth and plunge their souls into impenetrable darkness. Whenever a question comes up that respects the character or conduct of an intimate friend or relative on the one hand, or some enemy on the other, be on your guard lest personal feelings influence you and you be found to take sides against the truth. Beware lest you shut your eyes against the light and suffer yourself to be deluded and drawn into an attitude in which God will not go with you. He will have no sympathy with your wrong feelings nor go with you at all in any of your prejudices. His soul is infinitely upright and honest; and the moment you depart from the same state of mind, your fellowship with Him ceases and a dark cloud hangs between you and the mercy seat. Will you not examine yourselves and see whether something of this kind has not shut you out from God's presence?

27. Remaining in willful ignorance upon any important subject grieves the Holy Spirit. It is amazing to see how many there are who refuse to come to the light on some of the most important subjects that have ever agitated the church or the world. How many thousands of professors of religion will not examine the subject of the abolition of slavery, the subject of moral re-

form, of sanctification, of physiology, &c.; and they seem to remain not in accidental but in willful ignorance in the midst of all the light that is pouring around them. It is wonderful to see to what an extent ignorance prevails upon so many important questions, and especially to witness the manifest resistance of mind indulged in by many when these subjects are brought up.

28. All want of candor in the examination of important questions also grieves the Holy Spirit.

29. The indulgence of feelings of contempt for particular persons or for their sentiments, and all contemptuous expressions and all attempts to put down by ridicule, persons or sentiments or practices to which we feel opposed, grieves the Holy Spirit. By this I do not mean that things which are really ridiculous may not be treated according to their nature, but that serious and important subjects cannot be treated with contempt or ridicule without grieving the Holy Spirit. Some persons are always disposed to treat all subjects of dress, tight lacing, dietetics, and such like very important subjects, with contempt and ridicule. Now I cannot believe that any person who will indulge in this can enjoy the presence of the Holy Spirit. These certainly are feelings with which the Spirit of God can have no sympathy or fellowship whatever.

30. Making direct resistance to the truth whenever it has a personal application to you grieves the Holy Spirit. To general truth or to particular truth, or to almost any truth that has no direct bearing upon themselves, they will manifest no opposition. But when they perceive that it means *them*, they manifest the spirit of the Pharisees when they exclaimed, "Thus saying thou reprovest us also."

31. Justifying resistance to the truth on the ground that it is personal grieves the Holy Spirit. I have already said in this discourse that my object in preaching is to be as personal as I can, consistently with the general design of preaching to a popular audience, and as far as possible to "give to every one his portion in due season." And now if any of you feels disposed to complain if I point out the particular way in which you are grieving the Holy Spirit or because you suppose that I know you to be rebuked for your particular sin, you are entirely unreasonable. For certainly I do mean and ought to mean to preach about the particular sins of the persons whom I address. Preaching can do you no good except as you feel it to be personal and to mean you. I design to speak in love but with all plainness, and address myself to every man's conscience in the sight of God. I shall not therefore feel myself convicted of having done wrong if what I say should be complained of as having a personal application to anyone or everyone of my hearers, I would that I could so address you that every person should feel that I was telling him all that ever he did.

I say the more on this subject because the impression seems to be almost universal that preaching should not be personal, and consequently a kind of public sympathy is excited if anyone complains that the preaching had a personal application to him. And many individuals, if they are pierced by an arrow of truth, instead of repenting before God go about and complain as if they thought they were abused. They consider themselves rather as persecuted than as being seriously called upon to repent. Their business seems to be rather to repel an injury than to confess and forsake a fault. By this I do not mean to justify harsh and abusive language or any unreasonable attacks upon the character or conduct of individuals or classes of men either public or private. But I do mean to say that if when your faults are pointed out in love, if the reproof is not more public than your sin or the nature of the case demands, you are so far from having any right to complain, that you may be sure you grieve the Spirit of God if you do not accept the reproof with all thankfulness of heart.

32. Neglecting His solemn visitations and strivings and attending to other things grieves the Holy Spirit. Christ is represented as standing at the door of the heart and knocking, and in another place as waiting until His "head is wet with the dew." It is often truly shocking to see how little attention is paid to the manifest presence and agency of the Holy Spirit in professedly religious families. When they are aware that He is striving with some member of the family and has come to their house on the solemn errand of eternal salvation, they behave themselves with as little solemnity and pay as little attention to His awful presence and majesty as if He were only a servant of servants. Sometimes even the very individual with whom He is striving, and with whom He has taken up a solemn labor to bring him to repentance, will neglect attending to His directions and suffer almost anything to divert his attention from the great subject of his own salvation.

33. Suffering your thoughts and time to be swallowed up in business, amusements or anything else until you have settled the question of your unqualified submission to God grieves the Holy Spirit. No doubt many an individual has grieved the Spirit entirely away by suffering himself to be engaged with his business or amusement just at the time when his destiny was trembling on a moment's point.

34. Indulging the fear of men rather than of God grieves the Holy Spirit. How many ministers have grieved the Spirit entirely away by fearing men so much as not to declare to them all the counsel of God. And how often is it the case perhaps that [when] some of you are pressed by the Spirit up to the faithful discharge of your duty in warning and reproving those around, you dare not do it for fear of their ill will; and in the greatness of your unbelief, instead of assigning to yourself the real reason for your negligence, you persuade yourself that faithfulness on your part would do no good.

35. Standing out against any reform grieves the Holy Spirit. The world must be reformed in almost everything before it will be right. And benevolence is waking up to push reform into many departments that disturb the slumbers and severely run across the lusts, the self-indulgence, the pride and wickedness of both the church and the world. There is therefore the greatest danger that these efforts at reformation will find you indulging in some form of sin and sternly rebuke you. Now I beg of you to be on your guard lest you commit yourself against any manner or degree of reform demanded by the state of the world. As the spirit of reform continues to increase, your danger will increase. And hundreds of thousands, it is to be

feared, have already made shipwreck of what little spirituality they had by suffering themselves to be thrown into a state of opposition to the reforms of the day.

These are some of the ways in which the Holy Spirit is grieved. Let these serve to direct your thoughts to a thorough inquiry in regard to whether in these or in other respects you are grieving the Holy Spirit.

III. *The consequences of grieving the Holy Spirit.*

1. One of the consequences of grieving the Holy Spirit is to be abandoned by Him. If you continue to grieve the Holy Spirit, you may expect Him to abandon you forever. God's Spirit will not always strive with man. He gave up the Israelites because they vexed and grieved His Spirit. He abandoned the old world for the same reason. And many individuals and families and nations in every age of the world have been given up because they grieved the Holy Spirit.

2. Spiritual blindness. This follows as a matter of course from the absence of the Spirit's influences. Men are naturally blind and deaf to all the great truths which should sanctify their souls. Not that you have not naturally eyes and ears with which to see and hear were you well disposed, but "having eyes you see not, and ears, you hear not." And being unwilling to retain God in your knowledge you blind your own eyes and deafen your own ears and harden your own hearts. And when once the Spirit of God has given you up, your blindness, though voluntary, is as certain and eternal as your existence.

3. A conscience seared as with a hot iron is another effect of grieving the Spirit. This will naturally follow from your great spiritual blindness. A silent or seared conscience is a state of mind to be infinitely dreaded. For if its voice be silenced you may go on in security crying peace and safety until sudden "destruction cometh upon you." It is an unspeakable blessing to have a quick and tender conscience, one that will enforce the slightest obligation with great power. But you should by all means, as you would the murder of your own soul, avoid that which will silence your conscience and hush its warning voice.

4. If God abandon you, you will become the confirmed and complete slave of that sin, whatever it be, on account of which He has given you up. If it be some vile indulgence in some form of intemperance, the love of money, the love of pleasure, passion under any form, or infidelity or error—in short whatever sin has been persevered in until God has given you up or the Holy Spirit departed from you—that sin has become your master. It will chain you like a slave and rule over you with a rod of iron. It will impose on you its galling yoke until you shall be filled with your own ways.

How many cases of this kind have come under my own observation, where persons have tempted God by indulging in some form of sin until He has given them up to its reigning power; and then how feeble are all their efforts to overcome it. Their resolutions are as yielding as air. Every breath of temptation carries them away. And finding themselves all weakness and swept away by temptation as with a flood, they throw up the reins and drive furiously to destruction.

5. If the Holy Spirit abandon you, you may expect God to "send strong delusions upon you that you may believe a lie, that you may be damned because you obey not the truth but have pleasure in unrighteousness." It is said that an "evil spirit from the Lord troubled Saul," and that a "lying spirit" was suffered by the Lord to deceive Ahab to his own destruction. A man who grieves the Holy Spirit, who is hiding away from the light, receives not the truth but has pleasure in some form of unrighteousness. It is remarkable to see in how many ways the providences of God will help a man, in this state, forward to some fatal delusion. Infidel books or lecturers, universalist ministers or publications, wicked companions and associates, and oftentimes the prince of hell are suffered to delude and lead such a soul into impenetrable darkness and destructive delusion.

6. Self-disgrace may be and often is a consequence of being abandoned by the Holy Spirit. It is remarkable to see when an individual has grieved the Holy Spirit how blind he is in regard to the light in which his conduct is and will be viewed by those around him. If this be your case you will probably go from step to step, beginning perhaps with indulgence in levity; next you will discover an irritable spirit and show that you have no command of your temper; then a spirit of worldly-mindedness may develop itself; next a spirit of licentiousness may be plainly discerned by those around you; then some form of intemperance may get the mastery of you; then a spirit of exaggeration and perhaps of lying may take possession of your soul; and thus in the midst of your blindness [you may] wander on until you find yourself deeply disgraced in the eyes of men and forever lost in the eye of God.

7. You may be left to inflict the deepest disgrace on your family and friends and perhaps ruin many over whom you have influence. "A little leaven leaventh the whole lump." Men naturally have great influence over each other and with great facility do "evil communications corrupt good manners," because wicked example so falls in with the corrupt state of the human heart. It is exceedingly easy to influence individuals to sin because they are already so inclined to sin. A slight amount of temptation therefore may lead those around you to follow your example, until all together at last you sink to the depths of hell.

8. If you are a professor of religion and the Holy Spirit leave you, you will of course greatly wound and dishonor Christ.

9. You may be given up to Satan "to be led captive at his will." I have already adverted to the case of Saul and Ahab as being given up to Satan for their wickedness. Paul speaks of having delivered a certain man to Satan for the destruction of the flesh; and it doubtless often occurs when the Spirit of God has left a man that Satan takes full possession of his heart. Christ seems to teach this in the following language: "When the unclean spirit is gone out of a man, he walketh through dry places, seeking rest, and finding none. Then he saith, I will return into my house whence I came out; and when he is come, he findeth it empty, swept, and garnished. Then goeth he, and taketh with himself seven other spirits more wicked than him-

self, and they enter in and dwell there: and the last state of that man is worse than the first." Now here it is plainly taught by Christ himself that when the Holy Spirit has left a man, his heart is like a room swept and garnished, waiting to entertain the devil; and that he may be expected to take possession, to exert over him at least sevenfold more influence than ever before.

10. If the Holy Spirit leave you, you may expect to become very insensible and blind in regard to the state of your own soul. You may be left to think that you are engaged in religion and mistake the silence of your conscience for the peace of God, and the absence of all concern about your soul for a good hope through grace. It doubtless has often occurred, and I think I have myself seen cases, where persons seem to have the most undoubting assurance of mind that they were in a gracious state, when their temper and conduct manifest anything else than the Spirit of Christ. Christ himself represents some as being in such a state of delusion as to carry their false hopes and delusions to the very bar of God. He represents them as saying, "Lord, Lord, have we not prophesied in thy name? And in thy name cast out devils, and in thy name done many wonderful works?" But hear His answer: "Then will I profess unto them, I never knew you. Depart from me, ye that work iniquity."

11. If the Spirit leave you, you will have no heart to offer prevailing prayer; and if you attempt to pray you will find that your mouth is shut, and if opened it will only be opened to mock God. And you will find as a matter of fact that instead of being benefited you are only hardened by engaging in prayer.

12. You will wax worse and worse if abandoned of God. This may be true of you and still you not observe it; and yet if you will be honest with yourselves, if any of you have grieved the Holy Spirit away, by comparing your recent with your former experience, you may see that you are waxing worse and worse.

13. If the Spirit leave you, your damnation is certain, God has said. "Woe unto them when I depart from them." If left to yourself, remember that you are as certain of being lost as if you had already been a thousand years in hell.

14. If the Spirit abandon you, all things will work together for your destruction. The very means that should make you better will make you worse. The efforts that God makes to save those around you will only confirm you in your sins. In short all God's providences, with all the influences of His grace which surround you, will be but so many stumbling blocks to your poor blinded soul. The Sabbath with its cheerful light and solemn stillness will rise upon you but to harden your heart. "The sound of the church-going bell," the voice of the living preacher, the song of praise, everything in the sanctuary, everything within and without yourself will conspire to work out for you an exceeding great and eternal weight of damnation.

REMARKS

1. To grieve the Holy Spirit is great presumption. You are in danger every moment you persist in it of being given up forever. Remember there is a point beyond which forbearance in God would not be a virtue. Long-suffering as He is, God will bear with you no longer than is consistent with the public good. When the children of Israel had repeatedly grieved the Holy Spirit in the wilderness, until they came upon the borders of the promised land and were commanded to go up and take possession, through unbelief they began to murmur and went not up. This one instance of rebellion, added to those that preceded it, was too much for divine forbearance. And God is represented as lifting up His hand and taking a solemn oath "that they should not enter into his rest." Now take heed therefore lest you sin once too much. Are you not convinced from what I have already said that you have often grieved the Holy Spirit? Have you not often done it in many of the ways I have mentioned as well as in innumerable ways I have not mentioned? And now dare you do it again? If you do, it may be found to be true that you have grieved the Spirit once too much to be forgiven.

2. From this subject you can see the great forbearance of God. How many of you have grieved the Holy Spirit for days and for months and perhaps for years! How wonderful that God should spare you. He sent His ministers, His written word, His providences, and to no effect. Finally He came himself by His own Spirit, and has been abused by you in a thousand ways. And even now perhaps you are indulging some sin that grieves Him almost beyond endurance. If you persist you do it at the peril of your soul.

3. You see how to account for the blindness of great multitudes of professors of religion. Many of you can see how to account for your own hardness and blindness of mind, both you who are in and you who are out of the church.

4. You see why so many persons often pray for the influences of the Holy Spirit and yet do not receive His influences. It may be and doubtless often is because they have grieved Him entirely away.

5. Again it may be and doubtless often is true that many pray for the Holy Spirit who are continually grieving Him by the indulgence of some lust or by the neglect of some duty, or in some way doing that or indulging that which is so offensive to the Holy Spirit that He will not abide with them.

6. You can see from this subject that the Holy Spirit when He comes to many is like the "wayfaring man, that tarrieth but for a night." His visits are short and far between. The fact is their lives and tempers and habits are such that for them to dwell with God or He with them is out of the question.

7. Many ministers seem to have grieved Him away. Their ministry seems to be entirely barren. They preach and pray and perform other duties without unction, and of course without success. And while they continue their round of efforts it is plain to the spiritual members of their church that they have not the Holy Spirit. Their conversation during the week is not in heaven. Their preaching on the Sabbath has in it anything but the spirit, power and demonstration of the gospel.

Sometimes they seem to be sensible that they have grieved the Spirit.

Some years since, a young man who had been several years in the ministry came to me for advice, saying that he had grieved the Holy Spirit when studying theology, since which time he had never enjoyed His presence; consequently his ministry was barren. His soul was shut out from God and he felt that he must abandon the ministry, as God had rejected him in consequence of his sin.

A Christian brother, some months since, related to me another fact, worthy of all consideration by ministers of the gospel. An elderly minister made this confession in a revival of religion, into the midst of which he was providentially brought. Said he, "When I was young and for years after I entered the ministry, the Spirit of God was with me. A divine unction attended my preaching. I was instrumental in promoting several revivals of religion. But finally on account of pecuniary considerations I was led to change my field of labor. For this the Spirit departed from me. After this my ministry was barren and my soul was as the barren heath. The heavens became brass over my head and the earth iron under my feet. Thus many years have passed over me. Still the Spirit of the Lord has not returned."

8. This subject will enable us to account for the present state of so great a number of the professed ministers of Christ—the barrenness of their ministry, the worldliness of their spirit, their bitterness and jangling and prejudice, and everything that so much wounds and disgraces Christ.

9. Let us all take warning lest any of us while we think we are standing should suddenly and hopelessly fall. Beloved, let us walk softly before the Lord and look narrowly into all our ways. Let us see wherein we have been and are grieving the Holy Spirit.

And now let us all go down upon our knees and confess our infinite guilt in having, in so many ways and for so long a time, grieved the Holy Spirit, "whereby we are sealed unto the day of redemption."

Professor Finney's Letter of May 6, 1840

TO MINISTERS OF THE GOSPEL OF ALL DENOMINATIONS

Beloved Brethren: The Lord is in great mercy visiting our churches again with precious revivals of religion, and will you permit me to make a few suggestions in respect to the course to be pursued to preserve the converts from backsliding? You are aware that in the providence of God I have had an opportunity of being in some measure acquainted with the course of things in these blessed seasons of refreshing from the presence of the Lord. I have watched with the deepest interest the rise and progress and decline of these seasons and have inquired, with the deepest solicitude, after the best means of promoting them, and into the causes of their decline. After much reflection and observation upon the subject, there are a great many things that I would say to my beloved brethren, but for the present beg leave to drop a few suggestions in regard to the converts of these revivals.

It has long appeared to me that errors in the management and training of young converts have been a principal cause of the decline of revivals of religion in the churches. I am very far from being of the opinion that revivals in this country have declined, for many years, so deeply and radically as many have seemed to suppose. It has been sometimes predicted that the revivals that have prevailed within the last twenty years had so declined as that a long night of death and darkness would ensue like that which followed the revivals in the days of Whitefield and Edwards. I do not believe that any such thing has occurred or is likely to occur in this country, unless some revolutionary struggle or great and absorbing political question should, for a long time, divert the public mind. We have great reason for gratitude that the decline of revivals has, for the last twenty years or more, been but temporary. And I think the fact that there have been but temporary seasons of declension can be accounted for on the plainest principles of philosophy and common sense. But I pass over this part of the subject for the present, for the purpose of saying with respect to the converts:

1. That their future character and influence must depend under God upon the instructions they receive in the early stages of their Christian course. The notions that they first form, the shape and direction given to their religious character at first, will, in a great measure, establish their future influence and destiny. They therefore need *peculiar* instruction suited to their mental capacities, the infancy of their religion and the circumstances with which they are surrounded. I repeat it, their instructions need to be altogether *peculiar*. Infants should not be fed with strong meat, nor a child treated as a man. They ought to be made to see that they are children, that they are in a state of spiritual infancy, and have everything to learn. Too much pains cannot be taken, therefore, to show them the perfection of their ignorance on spiritual subjects. They need, therefore, to begin with the A B C of religious truth and duty and be, at the outset, well grounded in the *first* principles of the doctrine of Christ.

2. Their instructions should be very thorough. It is no doubt a great error to suppose that young converts should not be instructed to make those discriminations that distinguish between true and false affections, between selfishness and religion. Unless these discriminations are made and the convert rendered familiar with them, he will almost with certainty, for a time, imagine that he has much more religion than he really has, and afterwards come to be very doubtful whether he has any religion at all. If selfish affections and emotions are allowed to be intermingled with holy ones, without discrimination, all will at first be taken as religion. But this process long indulged will soon root out and annihilate all holy affections and leave the mind perpetually under the influence of selfishness. This selfish religion will soon so develop itself as to lead its possessor so utterly away from the Bible, as to force upon him the conviction that he is all wrong and that he has probably never had any religion. But if he can be led to make the necessary discriminations, selfish affections, instead of being puffed up by

them, will greatly humble him, put him on his guard to resist them and the occasions of them. He should therefore be hunted from every form and degree of selfishness. He should have a clear idea of what selfishness is and, from week to week, the multitudinous forms in which it appears should be pointed out and its deceitfulness exposed. When I have preached upon selfishness the question has often been asked me by professors, "Why do not ministers preach more about selfishness? Why is not the fact that all selfishness is sin made more prominent in the instruction of religious teachers? And why is it not known that selfishness and benevolence are eternal opposites, and that their existence in the same mind at the same time is utterly impossible?"

I confess that it has been to myself a matter of great wonder that the distinction between selfishness and religion is not made more prominent in the instructions of the pulpit, and that selfishness in so many forms, and in such disgusting degrees, is suffered to remain unrebuked in the church of God. If converts are suffered to indulge selfishness—if they are allowed to *indulge* it in any form or in any degree—it will inevitably eat out all their piety. Nay, their piety is gone already; for the *indulgence* of any form of selfishness is a *state* of absolute rebellion against God. Hence,

3. They should be searched to the very quick. Their business principles and habits and transactions should be thoroughly scrutinized and weighed in the balances of the law of supreme love to God and equal love to man. They should be made to see and feel that to pursue any employment or course of life for any selfish *end* or in any selfish *manner* is downright apostasy from God. It should be insisted upon that they adopt in heart and practice the law of universal love as their rule of life.

4. Young converts must be made acquainted with the nature and degree of their spiritual wants and dependence. They should be guarded with the utmost caution against a spirit of self-dependence on the one hand and esteeming their dependence on the other. They should be made to see and feel that their *cannot* is their *will not*, in other words, that their want of stability of disposition to do the will of God is the only difficulty in the way. But that this instability of disposition is so great, that they are as really dependent upon the influence of divine grace, as if obedience to them were naturally impossible. I am aware, my brethren, that in churches where they have revivals these truths are taught, or there would not be revivals; yet I have often thought that pains enough were not taken to make converts clearly apprehend the *depth* and the *nature* of their dependence.

5. I have found in my own experience that the greatest painstaking is required to give young converts a just and sufficiently affecting view of their necessities, and in the same connection to lead them to a just apprehension of the *fullness* and *nature* of the remedy. The law must forever serve as a schoolmaster to bring them to Christ. This as long as the world stands will be the use of the law in a world of sinners. But when they are brought to Christ, they should be brought to Him not only as a justifying but as a sanctifying Savior. No pains should be spared to make them understand not only that Christ has power on earth to *forgive* sins, but that

His blood *cleanseth* from the commission of all sin. The law, when properly exhibited, not only drives the sinner to Christ for pardon, but for sanctification. And the convert should be made to see that the main business of Jesus is to save him from the commission rather than the pardon of his sins.

6. I am fully convinced that pains enough are not taken to lead the convert to seek earnestly the "baptism of the Holy Ghost, after that he hath believed." My own instruction to converts in this respect has formerly been very defective. The fact that the baptism of the Holy Ghost is a thing universally promised or preferred to Christians under this dispensation, and that this blessing is to be sought and received after conversion, was not so distinctly before my mind formerly as it has been of late. I am satisfied that this truth is abundantly taught in the Bible and that the baptism of the Holy Ghost is the secret of the stability of Christian character. It is that water of life which Christ has promised that if they drink it, "they shall never thirst, but that it shall be in them a well of water springing up into everlasting life." Converts should therefore have their attention definitely directed to what this blessing is—its nature, how it is to be obtained, to what extent and with what degree of permanency it may be expected. In short, they need to be baptized into the very death of Christ and by this baptism to be slain and buried and planted and crucified and raised to a life of holiness in Christ. Anything short of this will leave the convert to inevitable backsliding; and to this attainment I am persuaded he may be led by suitable painstaking on the part of his religious teachers.

7. In order for this it is indispensable that he should be cut off from every kind and degree of unholy self-indulgence. His appetites and passions must be restrained and subdued, his body kept thoroughly under, and his whole being must be honestly, fully and sacredly set apart to the service of God.

8. Converts should be guarded with great caution against a self-righteous use of means, on the one hand, and an antinomian neglect of them on the other. Antinomianism and Arminianism are two extremes between which they must learn to steer, or they will certainly make shipwreck of their faith.

9. Converts should by all means be *kept* awake. If they are allowed to fall asleep, you might as well attempt to preach to the tombstones as to them. We may as well preach to dead men as to sleeping ones.

And now, beloved brethren, many of us have been and still are blessed with revivals of religion under our ministrations; and I pray you, let me inquire without offense, do we feel as we ought to feel the immense responsibility that at this time devolves on us, in what an immensely important sense Christ has committed the keeping of His honor and the training of His little ones to us? Shall these converts backslide through any neglect of ours? Shall the blessed work subside, react and disgrace religion, for want of a deep sympathy in us with the heart of Christ? Shall the converts be watched over as the apple of our eye, and shall our souls continue "to travail in birth" for them till Christ be fully formed in them the hope of glory?

I wish to make some remarks on the treatment of particular classes of converts, but must defer them till my next.

Your brother in the bonds of the gospel,
C. G. FINNEY

Professor Finney's Letter of June 3, 1840

TO MINISTERS OF THE GOSPEL OF ALL DENOMINATIONS

Beloved Brethren: In my last letter, I observed that I had some things I wished to say to ministers on the necessity of their being baptized with the Holy Ghost. I begin by saying that to me it seems very manifest that the great difference in ministers in regard to their spiritual influence and usefulness does not lie so much in their literary and scientific attainment as in the measure of the Holy Spirit which they enjoy.

The apostles appear to have been entirely different men after the baptism of the Holy Ghost from what they were before. They had been converted and called to the ministry and enjoyed the personal instructions of Christ, previous to His death; and yet they remained amazingly ignorant and ill-qualified for the work to which they were called until they were baptized by the Holy Ghost at the day of Pentecost. This baptism did not by any means respect principally the working of miracles, as some seem to have supposed, for they possessed the power of working miracles before. But its main design and bearing was to fill them with light and love and power in preaching the gospel. And as I said, after this baptism they appear to have been in almost every respect entirely different men from what they were before.

Now it seems that there are many ministers in the church at the present time, who have been converted and perhaps called to the ministry, who have never received the baptism of the Holy Ghost because they have never believed that any such thing was attainable nor looked for or expected it. They have had the gospel with but a slight measure of the Holy Spirit, just as the apostles had had the personal instruction of Christ but with so little of the Spirit's influences as never to have understood and felt its power. They are, therefore, as much in the dark and as poorly qualified for the work to which they are called as the apostles were previous to the day of Pentecost.

Now the thing which they need and must have, before they will have power with God or man, is the baptism of the Holy Ghost. Without this they will forever remain in the dark in regard to the spiritual wants of the church. And however learned, philosophical, metaphysical, logical or, if you please, theological their sermons may be, they will always be wide of the mark and never meet the necessities of the church until they are baptized with the Holy Ghost. They need to be set apart to the work by the anointing of God. They may have been called but not anointed because they have not sought the anointing. They are in some measure prepared intellectually but scarcely at all spiritually for their work. Hence they know not what to say to elevate the standard of piety among Christians. Many of them can produce conviction in the church; but how few of them as a matter of fact succeed in promoting the work of sanctification in the church?

Beloved brethren, take it not amiss that I speak thus plainly. I speak in love and, as I trust, in the bowels of Jesus Christ. Do you as a matter of fact promote the spirituality of your churches?

A great deal is said about a thorough preparation for the ministry at the present day. And certainly there cannot be too much said upon the importance of such preparation. But do permit me to ask, what in fact constitutes a thorough preparation for the ministry? Is it a mere college and theological education? By no means. These are important but they are far from constituting the principal part of a thorough education. Indeed they are as nothing when compared with the importance of the baptism of the Holy Ghost. The apostles were for the most part unlearned in the worldly acceptation of that term, and yet a more efficient class of ministers never existed. And what great numbers both of ministers and laymen, unlearned in human science, have been among the most efficient and powerful ministers and laymen in the church of God, while for the most part men that have been the most famed for human learning have been in a great measure inefficient and useless in the church of God! This by no means proves that human learning is unimportant; but it does prove beyond all gainsaying the paramount importance of the baptism of the Holy Ghost.

I would therefore repeat with *great emphasis* what I said at first, that the difference in the efficiency of ministers does not consist so much in the difference of intellectual attainments as in the measure of the Holy Spirit which they enjoy. And how abundantly do the facts that lie right upon the face of the church's history demonstrate the truth of the assertion. I do not hesitate to say that whatever the age or the learning of a minister may be, he is a mere child in spiritual knowledge, experience and qualifications for his office without the baptism of the Holy Ghost. He certainly will, and must forever, remain so. Until he knows what it is to be "filled with the Spirit," "to be led by the Spirit," "to be endued with power from on high" to fulfill his high and responsible functions, he is a mere child and by no means qualified to be a leader in the church of God.

A thousand times as much stress ought to be laid upon this part of a thorough preparation for the ministry as has been. Until it is felt, acknowledged and proclaimed upon the housetops, rung through our halls of science and sounded forth in our theological seminaries, that this is altogether an indispensable part of the preparation for the work of the ministry, we talk in vain and at random when we talk of the necessity of a thorough preparation and course of training.

I must confess that I am alarmed, grieved and distressed beyond expression when so much stress is laid upon the necessity of mere human learning and so little upon the necessity of the baptism of the Holy Spirit. What are we coming to? Of what use would ten thousand ministers be without being baptized with the Holy Ghost? Ten thousand times ten thousand of them would be instrumental neither in sanctifying the church nor in converting the world. There is so little said, so little preached, so little thought upon this subject, that the churches are in a great measure in the dark in respect to what constitutes a thorough preparation for the ministry. Consequently, when they employ young men from our colleges and theological seminaries, they take it for granted that they have engaged a minister who has taken a thorough course and is well furnished for his work. But alas! How sadly and almost universally are they disappointed. They find after all, as a matter of fact, that he is spiritually inefficient, in bondage to sin and lust, and but a mere babe in Christian experience.

Now I am sure that I do not say this to rail, but in the grief and anguish of my heart. It is a solemn truth, to which the testimony of the great mass of the churches can unequivocally be given.

And now, dearly beloved, unless ministers will wake up to this subject, unless they will seek and obtain this baptism for themselves, unless they will preach it to the churches, unless this truth be insisted upon through the whole course of education, unless a thousand times greater stress be laid upon it, both in theory and in practice, than has been, we multiply the number of ministers in vain. Numbers will but increase the janglings and strifes and party zeal and darkness and spiritual death of the church of God. I might appeal to the experience of all the churches in the land in confirmation of what I say.

Your brother in the bonds of the gospel,
C. G. FINNEY

3/17/18